CANADIAN LOCAL GOVERNMENT

CANADIAN LOCAL GOVERNMENT

An Urban Perspective

SECOND EDITION

ANDREW SANCTON

OXFORD

UNIVERSITY PRESS

OXFORD
UNIVERSITY PRESS

Oxford University Press is a department of the University of Oxford.
It furthers the University's objective of excellence in research, scholarship,
and education by publishing worldwide. Oxford is a registered trade mark of
Oxford University Press in the UK and in certain other countries.

Published in Canada by
Oxford University Press
8 Sampson Mews, Suite 204,
Don Mills, Ontario M3C 0H5 Canada

www.oupcanada.com

Library and Archives Canada Cataloguing in Publication

Sancton, Andrew, 1948-, author
Canadian local government : an urban perspective / Andrew
Sancton. -- Second edition.

Includes bibliographical references and index.
ISBN 978-0-19-900809-4 (pbk.)

1. Municipal government--Canada. I. Title.

JS1710.S36 2014   320.8'50971   C2014-905851-9

Cover image: Michael Wheatley/Getty Images

Oxford University Press is committed to our environment.
This book is printed on Forest Stewardship Council certified paper,
harvested from a responsibly managed forest.

MIX
Paper from
responsible sources
FSC
www.fsc.org
FSC® C103567

Printed and bound in Canada

1 2 3 4 — 17 16 15 14

CONTENTS

Preface and Acknowledgements   *xi*
Introduction   *xiv*

PART I   THE LEGAL AND POLITICAL FRAMEWORK   1

1 ▪ What Is Local Government?   3
Municipal Corporations in English Cities   3
Different Kinds of Canadian Municipalities   7
Special-Purpose Bodies   8
Financial Significance of Local Government   10
Conclusion   11
Resources   12
Study Questions   12

2 ▪ Why Local Government?   13
Imagining Provinces without Local Government   13
Functions of Canadian Local Governments   22
Conclusion   25
Resources   25
Study Questions   26

3 ▪ Central Governments and Local Governments   27
Constitutional Role of Federal and Provincial Governments   27
Provincial Statutes Relating to Local Government   29
Provincial Ministries and Ministers   32
Administrative Tribunals   33
Money   35
Reasons for Central Involvement in Local Issues   38
Municipal Organizations   41
Conclusion   45
Resources   45
Study Questions   46

4 ▪ Special-Purpose Bodies   47
School Boards   48
Police Boards   50
The Vancouver Board of Parks and Recreation   56
Library Boards   57
Local Transit Systems and Utilities   57
Inter-municipal Special-Purpose Bodies   61
Intergovernmental Special-Purpose Bodies   64
Local Special-Purpose Bodies with No Municipal Involvement   68
Conclusion   71
Resources   72
Study Questions   72

PART II   ADAPTING TO URBANIZATION   73

**5 ▪ Population Centres, Rural Areas, and Causes
        of Metropolitan Growth   75**
Approaching Urban–Rural Differences   75
Population Centres   78
Census Metropolitan Areas and Census Agglomerations   79
The Greater Golden Horseshoe   81
CMAs and Provinces   85
Causes of Growth in Canada's Largest CMAs   86
Conclusion   88
Resources   89
Study Questions   90

6 ▪ Annexations   91
The Expansion of a Hypothetical Urban Settlement   92
Montreal   94
Edmonton   96
London, Ontario   100
Calgary   107
Regina   109
Conclusion   109
Resources   110
Study Questions   111

7 ▪ Two-Tier Metropolitan and Regional Governments   112
Consolidationists versus Public Choice   113
The Municipality of Metropolitan Toronto   117

The Metropolitan Corporation of Greater Winnipeg   120
Regional Municipalities in Ontario   121
Urban, Regional, and Metropolitan Communities in Quebec   126
Regional Districts in British Columbia   129
Regional Commissions in New Brunswick   133
Regional Partnerships in Edmonton and Calgary   134
Conclusion   136
Resources   137
Study Questions   137

8 · **Amalgamations and De-amalgamations   138**
The Windsor Precedent   139
Winnipeg's Unicity   142
The Early 1990s: Newfoundland, Prince Edward Island,
    and New Brunswick   144
Cape Breton and Halifax   146
Ontario   149
Quebec   161
Conclusion   169
Resources   170
Study Questions   170

PART III   POLITICS AND MANAGEMENT IN CANADIAN URBAN GOVERNMENT   171

9 · **Municipal Politics, Councils, and Elections   173**
Municipal Politics and Political Parties   173
The Era of Municipal Reform   177
Local Political Parties in Canada   178
Size and Structure of Municipal Councils   182
Who Decides and When?   188
Openness of Meetings and of Votes in Municipal Councils   192
Is Being a Municipal Councillor a Full-Time Job?   194
Municipal Elections: Terms of Office, Turnout, and Minority
    Representation   197
Financing Municipal Campaigns   199
Conclusion   200
Resources   201
Study Questions   201

10 · Developers, Councillors, and Citizens   202
How Rural Land Has Become Urban in Ontario   203
Shopping Malls versus Downtowns   210
Old Buildings versus New Buildings   213
Neighbourhoods versus "Cataclysmic Change"   215
"New Reformers" and the Development Industry   217
The Development Industry Today in Toronto   220
Citizen Participation   222
Conclusion   224
Resources   225
Study Questions   225

11 · Mayors and Local Political Leadership   227
Legal Status of Mayors   228
Executive Committees   230
How Mayors Become Powerful   232
Urban Pluralism and Urban Regimes   237
Do Canadian Cities Have Urban Regimes?   230
Models of Mayoral Leadership   239
Conclusion   247
Resources   248
Study Questions   248

12 · Policy-making   249
Responding to Federal and Provincial Governments   251
Responding to Pressures for Economic Growth   254
Responding to Pressures from Citizens   258
Municipalities and Precommitment   262
Implementing Municipal Policy Decisions   264
Conclusion   265
Resources   266
Study Questions   267

13 · Senior Management and Labour Unions   265
Distinctive Features of Municipal Management   268
The Role of City Managers and CAOs   270
When Things Go Wrong   271
Contracting Out   273
Public–Private Partnerships   276
Municipal Unions   278
Conclusion   284

Resources   285
Study Questions   286

PART IV   FINANCIAL ISSUES   287

14 · Budgets, Grants, and User Fees   289
Local Government Finances   290
Municipal Budgets   295
User Fees   301
Financing Water   306
Conclusion   312
Resources   312
Study Questions   313

15 · The Property Tax   314
How Much Property Tax?   314
Determining Tax Payable for Individual Property Owners   316
Alternative Assessment Systems   321
Exempt Property and Payments-in-Lieu of Taxes   322
Who Pays?   323
Other Demands on the Property Tax   325
Alternatives to the Property Tax   326
Conclusion   328
Resources   329
Study Questions   329

16 · Conclusion: Canadian Local Government
in Comparative Perspective   330
Government Functions   331
Multi-Purpose versus Single-Purpose Authorities   333
Autonomy   334
Size   335
Why Canadian Local Government Is Important   337
Assessing Canadian Local Government   339
Resources   341
Study Questions   342

Notes   343
Bibliography   368
Index   381

PREFACE AND ACKNOWLEDGEMENTS

I have been teaching courses in Canadian local government at the University of Western Ontario for more than 30 years. Like all instructors, I have never found a perfect textbook. Until a few years ago, however, I resisted the temptation to try to write my own—there were always too many other projects and priorities and too many aspects of the subject about which I did not feel ready to write. By 2007, however, such excuses seemed feeble, especially when I came up against the persuasive reasoning of David Stover and Kate Skene from Oxford University Press Canada. They started the process that launched the first edition of this book in 2011, and now I am grateful that they have seen fit to publish a second edition.

I am under no illusions that other instructors and their students will find my attempt at a text to be perfect. Their priorities will doubtless be different from mine. All readers, however, have a right to know the kinds of influences that have shaped my own particular approach. Since the mid-1980s I have taught courses at Western designed for managers in Canadian municipalities, first in our Diploma in Public Administration program that was developed by the late Professor Allan O'Brien, and then in the Master of Public Administration program. Allan, a former mayor of Halifax and past president of the Federation of Canadian Municipalities, convinced me that, as a then young academic with no experience working in municipal government, I had something to offer our manager–students.

In retrospect, I think he was right. More importantly, for this book, my experience in these classes has profoundly affected how I approach my subject. It is a cliché to claim that instructors always learn from their students, but for me it has been obviously true. I lecture about the broad principles of local government organization and politics and am happily interrupted by managerial stories about how they relate to "the real world." I came to have a profound respect for the kinds of problems senior Canadian municipal managers must grapple with daily, a respect I hope is reflected in this book. The practical result of all this for my current readers is that, more so than in other texts, they will find this book rooted in practical problems and issues. But just as municipal managers need to be able to think abstractly as well as practically, this book does contain some abstract sections grounded in various theoretical approaches to the study of political science and public administration. Such sections are always meant to illuminate practical issues rather than to minimize them.

Given that non-managers will constitute the vast majority of my readership, how does my own personal history with such managers affect my approach in this book? Above all, it means that readers will learn about Canadian local government from the perspective of someone who takes it very seriously as a vital component of Canada's overall system of government. For me, local government is important for what it is and what it does, not simply as part of some broader theoretical argument about, for example, the nature of cities in capitalist economies or how market competition promotes efficiencies in local service provision. If both practising municipal managers and students of political science and public administration feel that this book engages them, then in my eyes it will have been successful.

One of the great attractions of life as a professor is being able to pursue one's own academic interests. Western has always been a most hospitable place for local government research, especially in recent years after my colleague and friend, Robert Young, obtained a very large grant from the Social Sciences and Humanities Research Council of Canada (SSHRC) involving the study of Canadian municipalities. The book that he and I co-edited for this project, *Foundations of Governance: Municipal Government in Canada's Provinces* (Toronto: University of Toronto Press, 2009), and the others that followed, have provided much important raw material for this text. From 1990 to 1995, I benefited from my own SSHRC standard research grant, a project that delivered less in published form than was originally promised. Some of the material from this project is published here for the first time, especially in Chapter 10. My debts to the SSHRC in general and Bob Young in particular are gratefully acknowledged. A sabbatical leave from Western in the second half of 2013 made possible the final push to complete this second edition.

Except for David Siegel at Brock University and for two reviewers of the original manuscript who remain anonymous, other colleagues have generally been spared prior exposure to what I have written here. David was especially helpful in his formal review, in making subsequent suggestions for improvement, and in sharing with me his experience as a very successful textbook co-author. Two of the anonymous reviewers for this second edition made helpful suggestions that guided my revisions. Christopher Leo, now retired from the University of Winnipeg, wrote an especially long and detailed critique, and I have tried to take account of many of his suggestions. My colleague Martin Horak commented on a draft of the new chapter on local policy-making. Thanks to Zack Taylor for causing me to correct what he kindly called "a microscopic factual error" in the first edition, and to Robert Williams and Jack Novak for helping out with my discussion in Chapter 9 of the size of the council in the Halifax Regional Municipality.

After having completed the original manuscript and the revisions for this second edition, I now more fully understand the challenges faced by all those who have previously attempted texts on this subject. I think especially, however, of Professor Donald J.H. Higgins of St. Mary's University, whose pioneering texts *Urban Canada: Its Government and Politics* (1977) and *Local and Urban Politics in Canada* (1986) paved the way for the rest of us among his generation of political scientists. Don's tragic death in 1989 took from us a scholar who had a great deal more to contribute.

I have received helpful and prompt guidance from my developmental editor at OUP Canada, Mark Thompson. Informed and skilful copy-editing was provided by Julie Fletcher. My thanks go to all who have been involved in this project. I, of course, remain solely responsible for all errors and omissions. I hope those who discover them will let me know.

Above all, textbooks are for students. This book is dedicated to all of mine: past, present, and future.

Andrew Sancton
asancton@uwo.ca
London, Ontario
August 2014

INTRODUCTION

M ost Canadians live in cities or their suburbs. Even a statement as simple as this raises many questions about how the words *cities* and *suburbs* are defined. These questions are crucial to the subject matter of this book and will be addressed at various points, especially in Chapter 5. Because Canada is primarily an urban nation, many Canadians confront significant urban problems every day: traffic congestion, expensive or ineffective public transit, homelessness, the ugliness of commercial sprawl. Many more use urban services that are usually taken for granted here, but which are highly problematic in some of the world's most populous cities: the supply of clean drinking water, the safe removal of liquid and solid waste, policing of public spaces so as to provide security for all who wish to move around. Local governments are intimately linked to urban problems and services, and that is one good reason why we should know about them.

As we shall see throughout this book, however, local governments often do not have exclusive jurisdiction over urban problems and issues; the most intractable problems usually involve other levels of government as well, sometimes in dominant decision-making roles. Analyses of the politics of urban problems often refer to *multi-level governance*, a process whereby various levels and varieties of government act collaboratively to address issues that transcend the jurisdictional responsibilities of each. This book focuses neither on urban problems nor on multi-level governance. It focuses instead on local governments as political institutions. Its objective is to attempt to answer all the big questions political scientists ask about any political institutions: How are they defined? Why do we have them? What do they do? How do they relate to other political institutions? How is power attained and distributed within them? How do decisions get made and implemented? Where does their money come from and how does it get spent? Answering these questions will require us to consider many important urban problems, but at its heart, this book is about local government, not about urban issues and problems. The book takes local governments seriously in that it assumes that we need to know as much about how our local governments work as we know about other levels of government. No one can pretend that studying the politics and government of Canadian local government has as much initial appeal as studying international terrorism, American presidential elections, or the dominance of the prime minister in Canadian government. But most readers will be—if they are not already—working and/or raising families in Canadian cities, relying on local public services, and paying property taxes. Knowing about Canadian local government facilitates urban living.

Although some of the material in the book is clearly relevant to local government in rural areas, individuals with special interests in rural local government will be disappointed. If this book gave as much attention to rural as urban, its subtitle would not be "an urban perspective." A more important disclaimer is that in the Canadian context, "local government" does not include any form of Aboriginal self-government. Although some of the administrative challenges of local and Aboriginal governance are no doubt similar, their political origins are so different that comparisons within a political and governmental context—which is the context of this book— are quite irrelevant. Aboriginal self-governance relates in some way to the concept of *nation*; local government does not. In Chapter 5, we shall touch briefly on the subject of Aboriginal Canadians who live in cities, but this is about as close as we shall get to Canada's First Nations.

This book is designed as a textbook for political science courses in Canadian local government at both the undergraduate and the graduate levels. It should also serve as a reference book on the subject for any interested citizen. It assumes no prior knowledge of local government and only a rudimentary knowledge of the basic principles of Canadian government. There are no elaborate theoretical frameworks, and every effort has been made to limit the use of academic jargon, except where it is absolutely necessary to understand particular contributions to our knowledge of urban governance. Long-time scholars in the field might be surprised by the fact that their names generally appear only in the notes but not in the main narrative. As much as possible, this is a book about Canadian local government, not about how various scholars have contributed to our current knowledge of Canadian local government.[1] Nor is it a book about the urban geography or sociology of Canadian cities.[2]

The four chapters that comprise Part I of the book are concerned with the legal and political framework of Canadian local government. More so than other levels of government, local governments are generally the result of some deliberate design, either by provincial governments or by groups of local citizens who at some point in the past have taken action, in accordance with provincial laws, to provide themselves with some degree of self-government. Because of this element of self-conscious design, we need pay some attention in these first chapters to the principles that are relevant for the institutional design of systems of local government.

Part II is concerned with how structures of local government are adapted to urbanization. Chapter 5 deals with different definitions and characteristics of Canadian urbanization. In one way or another, the remaining three chapters in this part deal with changing boundaries of local governments. The fact that boundaries of local governments—unlike those of national or provincial governments—are always open for discussion and change is a key distinguishing characteristic of local government. To ignore boundaries when studying local government is to ignore the essence of the subject.

Part III of the book is about power, politics, and management within major Canadian municipalities. This is the part of the book that will seem most familiar to readers acquainted with books about the politics of particular provinces and countries. Here we explore the roles and behaviours of local voters, councillors, mayors, developers, citizens' groups, and managers. Part IV is about money, a subject of great importance to all governments but one of special importance at the local level where much money is needed, where local governmental access to various tax resources is relatively limited, and where there is much debate about the desirability of change. In this section we explore the property tax in some detail, a subject of essential knowledge for anyone claiming to know anything about local government in Canada. The final chapter, by way of conclusion, addresses issues that relate to the future of Canadian local government.

Understanding the nature of political institutions almost invariably requires an understanding of their historical evolution. There is much history in this book, but it does not all appear near the beginning. Relevant historical background is covered wherever it appears necessary.

Canadian local government has its origins in Britain's deep historical past. If we have no understanding of these origins, there is much about local government in Canada that is difficult to understand. We examine these origins in Chapter 1, whose object is to define what local government is.

PART I
THE LEGAL AND POLITICAL FRAMEWORK

CHAPTER 1

What Is Local Government?

L *ocal government* is a slippery term, used in different ways in different places in different circumstances. For the purposes of this book, the term includes both municipalities and all other governmental entities comprising territories smaller than provinces and having their own governing bodies with some capacity for autonomous decision-making. At this stage, such a definition raises as many questions as it answers. The main purpose of this chapter is to explain what the definition means.

Nowhere in Canada can we find any kind of constitutional or legal definition of local government. The situation is different in many European liberal democracies in which local governments are legally established and protected by the national constitution and therefore comprise an important part of the state apparatus. In the United States, each state government has its own constitution, and most of these documents establish and define local governments in one way or another. Canada and other countries from the old British Commonwealth are distinct in not providing any form of constitutional recognition for local governments. The only way to understand what they are is to explore their historical origins. Such an exploration forms the first part of this chapter.

Municipal Corporations in English Cities

Municipal corporations—more commonly known in Canada as municipalities—are the most important components of Canadian local government. Canadian municipalities are the direct descendants of English municipal corporations. To understand the legal context of Canadian municipal government, we need to know about English municipal corporations, and to know about English municipal corporations we need to understand their relationship to the monarch. In Britain, the monarch is the government. Everything that the British government does is done in the name of the monarch. The prime minister is the monarch's prime adviser. Everyone who works for the government serves the Crown; hence the term *civil servant*. The reality, of course, is that the monarch decides virtually nothing herself, but symbolically she is everywhere.

The first English municipal corporations derived from royal charters. For example, the charter of the City of London can be traced back to 1067. By the mid-fourteenth century a distinct corporate body had emerged, consisting of a mayor, aldermen, and councillors, the forerunner of the City of London Corporation that exists today and governs the square-mile territory at the heart of London known as "the City."[1] Later municipal corporations were established by parliamentary statute rather than by royal charters. A municipal corporation is legally entitled to do whatever its charter or statute says it can do.

Municipal corporations act on behalf of themselves and their residents, not on behalf of the Crown. For many centuries in Britain there was great tension between the Crown and many municipal corporations. Some of the provisions in the Magna Carta of 1215 are directed at protecting municipal corporations against arbitrary royal action. Until the nineteenth century, municipal corporations carried on their business with little or no supervision from the monarch and his or her government, and certainly without any form of public control through democratic elections. Their "business" varied from place to place, but it usually involved regulating public markets and nuisances, investing in what we would now call public infrastructure, and raising funds through various charges and taxes. In fact, distinctions between municipal corporations and other corporations were hazy at best. Municipal corporations engaged in commercial trading, and some trading corporations with royal charters (e.g., the Hudson's Bay Company in Canada) were granted legal authority by the monarch to govern vast territories of land that had been claimed for Britain by colonial explorers.

The approval in Britain of the Municipal Corporations Act in 1835 started a long process whereby Britain's municipal corporations became part of a regularized, democratic system of local government that extended throughout the entire country. This process began at about the same time as Canada's first municipal corporations were established. Saint John, New Brunswick, Canada's first municipal corporation, had been created by royal charter in 1785 but municipal incorporations elsewhere in what is now Canada did not begin until the 1830s and 1840s. In 1849, the legislature of the pre-Confederation Province of Canada approved a Municipal Corporations Act (commonly known as the Baldwin Act, after its sponsor Robert Baldwin) for Canada West that provided the basis for Ontario's municipal system for more than a century.[2] By this time, municipal corporations in Britain, the United States, and Canada were increasingly being recognized as a form of government rather than as an unusual variant of a private business corporation,[3] although campaigns by business interests to remove such corporations from all forms of "municipal trading" (i.e., commercial business) were commonplace until well into the twentieth century.

After 1867, legislatures in all the Canadian provinces eventually approved laws that established townships, counties, or districts as the basic units of rural municipal government. Residents in urban settlements, if they followed certain procedures laid out in the various provincial laws, could then initiate a process whereby their settlements, depending on population size, became incorporated as villages, towns, or cities. Although all municipalities ultimately owe their existence to provincial law, it is important to realize that incorporated villages, towns, and cities often owe their original existence to initiatives taken by local citizens many years previously. Frequently, systems of municipal government seem so complex that it is impossible to imagine that a rational policy-maker in a provincial capital could ever have devised them. In reality, the complexity derives largely from the past actions of thousands of individuals in their different local communities rather than from a single omnipotent centre.

We have already seen that early English municipal corporations were quite separate from "the government" as represented by the monarch. But are today's municipalities part of "the government"? The answer is not as simple as it seems. For traditionalists, municipalities can never be on the same level as a government whose very existence is inseparable from the Crown. For strict federalists in the United States and Canada, it is clear that the federal constitution establishes two—and only two—levels of government, with governments at each of the two levels deriving their existence directly from the respective constitutions of each country. But, for all practical purposes, most citizens recognize that they pay taxes to, and are regulated by, three distinct levels of government: federal, provincial (*state* in the United States), and municipal.

Occasionally, however, it is still sometimes suggested that municipalities are not really governments at all. For example, in 1999, a senior adjudicator for Ontario's Chief Information and Privacy Officer ruled that the city of Toronto was not a government under the terms of

Ontario's Freedom of Information and Protection of Privacy Act. He refused to accept the city's contention that certain information it provided to a provincial ministry need not be made public because it would "reveal information received in confidence from another government,"[4] which is grounds for exemption under the Act. The adjudicator went on:

> if a municipality was considered a government for the purposes of section 15 of the Act, a letter from a local library board could be placed on the same footing, and qualify for the same exemption as a document received from the government of another nation. This would greatly expand the number of records that could be withheld from the public indefinitely.[5]

A much more common and authoritative position was expressed by the Supreme Court of Canada in 1997 when it was asked to decide whether the Canadian Charter of Rights and Freedoms applied to certain employment practices of the city of Longueuil in Quebec.

> The ambit of s. 32 of the Canadian Charter is wide enough to include all entities that are essentially governmental in nature and is not restricted merely to those that are formally part of the structure of the federal or provincial governments. As well, under s. 32, particular entities will be subject to *Charter* scrutiny in respect of certain governmental activities they perform, even if the entities themselves cannot accurately be described as "governmental" *per se*. Since municipalities cannot but be described as "governmental entities", they are subject to the Canadian *Charter*. First, municipal councils are democratically elected by members of the general public and are accountable to their constituents in a manner analogous to that in which Parliament and the provincial legislatures are accountable to the electorates they represent. Second, municipalities possess a general taxing power that, for the purposes of determining whether they can rightfully be described as "government", is indistinguishable from the taxing powers of the Parliament or the provinces. Third, and importantly, municipalities are empowered to make laws, to administer them and to enforce them within a defined territorial jurisdiction. Finally, and most significantly, municipalities derive their existence and law-making authority from the provinces. As the Canadian *Charter* clearly applies to the provincial legislatures and governments, it must also apply to entities upon which they confer governmental powers within their authority. Otherwise, provinces could simply avoid the application of the *Charter* by devolving powers

on municipal bodies. Further, since a municipality is governmental in nature, all its activities are subject to *Charter* review. The Canadian *Charter* is therefore applicable to the residence requirement at issue in this case. The particular modality a municipality chooses to adopt in advancing its policies cannot shield its activities from Charter scrutiny. All the municipality's powers are derived from statute and all are of a governmental character. An act performed by an entity that is governmental in nature is thus necessarily "governmental" and cannot properly be viewed as "private."[6]

This passage is a clear a statement as to why, for legal purposes at least, municipalities meet all the requirements for being "governmental entities," although they are notably never referred to as "governments." It is also very clear from the passage that the governmental authority of municipalities derives solely from provincial legislation and from nowhere else.

Different Kinds of Canadian Municipalities

If municipalities are clearly governmental entities, how do we determine which governmental entities are municipalities and which are not? The official name of Chatham–Kent in Ontario is the Municipality of Chatham–Kent, so that is a good clue that it is indeed a municipality. So are all incorporated places that are cities, towns, and villages. Things get more complicated when we think about rural areas or "governmental entities" whose territories seem quite large.

First, much of Canada's territory is not included in any municipality. Some territory is Indian reserves or territory belonging to autonomous First Nations, but most of it is simply unincorporated, meaning that there is no municipal government with jurisdiction in that area. The relatively few people who live in unincorporated areas pose a special challenge for provincial governments because they require some minimal government services (local roads, for example) that elsewhere are paid for and provided by municipalities. These same people often resist incorporation or inclusion in the territory of a neighbouring municipality because they rightly expect that they would end up paying higher taxes, even if they also would receive a higher level of local services.

Second, most populated agricultural areas are covered by rural municipalities. They go by such labels as *township*, *rural district*, or *county*. But the issue of terminology is not quite so simple. In Ontario's north, for example, many *geographical townships* are not incorporated and hence have no municipal government of their own (although some geographical townships are included within the territory of a municipality that has another name, such as Timmins or Greater Sudbury). In Ontario, Nova Scotia, and Alberta, some rural municipalities are known as counties.

In Ontario most counties are examples of what are known as upper-tier municipalities.[7] They provide some municipal services for the whole territory of the county, but this same territory also contains lower-tier municipalities (usually towns, villages, and townships) that provide more local municipal services. Ontario also has six *regional municipalities* that are generally more urban than counties. People who live within the jurisdiction of an upper-tier municipality are said to live within two-tier systems of municipal government.

In British Columbia and New Brunswick, *regional districts* and *regional services commissions* act respectively as upper-tier municipal governments in all places where there are also lower-tier municipalities. For otherwise unincorporated areas, they act as the single-tier of municipal government. Outside major cities in Quebec, *municipal regional counties* (MRCs) are similar to the upper-tier municipal authorities of British Columbia and New Brunswick. In provinces other than Ontario, Quebec, British Columbia, and New Brunswick, the entire municipal system is single-tier because no part of the province is covered by two distinct tiers (or levels) of municipal government. We shall analyze the historical evolution and relative merits of these different forms of municipal structure in Chapter 7.

Finally, Quebec has two *supra-regional governments* that cover the entire urbanized areas around Montreal and Quebec City. Some people living on the outer fringes of these areas are actually subject to three levels of municipal government: local municipality, MRC, and supra-regional (known in Quebec as the *metropolitan community*). Table 1.1 shows the total number of municipalities for each province, including the number of upper-tier and supra-regional municipalities, where applicable.

Special-Purpose Bodies

We saw earlier that when the Ontario information adjudicator was trying to determine whether he should consider municipalities to be governments, he was concerned that "a letter from a local library board could be placed on the same footing . . . as a document received from the government of another nation." Why did he refer to library boards when he was supposed to be concerned with municipalities? The answer is that

Table 1.1 Municipal Governments in Canada's Provinces, 2011

Province	Local Municipalities	Upper-Tier Municipalities	Supra-Regional Municipalities
Alberta	347		
British Columbia	151	27	
Manitoba	196		
New Brunswick	101	12	
Newfoundland and Labrador	280		
Nova Scotia	54		
Ontario	414	30	
Prince Edward Island	76		
Quebec	1,090	86	2
Saskatchewan	787		
Total	3,496	155	2

Source: Statistics Canada, 2011 Census of Canada, accessed 28 January 2014. Reproduced and distributed on an "as is" basis with the permission of Statistics Canada. Excludes census subdivisions that are not municipalities.

library boards in Ontario are both connected to municipalities and separate from them. Such boards and commissions are usually referred to as *special-purpose bodies*.

Special-purpose bodies are very similar to municipalities except that they are established to carry out a single governmental function, as distinct from municipalities, which have multiple functions. Those who govern special-purpose bodies are either democratically elected or appointed by people who are democratically elected. These bodies have the authority to levy a tax themselves, to claim tax revenues from another body, or to charge user fees for essential services or utilities. They also have the authority to make laws (i.e., binding rules) and to enforce them within their respective assigned territories. Although municipalities and most special-purpose bodies derive their authority from provincial law, some local special-purpose bodies (e.g., port and airport authorities) are under federal jurisdiction. We shall explore this further in Chapter 4.

Determining which local institutions qualify as special-purpose bodies, and therefore as *governmental entities*, is not easy. Fortunately, for our purposes, we do not have to make clear distinctions. We need only recognize that some special-purpose bodies are almost as powerful as municipalities and others are so weak that they are hardly like governments

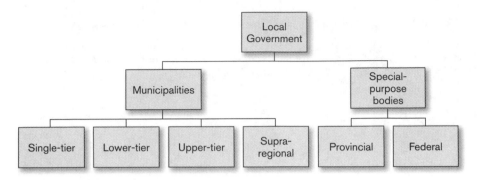

Figure 1.1 Components of Local Government in Canada

at all. Elected school boards with the authority to levy their own taxes are the strongest special-purpose bodies in Canada. Library boards in Ontario are among the weakest.

We can better understand the definition of special-purpose bodies by looking at examples of institutions that clearly are not special-purpose bodies. Committees of municipal councillors that report to the entire municipal council are not special-purpose bodies because they can make no final decisions themselves. The same applies to local advisory committees of citizens that may be appointed by any level of government. Business corporations that are partly or wholly owned by municipal governments are not special-purpose bodies because, unless specified by provincial law, they have no more authority than any other business corporation to appropriate taxpayers' money or to make any kind of binding rule or law. Local non-profit institutions such as hospitals and universities receive large sums of public money, mostly from provincial governments, but simply receiving public money does not make them special-purpose bodies.

Statistics Canada defines *local governments* as including municipalities and their associated "autonomous organizations, boards, commissions and funds . . . [and] school boards."[8] In short, local governments in Canada include municipalities and local special-purpose bodies. Such a definition is commonly accepted[9] but is far from crystal clear, as we shall explore in more detail in Chapter 4.

Financial Significance of Local Government

In 1913, local governments accounted for 36 per cent of government spending in Canada, while provinces were responsible for only 17 per

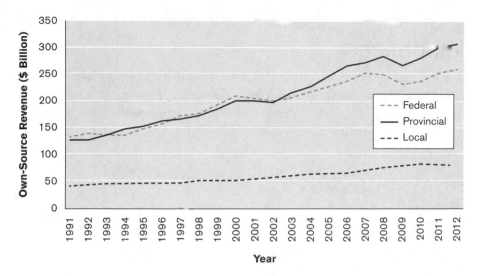

Figure 1.2 Own-Source Revenues for Federal, Provincial, and Local Governments

Source: Statistics Canada. Table 385-0032, Government finance statistics, statement of government operations and balance sheet, quarterly (dollars), CANSIM (database). Accessed 10 July 2014. Reproduced and distributed on an "as is" basis with the permission of Statistics Canada. In this table, Statistics Canada includes Aboriginal governments as "local."

cent. By 1948 the percentages were 14 and 18, respectively.[10] Since then, the proportion of provincial spending to the total has risen to the same level as the federal, while the proportion of total spending that is local remains much the same. Spending by local governments in Canada is significant and important, but it is wrong to claim that it is becoming more important relative to other levels of government.

Similar information can be found by looking at local government's share of the total revenue that each level of government raises from its own sources. By looking at "own-source" revenue for each level of government, we eliminate the effect of transfer payments from one level of government to the other. Figure 1.2 shows the total revenue raised by each level of government without counting transfers received from other levels.

Conclusion

In this chapter we have defined what local government is and looked at its financial significance in relation to other levels of government in Canada. But this information is only important in the real world if we know what it is that local governments actually do and what they spend their money on. This is what we turn to in the next chapter.

RESOURCES

See Andrew Sancton and Robert Young, eds., *Foundations of Governance: Municipal Government in Canada's Provinces* (Toronto: University of Toronto Press, 2009), which contains essays on the municipal systems of each of the 10 provinces.

STUDY QUESTIONS

1. Why is it not strictly accurate to say that people who work for municipalities are civil servants?
2. What is the difference between a single-tier municipality and an upper-tier municipality?
3. Do you currently reside in a two-tier municipal system or a single-tier system?

CHAPTER 2

Why Local Government?

[handwritten annotations:]
Progressive Conservative!
- Kill Bill 64 (one school division for all of Winnipeg).
- Provincial property tax (abolishments)

- Retain control of the education system ..

In theory, we do not need to have local governments at all, because what they do could be carried out directly by provincial governments. This chapter tries to explain why provincial legislatures—and the legislatures of most other democratic jurisdictions in the world—have established systems of local government within their borders. We then move on to discuss what Canadian local governments actually do. Not surprisingly, the functions of local government are generally related to some of the theoretical reasons why local governments have been created in the first place.

Imagining Provinces without Local Government

For most aspects of Canadian local government, provinces are central governments; they are the ones in control. For the purposes of this discussion, we shall refer only to provinces and local governments to keep things as simple as possible. For now, we need not worry about Canada being a federation, with two levels of government above the local.

It is not difficult to imagine provinces without local governments. This is especially so in Prince Edward Island, which has a total population only slightly in excess of 140,000. In many ways, the provincial government of PEI is little more than a local government itself, so it is not surprising that the provincial government makes many apparently local decisions.[1] For other provinces, especially the larger ones, imagining a complete absence of local government is much more difficult. In such a state of affairs, the province would make all the decisions about matters within its constitutional sphere of jurisdiction. It would decide how garbage gets collected, where buildings can be built, which teachers will teach in which schools, and how water supply systems will be built and financed. It would not necessarily have to make laws relating to each of these issues in each place, but it would have to establish its own procedures for deciding each of these issues, and many more.

A provincial government would have to address at least three major questions in the absence of any kind of local government:

1. Are all places going to be treated the same way?
2. If not, for which functions of government will there be local flexibility?
3. Will the bureaucracy remain in the capital city or will it be *deconcentrated* to outlying areas?

We will address each question in turn.

The question regarding equal treatment for all places is not about services being identical everywhere. Clearly, no one would contemplate having as many police officers patrolling a rural road as a busy downtown street. Levels of service can always be adjusted in accordance with some kind of rational formula to determine need (number of cars on the road, number of people living nearby, record of recent crimes in the area, etc.). But it would not be easy to develop for every government service appropriate formulas that would produce satisfactory results everywhere in a large province. Fair and efficient administration would be even harder. A small army of bureaucrats would be needed simply to collect all the required data.

Let us assume, however, that it is theoretically possible to work out the appropriate formulas and to administer them. Will these allow for flexibility? What can we do if citizens in one area want to be treated differently from those in another? For some matters—provision of health insurance, for example—the provincial government would be unlikely to allow variation. But what if people in one area of a province want more police (or recreational facilities or public gardens) than the formulas provide for? Or what if they want fewer so that their levels of taxation can be reduced? To accommodate such preferences, the central government would have to develop mechanisms for determining these preferences, for implementing them, and for taxing different groups of people at different rates so that each group pays for its own level of preferred services. Making these kinds of adjustments in taxes and service levels to allow for local preferences, while not impossible, would add a dramatic additional burden to the work of the provincial government.

As for centralizing, or deconcentrating, the machinery of government—that is, the bureaucracy—obviously the government could not manage all the different local activities from its headquarters in the capital city. Not only would large numbers of government employees be needed in major urban centres to actually provide the services, but their managers would have to be dispersed locally to ensure that central policies and procedures were properly followed. To the extent that central officials are located outside the capital, we say that the government is deconcentrated.

If this all sounds like some kind of bureaucratic and administrative nightmare, it is meant to. Many people think that having multiple layers of government—and multiple governments at every layer except for the whole country—is itself a nightmare. One of the major objectives of this chapter, and of this book as a whole, is to show that healthy systems of local government, while far from perfect, are preferable to the kind of centralized system described above. The argument here is not that local governments always work well and will always do what they are supposed to do.[2] Rather, if a system of government for any territory larger than a single small city includes a well-functioning system of local government, then it will work better than a centralized system containing no local government. The next section analyzes why this is so.

Efficiency

The most important reason that central governments establish systems of local government is to promote efficiency. Two senses of *efficiency* are relevant here. The first has to do with economies and diseconomies of scale, a concept from economics that refers to how unit costs change for different products depending on the number of units produced. For example, if electricity were required to serve a few isolated households, no one would decide to serve them by building a nuclear power plant; the cost would be too great for the small amount of electricity needed. Because there are economies of scale in nuclear generation of electricity, such a method could well be cheaper for each household if the whole system were designed to serve millions of people.

Sometimes it is assumed that there are economies of scale for every product. But common sense suggests that this cannot possibly be true. If there were economies of scale in commercial lawn mowing, we would expect to see entities such as a Canadian Lawn Mowing Company or, in this age of globalization, International Lawn Services Incorporated. The reason such companies do not exist is simple: there are no economies of scale in lawn mowing. A giant company cannot compete with a person who owns a single lawn mower and is able to move it around from customer to customer within a small area (and even that person cannot compete with an underemployed teenager who has free access to his parents' lawn mower when it is not being used to cut the family lawn).

The same factors are at work in government services. If citizens want their own highly sophisticated system for common defence against perceived external threats, they are going to be better off if they are part of a very large group who can pool their resources to buy all the latest high-tech equipment. But if the same citizens all desire that their residential neighbourhoods are served by well-maintained and attractive urban parks, they are not likely to be well served by a national "Ministry of Neighbourhood Parks." To prevent the diseconomies of scale that would emerge from having layers of bureaucrats supervising a national system of neighbourhood parks, it is simply more efficient to have hundreds of quite separate organizations providing such parks. In the real world, such organizations are part of local government.[3]

But there is also a different type of efficiency—*allocative efficiency*—that can be promoted by local government. Allocative efficiency in government involves ensuring that the bundle of services and taxes provided by government matches as closely as possible what people actually want. Local governments are well suited for promoting allocative efficiency. They provide a mechanism that enables citizens in different territories to adjust the level of government services to match what they want. Such a mechanism is, of course, far from perfect. Within the same small territory served by the same local government, young families might prefer that their tax money be spent to provide lifeguards for local wading pools while their older neighbours might want more large-print books in the public library. One way or another, the local political process works out compromises between these conflicting interests. The point is that different outcomes are likely in different places, and if the system is relatively open and democratic, such different outcomes reflect a crude measure of allocative efficiency.[4]

There is, however, a potential dark side to allocative efficiency. What if all the richer older people end up living close to each other and the poorer younger families live somewhere else? What if they are separated from each other by the boundaries that create different local governments for each group? If public education were provided exclusively by local governments, the old rich people could decide to have no schools at all, and the poor young families could not afford to provide schools for their own children. It is precisely to prevent such a state of affairs that public education in Western countries is now so closely supervised and controlled by central governments (provinces in Canada).

If citizens in the richer area use their local government to pay for a luxurious recreational and cultural centre that the poorer area clearly cannot afford, the issues are trickier. Some people will argue that it is unfair and therefore unacceptable for rich people to have better public facilities in their areas than poor people can have in theirs, especially if the two areas are relatively close to each other and the use of the luxurious facility is in some way restricted to residents of the area that paid for it. If this argument is extended to claim that rich people should not be allowed to keep their riches, then at least it is consistent. But the logic is hard to see if it is acceptable for rich people to use their riches to build swimming pools in their respective backyards but not to decide to pay high taxes to their local government to provide themselves with one superlative swimming facility. Can we reasonably accept that different people will have different levels of individual financial resources but that all local governments must have similar resources and provide similar levels of services? What about the differences in resources between the governments of Alberta and New Brunswick? More tellingly, what about the differences between the governments of Canada and Bangladesh?

Raising these questions shows that allocative efficiency is potentially a controversial concept. Sensible people can have legitimate disagreements about the extent to which societies should tolerate differences in service levels among their different local governments. But at a minimum, there is surely agreement that groups of citizens in different places, regardless of their financial resources, are likely to have different preferences for some government services and that it is wasteful to ignore such differences by providing a common level of services and taxes everywhere. Local governments enable differentiation in levels of service for different groups of citizens in different areas.

Two other potential arguments about how local governments promote efficiency need to be considered. The first has to do with the benefits of competition. By definition, if there are no local governments within a given jurisdiction, then the one central (e.g., provincial) government in that jurisdiction is a monopoly in the sense that it is the only provider of government services. Monopolies are notorious for being inefficient and for passing on their excessive costs to captive consumers. Establishing a system of local government involves establishing governments whose levels of services and taxes can at least be compared with each other. Citizens therefore have some idea about the relative efficiency of their own local governments and can at least vote accordingly. Indeed, a large body of literature considers the extent to which people and businesses actually move from one jurisdiction to another in search of the local government that best matches their preferences. This literature was originally sparked by an academic article by the American economist Charles Tiebout, who famously argued that governments can be made to be as efficient as private firms by ensuring that there are enough of them to compete with each other to attract taxpaying residents and businesses. Under Tiebout's assumptions, residents and businesses "vote with their feet" when they are dissatisfied with the actions of local governments, and the threat of losing taxpayers forces governments to be as efficient as possible. We need not accept fully the "public-choice" framework that flows from Tiebout's analysis in order to accept that competition among different local governments to do a better job can sometimes be beneficial.[5]

So far, the arguments about efficiency have related to local governments in general, both municipal governments and special-purpose bodies. But the last argument relates only to municipal governments, which, as seen in Chapter 1, are by definition responsible for a number of different governmental functions. The existence of municipalities enables them to benefit from *economies of scope*, which involve efficiencies deriving from the fact that an organization is doing more than one thing at a time. For example, a municipality can benefit from the fact that it can use its own parks and community centres to run recreational programs. Or under-occupied road maintenance workers can be used to fix sewers. If the central government were responsible for these functions (or if they were each provided by a different special-purpose body), then local coordination across different functional areas would likely be more difficult. Economies of scope for functions within the jurisdiction of the same municipality are not guaranteed. Most people can recall seeing municipal workers digging up a municipal roadway one day to fix a sewer only to have it dug up again a few weeks later to fix something else.

In fact, local governments in general do not have a popular reputation for great efficiency. Images of outside workers standing around waiting for equipment to arrive or of inside workers pushing paper from one office to another are probably predominant in many people's minds when they (infrequently) think about local government. Many such images are simply unfair and inaccurate. But that is not what concerns us here. What is relevant is that local government enhances the potential capacity of government in general to be more efficient. Perhaps the only institutions that would be less efficient than local governments in providing local public services would be agencies of central governments.

Participation

There are many exaggerated arguments about how the existence of local governments facilitates citizen participation in local decision-making. Such arguments often conjure up images of deliberative assemblies in ancient Athens, town meetings in New England, or the claim by the English political philosopher John Stuart Mill that local governments are "the chief instrument for the public education of the citizens."[6] What these images all have in common is an assumption that citizens have a keen interest in local issues, a recognition that these issues are to be settled by the actions of local governments, an understanding of how such institutions work, and a belief that their own actions will make a difference in the local decision-making process. In fact, however, much evidence suggests that each of these assumptions is wrong.

Paul E. Peterson, an American political scientist, urges us to recognize some of the harsh facts about local government, especially in North America, many of which we will return to in later chapters of this book. Turnout at elections is low, in part because party involvement is limited, making it difficult for all but the best-informed electors to know whom to vote for. Issues at the local level often seem technical and legalistic, especially in comparison with the broad policy issues with which national legislatures usually occupy themselves. Media attention to local politics is cursory at best, making it more likely that citizens actually know more about what is going on in their national capitals than in their city halls.[7] In these circumstances, how can anyone possibly claim that local government is even partially justified by its ability to enhance citizen participation?

The claim must be based on particular circumstances and issues rather than on generalized claims about the day-to-day activities of local government. Many citizens— even ones who have owned their own houses in the same neighbourhood for a long time— can go for years without having much participatory involvement in local government. They expect the normal municipal services, complain about taxes, and might even vote if they feel they know the candidates. But when someone proposes to make a significant change in their immediate built environment that is perceived to be negative, they often quickly become involved, fully expecting that "their" councillor will support their position. This is where local political activity can be intimate and highly participatory. Councillors generally do respond to groups of enraged local citizens; they encourage these citizens to show up at committee and council meetings; and the citizens actually watch their complaint get dealt with. Thousands of people in Canada become involved in local politics each year in precisely this way, and many subsequently run for election. Some of these people then get elected to decision-making positions themselves, and some of these subsequently enter provincial or federal politics. These are some of the ways that local government promotes meaningful citizen participation in politics.

This is not to pretend that all participation in local politics is prompted by ordinary citizens trying to defend or improve their neighbourhoods. Some people get involved because their livelihood involves local real estate and they know that local governments are very important to the local market. Others become involved in local politics because they are really interested in eventually making a political career at another level and they know that local politics is a good "training ground" and a place to get one's name known. In short, local government decision-making is often, if not usually, intimately connected to complex calculations about short- and long-term political advantage rather than to simply enabling ordinary citizens to have their say on issues that are of concern to them.

These considerations about the participatory and political aspects of local government should cause us to examine how they affect the capacity of local governments to be efficient. In the previous section of this chapter, local governments were portrayed as though they were neutral mechanisms for transforming citizen preferences into public policies and public services. An extreme example of this perspective is represented by the *public-choice* approach, wherein local governments are perceived as acting so much like private firms that their decisions are expected to be determined more by market forces than by preferences expressed through such political mechanisms as elections. But even if we dispense with the fiction that local governments are exclusively engaged in some kind of market competition with each other, we still cannot conclude that it is possible for them to somehow be non-political. The fact that the makeup of their governing boards (councils) is determined through a relatively open electoral process, and that people who get elected usually want to be re-elected, means that participation matters. This is good. Yet, as we shall see in more detail in later chapters, not all citizens are equal when it comes to participation, so not all citizen preferences are accurately and fairly represented in the local decision-making process. This is a fact that not only reflects badly on the capacity of local governments to promote participation but also undermines their capacity to allocate efficiently.

Having acknowledged all this, we are once again left to contemplate what our political life would be like in the absence of local government. Would there be alternative opportunities for citizens to become politically engaged? What participatory avenues would be open to citizens who wanted to affect a central-government decision that affected only their immediate area? Could such avenues be effective if the political or bureaucratic futures of those in the central government were in no way determined by what people in the area actually wanted? Indeed, if there were no local government, our collective political lives might well seem even more limited and powerless than they already are.

Pluralism

A pluralistic political system is one in which there are many sources of power. The opposite of a pluralistic system is a totalitarian one in which the state controls everything and no other sources of power are tolerated. Totalitarian states do not have local governments that are in any sense independent of the central state. In the aftermath of Nazi Germany, and to a lesser extent in the aftermath of the Soviet Union and its Eastern European empire, much attention focused on establishing local governments that could act as bulwarks against the re-emergence of totalitarianism. Although it is doubtful that the existence of local governments can prevent dictatorship at the centre, it is certainly true that local governments provide a source of political power that can serve as counterpoint to the central authority.

In liberal democracies, political power emanates from many sources, which is why these democracies are sometimes called *pluralist democracies*. Big businesses, trade unions, social movements (such as environmentalism), and interest groups (of which there are thousands, such as associations of pharmacists) are all sources of political power, either because they control financial resources and jobs (e.g., big business) or because they have the capacity to influence votes at election time. Unlike the other sources of pluralist political power mentioned above, local governments—especially municipal governments—can claim a special legitimacy based on the fact that their governing bodies are subject to election by universal franchise within their designated territories. This territorial base, combined with their special claim to democratic legitimacy, means that municipal governments can plausibly claim to represent people within these territories.

This doesn't mean they will necessarily get what they want from the central government, but it does mean they are a distinct voice in the pluralist universe. Although federal and provincial legislators represent distinct territories, the boundaries of their constituencies (which are designed to be roughly equal in population within any given province) mean that they often represent areas that are larger or smaller than those of the territorial communities that have the most meaning to people. Municipal boundaries can be more congruent with such communities (although we shall see in later chapters that this is not always the case), and so mayors, for example, have a potentially greater capacity to speak on behalf of territorial communities. If there were no local governments, there would be no mayors.

Functions of Canadian Local Governments

In practical terms, local governments exist to do what cannot be done so well either by central governments or by the private market. In the discussion earlier in this chapter about economies and diseconomies of scale in government services, we saw that some government services can be provided more efficiently if they are provided by organizations that are smaller than the central government. Such functions of government are natural candidates to be placed under the direct jurisdiction of local government. But as we shall see, some functions of government are carried out locally in the absence of such a compelling economic imperative. Such services tend to be closely supervised, and sometimes subsidized, by central governments.

If we were to look at local governments around the world,[8] we would find a huge variety in their functional responsibilities. Indeed, if we allow for central intervention and supervision, it is almost impossible to think of a government function that could not be provided locally. If we do not make such an allowance, it is almost impossible to think of government functions that would be exclusively local, because almost all local services are subject to some form of central guidance. In any event, in the discussion that follows, we shall not be attempting universally applicable descriptions of the functions of local government but shall instead be focusing on what local governments in Canada do. Even this is difficult, however, because considerable variation exists among the provinces.

Ontario is the special case.[9] Unlike other provinces, its municipalities are responsible, under close provincial supervision and with massive provincial subsidies, for delivering income and employment assistance for able-bodied people who have run out of money. The program is called Ontario Works but is more universally recognized as *welfare*. Again, unlike municipalities in other parts of the country, those in Ontario provide subsidized child care, with substantial provincial assistance, to low-income parents. Without provincial financial assistance, they are responsible for providing subsidized "social" housing to people unable to afford market housing. For child care and social housing, Ontario municipalities have considerable freedom in determining the levels of service, although they are required to maintain their current housing portfolios and "they cannot share higher costs for energy or mortgage debt service with tenants."[10]

In all Canadian provinces, municipalities—both urban and rural— have at least some legal authority to act in each of the following functions:[11] fire protection; animal control; roads (but only in the cities of Charlottetown and Summerside in PEI); traffic control; solid waste collection and disposal (but not in PEI); land-use planning and regulation; building regulation; economic development; tourism promotion; public libraries; parks and recreation; cultural facilities; licensing of businesses; emergency planning and preparedness; rural fences and drainage; regulation and/or provision of cemeteries; airports (though not major airports formerly operated directly by the federal government); and weed control and regulation of cosmetic pesticides (although recent provincial legislation in Ontario removes cosmetic pesticides from municipal jurisdiction).

The following are additional functions that are generally carried out by *urban* municipalities: public transit; regulation of taxis; water purification and distribution; sewage collection and treatment; downtown revitalization; and regulation of noise.

Urban municipalities are generally responsible for policing, except in Newfoundland and Labrador, where it is a responsibility of the Royal Newfoundland Constabulary, although various kinds of special-purpose bodies exist in different provinces (as will be outlined in Chapter 4) to insulate police from the direct control of municipal councils. Some urban municipalities obtain their policing through contracts with the Royal Canadian Mounted Police (RCMP) or with provincial police forces (Ontario and Quebec). The RCMP or provincial police forces generally provide policing in rural areas. Arrangements vary from province to province concerning the extent to which rural municipalities contribute to the cost. In Ontario, rural municipalities have paid the full cost since 1998.

As we have seen, Ontario is the only province in which municipalities have the statutory responsibility to provide social services and contribute to their funding. In Alberta, municipal governments contribute to the funding of certain preventative social service programs and lodges for low-income senior citizens. Arrangements for municipal seniors' residences in Ontario are similar, except that they are operated directly by cities and upper-tier municipalities rather than by separate non-profit corporations. In British Columbia, larger urban municipalities (especially the city of Vancouver) are engaged in social planning functions mainly aimed at attracting funding from other levels of government, coordinating the work of non-profit agencies, and providing modest municipal subsidies to various kinds of social service organizations, including community centres and non-profit child-care centres. In other provinces, there is even less municipal involvement in social services, ranging from none at all to minor expenditures for non-recreational programs in community centres and for the staffing of social planning groups.

Quebec and Ontario are the only provinces in which cities have any financial responsibility for the operating costs of social housing. In some other provinces, major cities provide land and/or capital contributions to new social housing units. The city of Vancouver manages subsidized housing for seniors and people with disabilities but has no financial responsibility for these units. Even the management costs are paid by other levels of government. Regional districts in British Columbia manage rental units for low-income people but make no financial contribution. In Calgary there has been a well-known and apparently quite successful "10 Year Plan to End Homelessness," but the main instigator is the non-profit Calgary Homeless Foundation, not the municipality.[12]

Municipalities in Ontario are responsible for providing land-ambulance services. The City of Winnipeg has a contractual arrangement with the regional health authority to provide ambulance services within its territory, but this appears not to be a municipal responsibility elsewhere in the province.

The regulation of air quality is a municipal (regional district) responsibility in British Columbia. Public health is explicitly a municipal responsibility only in Ontario, where it is often carried out through regional or county public health units. In Manitoba, municipalities are responsible for the inspection of food service establishments and for insect control.

Public utilities (other than water supply) are difficult to categorize. For example, electrical distribution in Ontario's urban areas is the responsibility of business corporations, most of which are still owned by municipalities. Some small municipalities own local telephone companies and others own their own natural gas distribution systems.

In many developed countries, municipal governments have direct responsibility for public education. In Canada, public education is the responsibility of local school boards, although their authority varies significantly from province to province. Only in Quebec do school boards still have the authority to levy their own taxes to help finance local schools.

We can conclude from all this that the core functions of Canadian local governments—especially municipalities—involve planning, regulating, protecting, and providing infrastructure services for our built environment. In the urban areas in which most of us live, such a responsibility is crucial to the quality of life, and this is why municipalities are so important. Notwithstanding the suitability of municipalities for controlling the built environment, no one can sensibly claim that each individual municipality should be able to do as its residents please. Most of us are now painfully aware, for example, that residential development that requires inhabitants to drive cars to live their everyday lives is damaging not just to the health of the individual residents but also to the environment that we all must share. That is why central governments are increasingly legislating the general principles under which municipalities regulate local development, and this in turn is why intergovernmental relations, in Canada and elsewhere, are becoming increasingly complex, leaving us much to contemplate in subsequent chapters.

Conclusion

The built environment is under local jurisdiction in Canada and most other countries because it is physically located in a particular place. For efficiency reasons discussed above, it makes sense that one central government is not directly responsible for all aspects of the built environment in hundreds of different settlements, large and small. By establishing local governments to manage the built environment—and to perform certain other services designated by central governments — we can concurrently provide valuable opportunities for political participation and engagement and enhance pluralism by creating alternative sources of political power rooted in elected territorial governments rather than in big businesses, trade unions, social movements, and interest groups.

RESOURCES

Lionel Feldman, ed., *Politics and Government of Urban Canada: Selected Readings*, 4th ed. (Toronto: Methuen, 1981), Part I, 1–86, contains classic and conflicting articles by Georges Langrod, Keith Panter-Brick, Leo Moulin, L.J. Sharpe, Robert A. Dahl, and Warren Magnusson on the relationship between local government and democracy.

STUDY QUESTIONS

1. What are *economies of scale* and why are they important in debates about local government?
2. What does it mean to "vote with your feet"? Should local governments pay attention to this phenomenon? Why or why not?
3. Do you believe that local governments in most provinces could be replaced by deconcentrated provincial governments? Explain your reasoning.

CHAPTER 3

Central Governments and Local Governments

Local governments are part of Canada's multi-level system of government. We saw in Chapter 1 that local governments are sometimes divided into two levels. But in this chapter we are concerned with the governments that cover larger territories than local governments, the ones that we have called central governments. Canada is a federation in which two levels of government, the federal and provincial, are established by the Constitution. In different ways, both of these levels of government have profound impacts on what local governments can and cannot do. This chapter is about those impacts and how municipalities organize themselves to respond.

Constitutional Role of Federal and Provincial Governments

Canada's written Constitution consists of the Constitution Act, 1867 (originally titled the British North America Act) and the Constitution Act, 1982 and their amendments.[1] No reference is made in these documents to the terms *local government* or *municipality*. However, the term *municipal* is mentioned twice, both times in section 92 of the Constitution Act, 1867, which is concerned with "exclusive powers of provincial legislatures." Subsection 8 lists "Municipal Institutions in the Province" as one of the exclusive provincial powers, and subsection 9 lists "Shop, Saloon, Tavern, Auctioneer, and other Licenses in order to the raising of a Revenue for Provincial, Local, or Municipal Purposes." Subsection 16 adds to provincial jurisdiction "Generally all Matters of a merely local or private Nature in the Province."

This is the sum total of what the Canadian Constitution says about provincial authority over municipalities, and it has been enough for judges, commentators, and politicians over the years constantly to claim that Canadian municipalities are "creatures of the provinces." Such a characterization is accurate as far as it goes, because municipalities under the Constitution rely on the provinces for their legal existence. A corollary to this statement is that any federal law purporting to alter the legal status of a municipality would be unconstitutional. But as we shall see throughout this chapter, there are many actions that the federal government can take—and does take—that directly affect what municipalities actually do.

For one thing, when the federal government is acting for purposes within its own spheres of jurisdiction, it is not bound by municipal regulations that might apply to other property owners or employers in the municipality. This is an important point, because the federal government is the country's largest property-owner and employer. In many Canadian municipalities—especially ones that contain or are near to major military bases, national parks, or other major federal facilities—the federal government's presence is crucial to the local economy. Federal policies concerning such matters as immigration, ports and airports, depreciation of buildings for income tax purposes, and the funding of research can also be crucial to local economies. So it is absolutely wrong to claim that, just because the federal government has no constitutional responsibility for Canadian municipalities, it is irrelevant to those municipalities. As we shall see, in recent years, municipalities have been especially active in seeking new funds from the federal government, an objective that is perfectly constitutional because the federal government faces few restrictions on its ability to spend. In any event, most federal funds destined for municipalities are channelled through their respective provincial governments.

To think more carefully about the meaning of the Constitution with respect to Canadian local government, it is interesting to contemplate whether the federal government could establish elected local special-purpose bodies within its field of jurisdiction. For example, as the result of an amendment to the Constitution approved in 1940, unemployment insurance is clearly within federal jurisdiction. What if the federal Parliament approved a law dividing Canada into multiple territories for this purpose and establishing local elected bodies in each territory to decide on local details of implementation? Such authorities would be local governments under federal jurisdiction. It is hard to see how such a law could be subject to a constitutional challenge. As we shall see in the next chapter, federally established authorities that operate ports and airports are essentially local special-purpose bodies, although the members of their governing bodies are not elected.

The National Capital Commission (NCC), comprising 15 members all appointed by the federal government, can be seen as a local special-purpose body under federal jurisdiction. In its earlier institutional manifestations it played a major role in drawing up and implementing a regional plan for the entire capital area, the most notable feature of which is a greenbelt around the original city of Ottawa. The NCC also is also responsible for significant green spaces and recreational areas on the Quebec side of the river. An important constitutional ruling of the Supreme Court of Canada in 1966 held that "the federal government had the power to plan for the National Capital Region, and to expropriate land for its purposes, including land for the Greenbelt."[2] This power related exclusively to the fact that the area in question was the federal capital. Similar federal powers do not exist in other Canadian cities.

Municipal institutions are not in any way protected by the Canadian Constitution. They are simply placed under provincial jurisdiction. It is wrong, however, to claim that there is no protection for *any* form of local government in the Constitution, because the Constitution contains important provisions relating to the ability of certain kinds of local minorities to control their own public schools. Section 93 of the Constitution Act, 1867 places education under provincial jurisdiction but protects the rights possessed by designated religious minorities (Roman Catholic and Protestant) in certain provinces (now Ontario, Saskatchewan, and Alberta) when those provinces entered Confederation. This means that, in the affected provinces, Roman Catholics have the right to elect their own school boards. By extension, it seems that public school supporters in those provinces have the same constitutional right. Since the passage of the Constitution Act, 1982, various decisions of the Supreme Court of Canada have held that the rights of French and English linguistic minorities in each province to minority-language education include rights to manage and control such education. But such rulings on language rights have done little to protect the local nature of educational governance because in six provinces a single French-language school board covers the entire province.[3]

Provincial Statutes Relating to Local Government

Unlike American states, Canadian provinces do not have their own written constitutions. Provincial legislatures are free to enact any kind of law they want, as long as it does not violate the Charter of Rights and Freedoms, impinge on federal jurisdiction or on the protected rights of religious minorities concerning education, or affect the office of Lieutenant-Governor (the Queen's representative appointed by the federal government). This means that no form of constitutional protection exists for municipalities in Canada, a situation contrasting with that in many American states where state constitutions provide for various kinds of municipal protection, often known generically as *home rule*.[4]

In Canada, every province has at least one general law, or statute, that establishes the basic rules for municipal government. In some provinces different laws exist for urban and rural municipalities. Many of Canada's largest cities, including Toronto, Montreal, Vancouver, and Winnipeg, are mostly exempt from such general laws because special provincial laws, often called *charters*, apply only to them. The existence of such charters must not be confused with the kind of "home rule" that exists in many American states. A city charter in Canada is nothing more than an ordinary provincial statute. It provides no extra constitutional protection for the municipality to which it applies. Its provisions can be changed by the provincial legislature at any time without any form of approval from the municipality. The only sense in which a city charter is especially important is if it grants more authority than that which is found in general provincial legislation applying to municipalities.

These general laws that apply to other municipalities are usually known as *municipal acts*, but what they are called doesn't really matter. What matters is what is contained within them. In the last decade or so, provincial legislatures have tended to try to simplify such laws by granting municipal governments various forms of general jurisdiction over a relatively wide range of subjects related to local affairs. Past practice involved detailed lists of exactly what it was that municipalities were allowed to make rules about. The apparent requirement for such lists derived from the fact that Canadian courts generally adopted what American jurists refer to as *Dillon's rule*, "as set down by Iowa Supreme Court Judge John F. Dillon in the 1860s, who equated municipalities with business corporations, both of them limited to the powers expressly granted through their incorporation."[5] *Express authority* (or power) refers to matters explicitly listed in provincial legislation as being under municipal jurisdiction. The advantage of having express authority was that, if a subject appeared on the list, it was extremely difficult for anyone to claim in a court of law that a municipality was acting illegally by attempting to regulate it. The problem, however, was that, every time a new local issue emerged, municipalities would have to ask the provincial legislature to amend the law to grant them the required jurisdiction. Now that the assignment of municipal jurisdiction is more general in most provinces, we can expect municipalities to test their jurisdictional limits and affected individuals and companies to challenge such apparent jurisdiction in the courts. The important principle here is that municipalities can do nothing without some kind of authorization by a provincial law. If a municipality is regulating taxi fares, it is doing so either because it has express authority to do so or because it is acting under a more general provincial grant of authority such as "all matters related to public vehicular transportation."

In recent years there has also been a provincial trend to grant *natural person powers* to municipalities. A *natural person* is an adult human being. With natural person powers, municipalities can generally do what persons can legally do, such as enter into contracts and borrow money. Municipalities already had most of these powers anyway, and no provincial law envisions municipalities doing *all* the things a person can do (e.g., get married, adopt children), so the granting of natural person powers has hardly caused a revolution in municipal law. Nevertheless, Tindal, Tindal, Stewart, and Smith are right to point out that the additional natural person powers granted to municipalities provide them with a wider range of tools to carry out their assigned functions.[6]

It would be a huge mistake to assume that the only places to look for such laws governing municipalities are in the general municipal statutes or in the special ones (charters) that apply in some of the large cities. For one thing, provincial governments often sponsor laws that apply only to particular municipalities or groups of municipalities. These laws are just as valid as more general ones, so any lawyer or researcher needs to know the contents of all of them. More importantly, a great many other provincial laws relate to a wide variety of subjects that grant authority to municipalities. For example, if one wanted to know what municipalities in a particular province could do with respect to controlling traffic, it might well be more fruitful to search in laws regarding roads and transportation than in the relevant Municipal Act. Some of these laws establish local special-purpose bodies and outline how such bodies will relate to municipal government. Laws having to do with municipal police forces and with land-use planning are especially relevant here.

So far we have not referred to private statutes. These are often of considerable importance in understanding how provincial law applies to particular municipalities. Private statutes are enacted by provincial legislatures only on the application of an individual, a municipality, or a corporation; they relate only to the particular interests of the applicant.

Municipalities frequently request private statutes so that they can solve some particular local problem for which there is no other legal remedy. These statutes are usually sponsored by the local member representing the area in which the statute is meant to apply; they are never sponsored by a cabinet minister. In dealing with private statutes, the legislature follows special procedures to make sure that any affected person or corporation gets a chance to demonstrate how their interests will be affected. All statutes that are not private statutes are known as *public statutes*. For most public-policy questions, researchers need only know about public statutes, but when we are studying the legal authority of particular municipalities in particular circumstances, we often need to know about the relevant private statutes as well.

Provincial Ministries and Ministers

Each province has a cabinet minister designated to look after the municipal system within the province. The most common title is Minister of Municipal Affairs, but other titles are used as well. For example, in British Columbia the person holding the title is the Minister of Community, Sport and Cultural Development. These ministers are all responsible for ensuring that legislation is in place and implemented so that municipalities can do their jobs effectively, efficiently, and democratically. In some provinces the legislation gives the minister considerable authority to control what municipalities do; in others there is much less in the way of central supervision. Similarly, the number of provincial public servants assisting the minister in carrying out these functions varies considerably. These and other matters of common concern are discussed at annual meetings of Provincial and Territorial Ministers Responsible for Local Government that are organized by the Canadian Intergovernmental Conference Secretariat.[7]

It is important to note that, even though municipalities are legally "creatures of the provinces," no provincial minister is in a hierarchical relationship with respect to municipalities; except in the most unusual circumstances specified by law, no minister can tell a mayor or municipal council what to do. Provincial law establishes municipalities as institutions that are separate from the provincial government. Provincial ministers responsible for municipal affairs frequently find themselves defending the desirability of municipal autonomy against attacks from ministerial colleagues who might wish to impose highly detailed rules about what municipalities can do concerning their own spheres of concern, such as roads. This defence is an important function, because almost all provincial ministers must deal with municipalities in one way or another. In general, ministries of municipal affairs are the only provincial ministries with a direct interest in enhancing the participatory and local democratic features of municipal activities. Other ministries tend to see municipalities only as convenient mechanisms for the local delivery of some of the provincial services for which they are responsible.

Some of these other ministries have responsibility for the smooth operation of local special-purpose bodies that operate within their spheres of jurisdiction. The best examples are the provincial ministries responsible for education: their relationship to school boards is analogous to the relationship between ministries of municipal affairs and municipalities. Similarly, provincial ministries responsible for policing are generally responsible for whatever local special-purpose bodies are established to govern local police services. A frequent dynamic within provincial governments is that, whenever uncertainty exists about who should have power over what at the local level, ministers of municipal affairs defend the interests of municipalities while the other ministers defend their respective special-purpose bodies. We shall return to this issue in the next chapter.

Administrative Tribunals

Many provincial statutes, especially those concerned with land-use planning, either require that certain municipal decisions be approved at the provincial level before they come into effect or provide opportunities for aggrieved local citizens to appeal such decisions to the provincial government. One mechanism for deciding on these approvals or appeals is to require action from the relevant minister. For matters of important policy in which the provincial government has a clear interest, it makes sense for the issue to require a ministerial decision. But no minister wants to be burdened with having to decide the exact meaning of a particular policy in every possible circumstance or to referee relatively routine disputes between citizens and their local governments. Fortunately, there is an alternative. Such matters can be referred to a provincial administrative tribunal.

Most provinces have some kind of administrative tribunal or tribunals relating to municipal affairs and/or land-use planning. The authority of each varies dramatically from province to province. The extremes are British Columbia and Ontario. In British Columbia there is no provincial appeal tribunal for local land-use planning, and general complaints about abuse of process or funds by municipalities go to a single provincial official, the Inspector of Municipalities. In Ontario, there is an extremely powerful tribunal, the Ontario Municipal Board, which we shall soon examine in a bit more detail.

In British Columbia, municipalities must gain approval of the Agricultural Land Commission[8] if they wish to authorize development within the province's reserve of agricultural land. Apart from that, regional districts and municipalities in BC have remarkable autonomy to make their own final decisions about the use of land. Provincial legislation does require that, prior to any changes in land-use regulation, municipal councils must consult with affected parties and hold at least one formal public hearing on the matter. Such changes directly affect the value of people's property, and the general common-law principle is that everyone potentially affected by the changes has a right to be heard and to be part of a fair process of decision-making. This principle also applies, of course, in the other common-law provinces (all except Quebec), which is why municipal decisions that directly affect particular individual interests can usually be appealed to the courts. But appeals to courts can only be based on the *process* by which the municipal decision-making process was carried out. Appeals to administrative tribunals are usually about the *substance* of the municipal decision, which is why they exist separately from the courts. Two of the most obvious differences between municipal councils on the one hand, and the federal and provincial legislatures on the other, are that municipalities are corporations exercising delegated authority from provinces and that they routinely make decisions directly affecting the property rights of particular individuals. These characteristics mean that municipal decisions are much more susceptible to various forms of appeal, thereby causing municipal decision-makers constantly to wonder if their actions on a particular matter will eventually end up in a court of law or an administrative tribunal.

Because of its great power and status within Canada's largest province, the Ontario Municipal Board (OMB) deserves special attention. It was created in 1906 as the Ontario Railway and Municipal Board, charged primarily with hearing applications for and regulating intra-provincial railways and street railways within municipalities.[9] It became the OMB in 1932 after its railway functions had atrophied and its supervisory roles concerning municipal finances and land-use planning had greatly increased.[10] The OMB has about 35 members, all appointed by the provincial cabinet for renewable three-year terms. Most are lawyers, land-use planners, or former municipal councillors. Almost all their hearings—conducted by panels comprising one to three members—now relate to land-use planning. Virtually all municipal planning decisions or non-decisions, ranging from a new official plan for an entire municipality to a minor variance in zoning affecting a single property-owner, can be appealed to the OMB. What the municipal council actually did or did not do is of little consequence to the OMB. It wants to hear the *reasons* for the municipal action and the *reasons* the appellants think the municipal council acted wrongly. This usually involves costly expert opinions on both sides that are gathered and cross-examined by the lawyers for the various parties involved in the dispute. If declared "provincial policies" appear to be relevant, then the OMB is supposed to take these into account as well.

The key point is that the OMB effectively substitutes its own judgment for that of the relevant municipal council. Because all the actors in any municipal decision-making process about the use of land in Ontario know that an appeal to the OMB is always possible for almost any conceivable reason, municipal decision-making is often seen as simply a step in the process rather than its culmination.[11] There has been much rhetoric in Ontario in recent years about the empowerment of municipalities in general and the city of Toronto in particular. But as long as the OMB maintains its power, Ontario municipalities will be among the weakest in North America when it comes to their ability to control their own land use. Meanwhile, all the lawyers and consultants involved in OMB hearings are powerful opponents of change to its authority. So are developers—and sometimes even citizen groups—who tend to believe that OMB decision-making is more predictable and consistent than that of elected municipal councils.

Administrative tribunals exist for local government functions other than land-use planning. For example, most provinces have some form of tribunal that regulates municipal police services, hears appeals from police officers about disciplinary issues, and investigates province-wide policing issues (investigating citizen complaints against particular officers is usually carried out by yet another body). In Ontario, the Ontario Civilian Commission on Police Services is also charged with refereeing disputes between municipal councils and local police services boards (which are special-purpose bodies) about the financing of local police services.

Money

Local governments, such as police services boards and municipalities, need money. Ultimately, the province decides how they can get it. Provincial legislatures approve laws that specifically authorize certain forms of local taxation, the levying of user charges, and formulas for the transfer of money from the provincial treasury to local governments. We shall examine these transfers further in Chapter 14; for now, however, we need to note that they can be for general purposes (unconditional) or for specific purposes (conditional). Specific-purpose grants are allocated on the condition that they are used to help finance an objective that the provincial government deems to be desirable, such as support for low-income housing.

Generally, provincial legislatures do not place restrictions on how organizations and individuals might voluntarily bestow funds on local governments, but Quebec legislation requires that federal funding of Quebec municipalities must receive prior provincial approval.[12] In Manitoba, British Columbia, and Saskatchewan, provincial governments have been explicit partners in tri-level *urban development agreements* involving the federal government and the cities of Winnipeg, Vancouver, Regina, and Saskatoon. In these agreements all three levels of government participate financially in attempting to remedy targeted urban problems. The agreements have received considerable academic attention,[13] but Vancouver's is probably the best known because it has provided for "Insite," the supervised injection site for drug addicts located in the Downtown Eastside. The agreements expired in 2010, but efforts by the Harper government to close Insite were blocked in 2011 by the Supreme Court of Canada on the grounds that closure would violate the Charter rights of the addicts benefiting from the service.[14] Prime Minister Stephen Harper, unlike Prime Minister Paul Martin (2003–6), has frequently expressed the view that the federal government should not be signing formal intergovernmental agreements with municipalities.

Provincial policies about local government funding are hugely important. In theory, a province could allow its local governments to have the same taxing authority as the province itself, so local personal and corporate income taxes, as well as sales taxes, could be implemented, just as they have been in some American states. In the past, there have been isolated examples of municipal income and sales taxes in Canada; Montreal's authority to levy a municipal sales tax was removed in 1964.[15] In fact, the main local tax has always been a tax on real (i.e., land and buildings) property. Issues relating to property tax often dominate local politics because revenues from it are crucial to the quality of local services. Property tax levels are often forefront in the minds of property owners, whether residential, commercial, or industrial. We shall return to the property tax in Chapter 15.

Whether municipalities should have access to other taxes has been a controversial issue in recent years. Municipal officials have often argued for new taxation authority, but what they seem most interested in is getting a guaranteed share of various federal and provincial taxes, especially sales taxes, including the federal Goods and Services Tax (GST). Effective in 2007, Toronto was granted the authority to tax land transfers, the renewal of motor vehicle registrations, public entertainment (such as movies), tobacco products, and alcohol served in bars and restaurants. So far, after huge political battles in council, Toronto has levied a land transfer tax of 2 per cent and an annual $60 municipal tax on vehicle registrations. After the election of Mayor Rob Ford in 2010, the city subsequently repealed the tax on vehicle registrations. Implementation of the other possible taxes has never taken place, the fear being such taxes would have the effect of driving customers of commercial operations elsewhere. This might not be a problem in downtown Toronto, but who would want to own a bar or movie theatre near the city's outer border if there were bars and movie theatres a few blocks away in a neighbouring municipality whose patrons were not required to pay the tax?

Municipalities have generally been more successful in obtaining *shares* of particular federal and provincial taxes. Their most important victory came in the 2005 federal budget when the Liberal government promised to send five cents a litre of its federal gas tax to Canadian municipalities for the next five years. In 2011 the Conservative government permanently extended this commitment. The money is allocated to each province in accordance with its share of the Canadian population. Allocation to the municipalities is determined by a federal agreement with each province.[16] In British Columbia and Ontario, the provincial association of municipalities is a party to the agreement, and in Ontario, the city of Toronto has its own agreement. The federal conditions for sharing the funds are relatively lax, resulting in the claim by municipalities that this is the way all federal funds should be disbursed locally. Nevertheless, even federal tax-sharing on gas is in fact a form of federal grant, subject to some real conditions: municipalities can only use the funds for "environmentally sustainable capital infrastructure." If the federal and municipal governments were literally sharing revenue from a common tax, the municipalities could make their own decisions about their portion of the rate in accordance with whatever intergovernmental agreement they were able to negotiate. They could then spend the proceeds as they wished, just as the federal government does.

Reasons for Central Involvement in Local Issues

So far in this chapter we have been assuming that provincial governments are involved primarily in laying out the basic legal and financial framework for local governments. We have also noted some recent federal initiatives, especially in relation to providing funds for local government. But federal and provincial governments often have policy objectives of their own when they take action with respect to local governments. Provinces are not merely fulfilling their jurisdictional obligations with respect to "municipal institutions," and the federal government is not simply being generous. This section analyzes two reasons central governments make policy decisions that are designed to regulate or to influence the policy decisions of local governments.

Externalities

Let us assume that a provincial legislature decides that local governments should take complete control over matters relating to waste water (sewage). Let us also assume that in one city electors choose a council whose majority is committed above all else to a clean environment. In a nearby city, however, electors choose a council that is committed to economic growth. There is nothing inherently wrong with different voters in different cities choosing councils with different political priorities. As we have seen in the previous chapter, allowing for such differences among voters' preferences in different places is one of the main reasons why local governments are established in the first place.

Let us also assume that the environmentally conscious council spends its taxpayers' money to make expensive investments in the best sewage treatment equipment available. Its tax levels rise. It approves tough laws preventing the unauthorized release of any sewage that might be environmentally damaging. Such laws cause some investors to decide not to locate their businesses within its boundaries because they worry about the costs of compliance. Depending on the existing arrangements for the financing of local government, the absence of new business investment could cause taxes for current inhabitants to rise still further. Furthermore, even with the adoption of such tough and costly policies, the state of the local environment might not improve. How can this be?

The answer could lie with the municipality next door. It might decide to attract business by keeping taxes low and therefore not investing in pollution-fighting infrastructure. It has decided to keep its regulatory regime to a minimum so as to make itself even more attractive to investors. To make all this tolerable to current residents, the council encourages new pollution-producing investors to locate their facilities near the municipality's outer boundaries, one of which happens to be upstream from the boundary with the environmentally conscious council. The latter would suffer all of the negative consequences of the former's policy and reap none of the benefits of its own.

The problem here is that the municipal boundaries would appear to bisect a single ecological area. In economists' terms, one municipality is able to foist its "negative externalities" on to another which, in turn, is not being rewarded for the production of "positive externalities."[17] Three possible solutions exist. The first is for the central government to take over the entire function. But a central government is unlikely to be able to manage effectively all aspects of sewage systems in every urban settlement within its jurisdiction. The second solution is to change the municipal boundaries. This approach will be discussed in subsequent chapters. The third is for the central government to intervene by introducing rules and regulations (perhaps accompanied by subsidies for anti-pollution investment) that ensure that no municipality can export its pollution to another. Such regulations appear to inhibit local autonomy, but, as demonstrated by the case of the environmentally conscious municipality, they also ensure that the designated policies of some local governments are not sabotaged by the contrary policies of their neighbours.

In principle, it is appropriate for central governments to intervene to prevent or punish negative municipal externalities and to encourage or reward positive municipal externalities. Such a proposition is easily acceptable in theory. Much of the everyday politics of central–local relations, however, involves disputes about what constitutes an externality. For example, in June 2013, the city of Ottawa asked the Ontario government either to take full responsibility for a road within its borders or to allow it to charge tolls at the city boundaries for the use of the road. The city's case was built on evidence that "about 20 percent of the drivers using the road at rush hour are from outside Ottawa."[18] The city's case was that it should not have to pay for the positive externalities generated by its road. The province did not accept the city's argument; if it did so, there would presumably be similar claims by other municipalities all over the province. There is no way to calculate all the positive or negative externalities generated by the services provided by any particular municipality.

Advancing Central Priorities

Sometimes a central government subsidizes particular local activities because it claims that they generate positive externalities for a wide area.

An extreme form of such a claim would be that more investment in subway systems in our major cities provides benefits even to rural Canadians because, without such systems, our cities cannot act efficiently as generators of economic growth. But it is probably more helpful not to unduly stretch the concept of externalities and simply acknowledge that central governments sometimes want to accomplish certain policy objectives of their own and can only do so by acting through local governments. To illustrate this point, we shall look at two ways in which the federal government has become involved in local issues: infrastructure subsidies and homelessness.

In Canada both the federal and provincial governments have subsidized local infrastructure, especially over the last decade.[19] As we shall see below, this has in part been a response to vigorous lobbying by municipalities. Responding to such lobbying enables federal and provincial politicians to benefit politically by "cutting ribbons" at official openings of new facilities. Americans refer to such centrally funded local projects as *pork* that is brought home by local legislators. But there can also be some very sound reasons why central governments might want to fund local infrastructure. One such reason became apparent after the worldwide financial collapse in 2008. Like many other national governments, the Canadian federal government wanted to inject money into the economy as quickly and productively as possible. Every major municipality in the country had a list of infrastructure projects that were waiting for capital funding. By granting money to municipalities for these "shovel-ready" projects, the federal government created jobs and stabilized the economy (their main objectives) while municipalities were able to accelerate their plans for infrastructure renewal. For different reasons, both levels of government were winners. In its 2013 budget, the federal government announced that programs for the subsidizing of local infrastructure projects (in addition to the sharing of the federal gas tax) would continue.[20]

Both the federal government and the provinces have a long history of involvement with Canadian municipalities to provide housing to people who cannot afford market rents.[21] Federal involvement began after the Second World War, when the government mandated its agency for guaranteeing private residential mortgages, the Central (now Canada) Mortgage and Housing Corporation (CMHC), to use its profits to fund major public housing projects in large cities. Over the years CMHC developed an increasingly sophisticated array of programs to provide different types of social housing, but, starting in the mid-1980s, it disengaged, leaving social housing primarily to the provinces. Nevertheless, a vestige of the commitment to fighting homelessness remains. A federal Homelessness Partnering Strategy (HPS) administered by Employment and Social Development Canada was allocated $135 million per year from 2011 to 2014. The funds do not actually provide housing but rather are aimed at supporting "activities that help ensure people who are homeless and/or at risk of becoming homeless are able to stabilize their living arrangements and circumstances and move beyond emergency needs."[22]

Except in Ontario, the provinces are now the main policy-makers and funders for social housing. Providing such housing fits well with their overall responsibilities for health and social services, because adequate housing is such an important component of human well-being. Nevertheless, provinces need physical locations for whatever social housing they assist in providing, and this is where municipalities come into the picture. Municipalities can provide land they own, or they can acquire land for social housing as part of the approval process for private housing developments (see Chapter 10). Municipal officials, both elected and appointed, invariably have key roles to play in determining the ways in which homeless people are treated within a community and how receptive nearby residents are likely to be to proposals for the construction of new social housing. Municipal opposition—or even indifference—can kill such proposals, but careful municipal planning can help ensure that social housing is seamlessly integrated into an overall pattern of neighbourhood development.

Central and local governments need each other in many fields of governmental policy-making. Central–local relations are not just about the central level telling the local what to do. We have seen examples of this in the previous paragraphs. But municipal leaders (and, to a lesser extent, leaders of local special-purpose bodies) do not simply assume that officials in other governments will look after their best interests and contact them whenever they see a need. Municipal leaders are active participants in the wider political process that shapes the environment in which all levels of government must operate. They do so mainly through municipal organizations.

Municipal Organizations

Municipalities organize themselves through the Federation of Canadian Municipalities (FCM) based in Ottawa and similar groups in each of the provinces. The existence of these associations points to an obvious tension in the status of municipalities within the Canadian political universe. On the one hand, they are clearly elected governments, having to deal daily with interest groups clamouring for lower taxes, a cleaner environment, better roads, and more housing for people who cannot afford market prices. On the other hand, from the perspective of the federal and provincial governments, municipalities make their case as though they themselves were just another interest group. There are too many municipalities for each one to make its own case and, in any event, they share a great many common interests. But once they join together in an association, they lose much of what makes them distinct. Precisely this problem helps explain why the city of Toronto is not a member of the Association of Municipalities of Ontario. It is so much larger than other municipalities in the province that its leaders believe they can do a better job themselves of representing the city's interests to the provincial government. Toronto remains, however, an active member of the FCM.

The FCM has existed since 1901. Its membership comprises almost 2000 municipalities—over half of the Canadian total. But most of the non-members are the very smallest. Many are indirectly represented by the 19 provincial and territorial associations of municipalities that are also FCM members. (Some provinces have both francophone and anglophone associations, and some have separate associations representing big cities and smaller and rural municipalities.) The FCM operates exclusively at the federal level, lobbying constantly to direct federal funds towards municipalities.[23] As already noted, in recent years it has been especially successful in relation to infrastructure (including the sharing of the federal gas tax) and in obtaining $550 million from the federal government for the Green Municipal Fund, which the FCM administers as loans and grants to Canadian municipalities to enhance community sustainability.[24] The FCM also managed in 2004 to convince the federal government to give municipalities a 100 per cent rebate on amounts that they pay for the GST.

The FCM has obviously favoured a strong federal presence in relation to matters of importance to Canadian municipalities. In the 1970s it was a firm supporter of the short-lived federal Ministry of State for Urban Affairs.[25] In 2004 Prime Minister Martin appointed a Secretary of State for Cities and Communities, but the cabinet position did not survive when Prime Minister Harper took office in 2006. In both of these cases, the federal plan was not to try to take over provincial jurisdiction in relation to municipalities but rather to coordinate more effectively the many federal activities with direct consequences for municipalities.[26] But this is a sensitive matter, especially in Quebec, so it is unlikely that yet another federal institution for cities will emerge anytime soon. Meanwhile, the FCM carries on its lobbying activities in whichever federal agencies seem relevant to the policy concerns of Canadian municipalities.

In the same way that provincial governments are much more important for the day-to-day activities of municipalities than the federal government is, provincial associations of municipalities are generally more important than the FCM. They are key players in any provincial policy-making that affects municipalities, and their annual conferences generally command the presence of a wide array of provincial cabinet ministers. Their main problem is the difficulty of building political unity among municipalities, except on the vaguest of principles. While all municipalities in a particular province might agree that their provincial government should transfer more funds to them, they soon disagree among themselves about the criteria for disbursement or the local programs to

Table 3.1 Provincial and Territorial Associations of Municipalities in Canada

Alberta Association of Municipal Districts and Counties

Alberta Urban Municipalities Association

Union of British Columbia Municipalities

l'Association des municipalités bilingues du Manitoba

Association of Manitoba Municipalities

Municipalities Newfoundland and Labrador

Association francophone des municipalités du Nouveau-Brunswick

Cities of New Brunswick Association

Union of Municipalities of New Brunswick

Union of Nova Scotia Municipalities

Association of Municipalities of Ontario

Federation of Prince Edward Island Municipalities

Fédération Québécoise des Municipalités

Union des Municipalités du Québec

Saskatchewan Association of Rural Municipalities

Saskatchewan Urban Municipalities Association

Northwest Territories Association of Communities

Nunavut Association of Municipalities

Association of Yukon Communities

Source: © Federation of Canadian Municipalities. Reprinted with permission.

which funds should be targeted. For example, large urban municipalities might want funds for public transit while rural municipalities might be preoccupied with the need to improve the drainage of agricultural land. It is often extremely difficult to reach inter-municipal agreement, which is another reason Toronto has left the Ontario provincial association. Much of the day-to-day work of provincial associations of municipalities involves participating in various forms of consultative committees established by provincial ministries, many of which can be of considerable significance for provincial policy-making. The associations' role, of course, is to ensure that the municipal voice is heard while important decisions affecting them are being made. Often they do a highly effective job. But municipal politicians in big cities usually feel they should be consulted directly on any matter of concern to them, which is another reason they sometimes feel they can get along without the associations.

Municipal interests are so different that, as can be seen in Table 3.1, six provinces have more than one association. In two cases (Manitoba and New Brunswick), separate associations exist for municipalities that operate at least partly in French. But far more significant for our purposes is the fact that in three other provinces (Alberta, Saskatchewan, and Quebec) separate organizations exist for urban and rural municipalities, meaning that municipalities in these provinces do not generally even attempt to arrive at common positions with respect to provincial policies. Whether this makes much difference in the overall scheme of things is unclear. For example, the Association of Municipalities of Ontario (AMO), representing both urban and rural municipalities in Ontario, is subdivided into eight caucuses and one distinct organization (for French-speaking municipalities), each of which elects varying numbers of representatives to a board of directors comprising 40 members.[27]

It is important to remember that, because both the FCM and the provincial associations represent the municipalities as corporate entities, they in fact represent the wishes of the people comprising the municipal councils. In short, they are controlled by elected municipal politicians. A panoply of other organizations represents *employees* of municipalities—everything from the Canadian Association of Municipal Administrators (CAMA) (comprising about 400 city managers, chief administrative officers, and other senior municipal appointed officials) to provincial associations of building inspectors, tax collectors, and municipal clerks. Such organizations are primarily concerned with providing services to their members, including opportunities for professional development, but they sometimes express policy to provincial governments as well, positions that are not always identical to those of their political masters. In summary, the network of municipal organizations in Canada is extremely complex, and identifying common objectives is often difficult as municipalities interact with the federal and provincial governments.

Conclusion

Despite the frequent assertion that municipalities are mere "creatures of the provinces," in practice they form an integral part of Canada's system of multi-level governance, even taking account of the Harper government's disapproval of formal tri-level agreements. In recent years, acting mainly through the FCM, municipalities have had a significant impact on federal politics and policies. They have certainly been successful in raising awareness across Canada about the need for all governments to invest more in physical infrastructure, much of which is built and maintained by municipalities.

For all kinds of reasons, municipal involvement with the provinces is much deeper than with the federal government. Indeed, provincial–municipal interactions are crucial to the everyday activities of almost all Canadian residents. We will analyze these interactions in their various forms throughout the rest of this book. One of the many complicated features of the provincial–municipal relationship is the existence of local special-purpose bodies, to which we turn for more detailed study in the next chapter.

RESOURCES

The website of the Federation of Canadian Municipalities—www.fcm .ca/home.htm—is the most useful website on the subject matter of this chapter. A thorough exploration of all of its parts, including the links to some of the FCM members and provincial organizations, provides a detailed portrait of multi-level governance in Canada.

For a sophisticated discussion by a political theorist of alternative approaches to the constitutional status of Canadian municipalities, see the following articles by Warren Magnusson: "Are Municipalities Creatures of the Provinces?" *Journal of Canadian Studies* 39, 2 (2005): 5–31; "Urbanism, Cities, and Local Self-Government," *Canadian Public Administration* 48, 1 (2005): 96–123; and "Protecting the Right of Local Self-Government," *Canadian Journal of Political Science* 38, 4 (2005): 897–922.

STUDY QUESTIONS

1. What is the constitutional status of Canadian municipal governments? Why is it not possible for them to have "home rule" under current constitutional arrangements?
2. What is "private legislation" and why is it sometimes important for local governments?
3. What are administrative tribunals and why are they important for municipalities in most provinces?
4. What are negative and positive externalities? How are they relevant for discussions of municipal autonomy?
5. Why is it often difficult for provincial associations of municipalities to arrive at common positions?

CHAPTER 4

Special-Purpose Bodies

We saw in Chapter 1 that local special-purpose bodies are local governments that have responsibilities only for a specific function, such as public education or policing. In Chapter 3 we noted that in some provinces, a particular form of special-purpose body, Roman Catholic school boards, have a degree of constitutional protection. Although less visible than municipal governments, special-purpose bodies deserve our attention because they make important decisions for communities and spend significant amounts of money. They are also important because their relations with municipalities can sometimes be quite difficult, and frequent proposals are made, from the municipal side at least, for their power to be curbed. Municipalities generally want to control local services and expenditures within their territories and special-purpose bodies are often a direct threat to their ability to do so. Any student of Canadian local government needs to know why special-purpose bodies were created and why they persist. As we survey different types of special-purpose bodies in this chapter, we shall attempt to address these issues. Unfortunately, so much variation exists among special-purpose bodies that it can be difficult sometimes to keep them all straight. But complexity is endemic to local government. Its institutions have generally been designed to help solve real problems in the real world rather than to look neat on an organizational chart. It is more important to gain a feel for the reasons behind this complexity than it is to know exactly how each different body is organized. Nevertheless, this chapter explores special-purpose bodies in some detail because the rest of the book will be primarily concerned with municipalities, and future chapters will deal with special-purpose bodies only in passing.

School Boards

The first schools in Canada were originally operated by the Roman Catholic Church in New France. Protestant churches opened schools after British conquest and settlement, especially in the early nineteenth century. Early legislation in the British North American colonies provided mechanisms for parents to organize and collectively finance public schools in their own immediate areas. Such legislation generally predated the establishment of municipalities. By the early 1840s, municipalities were more common and were generally made responsible for raising funds for schools from the general tax levies they charged on local property.[1] Meanwhile, locally elected school boards emerged out of the skeletal organizations of parents that had created the first public schools earlier in the century. In the Province of Canada (now Ontario and Quebec), the 1840s were marked by considerable uncertainty about whether school boards or municipalities were locally responsible for public schools. For a brief period, the Toronto municipal council was responsible for appointing school board members as well as paying for the schools themselves. In 1848 it closed the public schools during a dispute with the board about costs. The conflict was resolved in 1850 when the law was amended to provide again for the election of school board members and to establish their right to levy their own tax on property.[2] The fundamentals of this arrangement remained in place in Ontario until 1998.

Both before and after Confederation in 1867, legislatures in British North America reinforced the role of elected school boards as the local bodies in charge of public schools. In doing so, they were generally following American models, although there have always been many more examples in the United States of places where mayors and municipal councils retained some form of control over school boards and local schools.[3] Locally elected school boards were created in England and Wales in 1870, in large measure to emulate American success in providing basic education to large numbers of children. But they were abolished in 1902,[4] when local education became a direct responsibility of municipalities (or *local authorities*, as municipalities are generally known in Britain). The existence of relatively powerful local school boards is very much a North American phenomenon. Their importance did not derive from Britain or Europe.

Denominational Rights

A special feature of school boards in Canada has been the creation of rights for some Christian denominational minorities in some provinces to establish their own school boards. Such rights were first legislated in the Province of Canada in 1841 when Catholic and Protestant minorities were allowed to establish their own *dissentient* school boards in each township and parish. The general rights of these religious minorities in Ontario and Quebec were perpetuated and protected by section 93 of the British North America Act (now the Constitution Act, 1867) at the time of Confederation. They were extended to Manitoba, Alberta, and Saskatchewan when these provinces were admitted to Canada, but were controversially removed in Manitoba in 1890.[5]

The case of Newfoundland (now Newfoundland and Labrador) is especially interesting. When it joined Canada in 1949, school boards for Roman Catholics, Anglicans, Methodists, Congregationalists, the Salvation Army, Seventh Day Adventists, and two varieties of Presbyterians were all constitutionally protected. Pentecostals were added in 1954.[6] Under the terms of the Constitution Act, 1982, these constitutional guarantees can be amended only with the approval of the relevant provincial legislature and the Parliament of Canada. After considerable political turmoil, the guarantees to religious groups enabling them to have their own school boards were abolished in both Quebec and Newfoundland, in 1997 and 1998 respectively.

Linguistic Rights

Political agreement in Quebec was facilitated by the Supreme Court of Canada's interpretation of constitutional guarantees contained in the Canadian Charter of Rights and Freedoms (sections 1–34 of the Constitution Act, 1982) for linguistic minorities. English-speaking Quebecers, who had been holding on to Protestant boards so as to control their own local educational systems, became convinced that the constitutional protections for English-language school boards were just as secure as the religious guarantees had been. The end result of the Supreme Court's decisions on minority-language educational rights, as we saw in Chapter 3, was the establishment in all provinces of at least one minority-language school board. In 1996, the New Brunswick provincial legislature enacted the Progressive Conservative government's plan to replace all the province's school boards with one English-language provincial board and one French-language one. Local influence over schools was to be provided by elected parent committees for each school. However, in 2000, a Liberal government sponsored legislation that re-established school boards. In 2012 and 2013, the governments of Prince Edward Island and Newfoundland and Labrador respectively consolidated their English-language school boards into one board comprising

Table 4.1 Types of School Boards in Canadian Provinces

	English Public	French Public	English Catholic	French Catholic
Newfoundland and Labrador	1	1		
Prince Edward Island	1	1		
Nova Scotia	7	1		
New Brunswick	4	3		
Quebec	9	60		
Ontario	31	4	29	8
Manitoba	37	1		
Saskatchewan	18	1	9	
Alberta	41	4	16	1
British Columbia	59	1		

Note: Table does not include three school boards for indigenous peoples in Quebec and one in Nova Scotia.

Source: Websites of provincial ministries of education. Accessed 12 August 2013.

members appointed by the government. In these two provinces there is no longer any local government for education.

Current Status of School Boards

Although local elected school boards currently exist in eight provinces, their authority to levy their own taxes has been greatly eroded over the past few decades. Quebec is now the only province in which school boards have independent authority to levy taxes on property. Nevertheless, subject to varying degrees of control by provincial ministries of education, they still make many important decisions about local schools, decisions that can be crucial to the viability of particular communities and neighbourhoods. School trustees are generally elected at the same time as members of municipal councils, so voting turnout generally depends on municipal turnout. In Quebec, however, where school boards have their own election dates, turnouts have been abysmally low: only 7.75 per cent in 2007.[7]

Police Boards

As with public schools, policing in a rudimentary form existed in Canadian cities and towns before municipalities did. Originally, *constables* were appointed in Britain and in Canada by local justices of the peace, who also performed many of the local regulatory functions that were later passed on to municipalities. Constables were simply local citizens who took their turn in watching for fires, patrolling at night, issuing summonses, and making arrests. But their connection with justices of the peace marked the beginning of a kind of special status for police that has survived long since they became part of professional police forces in the late nineteenth century. In Charlottetown, Prince Edward Island, the city police force remained under the direct control of a local judge until as late as 1941. More commonly elsewhere, municipal councils themselves initially inherited some of the judicial authority of justices of the peace. The original law incorporating the city of Toronto established the elected council as the "Mayor's Court of the City of Toronto," whose jurisdiction extended over "crimes and misdemeanours arising within the City,"[8] Because of these early judicial functions, mayors are sometimes anachronistically referred to as "chief magistrates."

Although municipal councils have long since lost their judicial functions, police officers, when performing their duties in Britain and Canada (but not in the United States), are still considered to possess a degree of legal independence from their political masters that is not extended to other government employees. The exact nature of such independence will be discussed later. In any event, just as the council of the city of Toronto once had complete control over public education, it also had complete control over policing from 1834 until 1858, at which time a new law for Upper Canada required that each city (but not other types of municipalities) establish a Board of Commissioners of Police, comprising the mayor and up to two local magistrates or two citizens appointed by the council.[9]

Ontario remains as the province in which police boards are the most powerful. No municipal council has direct control over a police service, although municipal appointees always comprise the majority of board members. Budgets for police services are drawn up by the police services board; if the municipal council does not approve it, the board can appeal to the Ontario Civilian Commission on Police Services, which will make the final determination. The situation is similar in British Columbia, except that there are only 11 municipal police boards, one for each of the municipal police services. Most BC municipalities are policed by contract with the RCMP. Under these circumstances, municipal police boards are not required. Where they are required, the boards are chaired by the mayor; one other member (not a councillor) is appointed by the municipal council; and up to five members are appointed by the provincial government.[10] If disagreement arises between a municipal council and a board about the budget, the final decision is taken by the provincial director of police services, an official in the Ministry of the Attorney General.

Local police boards are also mandatory for municipal police services in Alberta, Saskatchewan, Manitoba, and Nova Scotia, but final responsibility for the police budget rests with the municipal council. In New Brunswick, police boards are optional. In Newfoundland and Labrador, municipal policing is carried out by a provincial force, the Royal Newfoundland Constabulary. Quebec and Prince Edward Island are the only provinces in which no municipal police boards exist.

Quebec deserves special attention because, like Ontario, it contains large cities but, unlike Ontario, municipal councils directly control the police. However, the chief of the Montreal police service, the second largest municipal police service in Canada, is appointed by the Quebec government. The chief reports to the municipal council in the same way as any other department head. Under Montreal's legislative charter, the council must establish a public safety committee made of councillors and one provincial appointee, but its functions are purely advisory.[11]

With respect to the governance of municipal police in Canada, at least two important questions must be asked: (1) Is there any sense in which the police are constitutionally independent of the municipal corporation that they serve? (2) To the extent that they are, do they need a special-purpose body to protect such independence?

Independence of Police Officers

Are municipal police constitutionally independent of their respective municipal corporations? This important legal question has received considerable attention from judges and scholars in the Anglo-American democracies. The question is essentially the same whether it involves the RCMP in relation to the federal government, provincial police forces in relation to provincial governments, or municipal police forces and municipalities: To what extent do constitutional conventions allow civilians to direct the activities of police officers? This has been an issue of considerable political controversy in Canada in recent years, the most notable recent example being how Ontario politicians and civil servants related to the Ontario Provincial Police (OPP) in 1995 during the occupation of Ipperwash Provincial Park by the Chippewas of the Kettle and Stoney Point First Nation. The fact that the OPP shot and killed Dudley George, one of the occupiers, led to the creation in 2003 of a judicial inquiry, presided over by Mr Justice Sidney Linden. Mr Justice

Linden devoted an entire chapter of his report[12] to "Police/Government Relations." Linden's treatment of this subject was backed up by extensive legal research.[13]

Linden cites a famous British judicial decision in 1968, which has had a huge influence in advancing the cause of police independence. In the decision, Lord Denning wrote that no police authority can tell a chief constable what to do. "The responsibility for law enforcement lies on him. He is answerable to the law and to the law alone."[14] In 1999 the Supreme Court of Canada stated that "A police officer investigating a crime is not acting as a government functionary or as an agent of anybody. He or she occupies a public office initially defined by the common law and subsequently set out in various statutes." The Court noted that this principle "underpins the rule of law" and "is one of the fundamental and organizing principles of the Constitution."[15]

But Mr Justice Linden was quick to point out that both federal and provincial statutes in Canada *do* give ministers of the Crown authority to direct many police activities and that the Supreme Court has never questioned the constitutional validity of these statutes. What ministers clearly *cannot* do is direct police activities with respect to particular criminal investigations. The Ontario Police Services Act states that municipal police service boards "shall not direct the chief of police with respect to specific operational decisions or with respect to the day-to-day operation of the police."[16] This provision reinforces the prohibition against civilian involvement in criminal investigations, but it also widens the sphere of police independence to include "specific operational decisions." It is important to note, however, that in Canada there is no constitutional protection for police independence in *all* operational decisions. Such protection only applies with respect to criminal investigations.

In theory, Parliament or a provincial legislature could approve a law overriding constitutional conventions about police independence in criminal investigations and authorizing civilian government officials to direct such investigations. Any such law would no doubt be challenged on the grounds that it violates the Charter of Rights and Freedoms. But the key point here is that the police are not alone among municipal employees in being immune from certain kinds of administrative or political direction. For example, provincial laws prevent any employers, including municipalities, from directing professionals such as physicians, lawyers, and accountants in the carrying out of their professional responsibilities. If we consider the police as professional investigators of criminal activities, their position is really no different.

The Necessity of Police Boards

To what extent do municipal police services need special-purpose bodies to protect their constitutional independence? In light of the previous discussion, the answer should be obvious. Because municipal police have the same constitutional status as the RCMP and provincial police services and because these police services (and many municipal police services in Canada) are not governed by special-purpose bodies, there is no obvious reason why there should be any local special-purpose bodies for police. Whether they exist or not is simply a matter of provincial policy and law. In Ontario, where police service boards are especially strong, there have been many proposals over the years that these boards be abolished or at least made optional, with the decision about their existence to be taken by the municipal council.[17] Police organizations have successfully defended their special-purpose bodies, in part by appealing to the unique constitutional status of the police. But as we have seen, the principle of non-interference in criminal investigations does not require that police be governed by special-purpose bodies. With no obvious necessity for local police special-purpose bodies, there can be no obvious conclusions about how they should be structured or how they should relate to municipal councils. Generally speaking, police organizations want them to be almost totally independent of municipal councils, while the councils want to be able to control expenditures without taking on direct responsibility. Even in cities where police special-purpose bodies are weak or non-existent, most individual councillors are reluctant to criticize police practices in public for fear of being tarred as anti-police.

Excessive emphasis on the notion of police independence and the continued existence of strong local police special-purpose bodies combine to severely limit political debate in Canadian municipalities about police priorities and policies.[18] In the case of the Ipperwash occupation, the issue was not whether the relevant provincial minister could issue general instructions to the OPP (Mr Justice Linden concluded that he could), but whether the government's position was communicated to the OPP clearly and through the correct channels. With regard to municipal police services, it is obvious that mayors, individual councillors, and even individual members of police service boards cannot attempt to instruct any police officer about what to do about anything. Acting collectively and officially, however, municipal councils or police boards (depending on which group has the statutory authority) can and should openly instruct chiefs of police about matters of policy. Mr Justice Linden was not afraid to take on the difficult task of outlining the distinction between a policy decision and an operational decision. He claims, for example, that a decision about whether to use force or to negotiate with protestors is a policy decision "even when the policy was first made in the context of a specific dispute," but that such a policy decision "should be generally applicable to similar disputes."[19] It is rare indeed for a municipal council or a police services board to have an open debate about such an issue.

In July 2010, the Toronto Police Services Board (TPSB) appointed a retired judge of the Ontario Court of Appeal, John W. Morden, to conduct a review of the actions of the Toronto Police Service during the G20 summit in Toronto in June of the same year. The review was initiated primarily because of concerns that the police had used excessive force in dealing with widespread public demonstrations and disorder. Although Morden addressed the issue of police independence,[20] it was much less central to his inquiry than it was to Linden's and his recommendations on this subject, though consistent with Linden's, were less comprehensive. However, unlike Linden, Morden addressed many issues directly related to the role of Ontario's municipal police services boards. For example, he expressed dissatisfaction about the limited role played by the board in setting Toronto police policy concerning the summit.[21]

Particularly interesting for our purposes is Morden's discussion of complaints by the RCMP about the behaviour of Toronto city councillor Adam Vaughan, who was also a member of the TPSB. Morden writes:

> On February 11, 2010, Councillor Vaughan issued a newsletter to the residents of his ward. In it, he summarized information that he had learned regarding the plans for the G20 Summit. Councillor Vaughan stated as follows:
>
> > As your councillor I will continue to work to try and move the summit, and if it can't be moved, mitigate its impact. I will also use my seat on the Police Services Board to make sure the interests of the ward and the city are respected as security issues come forward. I have received a "classified" briefing so far. There will be serious disruptions. The security perimeter will be much larger than the area affected by the recent NFL games, and the protests are expected to be larger than last spring's Tamil demonstrations.[22]

The RCMP complained to the Toronto police chief that Councillor Vaughan in this part of his newsletter was divulging classified information, and this complaint was acknowledged by the rest of the board. The board was also concerned that Vaughan's reference to making sure that the interests of his ward were protected could be viewed as an attempt to "to influence operational decisions."[23] Morden concluded the following about Councillor Vaughan's newsletter:

> The reference to there being "serious disruptions" during the G20 Summit does not, in and of itself, contain any confidential information. In addition, given the nature and size of the event it is my view that it was common public knowledge that the G20 Summit would result in serious disruptions and that the types of possible disruptions had already been discussed between the Toronto Police Service, the City of Toronto, and various organizations and individuals that might be impacted. Similarly, Councillor Vaughan's suggestion that he will use his membership on the Board "to make sure the interests of the ward and the city are respected as security issues come forward" does not violate the Code of Conduct Regulation. The Code of Conduct Regulation prohibits Board members from interfering with the Toronto Police Service's operational decisions and responsibilities. Councillor Vaughan's statement does not, without more, violate this prohibition. Accordingly, I find that the Board's reaction to Councillor Vaughan's newsletter was unwarranted in the circumstances.[24]

This is an important statement about the ability of municipal councillors who are members of police services boards in Ontario to perform their legitimate functions in relation to the people who elected them.

The Vancouver Board of Parks and Recreation

The provincial legislation that establishes and governs the city of Vancouver (the Vancouver Charter) requires that there be a park board whose members are directly elected for four-year terms at the same time as the Vancouver city council. The board currently has seven members, but this number can be changed by the city council.[25] The board has its origins in the city's acquisition of Stanley Park from the federal government in 1887. Stanley Park was initially managed by a park committee established by council, but this became a directly elected board in 1890. The board subsequently became responsible for other parks and for recreation programs. Although it raises some funds from user fees, it relied on grants from the city council for more than half its 2011 operational budget of about $103 million.[26]

The continued existence of the board no doubt reflects the great attachment that citizens of Vancouver have for their parks, especially Stanley Park. Nevertheless, financial control of the city's parks and recreation programs rests firmly with the city council, because it determines annually the amount of money that is transferred to the park board.[27]

Library Boards

Large cities in Canada operate public libraries. Except in Quebec, these libraries are governed by special-purpose bodies made up of municipal councillors, citizens appointed by municipal councils and/or school boards, and sometimes provincial representatives. Nowhere are the boards directly elected. The boards are reliant on municipal councils for funds, but generally have considerable freedom to make policy on non-financial matters, especially relating to decisions about collections policies. In fact, this is one of the main reasons for having the boards: to ensure that decisions about what books to order are not decided by councillors who might have little or no interest in libraries or who might not be sufficiently committed to principles relating to the free flow of a wide variety of religious, social, and political information. Another reason is that the boards are seen as better able than councils to harness the enthusiasm and commitment of library users. In smaller communities, and especially in smaller provinces, public libraries are often run directly by the province or by provincial–municipal partnerships. In these latter cases, library boards facilitate representation from the various municipalities that are involved in a region-wide multi-municipal system.

Local Transit Systems and Utilities

Many local special-purpose bodies exist because they provide a service that in large measure is financed by user fees. In short, they are operating a form of business, even if that business is significantly subsidized from the public purse. A common belief in Canada and elsewhere is that services generating significant independent revenues should have a degree of freedom from the direct control of municipal councils so that they have the flexibility to respond quickly to use their revenue where it is needed most to meet their business objectives. In fact, however, there is not much logic behind different institutional arrangements for different revenue-producing local services. For example, public transit services are usually run by special-purpose bodies even though they receive significant public subsidies, while water supply systems are usually directly run by municipalities even though they have become increasingly self-financing in recent years as water meters have become almost universal in most towns and cities.

Most local public services for which there can be user fees were originally provided by private companies. British North America's first water mains were built in Montreal by Joseph Frobisher's Company of Proprietors of the Montreal Water Works. Toronto started to receive a communal water supply in 1843, when the Toronto Gas, Light and Water Company began pumping from Lake Ontario.[28] Companies operating street railways appeared in both cities in the 1860s[29] and electricity companies in the 1880s.[30] In each of these cases the municipal council had to grant the company a franchise, meaning that the company was granted the exclusive right to install infrastructure for its service on municipal land within a defined territory. Franchises of this nature are generally granted when the service in question can be provided, in practical terms, by only one supplier within a given territory. Because there cannot be competing systems of underground water pipes, or of rails and wires on public streets, we say that the service is a *natural monopoly*. The alternative to granting a franchise is for the government to run the service itself. In the case of municipal governments, they often do so through special-purpose bodies.

Utilities and Private Companies

Before examining such special-purpose bodies in more detail, it is interesting to think about various natural monopolies that are still usually in the hands of private companies. In Canadian cities, the most common ones are natural gas distribution systems, traditional telephone lines or fibre optic cable, coaxial cable (used by cable TV companies), and district heating and cooling systems (found in the downtown cores of some major cities). Companies that benefit from having natural monopolies require heavy regulation to prevent them from taking unfair advantage of their monopolistic position. Such regulation occurs through the terms of their franchise agreements or through regulatory institutions established for this purpose. Natural gas distribution systems are generally regulated in Canada by provincial governments; various telecommunications cable systems are regulated federally by the Canadian Radio-television and Telecommunications Commission (CRTC); and district heating and cooling systems are overseen by municipal governments. But even the natural gas and telecommunications companies are subject to municipal regulation concerning the physical placement of their pipes and wires.

Federal and provincial regulation of these natural monopolies has changed dramatically in recent decades. For both natural gas and telecommunications, regulators have generally forced the owners of distribution systems to open up their systems to other service providers to create new forms of market competition. For natural gas, however, there is always only one physical system for distribution. For telecommunications, new technology has allowed competition even in distribution systems, especially in relation to telephones and broadband Internet provision. These systems are subject to strong competition from wireless providers. Hundreds of television channels are distributed by competing providers of coaxial cable and satellite service. As far as wires are concerned, however, there is no more than one network of fibre optic cable and one network of coaxial cable in any given Canadian territory.

Although most Canadian city-dwellers are familiar with such private companies as Heritage Gas (Nova Scotia), Bell Canada (telephones in Ontario and Quebec), and Shaw Communications (cable TV in western Canada, and satellite TV in other parts of the country), many might not be aware that various municipal governments in different parts of the country have provided some of these services themselves for quite a long period of time. For example, Thunder Bay in Ontario owns its own telephone company, and the cities of Kitchener and Kingston in Ontario operate natural gas distribution systems that are run by the same divisions of the municipal government that are also responsible for the water supply system. Especially interesting for students of Canadian municipal government is the fact that two of Canada's major utility corporations, EPCOR and Telus, had their origins as line departments of the city of Edmonton, providing electricity, natural gas, and telecommunications services within the city limits. Since being privatized by the city, many of their operations have spread throughout Canada (e.g., wireless telephone service from Telus) and to many parts of the world.

In most parts of Canada, electricity is distributed to consumers through wires owned by provincial Crown corporations (Hydro-Québec, BC Hydro, etc.). Until 1998, electricity distribution networks in most cities and towns in Ontario were operated by municipal special-purpose bodies generally known as *public utilities commissions* (which often ran the water supply system as well) or by *hydro commissions* that bought their electricity from Ontario Hydro. Since then, however, Ontario municipalities have been required to transfer their electricity operations to corporations established under the Ontario Business Corporations Act. This means that, in legal terms, they have similar corporate structures to those of private businesses in the province, except that in most cases the sole shareholder remains the municipal corporation. In some ways, a municipally appointed board of directors of a municipally owned corporation established to distribute electricity is very similar to a local special-purpose body, even though in legal terms it is just like a private corporate board of directors. Under the 1998 provincial legislation that established these arrangements, municipalities are free to sell their electricity distribution systems, but almost all remain municipally owned in one form or another.[31]

Transit in Toronto and Montreal

Special-purpose bodies for user-fee services are particularly important in public transit, especially in Canada's two largest provinces, Ontario and Quebec. The largest municipal transit system in Canada is operated by the Toronto Transit Commission (TTC), the current members of which are five Toronto city councillors and four Toronto citizens, all appointed for two-year terms by the Toronto city council. The TTC has direct responsibility for constructing, maintaining, and operating Toronto's subway, streetcar, and bus system, but it is far from being totally independent because it relies on city council for funds to make up the difference between its total costs and its revenues, almost all of which derive from user fees (fares). In 2011, the city contributed $432 million of the TTC's total operating expenses of $1.769 billion.[32] It is therefore a crucially important part of the city's annual budget. Nevertheless, the TTC does not appear in the city's official chart of its "administrative structure"[33] and its General Manager of Transportation Services has no administrative responsibility for the TTC. The councillor serving as chair of the TTC often speaks publicly on behalf of the commission, but the commission's formal independence certainly does not prevent the city's mayor, who is usually not a member, from vigorous involvement in political debates involving the TTC.

Arrangements for transit in Montreal are similar. The Société de transport de Montréal (STM) is governed by a board of directors comprising 10 members, 7 of whom are elected municipal officials.[34] Three members are transit users' representatives. It is quite clear, however, that the special-purpose bodies for transit in Montreal and Toronto are dominated by city councillors. Apart from the administrative convenience of separating a huge transit operation from an even larger municipal corporation, it is difficult to see why these special-purpose bodies exist. In many respects they are simply products of the historical development of each transit system. But this history is itself important for understanding some of the issues involved in the existence of special-purpose bodies for transit.

The Toronto and Montreal transit systems were private companies taken over by the municipalities in 1920 and 1951 respectively. In each case, the advocates of municipalization promised to continue to run the system like a business while simultaneously improving service. The Toronto Transit Commission (TTC) originally comprised three prominent local businessmen appointed by the council. As early as 1925, commission members clashed with city council as they tried to maintain financial self-sufficiency, while certain councillors pushed for policies that served their own particular political interests.[35] But the TTC was managed so successfully as a business (aided eventually by wartime prosperity combined with the absence of new automobiles) that it accumulated a reserve fund of $25 million that was used to finance most of the initial construction of the Toronto subway.[36]

By 1953, automobile sales were exploding and it became increasingly difficult for the TTC to be self-financing. By the time construction for the Bloor Street subway started in 1955, the TTC itself was able to finance only 45 per cent of the cost.[37] As the years went on, the TTC required more extensive capital subsidies, and then operating subsidies, although it remained in better financial shape than virtually all other North American transit systems. Not surprisingly, as municipal politicians became increasingly responsible for financing public transit, they were less likely to want to have the system governed by outsiders, which explains why most of the members of the TTC are now city councillors and why key budgetary decisions are taken by the council as a whole. As far as transit decision-making is concerned, this situation is not much different from places such as Calgary and Winnipeg where the transit systems are just another department of city government reporting to city council in the same way as other city departments.

Inter-municipal Special-Purpose Bodies

Inter-municipal special-purpose bodies are established so that two or more municipalities can partner with each other to provide a particular service. A special-purpose body, comprising representatives from the participating municipalities, acts as the governing body of the partnership. These kinds of special-purpose bodies can be required by provincial policy or they can result from voluntary inter-municipal agreements. We shall briefly examine examples of both, starting with conservation authorities in Ontario.

Conservation Authorities in Ontario

Most of the territory of the populated portions of Ontario is covered by 36 special-purpose bodies known as conservation authorities.[38] Their existence derives from provincial legislation approved in 1946 that was designed to facilitate inter-municipal co-operation for the purposes of flood protection. Perhaps their most notable feature is that their boundaries are constructed so as generally to follow boundaries of watersheds rather than of municipalities. This means that some municipalities belong to more than one conservation authority. Boards of directors of conservation authorities comprise municipal councillors from each participating municipality chosen by the municipal council as a whole. Municipal voting strength on each board generally correlates with its financial contribution, which in turn relates to each municipality's share of the assessed value of property within the authority's territory.

Although the original conservation authorities were designed to result from local initiative, municipalities are now required to participate, largely because the authorities form a crucial part of Ontario's land-use planning and water-source protection policy. In this regard, their actions are tightly regulated by provincial policy, but this does not mean there is no room for local variation, especially in revenue-producing activities such as the provision of campgrounds on authority land. In other provinces the functions carried out by conservation authorities in Ontario are generally carried out by the province itself.

TransLink in British Columbia

The South Coast British Columbia Transportation Authority, commonly known as TransLink, is an important example of a provincially mandated inter-municipal special-purpose body. TransLink is charged with overseeing roads and public transit in the Vancouver metropolitan region. The history of institutional arrangements for the provision of roads and public transit in British Columbia in general and Vancouver in particular is quite complex.[39] The latest major changes for the Vancouver region were made in 2007 but significant amendments were enacted in 2014. The legislation provides for an eleven-person board of directors chosen by the Mayors' Council on Regional Transportation, comprising the mayors of 21 municipalities and the chief of a First Nation served by the system. Each mayor or chief casts one vote for every 20,000 people residing within his or her municipality. In appointing the board, however, the council can choose only from among a list of 15 potential nominees (none of whom can be elected officials). The list of nominees is established by a screening panel comprising one appointee named by each of the following: the provincial government; the Mayors' Council; the Institute of Chartered Accountants of British Columbia; the Vancouver Board of Trade; and the Greater Vancouver Gateway Council (a business group concerned primarily with import-export issues). Since 2014, the

Mayors' Council also can appoint two of its own members to the board and must approve transportation plans, levels of municipal funding, fare increases, and borrowing limits for the authority. TransLink is the most complex and powerful regional transportation authority in Canada. It plans for future development for both public transit and roads; allocates funds for major improvements in the road system; and, either directly or indirectly, is responsible for the operation of public transit in the entire area. In addition to drawing on property tax revenues from member municipalities, it also has direct access to funds from taxes on parking lots and gasoline. For many residents of the Vancouver area, it is probably the branch of local government that has the most immediate impact on their daily lives. Relations between TransLink and municipal councils in metropolitan Vancouver are stormy at best. Municipalities object to the fact that they have such limited control over Vancouver public transit, especially because their own revenues from property taxes help finance TransLink.

Inter-municipal Water Authorities

As one would expect, inter-municipal special-purpose bodies that result from particular agreements among particular municipalities take a wide variety of forms. Many are established to operate particular municipal facilities built by more than one municipality. Rinks, fairgrounds, and other athletic facilities are perhaps the most common examples. But some crucial municipal services are also run by inter-municipal special-purpose bodies. For example, London, Ontario, receives its water from two treatment plants, one on Lake Huron and the other on Lake Erie. Each system is governed by an inter-municipal special-purpose body, because municipalities situated along each of the pipelines connecting the plants to London can opt into the system so as to use treated lake water rather than water from wells. Representatives from London's city council dominate each governing body, but all municipalities served by the system are represented as well. Interestingly, each of the *joint boards of management* has contracted out the management of their treatment plants and the pipelines to the Ontario Clean Water Agency (OCWA), which is a Crown agency of the Ontario provincial government.

One of Canada's most durable inter-municipal special-purpose bodies is the Buffalo Pound Water Administration Board, which has supplied treated water since 1951 to both Regina and Moose Jaw, which are 60 kilometres apart. The board's water treatment facility is at Buffalo Pound Lake, located a little to the north of both cities but closer to Moose Jaw.[40] The board is made up of three members: two senior administrators (one from engineering and one from financial services) from Regina, and one (an engineer) from Moose Jaw. Because the population of Regina (193,000) is more than five times that of Moose Jaw (33,000), the latter has the majority of members on the board. In reality, though, both sides must agree on significant changes, regardless of the makeup of the board. Because the board members are municipal staff, they are careful not to stray far from the political direction of their respective councils. Although the board is technically a separate legal entity and is therefore the employer of the plant's workers, collective agreements tend to follow settlements in Regina, which are in turn similar to those in most urban municipalities in the province. Most of the board's human resources functions are carried out by Regina's human resources department. Water rates are set by the board. Both councils seem to accept the notion that the setting of the rates is a technical issue appropriately determined by staff. In any event, the senior staff who are members of the board have never acted in such a way as to provoke political controversies about rate levels. Financial services for the board are provided by Regina.

This long-standing inter-municipal body has provoked little or no controversy or disagreement over the years. Why has it been so successful? Perhaps because the municipalities are far apart and consequently there are no inter-municipal irritants relating to other subjects that can impinge on a good working relationship concerning water. Perhaps it is because the board membership comprises senior staff rather than elected politicians who might want to use the board for other political purposes. Why has staff control of the board not itself caused difficulty in terms of accountability? Although formal mechanisms are not in place, staff members seem extremely sensitive to the need to consult with their respective councils on any issue that goes beyond the technical concerns of the water treatment plant itself. Why do administrative costs of running a completely separate board appear not to be an issue? The answer here surely relates to the informal arrangements whereby many of the non-engineering functions are in fact carried out by the City of Regina. The Buffalo Pound Water Administration Board stands as an apparently permanent voluntary inter-municipal institution. It shows that municipalities can get along with each other for a productive purpose over a long period of time.

Intergovernmental Special-Purpose Bodies

To the extent that police services boards (discussed above) contain representatives of both provincial and municipal governments, they are intergovernmental special-purpose bodies. But there are also other inter-governmental special-purpose bodies whose services are not directly financed by municipalities. As we saw above in regard to local transit systems and utilities, there are often few practical differences between institutions formally established as special-purpose bodies and others established as government-controlled corporations. Major ports and air-ports in Canada are operated by corporations established by the federal government, and their boards include representatives appointed by all three levels of government. The reason for federal leadership is that ports and airports are under federal jurisdiction. During the 1990s, significant changes were made to legislation governing Canada's major ports and airports. In general, less important ones were turned over by the federal government to a wide variety of private and public bodies, including municipalities. The establishment of local boards for major ports and airports was primarily an attempt to promote entrepreneurialism and better adaptation to local circumstances.

Federal Port Authorities

The Canada Marine Act became law in 1998. Under its provisions, 18 local port authorities have been established (Table 4.2).

The Act provides that both provincial and municipal governments listed in the regulations establishing each authority are entitled to name a minority of the members of the boards of directors, although the members cannot be elected politicians. The work of these authorities is extremely important for the economic development of the communities in which

Table 4.2 Canadian Port Authorities

Belledune Port Authority (near Bathurst, NB)	Saguenay Port Authority
Halifax Port Authority	Saint John Port Authority
Hamilton Port Authority	Sept-Îles Port Authority
Montreal Port Authority	St. John's Port Authority
Nanaimo Port Authority	Thunder Bay Port Authority
Oshawa Port Authority	Toronto Port Authority
Port Alberni Port Authority	Trois-Rivières Port Authority
Prince Rupert Port Authority	Vancouver Fraser Port Authority
Quebec Port Authority	Windsor Port Authority

Source: Transport Canada, www.tc.gc.ca/eng/programs/ports-cpalinks-1109.htm

the ports are located. In the cases of Vancouver, Halifax, Montreal, and Thunder Bay, it is of considerable importance to the entire Canadian economy.

The Toronto Port Authority (TPA) does not have much of a port to run, but its activities have been politically contentious because, despite the fervent opposition of David Miller, the former mayor of Toronto (2003–10), it has successfully expanded the operations of its small airport on Toronto Island, now known as the Billy Bishop Toronto City Airport. The friction between Mayor Miller and the Toronto Port Authority was one of the most dramatic examples in recent decades of an open conflict between a special-purpose body and an associated municipal government. While tension remains over whether jet planes will be allowed to use the airport in the future, the TPA, as a major landowner in the area, also has a major role to play in multi-level government efforts to redevelop the Toronto waterfront.[41]

Unlike the TPA, the Vancouver Port Authority is very much involved in shipping. It operates the largest port in Canada. Its decision in early 2013 to approve the building of facilities that would double the port's capacity to export coal provoked significant opposition from local environmentalists who objected to the plan to develop Vancouver as the largest coal-exporting port in the world. The port authority's position was that the wider environmental issues raised by the objectors were outside its mandate.[42]

Federal Airport Authorities

Canada's National Airports Policy was articulated during the 1990s as part of an effort to systematize the federal government's approach to the country's wide variety of airports, ranging from Pearson in Toronto to isolated landing strips in the Far North. For our purposes, the most important part of the policy is the designation of 26 airports as part of the National Airports System. These 26 airports serve a provincial capital and/or serve 200,000 passengers annually. Each is governed by an airport authority (Table 4.3) with its own board of directors, some of whose members are nominated by the governments of the provinces and municipalities they serve.

These airport authorities are supposed to be self-financing, even after paying annual rents to the federal government for the land on which the airports are situated. Consumer and business groups complain that this policy has greatly contributed to the high cost of flying in Canada and has thereby hindered economic development in some communities. Many of these authorities manage more than one airport. For example,

Table 4.3 Canadian Airport Authorities

Aéroports de Montréal	Prince George Airport Authority Inc.
Aéroport de Québec Inc.	Regina Airport Authority
Charlottetown Airport Authority Inc.	Saint John Airport Inc.
Edmonton Regional Airports Authority	Saskatoon Airport Authority
Fredericton Airport Authority Inc.	St. John's International Airport Authority
Gander International Airport Authority Inc.	The Calgary Airport Authority
Greater London International Airport Authority	Thunder Bay International Airports Authority Inc.
Greater Moncton International Airport Authority Inc.	Vancouver International Airport Authority
Greater Toronto Airports Authority	Victoria Airport Authority
Halifax International Airport Authority	Winnipeg Airports Authority Inc.
Ottawa Macdonald-Cartier International Airport Authority	

Source: Transport Canada, www.tc.gc.ca/eng/programs/airports-mapcaa-64.htm

the Edmonton Regional Airports Authority manages four, including the Edmonton city airport that, for a long period of time, offered short-haul scheduled flights after Edmonton International airport was built. The airport authority in Montreal converted that city's second airport, Mirabel, into a cargo-only facility and centralized all passenger flights at Trudeau airport in Dorval.

As we have seen, Toronto's Billy Bishop airport, located on Toronto Island, is *not* operated by the Greater Toronto Airports Authority (GTAA). The GTAA has been involved in ongoing studies about developing a second Toronto airport on federally owned land in Pickering, east of Toronto, but any action on such a project is a long way off. Most of the territory of Pearson airport, west of Toronto, is actually part of the city of Mississauga. There has been considerable conflict between the GTAA and Hazel McCallion, Mississauga's long-serving mayor. The issues involved municipal nominees to the GTAA board of directors, airport noise and its impact on present and future residential development, and the extent to which the GTAA has to comply with various municipal rules and regulations. In general, McCallion achieved little success in her various battles with the GTAA, a state of affairs to which she was otherwise unaccustomed.[43] In early 2014, other municipal leaders in the Toronto area expressed dissatisfaction with the GTAA for briefly closing

Pearson airport during extremely cold weather, thereby causing much inconvenience for both Torontonians and visitors.

The boards of the airport authorities themselves make new appointments to the board, even in the cases of the provincial and municipal nominees. For Mayor McCallion, this was a major irritant, especially when the GTAA turned down two of Mississauga's original nominees.[44] Regardless of who formally makes the appointment, members of any board are legally required to act in what they consider to be the interests of the board itself, not in the interests of the body that nominated them. This is a major reason that, simply because municipalities often name members to various special-purpose bodies, the municipalities do not necessarily have direct influence over the members' actions.

Agence métropolitaine de transport in Montreal

We have seen that the intergovernmental authorities for ports and airports have involved all three levels of government. The Agence métropolitaine de transport (AMT) in Montreal, which is charged with planning for public transit for the whole metropolitan region, is an example of a body that involves only the provincial and municipal levels. Established in 1995, it also operates the commuter rail system, whose operating deficits are funded by the provincial government and by area municipalities. The Quebec government appoints four of the seven board members, including the chair, while the other three members are municipal elected officials, one each from the cities of Montreal and Laval and another representing the other municipalities in the region.[45] The AMT is not nearly as strong an authority as TransLink in Vancouver because it has no jurisdiction over road development and because, except for commuter rail, it has no operational control over public transit.

Local Special-Purpose Bodies with No Municipal Involvement

All of the local special-purpose bodies examined so far have involved municipal governments in one way or another. Even school boards, which in most provinces have been remarkably independent of municipal government, have relied on municipalities for the administration of elections and/or the collection of property taxes. In recent years, however, some provincial governments have established boards and agencies to make particular public policy decisions for particular defined territories. To the extent that these boards and agencies have a degree of independence from provincial governments and otherwise meet the definition of local government outlined in Chapter 1, they can be considered local special-purpose bodies. The first such body to be discussed, Metrolinx in Toronto, is similar in purpose to TransLink in Vancouver and the AMT in Montreal.[46]

Metrolinx in Toronto and Hamilton

The Greater Toronto Transportation Authority was created in 2006, but its name was changed to Metrolinx in 2009. Its territory covers the cities of Toronto and Hamilton and the regional municipalities of Durham, York, Peel, and Halton. Its main functions are to plan the future public transit system for the area and to operate GO Transit, the existing commuter rail and regional bus system. In the past, municipalities have helped subsidize GO Transit and have been represented on the Metrolinx board and its predecessors. In accordance with amendments to the Metrolinx Act in 2009, the provincial government now appoints all 15 members of the Metrolinx board, none of whom are elected officials. As we shall see in Chapter 5, this is part of a clear effort by the Ontario government to take greater control of major urban issues facing the larger Toronto region rather than to leave such issues in the hands of local elected officials. Metrolinx makes important decisions about fares and services for GO Transit, and in 2008 it approved *The Big Move*, a comprehensive transit plan for the entire area.[47] While Metrolinx favours a comprehensive network of Light Rail Transit (LRT), Mayor Rob Ford has pushed for subways within the city of Toronto rather than LRT, which he claims blocks roads and provides second-rate service. The Ontario government will ultimately decide.

Regional Health Authorities

The greatest growth in non-municipal local and regional special-purpose bodies has been in health care. Regional health authorities exist in one form or another in all provinces except Alberta, Nova Scotia, and Prince Edward Island.[48] Excluding authorities that are province-wide in scope, Table 4.4 shows the number and name of these authorities in the remaining eight provinces.

In all cases, members of the boards of the authorities are named by the provincial government and receive virtually all of their funds from that source. Their mandates vary from province to province, but one of their main common objectives is to enable regional community leaders rather than provincial bureaucrats to develop mechanisms for local health institutions, especially hospitals, in order to use resources more

Table 4.4 Sub-provincial Health Authorities

British Columbia: 5 health authorities

Saskatchewan: 12 regional health authorities

Manitoba: 5 regional health authorities

Ontario: 14 local health integration networks (LHINs)

Quebec: 18 Agences de la santé et des services sociaux

New Brunswick: 2 regional health authorities

Newfoundland and Labrador: 4 regional health authorities

Sources: Websites of provincial ministries of health. Accessed 19 August 2013.

rationally. Another common function is the provision of public health programs, such as vaccinations and services for pregnant women. In Ontario, however, public health programs are delivered and partially financed either by municipalities or by special-purpose bodies (boards of health, district health units) that are directly linked to municipalities.

Regional health authorities have the potential to become extremely important, but their track record since they were first introduced in some provinces in the 1970s and 1980s has not been especially impressive. Some local hospital leaders have been reluctant to take orders from regional authorities and have sometimes successfully used their influence at the provincial level when regional decisions have gone against them. The problem with the regional boards is that they lack democratic legitimacy. Few of us could name a member of our own regional health authority. There have been attempts to elect members of regional health boards in Quebec and Saskatchewan, but turnouts were so abysmally low that such practices have been neither continued nor adopted elsewhere.

A major report for the Quebec government in 1999[49] recommended that upper-tier regional municipalities take over some responsibility for health and social services. The recommendation met with almost unanimous opposition from all affected parties and was never implemented. It is therefore highly unlikely that local and regional decision-making for health and social services will become more closely linked to municipal government in the foreseeable future. Elections at the local level in Canada will likely have little to do with health; board members of regional health authorities will almost certainly not think of themselves as being involved in local politics. Similarly, Canadian students of health policy and of local government will likely pay little attention to each other.

Conclusion

This chapter has shown that there is a huge variation in the nature of Canadian local special-purpose bodies. Some might think that the net has been cast too wide. If we restrict our definition to ones clearly linked to municipal government, then some scholars claim that school boards do not qualify.[50] For some, library boards might be too weak to qualify as local governments. Non-profit or Crown corporations established by other levels of government are obviously suspect, even if they do operate major local public facilities such as ports and airports and even if their boards do contain municipal nominees. Inclusion of regional health authorities is perhaps questionable, but if we exclude them, then what justification would we have for including Metrolinx, an institution that, in form and finance, looks remarkably like Ontario's LHINs? One difference is that the territory covered by Metrolinx is much larger than any of the Toronto-area LHINs, so that LHINs are more "local" than Metrolinx. But it would be absurd to exclude Metrolinx from a textbook concerned with the local governance of Canadian cities just because elected municipal politicians have been recently removed from its governing body. Similarly, it would be absurd to exclude Metrolinx and include TransLink just because of differences in financing and in mechanisms for making appointments to their respective boards.

The difficulty of defining and categorizing local special-purpose bodies is one of the features of local government that makes its study complex and complicated. As we shall see, one of the reasons for promoting municipal amalgamations is that they sometimes eliminate the need for inter-municipal special-purpose bodies. Within particular municipalities, there are often frequent calls to eliminate particular special-purpose bodies such as police services boards or transit commissions. Without any local special-purpose bodies, local government in Canada would definitely be simpler and easier to understand, but it would likely not be better equipped to improve the quality of our urban life. Municipal councils can do a great deal, but they are not necessarily well-suited to govern our schools, and perhaps not even our police services. There are strong reasons that various utilities that can raise their own revenues from consumers might be better off being run as separate business-like operations. And there are certainly reasons that inter-municipal special-purpose bodies should not always be replaced by amalgamated municipalities. Amalgamating the cities of Regina and Moose Jaw because they share the same water treatment plant, for example, does not seem like enlightened public policy. So even if we could all agree that it would be best to eliminate special-purpose bodies, it would never be possible in the real world. Through the remainder of this book, we shall see many reasons why special-purpose bodies of one sort or another will always be with us.

RESOURCES

Special-purpose bodies are no longer merely a seemingly obscure aspect of local government. They are receiving increasing attention from scholars of multi-level governance, especially specialists in the politics of international organizations such as the European Union. For an important article that refers to "general-purpose jurisdictions" (such as municipalities) as "Type I Governance," and "task-specific jurisdictions" (special-purpose bodies) as "Type II Governance," see Liesbet Hooghe and Gary Marks, "Unraveling the central state, but how? Types of multi-level governance," *American Political Science Review* 97, 2 (2003): 233–43.

STUDY QUESTIONS

1. What obstacles, if any, are there to Canadian municipalities taking direct control over local public education? Would you support such a move? Why or why not?
2. To what extent in Canada do municipal councils have direct control over municipal police services? Do you think they should have more or less control?
3. What are some examples of federally controlled local special-purpose bodies in the area of Canada in which you live? Check their websites and discuss what they are trying to do to promote economic development and/or enhanced quality of life in your area.
4. Are special-purpose bodies undemocratic? Why or why not?

PART II
ADAPTING TO URBANIZATION

Population Centres, Rural Areas, and Causes of Metropolitan Growth

Part I of this book was concerned with understanding what local governments are and how they fit into the overall Canadian governmental system. Part II shifts the focus to examining how our system of local government has adapted to the increasing importance of urban areas relative to rural areas. Invariably our cities and towns have expanded outward, a phenomenon that local government has both sponsored and often attempted to control. To begin to understand what is at issue here, we need first to know more about the differences between what is rural and what is urban, and how these differences affected the policies of local and provincial governments. We also need to know how Statistics Canada (an agency of the federal government) defines different kinds of human settlements. Such data are essential for any analysis that attempts to understand the links between Canada's systems of local government and the governance of our cities.

Approaching Urban–Rural Differences

Distinguishing urban from rural is not easy. In fact, starting with the 2011 census, Statistics Canada no longer uses the term *urban*. According to Statistics Canada, Canadians now live either in various types of *population centres* or in rural areas, which are the vast territories of Canada not included within population centres. The problem for Statistics Canada was that it had been using the term *urban* to describe settlements with populations as small as 1000. Because social scientists still use the term to refer to much larger places, it is important that we begin by surveying the term's two most important senses in the academic literature. The first is its demographic sense. According to this approach, three main population variables—size, density, and economic heterogeneity—determine the extent to which a place is urban. Relatively large numbers of people living close to each other who are engaged in diverse economic activity are living in an urban environment, a place ordinary people using everyday language are likely to call a *town* or a *city*, depending on its size.[1] But a labour camp where hundreds of workers are living close to each other (for example, to work in a mine) is not a town because insufficient diversity of economic activity takes place there. Because we do not have labour camps in Canada, we can assume that all places where large numbers of people live close to each other are urban areas. Some might want to consider a place like Fort McMurray in Alberta a labour camp, because so many Canadians, some without their families, have migrated there to work in the oil sands. Although accommodation for families is very expensive in Fort McMurray, it is clearly an urban settlement rather than a labour camp. Entrepreneurs are as free as Canadians anywhere else to open businesses there—and many have done precisely that in the hopes of attracting dollars earned by oil-sands workers. In so doing these entrepreneurs have created an urban economy, although one that is not nearly as diverse as those in larger cities such as Toronto, Montreal, and Vancouver.

Defining urban places simply as places in which relatively large numbers of people live close to each other is not really very helpful. The obvious questions are: How many people? How close? The answers are inevitably going to be arbitrary and subject to dispute. This is why Statistics Canada no longer bothers.

Before turning in more detail to how Statistics Canada solved its own particular problem, we must acknowledge the second approach to defining what is urban. This is the socio-cultural approach, in which being urban is more a state of mind than a demographic fact.[2] According to this approach, people can be urban in orientation even if they are farmers: they can use the Internet; watch satellite television; go on southern vacations in the wintertime; send their children to college and university; and be quite at home enjoying life in a big city when they attend meetings of organizations in which they are active (such as churches, agricultural groups, service clubs). In short, they live a kind of lifestyle that once was available only to people who lived in cities but now is available to all citizens of advanced liberal democracies. According to this socio-cultural approach, non-urban people, on the other hand, live in traditional ways similar to their grandparents' and great-grandparents', eschewing modern technology and feeling out of place when required to go to "the city" for such services as specialized medical care. Using this approach to defining *urban,* we should analyze degrees of urbanity by observing lifestyles or administering questionnaires.

The approach we use to define what is urban has profound implications for determining our approach to the organization of local government. If we adopt the demographic approach, we are likely to conceptualize the needs of urban and rural areas as being quite different from each other, and therefore we would likely want to have distinct institutions of local government for urban and rural areas. If, however, we accept that we will find many urban-oriented people living in relatively isolated physical locations, then the notion of having distinct systems of urban and rural local government might make little sense unless, of course, people with socio-culturally urban attitudes live in the country precisely because they do *not* want to live close to thousands of other people in a demographically urban environment. We shall return in later chapters to the important issue of how the different approaches to defining *urban* affect policy decisions about the organization of local government.

In the meantime, a crucial point needs to be made about the difference between urban and non-urban. Urban areas require more government services, and the kinds of additional services they require are generally supplied by local governments. Imagine a resident of a condominium in downtown Vancouver and somebody else who lives on a farm in rural Manitoba. The ordinary day-to-day life of the downtown resident will be highly dependent on the following public services:

- water supply for drinking and cleaning;
- sewage treatment so that the streets and harbour are not filthy and a hazard to health;
- building regulation, street lighting, and fire protection for security in the built environment;
- frequent and visible police patrol to ensure public order among thousands of strangers;
- public transit for mobility, including journeys to and from work.

These are just some of the essential public services that city-dwellers require. If they are going to be living in a city in the first place, they likely will expect a wide range of nearby cultural and recreational amenities as well, the provision of which will almost certainly require government assistance, if not direct involvement.

Like the city-dweller, the farm resident requires public roads, but there will likely be few demands, even from farmers who might be socio-culturally urban, that the government control noise and congestion or that it provide cleaning and lighting for the roads. The farm will have its own well, water pump, and septic system. There might or might not be garbage collection. There will be no regular police patrol, and strangers in the area will be rare and remarked upon by vigilant neighbours. Fire insurance rates will be high because response times from volunteer firefighters will be relatively long, and their ability to fight the fire will likely depend on ready access to a nearby surface water supply. Unlike city residents, however, farmers often need governments to make special provisions for draining land, for allocating surface water for irrigation, or for ensuring that fences between properties are maintained. Such matters are relatively minor compared to the needs of the urbanite.

It is important to acknowledge that many crucial government services are equally important to all citizens regardless of where they live: medical care; income security for the old, disabled, and unemployed; national defence; large-scale environmental protection. It is no accident that policy for these governmental functions is not determined at the local level. Rural residents do require police for the enforcement of criminal law, but rural policing is based much more on response to particular incidents than on regular patrol. Public education is, of course, another government function that is now universally acknowledged to be vital for all children, regardless of where they might live. Interestingly for our purposes, this is precisely why educational policy-making has become more centralized in recent decades and why school boards have commonly had their territories expanded to take in both urban and rural areas. Rural children quite properly now have access to many of the same educational facilities and opportunities as their urban counterparts, even if long bus rides are the frequent trade-off.

Population Centres

For Statistics Canada, a population centre is an "area with a population of at least 1,000 and no fewer than 400 persons per square kilometer." There are three groups of population centres:

- small population centres, with a population between 1000 and 29,999
- medium population centres, with a population between 30,000 and 99,999
- large population centres, with a population of 100,000 or more.[3]

According to the 2011 census, Canada contained 857 small population centres, 54 medium population centres, and 31 large population centres.[4] Five population centres straddle provincial boundaries:

Campbellton (New Brunswick and Quebec), Hawkesbury (Ontario and Quebec), Ottawa–Gatineau (Ontario and Quebec), Flin Flon (Manitoba and Saskatchewan) and Lloydminster (Alberta and Saskatchewan).[5] It is important also to note that many population centres include all or parts of a number of different municipalities; that not all municipalities contain a population centre; and that some municipalities contain more than one population centre (the single-tier municipality of Chatham–Kent in southwestern Ontario contains five). In short, the delineation of boundaries of population centres by Statistics Canada is almost completely unrelated to the existence of municipal boundaries. All Canadians who do not live in population centres are classified as *rural*. In 1871, more than 80 per cent of Canadians lived in rural areas; in 2011 only 18.9 per cent of the population fell into this category.[6] At the other end of the spectrum, 60.0 per cent of Canadians in 2011 lived in large population centres.[7]

Census Metropolitan Areas and Census Agglomerations

Because of the complexity of our settlement patterns, Statistics Canada has developed sophisticated ways of quantifying various ways in which the country's population centres are connected to their respective rural hinterlands. The starting point for these calculations is the concept of a *core*, which, unlike a population centre, always corresponds with the boundaries of a municipality or contiguous group of municipalities. A core comprises the territories of all the municipalities, of which at least 75 per cent of the population resides in a population centre of more than 10,000. If the population of a core is less than 50,000, it is the starting point for the construction of a *census agglomeration* (CA); if it is more than 50,000, it is the starting point for a *census metropolitan area* (CMA). Municipalities are added to urban cores to create CMAs and CAs as a result of calculations deriving from commuter flows; these flows are determined from questions asked in the previous census about place of work. If more than 100 commuters in a municipality are near an urban core, and if 50 per cent of the employed labour force in that municipality works in the urban core, then that municipality is added to the CA or CMA. A municipality is also added if it attracts more than 100 commuters and more than 25 per cent of its employed labour force lives in the urban core.[8] In 2006, 35 per cent of all the rural residents of Canada actually lived within the territories of CMAs and CAs, indicating that they have ready physical access to urban life. In fact, as we know from the definitions of CMAs and CAs, a significant number of them are commuting to work in the cores.[9]

If the population of a core in a CA falls below 10,000, then the area no longer exists as a CA. Once an area becomes a CMA, however, it remains so regardless of what happens to its population.[10] Table 5.1 shows the population of all the CMAs and CAs with populations of more than 100,000 as determined by the 2011 census. One of the obvious difficulties with the table—resulting from the practice of treating CMAs as permanent—is that, because the Toronto, Oshawa, Barrie, Hamilton, St. Catharine's–Niagara, and Kitchener CMAs are contiguous, it is difficult to use CMA population data to obtain a full picture of the territory and population of the entire Toronto metropolitan region.

Table 5.1 Population Counts for CMAs and CAs with Total Populations over 100,000, 2006 and 2011 Censuses

Geographic Name	Population, 2006	Population, 2011	% Change
Toronto (ON)	5,113,149	5,583,064	9.2
Montreal (QC)[a]	3,635,556[b]	3,824,221	5.2
Vancouver (BC)	2,116,581	2,313,328	9.3
Ottawa–Gatineau (ON/QC)	1,133,633[b]	1,236,324	9.1
Calgary (AB)[a]	1,079,310	1,214,839[b]	12.6
Edmonton (AB)	1,034,945	1,159,869	12.1
Quebec (QC)[a]	719,153b	765,706	6.5
Winnipeg (MB)	694,668	730,018	5.1
Hamilton (ON)	692,911	721,053	4.1
Kitchener–Cambridge–Waterloo (ON)	451,235	477,160	5.7
London (ON)	457,720	474,786	3.7
St. Catharines–Niagara (ON)	390,317	392,184	0.5
Halifax (NS)	372,858	390,328	4.7
Oshawa (ON)	330,594	356,177	7.7
Victoria (BC)[a]	330,088	344,615	4.4
Windsor (ON)	323,342	319,246	-1.3
Saskatoon (SK)	233,923	260,600	11.4
Regina (SK)	194,971	210,556	8.0
Sherbrooke (QC)	191,410[b]	201,890	5.5
St. John's (NL)	181,113	196,966	8.8

Table 5.1 *continued*

Geographic Name	Population, 2006	Population, 2011	% Change
Barrie (ON)	177,061	187,013	5.6
Kelowna (BC)	162,276	179,839	10.8
Abbotsford–Mission (BC)	159,020	170,191	7.0
Greater Sudbury/Grand Sudbury (ON)	158,258	160,770	1.6
Kingston (ON)	152,358	159,561	4.7
Saguenay (QC)	156,305[b]	157,790	1.0
Trois-Rivières (QC)	144,713[b]	151,773	4.9
Guelph (ON)	133,698[b]	141,097	5.5
Moncton (NB)	126,424	138,644	9.7
Brantford (ON)[a]	124,607	135,501	8.7
Saint John (NB)	122,389	127,761	4.4
Thunder Bay (ON)	122,907	121,596	-1.1
Peterborough (ON)	116,570	118,975	2.1
Lethbridge (AB)	95,196	105,999	11.3
Chatham–Kent (ON)	108,589	104,075	−4.2
Cape Breton (NS)	105,928	101,619	−4.1

[a] indicates that the population count excludes data from one or more incompletely enumerated Indian reserves or Indian settlements.
[b] indicates that the area of the CMA or CA changed between 2006 and 2011. Population counts from 2006 have been changed to reflect the population of the area in 2006.

Source: Adapted from Statistics Canada, Population and dwelling counts, for census metropolitan areas and census agglomerations, 2011 and 2006 censuses. Accessed 20 August 2013.

The Greater Golden Horseshoe

As we have just noted, six CMAs in the Toronto area are contiguous. Because the rules used by Statistics Canada prevent the merger of CMAs, the Toronto CMA simply does not capture the entire territory and population of the area that we usually think of as the Toronto city-region. The boundaries of the Toronto core abut the boundaries of the Oshawa CMA to the east and the Hamilton CMA to the west. Under current rules, these boundaries will not change, whatever happens to the commuting patterns of residents of these CMAs into Toronto. In a recent discussion of "The Greater Toronto Region," three geographers have written that "There is no single or widely accepted definition of the geographical extent of the Toronto region."[11] They go on to list five different possibilities, with their respective populations, according to the 2011 census (growth rate in per cent since 2006 is in brackets):

- City of Toronto (municipality): 2,615,060 (4.5)
- Toronto CMA: 5,583,064 (9.2)
- Greater Toronto Area (GTA): 6,054,221 (8.6)
- GTA + City of Hamilton (GTAH): 6,574,170 (8.1)
- Greater Golden Horseshoe: 8,695,100 (8.0)[12]

The GTA was once an area used for planning purposes by the Ontario government, but it now has no official standing, even though it is frequently used in the media for weather forecasting and traffic reports. It comprises the city of Toronto and the regional municipalities of York, Peel, Halton, and Durham (see Figure 5.1). The GTAH is the area covered by Metrolinx (see Chapter 4).

In 2006, the government of Ontario officially defined a still larger area as the Greater Golden Horseshoe (GGH). We shall explore it further, not just because it provides a good picture of the reality of Canada's largest city-region, but also because it is the territorial basis for the most ambitious foray by any Canadian province into the complex field of large-scale urban and regional planning. The 2011 populations of its municipal component parts (as shown on Figure 5.1) are listed in Table 5.2. Because the total population of Ontario in 2011 was 12,851,821, this meant that two-thirds of Ontario's population lived in the GGH.

The Ontario government has enacted two major laws designed to control the future use of land within the GGH. The first was the Greenbelt Act, 2005. It essentially prevents all new urban development in the designated Greenbelt area shown in Figure 5.1.[13] Much of this land, especially the Niagara Escarpment, had already been protected by previous legislation. But the new Greenbelt clearly encircles Toronto with a view to preventing continuous urban sprawl and to providing ready access to the countryside for urban residents.

The companion legislation was the Places to Grow Act, 2005. This legislation, by granting the government enhanced authority to plan for new growth and infrastructure, potentially applies throughout Ontario. Under the terms of the Act, in 2006 the government proclaimed the Growth Plan for the Greater Golden Horseshoe.[14] This plan lays down procedures by which an expected 3.7 million new GGH residents will be accommodated by 2031. The main theme is intensification. By 2015, 40 per cent of all new residential development will be required to take place within established built-up areas. The plan also designates some

Figure 5.1 Greater Golden Horseshoe Showing the Greenbelt and Boundaries of the Toronto CMA

Source: Adapted from Andrew Sancton, *The Limits of Boundaries: Why City-Regions Cannot Be Self-Governing* (Montreal and Kingston: McGill-Queen's University Press, 2008), 29.

established communities outside the Greenbelt as areas for expansion and sketches out plans for new transportation and environmental infrastructure to enable this to occur in an orderly and sustainable fashion.

These initiatives from the Ontario government merit our attention because they illustrate two important facts about Canada's largest metropolitan region:

1. Because the concept of the CMA is no longer useful in defining the territory of Toronto's built-up area and its area of economic

Table 5.2   Population of the Municipal Units of the Greater Golden Horseshoe

Municipal Unit	Population	% Growth since 2006
City of Toronto	2,615,060	4.5
Region of Peel	1,296,814	11.8
Region of York	1,032,524	14.2
Region of Durham	608,124	8.4
City of Hamilton	519,949	8.6
Region of Waterloo	507,096	6.1
Region of Halton	501,689	14.2
Simcoe County, Barrie, and Orillia	446,063	5.7
Region of Niagara	431,346	0.9
Wellington County and Guelph	208,360	4.0
Peterborough County and Peterborough	134,933	1.4
Brant County and Brantford	136,035	8.7
Northumberland County	82,126	1.4
City of Kawartha Lakes	73,214	-1.8
Dufferin County	56,881	4.5
Haldimand County	44,876	-0.7
GGH Total	8,048,993	8.0

Source: Statistics Canada, Population of the Municipal Units of the Greater Golden Horseshoe. Accessed 22 August 2013. Reproduced and distributed on an "as is" basis with the permission of Statistics Canada.

Table 5.3   Provinces (except Ontario) Listed According to Extent Population Is Dominated by Largest CMA or CA in the Province

Province	Population	Largest CMA/CA	Population	% of Total Population
Manitoba	1,208,268	Winnipeg	730,011	61
British Columbia	4,400,057	Vancouver	2,318,328	53
Quebec	7,903,001	Montreal	3,824,221	48
Prince Edward Island	140,204	Charlottetown	64,487	46
Nova Scotia	921,727	Halifax	390,328	42
Newfoundland and Labrador	5,145,369	St. John's	196,966	38
Alberta	3,645,257	Calgary	1,214,839	33
Saskatchewan	1,033,381	Saskatoon	260,600	25
New Brunswick	751,171	Moncton	138,644	18

Source: Statistics Canada, 2011 Census of Canada www12.statcan.gc.ca/census-recensement/2011/dp-pd/prof/details/page.cfm?Lang=E&Geo1=CMA&Code1=305&Geo2=PR&Code2=13&Data=Count&SearchText=moncton&SearchType=Begins&SearchPR=13&B1=All&Custom=&TABID=1

influence, the province has determined its own definition of the area, the GGH.

2. Because two-thirds of Ontarians live in the GGH and because planning for its future infrastructure is so crucial to the province's economic future, the government of Ontario has taken direct charge of large-scale planning within the GGH.

As we shall see, these actions by the Ontario government are potentially of great importance for understanding the role of local government in Canada because they suggest the possibility that, in the future, provincial governments might be the most important institutions in determining the outward physical growth of our largest cities.

CMAs and Provinces

If there is any possibility that developments in Ontario will be replicated elsewhere, then there will have to be similar examples of a single city and its region dominating the provincial population. For other provinces, the largest CMA in the province is the best indicator of such dominance, because there are no examples outside Toronto where CMAs are contiguous.

Table 5.3 shows the populations of each of the other nine provinces, together with the population of its largest CMA (or CA in the case of Prince Edward Island). The provinces are listed in order of the extent to which the population is dominated by that of the largest CMA.

Anyone with even the most elementary understanding of Canada's urban geography will be able to understand most of the reasons why this list takes the form that it does. Except for the last three provinces on the list, all are dominated by one city. The extent of the domination roughly reflects the general level of urbanization within the province. Three Atlantic Provinces (PEI, Nova Scotia, and Newfoundland and Labrador) are at the bottom of the group of provinces that have only one clearly dominant city because, relative to other provinces, their populations are dispersed in small towns and rural areas. This applies especially to New Brunswick, which is at the very bottom of the list. It has no one dominant city. In addition to Moncton, the Saint John CMA (2011 population of 127,761) and the Fredericton CA (94,268) vie for supremacy. This factor, along with tensions between north and south and between French and English, ensures that New Brunswick is not an easy province to govern.

Alberta and Saskatchewan merit special attention. They are the only two provinces with two major competing CMAs. In neither province is the provincial capital the largest, in part, perhaps, because electoral pressures have caused successive provincial governments to ensure that provincial largesse has been distributed more or less equally between the two cities and therefore between northern and southern portions of the province. If the governments of Alberta and Saskatchewan were ever to become as directly involved in large-scale urban planning as the government of Ontario is for the Toronto area, they would have to do so in a very careful and even-handed manner for each of their two major metropolitan regions. Such a path would be fraught with difficulty, which makes it unlikely that either province will follow it any time soon. Instead, they have tried to structure municipal institutions in such a way that local authorities can carry out this task in each region. To varying degrees, this has been the path followed in other provinces as well. Such initiatives have taken quite different forms and have met different levels of success. Analyzing them is an important objective of the remaining chapters in this part of the book.

Causes of Growth in Canada's Largest CMAs

Clearly, the proportion of Canadians living in population centres, especially in the largest CMAs, has been increasing dramatically for many decades, and this trend is by no means unique to Canada. An important feature of the well-known process of globalization has been a massive movement of humanity from the countryside to the city in the developing countries. Urban life has attracted rural migrants not because it offered instant wealth in orderly residential neighbourhoods, but because urban opportunities, even in makeshift housing on the edges of huge Third World cities, seemed superior to a lifetime of subsistence agriculture in an economically stagnant countryside. Recent growth in Canada's cities has *not* been the result of internal migration from rural areas. In Canada and other developed countries, this process of rural migration to cities accompanied industrialization, which began in Canada in Montreal in the second half of the nineteenth century.[15]

Globalization involves a massive increase in world trade, much of it fuelled by low-cost manufacturing in Third World cities that sucks people from the countryside. This trade is in turn financed and managed not by national governments but by major banks and transnational corporations, most of which have tended to concentrate in established financial centres whose relative importance in the world has dramatically increased—New York, London, and Tokyo being the prime examples. A key feature of globalization is the way it constructs links among urban economies throughout the world that apparently bypass the traditional rules and regulations imposed by national governments. The main objective of powerful international entities such as the World Trade Organization is to decrease the capacity of national governments to impose national rules and regulations respecting international trade.

What does all this have to do with Canadian local government? The answer is complex. First, it makes us pay more attention to cities. Anyone concerned with Canada's international competitiveness (which effectively means the future quality of life for Canadians) must be concerned about how our major cities will fit in the global network.[16] Can Toronto's banks be major players in international finance? Can Montreal build on its obvious potential as a bridge between Europe and North America? What will Vancouver's role be in the network of Pacific cities? Will hydrocarbons remain important in the world economy such that Calgary and Edmonton become major international cities as Alberta's resources become increasingly crucial for global prosperity?

When we refer to cities in this context, we are clearly not referring only to the central municipalities of Toronto, Montreal, Vancouver, Calgary, and Edmonton. We are referring at least to the CMAs, and possibly to larger entities such as the GGH and the entire Calgary–Edmonton corridor. With some exceptions that we shall explore in the next few chapters, there are no municipal governments that correspond to these areas. In any event, municipal governments do not have jurisdiction over many of the matters that directly relate to a city's international competitiveness. For example, the city of Toronto can do nothing about the regulation of the banks and other financial institutions whose headquarters are so important for its economy. It is true that municipalities, through their control over the built environment, can take some action to make their cities more attractive or less attractive to creative entrepreneurs,[17] but they cannot bring the ocean to Winnipeg or ski hills to Toronto. Just because globalization has caused cities to become more important in the global economy, it does not necessarily follow that municipal governments will become more important.

But globalization has had another profound impact on large Canadian cities. Globalization has caused new patterns of international migration that have brought in waves of new immigrants.[18] Just as rural migrants flocked to cities in developing countries, many who met with some success in these cities have foreseen even greater opportunities in developed countries. As birth rates fell in these countries and as their citizens showed less willingness to take on many of the less pleasant service jobs in big cities, the doors for immigrants opened. Canada was no exception. The result has been a dramatic change in the ethnic

Table 5.4 Selected Population Characteristics of Canada's Census Metropolitan Areas with Populations over 500,000, 2011

CMA	% Visible Minority	Foreign-born	Aboriginal Identity
Toronto	47.09	46.0	0.7
Montreal	20.3	22.6	0.7
Vancouver	45.26	40.0	2.3
Ottawa–Gatineau	19.2	19.4	2.5
Calgary	28.1	26.2	2.8
Edmonton	22.4	20.4	5.4
Quebec	3.1	4.4	0.9
Winnipeg	19.7	20.6	11.0
Hamilton	14.3	23.5	1.7

Source: Statistics Canada, *2011 Census of Canada*.

makeup of large Canadian cities.[19] Table 5.4 shows the high proportions of foreign-born and visible minorities in the Toronto and Vancouver CMAs, and some of the relatively low proportions elsewhere, especially in Quebec City. The table also shows the percentage in each of these CMAs who responded to the 2011 census questionnaire by stating that they identified with at least one Aboriginal group (North American Indian, Métis, or Inuit). Especially in western cities such as Winnipeg and Edmonton (and Saskatoon and Regina), this percentage has been increasing significantly in recent years as Aboriginal people move to the city for reasons similar to those of rural-to-urban migrants in developing countries.[20]

Much more could be written about the changing demographics of Canadian cities. For example, increasing evidence indicates that downtown areas of the largest Canadian CMAs are becoming residential areas for the wealthy[21] and that lower-income city-dwellers are moving to the inner suburbs where housing is generally cheaper. All of these factors are profoundly important for understanding the contextual background for the study of urban politics, which is the focus of Part III of this book.

Conclusion

Local governments do not exist in isolation from the urban and/or rural environments in which they are located. Indeed, as we have seen, whether an area is urban or rural in its essential characteristics is a major factor in determining the nature and extent of public services that its local governments are expected to provide. Observers frequently and rightly claim that Canada is becoming increasingly urban and that this process has profound implications for government at all levels. In order to understand such claims, we need to know about the various demographic measures used by Statistics Canada to classify different kinds of urban and rural areas. In the Toronto area, however, Statistics Canada has been unable to adapt its traditional census classifications to the full territorial extent of the sprawling city-region. That is why, in this chapter, emphasis was placed on the Greater Golden Horseshoe, a territory defined by the Ontario government. Three other provinces—Manitoba, British Columbia, and Quebec—also contain dominant metropolitan areas. In the future, we shall have to observe carefully to see if each of these provinces follows Ontario's example and becomes the lead player in large-scale planning for the major metropolitan area in the province.

Meanwhile, all provinces—including Ontario—have structured their systems of local government to take account of the differences between rural and urban and to provide mechanisms to enable these systems to adjust to various patterns of urbanization. This is the subject of the next three chapters.

RESOURCES

The Canadian census—conducted every five years—is an exceptionally valuable resource, and students of local government should know how to use it. The most recent census was conducted in 2011. For basic population data for many of the census areas outlined in this chapter, see www12.statcan.gc.ca/census-recensement/index-eng.cfm?HPA. In 2010 the federal government unexpectedly announced that it will no longer be compulsory for randomly selected Canadian citizens to answer the more detailed (long-form) census questionnaires; this change thereby casts doubt on the future accuracy of data (such as those relating to place of birth and Aboriginal identity) derived from these questionnaires. The voluntary answers are now referred to as the National Household Survey (NHS). Results from the NHS can be accessed through the link on the website referred to above. Data in Table 5.4 is from the NHS. The Table does not compare 2006 and 2011 data because they were collected in quite different ways.

STUDY QUESTIONS

1. Is it possible to live in the countryside and to have an urban lifestyle at the same time? Explain your reasoning.
2. What do we mean when we say that less than 20 per cent of the Canadian population is rural? How does Statistics Canada classify the remaining portion of the population?
3. Explain the differences between the Toronto CMA and the Greater Golden Horseshoe. Do you think one is superior to the other in defining the real nature of the Toronto area? Explain your reasoning.
4. What have been some of the impacts of globalization on large Canadian cities? Has globalization bypassed smaller places?

CHAPTER 6

Annexations

This chapter is about how the boundaries of urban municipalities—cities, towns, and villages—are adjusted to accommodate urban expansion. It focuses primarily on how this process has occurred incrementally, traditionally, and locally rather than being the result of major interventions by provincial governments. Such interventions and reorganizations, especially important in the big cities of Ontario and Quebec, will be the focus of chapters 7 and 8. Residents of big cities in eastern Canada can perhaps be excused for thinking that annexations are no longer of much relevance. But in early 2014 annexation procedures in one form or another were being followed in dozens of Canadian municipalities, including Edmonton, Grande Prairie, Lloydminster, Regina, Kamloops, Trail, Prince Rupert, and Brantford.

Both municipal annexations and amalgamations are considered here. The distinction between *annexation* and *amalgamation* is somewhat technical and not always of great significance in the real world, but it needs to be acknowledged. An *annexation* takes place when a municipality absorbs *some* of the land under the jurisdiction of an adjoining municipality. An *amalgamation* is when two or more municipalities come together such that the territory of all of them is placed under the jurisdiction of a single municipality. According to this technical and legal distinction, if a municipality of one million people comes together with a municipality of five hundred, the result would be an amalgamation. But in everyday language—even among municipal professionals—we would be much more likely to state that the larger municipality annexed the smaller than to say that they amalgamated with each other. In the real world, the large annexes the small, and equals amalgamate.

Most of the focus in this chapter is on annexations, even if the events described technically were amalgamations. This is because we shall be using the language used at the time by the participants in the process. The first section of the chapter looks at municipal annexation in general by discussing a hypothetical urban settlement. Then we move on to important historical and current Canadian case studies in Montreal, Edmonton, London, Calgary, and Regina. Each of these cases—even those from long ago—are important, not just for understanding how annexation works but also for understanding some of the big political and environmental issues associated with the outward expansion of built-up urban areas.

The Expansion of a Hypothetical Urban Settlement[1]

We saw in Chapter 1 that municipalities in Canada have been created in the past either as the direct result of a local initiative approved by the province or as a direct result of action initiated by the province itself. For the purpose of this hypothetical example, it does not much matter how the municipality came into being. Our starting point is a city incorporated as a municipality. This means, among other things, that it has defined boundaries. Forward-thinking local officials would have done everything possible to ensure that the boundaries included rural land beyond the built-up area so that there would be room for expansion within the municipality. Most businesses and residents within any town or city have always favoured at least moderate growth. Businesses want growth to expand profit-making opportunities, and residents generally favour growth because it enhances property values and provides job opportunities for future generations. Eventually economic growth will mean that all the land within the municipality's boundaries becomes built up. What happens then?

It is conceivable that city authorities will do nothing and that whoever has jurisdiction over land use in the adjoining rural area will prohibit further growth there. In this unlikely situation, further growth is virtually impossible: the city is stymied. In the short term, property values might increase because of the scarcity of urban land and buildings, but in the longer term the area is likely to slip into obscurity as other nearby cities absorb new growth. A much more likely possibility is that the rural authorities will allow urban growth adjoining the city boundaries. Such action raises all kinds of questions, many of which are of great practical importance today in many communities across Canada. What kind of urban infrastructure will be available in the rural area and who will pay for it? How will urban residents and businesses in the rural municipality get along with the farmers? Will it be cheaper to live and do business in the rural area and, if so, will the urban municipality experience an exodus? Will city officials resent their neighbour's growth, or will they help facilitate it so that the area as a whole can continue to expand? These questions all relate to *fringe development* in rural municipalities, and they are the subject of considerable concern to policy-makers in all provinces.

Another possibility is that the city would attempt to annex land from the rural municipality either before or after the fringe development occurs. If it happens beforehand, affected property owners (including farmers) are likely to be in favour because annexation by an urban municipality is almost sure to raise the value of their land in anticipation of nearly certain development. If annexation happens afterwards, affected property owners might be opposed if they sense that annexation to the city will cause taxes on their property to increase.[2] Depending on how easy it is to incorporate municipally, property owners on the urban fringe might attempt to create their own new suburban municipality in an effort to prevent annexation. In any event, officials in the rural municipality are unlikely to favour either annexation or suburban incorporation, at least not unless their municipality gets some form of financial compensation. The central government (provinces in Canada) needs some kind of procedure to determine if and how annexations and new incorporations are to occur. In Canada such procedures have involved inter-municipal negotiations, referendums, administrative tribunals, and provincial legislation. We shall examine examples of these various procedures in the cases that follow later in this chapter.

Even efficient and fair procedures for annexations do not solve all problems. For example, if a rural municipality continually loses land to an urban neighbour, there comes a time when its own viability is in doubt. At that point someone will have to decide if all of it should be absorbed by the city, even if that means including a large and continuing agricultural area within the urban boundaries, or if the rural remnant should be attached to some other rural municipality. Another problem that can emerge is that two urban areas can keep expanding through annexation such that they eventually become contiguous. In these circumstances, it is unlikely that one will be able to annex future land for growth from the other.

This discussion has shown how urban areas (called *population centre*s by Statistics Canada, as we saw in the previous chapter) can evolve in such a way that they contain many separate municipalities:

- Adjoining rural municipalities might have become urban over time.
- New urban municipalities might have been established within a former part of a rural municipality.
- Two previously distinct urban areas might have grown into each other.
- All or some of these processes might have occurred simultaneously.

Since the mid-nineteenth century, many politicians, civil servants, academics, and sometimes even real-estate developers have observed such phenomena with growing concern. They refer to the tendency for increasing numbers of municipalities within a single urban area as *fragmentation*, and they have worked hard to reverse the trend by advocating some form of *consolidation* of municipalities. If annexation has not been possible or desirable, they have promoted other consolidationist alternatives, to be discussed in the next two chapters. Before then, however, we shall look at important Canadian examples of locally generated annexations and amalgamations.

Montreal

The city of Montreal was first incorporated in 1833, but the charter expired in 1836 and was not immediately renewed because of the political turmoil that resulted in the Rebellion of 1837. A new charter for the city was granted by the governor general of the United Province of Canada in 1840, when the city's population was 31,000.[3] The city's boundaries encompassed only the area bounded roughly by Mount Royal and the river, and Atwater and Papineau streets. In the first few years after incorporation much of this land remained rural. By 1845 there were nine other incorporated municipalities on the island of Montreal, all rural parishes. But as industrialization in Montreal took hold, much of the urban development actually took place outside the city's official boundaries. By 1881, 27 other municipalities were on the island, most of which were villages that had been incorporated by local initiative after the Quebec legislature approved new laws facilitating the incorporation process. Two of the new municipalities were towns: Lachine and Saint-Henri.[4]

The Annexation of Maisonneuve

Between 1881 and 1921, 51 new municipalities came into being on the island of Montreal, but many lasted only a few years before agreeing to be annexed by the city of Montreal. The first of dozens of such annexations occurred in 1883, when most of the urbanized part of the town of Hochelaga joined Montreal. The last was Maisonneuve in 1918. In the interval, Montreal absorbed all or parts of 31 other municipalities, increasing its territory by a factor of five. The annexations invariably occurred because property owners in the annexed areas, believing they would be better off financially within the city, agreed to it. In most cases their municipalities were virtually bankrupt.[5]

Maisonneuve was the most dramatic example.[6] Its financial difficulties were actually the result of a major scam. One contemporary Montreal opponent of the annexation objected because city taxpayers would end up holding Maisonneuve's massive debt: "The bunch of 'get rich quick' artists that undertook the exploiting of Maisonneuve bought farm land, blocked them out into city streets, had sewers built, water mains laid, permanent pavements and sidewalks installed, out of the civic treasury through miles of vacant land, with not a house erected thereon."[7] In addition to a city hall, market, and fire station, the "get rich quick" artists also used money borrowed on behalf of Maisonneuve to buy land for a huge park at inflated prices from provincial politicians (the park later became the site of the stadium for the 1976 Olympic Games, when another round of municipal indebtedness began). Immediately after Maisonneuve joined Montreal in 1918, it accounted for 5 per cent of the city's population, 3.5 per cent of its taxable property, and 16 per cent of its debt.[8]

Maisonneuve's unfortunate story unfolded in the general absence of provincial regulation relating to land development, municipal indebtedness, and conflicts of interest. Developers used municipalities that they controlled in order to borrow money from lenders who assumed that they would eventually be repaid by the municipal taxpayers if the development was financially successful, or by the city of Montreal if it was not. Until 1918, the city was anxious to annex whatever land it could on the grounds that a bigger municipality would eventually be more beneficial to its property owners than a smaller one surrounded by bankrupt suburbs. The problem was that this policy eventually became financially unsustainable, even for an otherwise prosperous municipality such as Montreal. The city ended up absorbing the financially troubled suburbs, while those that were financially successful, such as Westmount, Outremont, and Mount Royal, remained independent. Nevertheless, according to the 1921 federal census, the city of Montreal included 78 per cent of the population of the metropolitan area (i.e., the CMA, although it was defined differently then). In the absence of further annexations, and with suburban municipalities growing at a faster rate than the city, this percentage had been reduced to 54 by the time of the 1961 census.[9]

"One Island, One City"[10]

In 1960, the city's charismatic young mayor, Jean Drapeau, began a campaign to annex all of the island's municipalities to the city of Montreal. His vision was "One island, one city." This was just one of his many grandiose schemes, which included the building of Montreal's subway system (the Métro), Expo 67, and the 1976 Summer Olympics. Knowing that most suburbs would resist his plan, Drapeau tried to get the Quebec government to amend the legislation relevant to annexation so as to enable the Montreal city council to decide on an annexation without the approval of the other municipality. The only check on the city would be that any of its proposed annexations would have to be approved by the Quebec Municipal Commission, a quasi-judicial administrative tribunal charged with, among other things, sorting out inter-municipal disputes. The existing legislation required the approval of both councils and approval by a majority of voters in a referendum in the municipality that was proposed to be annexed. The Quebec government refused Drapeau's request for a change in the procedures.

Drapeau tried again in 1963. This time the province agreed that, if the city could convince the council of a suburban municipality to agree to annexation, it would go ahead unless a designated number of citizens requested a binding referendum. If, however, the suburban council refused the city's request, the issue would go straight to the Quebec Municipal Commission for a decision. Under this system, Montreal annexed two suburban municipalities, one of which, Rivière-des-Prairies on the eastern tip of the island, was not contiguous with the rest of the city. In 1968, the municipality of Saint-Michel, which had been under the supervision of the Quebec Municipal Commission due to municipal corruption, was also annexed after a favourable referendum and the passage of a special Quebec law. Finally, in 1982, residents of east-island Pointe-aux-Trembles voted for annexation. In each of these cases the annexed suburbs had been in grave financial difficulty. Their residents agreed to annexation because the city of Montreal agreed to take over their municipality's debts. Like his predecessors decades before, Mayor Drapeau had added territory to his city, but at considerable financial cost. The city's territory was not further extended until 2002, a development that will be discussed in Chapter 8.

Edmonton

Edmonton was incorporated as a town on the north bank of the North Saskatchewan River in 1892. Strathcona was incorporated as a town on the south side in 1899. Strathcona was the terminus of a CPR spur line from Calgary and was the area's main rail link until the Grand Trunk Pacific railway (now part of Canadian National Railway, or CN) arrived in Edmonton in 1905. In 1907, Strathcona was chosen by the provincial government as the site for the new University of Alberta. In 1905, Edmonton was chosen by the federal government to be the capital of the new province of Alberta. As both the capital and the location of the station for the east–west rail link, Edmonton had won the battle for supremacy over its southern neighbour. "There was virtually no opposition"[11] when Strathcona amalgamated with Edmonton in 1912. This and other amalgamations and annexations that occurred until 1917 increased the city's size from 7.2 square miles to 41.2.[12] There were no further increases in territory until 1947. Between 1947 and 1980, 19 separate annexations added 55,474 acres to the city's territory.[13]

The Annexation Battle of 1979–80

On 22 March 1979, the city of Edmonton launched the most dramatic local annexation initiative in Canadian history. On that date the city applied to Alberta's Local Authorities Board (LAB):

> to annex completely two adjacent municipalities (the City of St. Albert and the County of Strathcona) and significant portions of two others (the County of Parkland and the Municipal District of Sturgeon). The application, if approved, would have increased the City's area from 79,962 to 547,155 acres and its population from 482,500 to 568,286 (1978 data). Subsequent hearings before the LAB (from September, 1979 through July, 1980) consumed 106 days of testimony, witnessed the filing of 299 exhibits and produced 12,235 pages of transcript. The City alone produced more than 30 expert witnesses before the Board: 183 witnesses were heard in all.[14]

Writing just after the hearings were finished, one of the expert witnesses for Strathcona County stated that:

> The Edmonton annexation case will have been the longest, probably the most complex and certainly the most costly adversary process in Canadian local government history. A conservative estimate of the direct cost only, as represented by payment by involved municipalities to consultants and lawyers, will exceed $4 million![15]

The city's aim was to establish itself as the single municipal government for the entire metropolitan area (81 per cent of the CMA population of 657,057 lived within the city in 1981).[16] Its expert witnesses advanced a wide array of arguments in claiming that its policy would lead to better land-use planning, more effective use of urban infrastructure, and economies of scale in the provision of many municipal services. On the other side, witnesses presented evidence from elsewhere, especially the United States and Britain, to counter these assertions. There was much squabbling among the lawyers as to what qualified as "evidence." Two of the city's expert witnesses later observed:

> Despite the fact that the issues before the Board were of a nature that could not be "proved" in the judicial sense much of the subsequent proceedings developed in an adversarial manner. This involved attempts to discredit city witnesses; to make them "prove" by way of evidence or personal knowledge matters that were common knowledge; and generally to attribute to the City undesirable motives governing its pursuit of annexation.[17]

One of the "undesirable motives" probably was the frequent claim that all the city was really interested in was taking control of "refinery row," located just to the east of Edmonton's eastern boundary in Strathcona County. In its written argument to the LAB, the city stated:

> The single and obsessive objective according to which Strathcona has managed land use since the early 1950's is to preserve the unearned, windfall industry which happened to locate within their boundaries in the early 1950's.[18]

Windfall industry refers to the oil refineries. Property tax revenue from this area was so lucrative that both sides in the dispute were willing to spend large sums of money to defend it (Strathcona) or gain access to it (Edmonton).

The LAB's decision was released in December 1980. The decision was almost completely congruent with what the city asked for, thereby taking a very broad view of the virtues of annexation:

> We see annexation as an essential tool in fashioning the planned development not only of the annexing authority, but the region to which it contributes in giving a lifestyle. In the past years, this tool has been put to limited purpose. It has been looked upon as a means

of satisfying the annexing authority's immediate need for land, or of a developer to bring land within the City. . . . No adequate consideration has been given to using the tool as an instrument designed to further regional development other than on a narrow sectional basis. . . . We have looked at "annexation" as a tool designed to achieve not only land for immediate use, but also to achieve jurisdictional power to plan and control growth in the region in which the City is located.[19]

Nobody was happy with the report. The targets of the annexation were bitterly disappointed. But even supporters of annexation stated that "Certainly students of metropolitan development will be disappointed at the absence of any detailed analysis as the basis for the recommendations."[20] The lack of explanation was justified on the grounds that the less detailed the analysis, the more difficult it would be that opponents could find grounds for appealing the board's decision to the courts.[21]

In any event, the provincial cabinet had the legal authority to override an LAB decision. Faced with massive opposition from residents of Edmonton suburbs, this is exactly what it did. In June 1981, Edmonton was allocated 86,000 acres of new land, much of it undeveloped in Strathcona County to the northeast of the city. Some of it was not even included in the LAB allocation but had been purchased by the city through Royal Trust, presumably so as to prevent windfall gains to private landholders.[22] The city gained a slice of refinery row, but much was left in Strathcona County. The key political point was that the annexation affected relatively few suburban residents. To this day the city of St. Albert remains independent of Edmonton, as does Sherwood Park, a residential suburb within Strathcona County. In 2011, the population of the city of Edmonton made up 70 per cent of the total population in the Edmonton CMA.[23]

In the end, the decision about the Edmonton annexation was very much a political compromise. The city got some of what it wanted, but the suburbs kept almost all of what was most important to them. Such a compromise required the skill of the politician, not the skill of the planning consultant, the lawyer, or the expert witness. All of the resources expended at the LAB were in vain. Since 1980, an annexation proposal of this size has never been argued before a Canadian quasi-judicial administrative body. As we shall see in Chapter 7, relations between Edmonton and its suburbs remain strained.

Annexation Proposals in 2013

Meanwhile, in 2013, Edmonton launched its first annexation effort in 30 years by announcing that it wanted to extend its southerly boundary by annexing 39,000 acres that are currently part of Leduc County and the town of Beaumont. The area in question includes the Edmonton International Airport, which is currently in the county. The city's position is that it is best equipped to provide the infrastructure needed for the area's optimal development and that the annexation would ensure the "healthy land supply that Edmonton needs in order to retain its competitive edge as a strong central city."[24] To complicate matters, Beaumont has proposed that *it* annex some of the same land from Leduc County that is coveted by the city. A definitive resolution is expected to take between two and five years. Although not on the same scale as Edmonton's 1979 proposal, the prospects for inter-municipal acrimony are almost as great.

London, Ontario

London separated politically from Middlesex County and became a single-tier city in 1855. It has remained so ever since, and was not directly affected either by the implementation of two-tier regional government systems in the 1960s and 1970s or by the municipal "restructuring" sponsored by the Harris government in the late 1990s and early 2000s. Since 1855, however, its boundaries have constantly been expanded through annexations, both large and small. In the early 1960s and again in the early 1990s, large annexations allowed London to avoid the dramatic changes that affected many other Ontario cities later in each decade. In this discussion of London's annexations, we shall refer only to those of 1885, 1961, and 1993, focusing most on the last. But each has something special to teach us about municipal annexation.

London East

London (not Edmonton) was Canada's first major oil-refining centre and the original headquarters of the Imperial Oil Company. This was a result of its good rail connections and its proximity to the oil fields of Lambton County, where Canada's first oil discoveries were made in the 1850s. Significantly, in the 1860s London's first refineries were built in London Township, *outside* the city's then-eastern boundary (Adelaide Street) adjacent to the Great Western Railway (now part of CN). Timothy Cobban has argued that such a location was chosen to escape "the regulatory reach of city council"[25] because refineries then and now are perceived as obnoxious neighbours for urban residents. Nevertheless, as the refineries grew, service industries and workers located nearby, all outside London's boundaries. Cobban reports that:

In March 1872, London council announced its desire to annex "that portion of ratepayers in the vicinity of Refiners in Township of London," and went about it gently, striking a committee to hold meetings with the refiners in the hopes of "procuring their assent." That assent was not forthcoming, and, despite frequent reports of "progress" from the committee's chairperson, the annexation movement faltered.[26]

Meanwhile, the number of complaints from residents within the city boundaries about noise and noxious odours from the refineries continued to grow.

In 1874, the response of the refiners was to take steps to incorporate their area so as "to put an end to these repeated attempts at 'forcing the suburb into the city.'"[27] The village of London East became a legal entity on 4 January 1875. In 1880, four of the refining companies in London East merged to form Imperial Oil. But despite all this apparent success, all was not well in London East. Cobban describes what happened in the autumn of 1884 when the railway's car works caught fire:

> The city's fire brigade was summoned, as was customary for large conflagrations in London East, for the suburb had no professional fire service of its own. The twenty-man fire brigade raced to Adelaide street, the city's boundary, with teams of horses pulling boiler pumps, hose carts and ladder wagons, but there they waited for either a $100 indemnity fee from London East or the Mayor's special permission to proceed, as per their instructions from city council. When neither materialized, they eventually crossed the boundary anyway. Once they finally arrived at the fire, they discovered that that the nearest water hydrant held no water. Although the suburb had laid a network of water mains and fire hydrants two years earlier, it had not been able to secure its own water source, and had been refused in its attempts to purchase access to the city's water system. By the time the fire brigade secured a source of water, the car works had been engulfed for two hours. Hours later, it had burnt to the ground, destroying $200,000 worth of the railway's plant and equipment and displacing its four hundred employees.[28]

The next year London East agreed to annexation on the condition that the city would not force the removal of the refineries as long as they stayed in their original area. In any event, by 1883, most of London's refining operations had moved to Petrolia, where they stayed until 1898 when Standard Oil purchased Imperial and moved the refineries to Sarnia.[29]

London East was no more, but it had been the centre of petroleum manufacturing in Canada for two decades. There was no longer any reason for its being a separate municipality—and it had proven incapable of doing what urban municipalities are supposed to do, such as to provide water and protect property.

Victory at the OMB

Prior to 1993, London's biggest annexation occurred in 1961. It had been a long time in the works, as London had been trying to take control over land being developed outside its boundaries throughout the 1950s.[30] In particular, it coveted a heavily industrialized area to the east on Oxford Street on the way to the airport, land now partly occupied by 3M and General Dynamics; land to the south connecting the city to the newly constructed Highway 401; and to the north, the land occupied by the University of Western Ontario. City officials also were concerned that population growth was much greater in the surrounding townships in Middlesex County than in the city, and that two in particular—London Township and Westminster—could themselves become rival urban centres. In 1958 the London city council approved a bylaw calling for the annexation of 24,000 hectares from four adjoining townships, an amount of land that would increase its territory by a factor of more than seven. About one-sixth of the land in the townships had already been developed. In accordance with the province's then legal requirements for municipal annexation, the 1958 bylaw was referred to the OMB. A three-member panel held hearings on the matter in London for seven full weeks at various times between April and December 1959. Ten different lawyers representing 14 different organizations and individuals were given formal standing. In May 1960, the panel released its 38-page decision in which it awarded the city 12,220 hectares, or about half what it had asked for, all from the townships of London and Westminster. The annexation was ordered to take effect on 1 January 1961. While the city had requested sufficient land to enable it to plan the outward expansion of the urban area over a 25-year period, the OMB awarded an amount that "contains all the present development which is part of the London community as well as lands adjacent or proximate where the further development envisaged in this decision can be expected to take place within a reasonable time in the future."[31]

The members of the OMB panel clearly believed that their function was to determine the structural arrangements that promoted "the greatest common good." They explicitly rejected the view that municipalities themselves had interests that merited consideration:

Many opinions expressed as to desirable municipal boundaries seem based on a hypothesis that a municipal corporation is much the same as a mercantile corporation. Indeed, many submissions made at the hearing and particularly many of those made in opposition to annexation seem to assume that municipal corporations possess certain vested interests and rights which they are entitled to assert and retain against the whole world, as it were. The Board is of the respectful opinion that any claim of this nature made by a municipal corporation must be regarded only in the light of the best interests of all the inhabitants of and other ratepayers in the whole area in question.[32]

This is an important statement, because it clearly expresses the view—to become much more prevalent in Ontario and other provinces later in the decade and beyond—that annexation issues were not about short-term disputes between municipalities but rather about making public policy for urban areas. The notion that municipal corporations did not "possess certain vested interests and rights" in this context would have been shocking indeed to the people who established the first municipal corporations in medieval England (see Chapter 1).

As far as participation by interested members of the public was concerned, the OMB decision made reference only to a "very large number of petitions," all of which expressed a fear that annexation would cause "an increase in taxes."[33] Board members were obviously skeptical about the petitions, because they noted that "it was impossible to determine the circumstances under which a great many if not most of the names were obtained. . . . [I]t is not surprising to find a substantial and even spirited response to any petition circulated for the purpose of keeping taxes down."[34] The decision also notes that there were no expressed objections "by petition or otherwise" from any ratepayer within the city and that the Board "has neither the duty nor the right to permit the wishes of a part only of those concerned to outweigh its findings of what is clearly in the best interests of all the inhabitants and ratepayers in the whole area."[35] There can be no doubt that OMB panel members were effectively saying that their job was to represent the interests of the silent majority. This is as close as they came to being concerned with the role of the public in a process that was otherwise dominated by lawyers, experts, and developers.

A brief passage in the decision relates to the position of the local federation of agriculture. Federation members objected to having their farms placed under the jurisdiction of a municipal government concerned with urban, rather than rural, administration. They were especially concerned about high levels of urban taxation. By not granting the city's full territorial demands, the Board effectively agreed with the federation's position. In a position contrary to that adopted by the province in the 1990s, the Board stated that "[n]o farmlands should be included except those within the area of the present urban development and those that will be so developed within a reasonable time." It then wryly predicted that owners of such land would not object, because "they will very probably be able to sell their land for subdivision before long in any event."[36]

The 1960 OMB decision on London's annexation is a well-reasoned, comprehensive document. In retrospect, it served the city well. Had the annexation not taken place in 1961, London would have had imposed on it a two-tier regional system of the kind implemented in other Ontario cities a few years later, systems to be described in the next chapter. But the virtues of the *process* involved in the 1961 decision are less obvious. Even the OMB panel members themselves referred to the hearings on the London annexation as "lengthy, very costly, and dislocating."[37]

Arbitration

By the late 1970s, there had been many other examples in Ontario—notably in Barrie—of protracted OMB hearings on annexation. Perhaps because it was clear by this time that no new two-tier regional governments would be established, the issue of improving boundary-adjustment procedures had become a priority. In 1979, the Ontario government established a pilot project in the city of Brantford and Brant County to settle a local boundary dispute through negotiation rather than by quasi-judicial hearings conducted by the OMB. The experiment was successful. It resulted in the passage of the Municipal Boundary Negotiations Act, 1981, a law designed to reduce drastically the role of the OMB and to replicate the Brantford experience in other parts of the province.

By the early 1980s officials in London were again complaining that they were running out of land for industrial development. But nothing happened until 18 November 1988 when the city informed the Ministry of Municipal Affairs that it wanted to "proceed as expeditiously as possible under the provisions of the Municipal Boundary Negotiations Act, 1981" to annex "certain lands from the Township of London and the Town of Westminster."[38]

The first stage of the process involved investigation by a ministerial "fact-finder" who reported on issues relevant to the three municipalities involved. But the conclusion, reiterated in a cover letter from the Minister of Municipal Affairs, stated that "the area affected is much more extensive than identified by the City in its proposal and the issues must be approached in a more comprehensive manner."[39] This ministerial declaration, made in what would be the last few months of the provincial Liberal administration, was probably the most significant decision made in the entire process—and it had nothing to do with either fact-finding or negotiations.

Negotiations among the parties went nowhere, in large part because the province's chief negotiator kept insisting on "comprehensiveness." In 1992, the NDP Minister of Municipal Affairs departed from procedures outlined in the Act and appointed an *arbitrator*, promising that he would implement whatever the arbitrator recommended. However, the arbitrator was given restrictive terms of reference stating what must be recommended:

> [t]hat there be a government structure comprised of elected people and based on the principle of representation by population, with responsibility for at least planning and servicing to cover the area reasonably anticipated to be within the City of London's area of major influence for at least twenty years, including:
>
> • future urban areas dependent upon London-centred infrastructure
> • London Airport
> • sufficient lands adjacent to the Highway 401/402 corridor.[40]

The arbitrator was John Brant, a local businessperson. He held 11 public meetings in London and the surrounding area in early 1992. The public hearing process seemed to be an enormous success. Meetings were well attended and well reported in the local media. Brant went to great pains to have everyone feel relaxed, and he seemed genuinely open to all the ideas presented, especially if they came from "ordinary citizens." Herein lay a serious problem: his terms of reference did not allow him to be open to all ideas, especially to those of the vast majority of presenters who wanted to keep things roughly as they were.

The arbitrator's report was released in early April 1992. It contained 21 discrete recommendations, which "can only be considered in their entirety: they are completely interrelated and balanced to provide an optimal opportunity for the entire area. They must be implemented as though they were one."[41] On the crucial subject of the city boundaries, Brant allocated to London 26,000 hectares from the four adjoining municipalities. The town of Westminster was to be eliminated.

In a newspaper interview a few weeks later, Brant reflected on the arbitration process. When asked if he was surprised about the overwhelmingly negative public response to his report, he stated:

There was a large number of people who were anxious that London not expand or that London's expansion be minimized. Those people had hoped to persuade me to break my mandate. . . . People are coming back to me and saying "you didn't hear us, you didn't listen." The truth of the matter is that they didn't read the terms of reference. . . . The nice thing about the process was that the terms of reference were always clear. . . . I never really challenged the terms of reference. . . . I didn't have any problem with the terms of reference.[42]

Brant was also asked about the relative importance of what he heard at the public hearings, compared to "the material . . . received outside the public process." His answer: "If I had to pick a number, it would be a 50–50 impact."[43]

From the minister's point of view, the whole purpose of the arbitration process was to relieve him from having to make a decision about which people in municipalities surrounding London held very strong views. But because the arbitration process he initiated had no legal status, its results could only be implemented by legislation. As soon as the minister started talking about the legislation, different groups—including a backbench MPP from his own party who represented much of the area to be annexed—started to lobby for their preferred approach. It soon became evident that Brant's decisions would not be implemented in their entirety. Indeed, a whole new debate had begun. It took eight months after Brant's report was released for this debate to be completed. Nevertheless, on 1 January 1993, the town of Westminster ceased to exist and London had its new boundaries.

More than 20 years after the annexation, the land around the intersection of highways 401 and 402 still has not been developed. On 12 January 2009, the local daily newspaper reported that London's senior provincial cabinet minister was proposing that federal and provincial infrastructure money be used to build a new sewage treatment plant in the area to enable industrial development. There was no indication that this was a project for which annexation had been enacted in 1992!

The 1992 London annexation had ramifications for Ontario as a whole. As we shall see in Chapter 8, when the Progressive Conservatives led by Mike Harris were elected to office in 1995, they soon developed procedures whereby one person would be sent into an area to decide on municipal amalgamations. These procedures were a direct result of lessons learned from the arbitration experiment in London in 1992. One of the lessons learned was that it was better to authorize one person to make a final binding decision so that additional legislation would not be needed.

Calgary

Calgary, located at the confluence of the Bow and Elbow rivers, developed as a significant urban settlement after 1874, when the CPR chose it as a town site and maintenance repair depot.[44] More than any other city in Canada, its territory has grown as a result of a long series of incremental annexations,[45] the latest occurring in 2011. The general pattern has been for developers to buy land in adjacent rural municipalities and, when they are ready to develop, to request annexation by the city so as to obtain access to water supply and sewer systems.[46] The Local Authorities Board (LAB), a body discussed earlier in this chapter with reference to Edmonton, was charged by the province with reviewing annexation agreements and, in cases of dispute, resolving them.

With only a few exceptions, Calgary's outward expansion has not been hindered by the presence of other incorporated urban settlements, because the adjacent land was largely unsettled and primarily used for ranching. The notable exceptions were Bowness and Montgomery to the west and Forest Lawn to the east. All were absorbed by Calgary in the early 1960s. The process merits our attention.

Aftermath of the McNally Report

The first point to note is that Calgary's expansion at this time was inspired partly by the report of a provincial royal commission in 1956 headed by Frederick McNally that was charged with investigating problems of metropolitan growth in both Edmonton and Calgary. The McNally report favoured a single municipality for the entire urban area in both cities, but implementation of this principle turned out to be much easier in Calgary than in Edmonton because the former was more of a farming area and had fewer surrounding urban settlements. McNally specifically recommended that Calgary absorb its three urban neighbours and that its total territory be expanded from 40 square miles to 105.[47] The provincial government in Alberta never undertook to implement the McNally recommendations, but the behaviour of many of the important players was clearly influenced by them. The city of Calgary took great comfort from the fact that McNally was endorsing its long-standing annexation strategy, even if the same report severely criticized some of its haphazard planning processes.

In 1958, Calgary applied to annex valuable land between it and the town of Forest Lawn (population 4000). The town responded by applying to annex the same land. By 1961, the city had consolidated various annexation proposals in different parts of the city, and they were all heard together by the Board of Public Utilities (predecessor of the LAB) in 1961. In its decision, the board stated: "The essential question . . . is not as to whether Calgary should be allowed to annex Forest Lawn but rather which municipality should be allowed to annex the territory common to both applications." Observing that Calgary was better suited to this end, the board recommended annexation of the disputed land, and added the town of Forest Lawn as well, on the grounds that it had no future otherwise. The other annexations to the north, south, and northwest were accepted without opposition.[48]

Forest Lawn was a working-class suburb on the east side of Calgary. Bowness and Montgomery were struggling suburban towns to the west, both without water and sewer services at the time of the McNally report. Max Foran has described their fate:

> The City annexed the Town of Montgomery in 1963. In approving the application initiated by the Town through resolution and petition [by its council], and supported by the City, the Local Authorities Board described the community of 5,200 as a logical extension of Calgary's residential area. In the years following the McNally Commission the Town had installed its own utilities that had been connected to the City before the annexation was processed. The City had done well. In October 1963, the Town of Bowness voted 1003 to 397 for annexation to the City. Though not overly happy with the financial implications, the City did not oppose the bid. . . . With the annexation of Bowness and its population of 10,000 the City had expanded its area to 154 square miles.[49]

A map produced by the City of Calgary (www.calgary.ca/PDA/LUPP/Documents/Publications/annexation-history-map.pdf) shows all of Calgary's annexations, including the many that have taken place since 1964. The latest was in 2011. As we shall see in the next chapter, Calgary's relations with its surrounding rural municipalities, especially Rocky View County to the north, have become increasingly bitter, and future annexations, if they happen at all, will be difficult at best.

In any event, like most North American cities, the city of Calgary now contains important fringe development outside its municipal boundaries. Furthermore, its current boundaries are coming closer and closer to non-contiguous urban municipalities, in the same way that they approached Forest Lawn, Bowness, and Montgomery in the 1950s. Such places as Airdrie, Crossfield, Cochrane, Chestermere, and Okotoks are growing even faster than Calgary itself. The more Calgary grows, the more its neighbouring municipalities will grow and the more they will become integrated into the urban area that is focused on Calgary as the central city. The strategic choice that Calgary faces is whether it should work co-operatively with these urban governments or whether it should attempt to absorb them as part of a continuing commitment to include all of the CMA within its boundaries. If it chooses the latter course of action, future annexation battles will be much nastier than those it has won in the past. If it chooses the former, Calgary's inter-municipal issues and problems will start to resemble those of other major metropolitan areas in Canada and elsewhere,[50] problems we shall address more fully in the next two chapters.

Regina

In 2013 the city of Regina officially launched an effort to annex significant amounts of land from Sherwood, the rural municipality that completely surrounds it. The city's claim was that it needed land to accommodate a population of half a million in the next 50 years. Sherwood's response was that previous annexation bids by Regina in the 1970s had been based on similarly optimistic growth projections that never came close to being met. Regina's population has certainly been growing in recent years (see Table 5.1), which explains the current pressure to do something. Sherwood has seized the opportunity to allow fringe development just outside Regina's borders, which is exactly why the city wants to take control. The provincial government appointed a mediator in an effort to bring the two sides together, and a settlement was reached in November 2013. On 1 January 2014 the city of Regina gained an additional 8500 acres from Sherwood, increasing the size of its territory by about 23 per cent.[51]

Conclusion

For Canada's biggest cities, it is unlikely that we shall ever see many more locally driven annexations, except perhaps in Edmonton and Calgary. As we shall see in the next two chapters, for most large Canadian cities, their respective provinces have stepped in and imposed their own solutions to problems of urban expansion.[52] Even in Edmonton and Calgary, the most recent annexation battles have demonstrated the costs and perils of arguing an annexation case at a quasi-judicial tribunal and of attempting a local settlement through negotiation. In the much smaller city of Barrie, Ontario, in 2009, attempts at a mediated local settlement of an annexation issue failed, causing the Ontario government to step in with a legislated solution, the Barrie–Innisfil Boundary Adjustment Act, 2009.[53]

But in hundreds of smaller towns and villages across Canada, annexation remains the most common way for urban municipalities to expand their boundaries to accommodate urban development. All provinces have attempted to develop mechanisms for enabling small-scale annexations that are both fair and not unduly costly for the participants. Everyone wants to provide opportunities for all the arguments to be advanced and considered, but no one (except lawyers and consultants) wants to replicate the Edmonton annexation hearings conducted by the Alberta LAB in 1980. Whatever desirable mechanisms have been developed, there is always the possibility that a local annexation process will break down and that someone will appeal to the province to settle the issue with legislation. In some provinces (e.g., Ontario), such legislative interventions have been quite common; in others (e.g., British Columbia), local municipalities are generally left alone to work out their differences. In any event, when it comes to structuring municipalities so that they can both guide and respond to urban expansion, provinces have ways of responding other than relying exclusively on annexations. It is to these other responses that we now turn.

RESOURCES

If you live in a town or a city, go to its website, public library, or municipal archives and try to obtain a map showing how the municipal boundaries have expanded since the town or city was first incorporated. See if you can determine the procedures used to make the changes and whether they caused much political conflict at the time. Sometimes there is still evidence within towns and cities of municipal boundaries that were eliminated by annexation many decades ago. For example, there can still be quite different types of development on each side of the old boundary. Try to find examples of such evidence. If you are familiar with an urban area that is bisected by municipal boundaries, try to explain how they have survived and what impact they appear to have on the nature of urban development in the two municipalities.

STUDY QUESTIONS

1. How did developers make money in Maisonneuve prior to its amalgamation with Montreal?
2. Do you agree with the claim by the OMB in its 1960 London decision that municipalities do not have interests that need to be considered in boundary disputes? Explain your reasoning.
3. What was wrong, in your view, with the Alberta LAB process in relation to the Edmonton annexation dispute in the late 1970s and early 1980s?
4. What might prevent Calgary from continuing to annex indefinitely? Are there any reasons why the province of Alberta should prevent such expansion?

CHAPTER 7

Two-Tier Metropolitan and Regional Governments

We learned in the previous chapter that, in most places, annexations cannot go on forever. Eventually, the boundaries of the central city run up against incorporated suburbs or other urban municipalities that can sometimes be as old as the central city itself. Residents of such places are not likely to agree to be absorbed, unless, of course, their own municipalities have become virtually bankrupt and are unable to provide the services that the central city can. In the absence of any intervention by the provincial government, the resulting situation will be one in which there is a single built-up urban area comprising a central-city municipality surrounded by a number of independent suburban municipalities. For many analysts of urban governance, such a situation is a problem, one that is often referred to as the *metropolitan problem*. For others, a multi-municipal–urban area is desirable.

The first objective of this chapter is to understand the nature of the disagreement between these two positions, one of which we can label as the *consolidationist* position, the other as *public choice*. The disagreement goes far beyond Canada. In the real world of Canadian municipal government, however, the consolidationist position has predominated. For most of this chapter we shall be examining two-tier systems of urban municipal government that have been championed by consolidationists. Their position has been that, in the absence of continuous annexation, an alternative solution to governing the entire urban area is to establish a metropolitan level of municipal government on top of the existing municipalities to provide a level of government that can address problems facing the whole area.

Some consolidationists actually prefer two-tier metropolitan systems to large, single-tier systems resulting from annexations because the retention of local municipalities provides for an element of local control, which might be much needed in a very large urban area. Others see two-tier systems as a second-best solution because they add to the complexity of municipal government. This latter view was clearly the approach taken by the McNally Commission in Alberta in the 1950s when it stated its preference for continuing annexation in Edmonton and Calgary rather than following Ontario's example of establishing a two-tier metropolitan system for Toronto, a process that we shall carefully examine in this chapter. The public-choice approach has rarely been articulated in Canadian debates about organizing the municipal government of our large cities. It did, however, receive some attention in debates in the 1990s when, as we shall see in the next chapter, provincial governments in eastern Canada enacted large-scale municipal amalgamations to create single-tier systems for large urban areas.

After examining the differences between consolidationists and advocates of public choice, the chapter will then focus on the emergence of two-tier systems of urban government in Canada. These systems have taken quite different forms at different times, so much so that sometimes the distinction between single-tier and two-tier systems appears to break down. This has been especially true with the creation of regional districts in British Columbia, metropolitan communities in Montreal and Quebec City, and new institutional arrangements for the Edmonton and Calgary regions.

Consolidationists versus Public Choice

Consolidationists believe that each metropolitan area needs a municipal government capable of making decisions on at least some of the municipal issues facing the entire area. For our purposes in this discussion, *metropolitan areas* corresponds to the Canadian *census metropolitan areas* (CMAs) discussed in Chapter 5. In the English-speaking world, consolidationists first articulated their positions in the nineteenth century with reference to the governance of large cities in Britain and the United States, especially London and New York. An upper-tier London County Council (LCC) was established in 1888.[1] In 1898 in New York, 15 cities and towns and 11 villages in five separate counties were brought together, after local approval through referendums, to create a single city with 5 distinct boroughs.[2] The arguments justifying these institutional changes are basically the same as those used today to justify similar proposals. There are four main arguments:[3]

- *Efficiency.* Some, if not all, municipal services benefit from economies of scale. This means that the more people served by a particular municipal service, the cheaper it will be to deliver a single unit of that service. To the extent that there are economies of scale in municipal services, they can be provided more efficiently with municipal governments that are larger.

- *Planning for infrastructure and environmental protection.* Metropolitan areas need public infrastructure such as roads, fixed-rail transit systems, water and sewage systems, major recreational facilities, and so on. Although it is quite conceivable that individual municipalities could provide these for themselves, a metropolitan area requires coordinated infrastructure development so roads and transit systems connect with each other and one municipality's sewage does not pollute another's water supply. A single municipal authority is required to provide such coordination.

- *Equity.* People who live in the same metropolitan area should have roughly the same level of municipal services, regardless of the financial resources of the particular municipality in which they live. Consequently, there should be a single municipal authority providing all or some of these services itself or, at a minimum, it should channel financial resources from richer areas to poorer areas to provide at least a degree of equalization.

- *Economic development and promotion.* Global investors in new enterprises have hundreds of potential locations. Metropolitan areas are in competition with each other for such investment. Investors do not care about municipal boundaries but they do care, for example, what the Vancouver metropolitan area has to offer compared to Seattle. Individual municipalities within the same metropolitan area should not each be promoting their own advantages on the international stage. A single municipal authority is required that can act on behalf of the entire area.

Although the relative importance of each of these arguments has varied from time to time and place to place, in one form or another each is almost invariably present in any debate about the organization of municipal government in metropolitan areas. As we shall see, however, changes in the real world are not usually brought about as a result of abstract debates. Usually, some form of crisis or precipitating event causes any significant change in the pattern of municipal organization.

The consolidationist position is built on at least two major assumptions:

1. Central governments (provinces in Canada) are unwilling or unable to step in themselves and attempt to solve whatever policy

problems result from having more than one municipality in the same metropolitan area.

2. Having multiple municipal governments in the same urban area creates only problems, and not advantages.

This second assumption is the main target of those who favour the public-choice position.

In its urban setting,[4] public choice has its origins in the 1956 academic article written by Charles Tiebout, which we discussed briefly in Chapter 2. The key insight of Tiebout's article is that multiple municipalities in a metropolitan area can be seen as being like competing private firms, each one providing its own distinct mix of goods and services at its own price levels. Rational consumers can pick the one that provides the mix they prefer at the price they prefer. Multiple competing municipalities are beneficial for consumers in the same way that multiple competing grocery stores are beneficial. Food is just as essential for urban life as the services provided by municipalities. But in our market economy some people end up shopping in bargain stores with poor-quality products and others use their money to patronize specialized gourmet stores. For Tiebout, municipalities were similar. Residents who did not like the services on offer in their municipality could "vote with their feet" by moving to another one, just as high-income people shop at more expensive grocery stores if they experience poor quality at the cheaper ones. (Many people, of course, such as the poor and the elderly, are not in a position to vote with their feet, just as they often are not in a position to buy expensive groceries or, for that matter, to access less expensive grocery stores.) In this way, residents not only could get what they most wanted—and could afford—in local services but the services likely would be provided efficiently, because a municipality that provided poor services at high cost would end up with no residents at all and everybody working for it would be out of work.

It is not difficult to see some of the obvious flaws in Tiebout's approach:

1. Tiebout did not take into account that most people decide where to live because of proximity to their work, or their partner's work, or because of the location of other family or loved ones.

2. Even if work and family were not an issue, most people do not keep careful track of levels of municipal services and taxes in various municipalities so are unlikely to maximize their choices in the way Tiebout suggests.

3. Even if residents possessed all the necessary information, the costs of moving homes are such that residents would be unlikely to do so

merely to obtain marginal gains in municipal services in relation to tax levels.

Academic debates have evolved around each of these points.[5] The details need not concern us here. But at a bare minimum, the "Tiebout hypothesis" suggests that we should pay more attention than consolidationists do to the virtues of providing an element of choice to residents of large cities.

Public-choice scholars challenge the view that only big governments can solve big problems; they generally conclude that big governments often make big problems worse. In urban settings, their approach is in direct conflict with that of the consolidationists. Often, public-choice scholars provide empirical evidence to undermine the consolidationists' most cherished views. For example, public-choice scholars discovered that, for a great many municipal services, there were few economies of scale and that, for some, diseconomies of scale set in at relatively low population levels. They attributed their findings to the fact that larger municipalities generated more layers of management, stronger unions demanding higher wage levels, and a decreased ability to adapt service levels to exactly what residents desired.[6]

Public-choice scholars also discovered that consolidationists had underestimated the likelihood that small governments would work together and with private contractors to overcome the disadvantages of smallness. When large infrastructure was needed, public-choice scholars looked to central governments and/or multi-municipal special-purpose bodies to step in. As far as equity issues were concerned, they argued that larger central governments were best suited to redistribute income and resources from the rich to the poor. Finally, public-choice scholars have simply not taken seriously the view that potential investors in a metropolitan area will be positively influenced by the existence of a single government, one of whose roles is to attract their attention. The public-choice view is that investors know what they are looking for anyway and, like consumers, are going to appreciate having a choice of municipalities in which to locate.[7]

Before moving on to look at real-world accomplishments by Canadian consolidationists it is important to re-emphasize that, until very recently, the public-choice perspective has hardly been present in Canadian debates about municipal organization in urban areas. People who have resisted consolidationist solutions have only rarely articulated views that have explicitly, or even implicitly, echoed public-choice perspectives. Consequently, they have often appeared as stubbornly resistant to change or as unprincipled defenders of privilege. But during many

of the institutional changes to be discussed in this chapter, consolidationists dominated the debates because two-tier solutions in themselves
were relatively non-controversial—they involved adding a level of municipal government, not amalgamation. From the 1950s to the 1970s—
before today's high levels of pessimism about the ability of governments
to solve problems—the idea of adding a level of municipal government
in metropolitan areas seemed like a sensible, pragmatic response to complex problems caused by rapid urban growth.

The Municipality of Metropolitan Toronto

In her definitive account of "the political dynamics of urban expansion
in the Toronto region," Frances Frisken observed:

> Until the early part of the 20th century, Toronto grew by annexation
> in the same way as many other North American cities, taking in small
> municipalities or suburban districts that are still well known by their
> original names (for example, Yorkville, the Annex, Parkdale, North
> Toronto, Moore Park). In 1912, however, City Council ruled out fur-
> ther annexations, having decided that the costs of providing services
> to annexed districts exceeded any benefits they might bring to the
> city. Council held firmly to that position in the face of later requests
> for annexation from the suburbs of York and East York, which viewed
> annexation as a way to secure better services, particularly those offered
> by the Toronto Transportation Commission.[8]

Early proposals for a two-tier form of metropolitan government emerged
at the same time as annexation was losing its appeal,[9] just as they did in
Montreal.[10]

By 1949, with uncontrolled and rapid urban development taking place
all around its borders, especially in the rural townships of Etobicoke,
North York, and Scarborough, the Toronto city council reversed its position on annexation, voting 19–2 to annex all of its adjacent suburbs.
All of the suburbs objected, but only Mimico proposed an alternative: a
special service board to provide major regional infrastructure. In 1950,
Premier Leslie Frost referred both Toronto's and Mimico's proposals to
the OMB for resolution.[11]

In January 1953, the OMB chair, Lorne Cumming, announced that
he was recommending a compromise solution: the creation of a two-
tier federated form of municipal government comprising the city of
Toronto and 12 surrounding municipalities.[12] A few months later the

Ontario legislature enacted this proposal, and on 1 January 1953, the Municipality of Metropolitan Toronto came into being. Its main initial functions were to build new arterial roads and water supply and sewage systems. One of the arterial roads was the Gardiner Expressway, named for the very successful first chair of the "Metro Council," Fred Gardiner. In 1957, a Metro police service was created, and later most municipal social services costs were moved to the Metro level. Costs were paid for by each municipality in proportion to its share of total taxable property assessment within the boundaries of the new Metro system. In 1954, this meant that the city of Toronto was paying 62 per cent of the cost. Despite its heavy financial commitment to Metro and despite the fact that it comprised 57 per cent of Metro's population, the city was given only 12 of the 24 seats on Metro's governing council. In its early years, there can be little doubt that the main purpose of the Metro system was to use the city's resources to finance new infrastructure in the suburbs.

By 1963, the city's shares of Metro's taxable property assessment and population had declined to 44 per cent and 38 per cent respectively, but it still held half the seats on Metro council. Greater violations of the principle of representation by population could be found among the suburbs. North York, with a population of 308,000, was still allocated only one seat; so was Swansea, with its population of 9000. In the same year, Premier John Robarts appointed H. Carl Goldenberg of Montreal to review the entire Metro system. In 1965, the Goldenberg commission recommended that the 13 municipalities be consolidated into four and that each be represented on the Metro council in proportion to its population. In 1966, much of the report was implemented, except that six consolidated lower-tier municipalities were created (Toronto, York, East York, Etobicoke, North York, and Scarborough) instead of four.

The most important structural change within Metro since 1966 was the reorganization of Metro council in 1988. In 1977, a Royal Commission headed by former Ontario Premier John Robarts recommended a council composed of the mayors of the six constituent municipalities and 27 councillors directly elected from specially designated Metro wards. Each of the 27 Metro councillors would also sit on the local council of his or her respective lower-tier municipality. As a result of yet another study on the same issue in 1986, the direct election of 28 Metro councillors was implemented in 1988. Under this scheme, local mayors still sat on Metro council but Metro councillors had no role on lower-tier councils.

As we shall see in the next chapter, Metro was abolished in 1998. In its early years, however, there can be little doubt that it was a huge success. It attracted the attention of students and practitioners of urban governance from around the Western world. In London, England, the boundaries of the old LCC had never been extended, and it was now more like a central-city government than a metropolitan one. Metro Toronto was a unique two-tier metropolitan federation of the type that many consolidationists had been advocating for years. As Frisken notes, both domestic and international observers "were virtually unanimous in concluding that Metro had accomplished its principal objective: to speed up the provision of infrastructure to support suburban population growth and industrial expansion."[13]

By the late 1960s, however, Metro obviously had become less effective. Not much new suburban infrastructure was needed, because Etobicoke, North York, and Scarborough were already largely built out (and, as we shall see in Chapter 10, development companies were by this time expected to build and/or pay for most of the new infrastructure, anyway). In addition, increasing political conflict existed within Metro council between representatives of the city of Toronto and the suburban members, some of which related to the refusal by the new suburban majority on the council to help finance the rebuilding of old infrastructure in the inner city. But the most serious conflict revolved around the desire of the suburban majority to build a new network of expressways to allow better suburban automobile access to downtown. The proposed north–south Spadina Expressway was to be the first link in the network, and construction south of Highway 401 began. But city politicians (backed by very strong citizens' groups) resisted. In 1971, the new provincial premier, Bill Davis, announced legislation to overturn Metro's (and the OMB's) decision on the matter, famously stating, "If we are building a transportation system to serve the automobile, the Spadina Expressway would be a good place to start. But if we are building a transportation system to serve people, the Spadina Expressway is a good place to stop."[14] As a result of provincial legislation, the expressway (now known as the Allen Road) ends at Eglinton Avenue rather than cutting through inner-city neighbourhoods on its way to a proposed new east–west expressway that also was killed.

If Metro was to maintain its mission to plan and finance new suburban infrastructure, its boundaries would have had to be extended. But suburban municipal politicians beyond Metro had worked out their own ways of planning and financing infrastructure and, as we shall soon see, the Ontario government facilitated their desires to remain free of Metro by providing them with their own two-tier regional governments. By the time the Ontario government provided for direct election to Metro council in 1988, Metro simply did not have that much to do, a fact reflected

in the lack of serious competition for Metro seats in the municipal elections that followed. Those who were elected (or sometimes acclaimed)
were reduced to squabbling with lower-tier councillors about who was to
be blamed for whatever was going wrong. Ten years later, Metro was no
more. By this time there were few who would mourn its loss.

The Metropolitan Corporation of Greater Winnipeg

In the late 1950s there were 19 separate municipalities in metropolitan
Winnipeg, with about half of the population living in the central city.
Area-wide special-purpose bodies dealt with water supply, sewage, public transit, and regional planning. In 1960, the Progressive Conservative
government of Manitoba, led by Duff Roblin, introduced legislation to
bring these special-purpose bodies together into a new multi-functional
metropolitan government, the Metropolitan Corporation of Greater
Winnipeg. In some respects Metro Winnipeg, which began its work in
1961, was modelled on Metro Toronto. But the Manitoba government
provided for a Metro council quite different from the original one in
Toronto. There were to be only 10 members and all were to be elected to
serve only on the Metro council. The law also provided that each Metro
electoral district had to include parts of at least two separate municipalities. All these stipulations were designed to ensure that Metro councillors were loyal primarily to the objectives of Metro itself, rather than to
those of the constituent lower-tier municipalities.[15]

The man who was director of planning for Metro Winnipeg from
its creation until 1967 has provided this fascinating comparison of the
metro systems in Winnipeg and Toronto:

> Unlike the Metro Toronto system, there was no direct link with the
> councils of the area municipalities through the membership of their
> mayors and some of their councillors on Metro Council. Throughout its
> life the Metro government was repeatedly faced with real or imagined
> accusations of disregarding the municipal problems and points of view.
> Furthermore, when the original metro–municipal conflicts arose, these
> quickly became public issues and were debated in the news media. This
> minimized the possibility of negotiated settlements of issues such as
> happened in Metro Toronto's committee rooms. Advocates of "open-
> ness" in local government may argue that the public conflict caused by
> the Winnipeg system was beneficial in that it made sure the public was
> aware of, and could participate in, the resolution of the metro–muni-
> cipal issues; on the other hand, the protagonists quickly assumed firm

positions on issues making negotiation and compromise much more difficult.[16]

Metro Winnipeg successfully modernized much of the area's infrastructure and ended the practice of dumping untreated sewage into the Red and Assiniboine rivers. It also adopted a metropolitan plan that guided the area's urban development for many years after it had been abolished.[17] But the political conflicts between Metro and local politicians, especially Winnipeg's popular long-time mayor, Steve Juba, were too damaging. When the NDP was elected in Manitoba in 1970, one of its first major acts was to merge Metro and its constituent municipalities into a "unicity." We shall examine this process in the next chapter.

Regional Municipalities in Ontario

The territory of southern Ontario was divided into counties in the nineteenth century, all of which, until the late twentieth century, were upper-tier units of rural government. When an urban area in southern Ontario became large enough to be classified as a city, it became separate politically from the county of which it was a part and became a single-tier municipal government. In our discussion of annexations in London, Ontario, we noted that London has been a single-tier municipal government since it became a city in 1855. When Metro Toronto was created in 1953, the city of Toronto became the first city in Ontario's history to be part of a two-tier system of municipal government. From 1969 to 1974, 10 two-tier regional municipalities were created in Ontario, and all involved establishing at least one city as a lower-tier government within the system. Ontario's regional municipalities were clearly modelled on Metro Toronto. As we saw in our discussion of Metro Toronto, by the late 1960s the number of its constituent municipalities had been reduced from 13 to 6, and policing and social services had become Metro responsibilities. When each of the regional municipalities was established, these reorganizations that had been accomplished incrementally in Metro Toronto were carried out all at once. Indeed, the rearrangement of lower-tier municipal boundaries by the province was often more controversial than the establishment of the regional municipality.

Stewart Fyfe has provided us with an excellent list of the main elements initially common to all or most of Ontario's regional municipalities.

1. An upper-tier unit is created for the large urban centre and its hinterland. The old county boundaries have commonly but not universally been followed.

2. There is a reduction in the number of local municipalities, mainly by consolidation, together with large annexations, to give the urban centre more control over its hinterland.

3. The council is composed of members of local councils . . . and roughly in accordance with population. The chairman is appointed by the province for the first term, following the Toronto precedent. Thereafter he [or she] is to be chosen by the council, following the county model and that of Toronto also.

4. The regional municipality is responsible for public health, police, regional planning, arterial roads, sewage disposal, bulk water supply treatment, garbage disposal, capital borrowing, welfare [social services], and regional parks. . . .

5. Local municipalities are responsible for local planning, roads, parks, local sewers, water distribution, garbage collection, fire protection, street lighting, and tax collection.

6. The regional municipality is financed by a requisition on the local municipalities, in proportion to their share of the total [property] assessment.[18]

Table 7.1 lists Ontario's regional municipalities, showing the dates they came into existence and of abolition (if applicable) and the most populous municipality (in 2011 or at time of abolition) within each.

Regional municipalities were never very popular, in part because they were created at a time of considerable inflation and many residents attributed greatly increased tax bills to their creation, and, in part because of the upheavals caused by the lower-tier boundary changes. Throughout their existence, debates have continued about exactly how they should be structured, many of these debates mirroring those already discussed for Metro Toronto and Metro Winnipeg. Over time, most took on more functions than they were originally assigned, especially relating to water supply and sewers. In any event, in 1999, the Ontario government introduced legislation to abolish four of them: Ottawa–Carleton, Hamilton, Sudbury, and Haldimand–Norfolk. The legislation will be briefly discussed in the next chapter.

All of the remaining six regional municipalities are within the territory of the Greater Golden Horseshoe (see Chapter 5). The existence of Peel, York, and Durham immediately adjacent to Metro Toronto was one of the factors that prevented the extension of Metro's boundaries in the 1970s and 1980s, hence stopping it from continuing as a genuine government for the entire metropolitan area. Dissatisfaction with regional municipalities remains in these areas, but most residents seem to prefer the status quo to either of the two main alternatives: complete

Table 7.1 Regional Municipalities in Ontario, Showing Year of Implementation and Abolition (If Applicable) and Name of Largest City

Regional Municipality	Years	Largest City
Ottawa–Carleton	1969–2000	Ottawa
Niagara	1970–	St. Catharines
York	1970–	Markham
Peel	1973–	Mississauga
Halton	1973–	Oakville
Waterloo	1973–	Kitchener
Hamilton–Wentworth	1973–2000	Hamilton
Sudbury	1973–2000	Sudbury
Durham	1973–	Oshawa
Haldimand–Norfolk	1974–2000	Nanticoke

Sources: Stewart Fyfe, "Local Government Reform in Toronto: 1853–1973," in R. Charles Bryfogle and Ralph R. Krueger, eds., *Urban Problems*, rev. ed. (Toronto: Holt, Rinehart, and Winston, 1975), 360; Statistics Canada, *2011 Census of Canada*. Abolition dates derive from Ontario's Fewer Municipal Politicians Act of 1999, which is described in Andrew Sancton, *Merger Mania: The Assault on Local Government* (Montreal and Kingston: McGill-Queen's University Press, 2000), 154–9.

amalgamation (which is what happened in the other regions in 2000) or becoming part of some form of extended Metro Toronto, an option that did seem a real possibility in the 1990s (as we shall see in the next chapter) but which is now off the table.

Rather than review in detail all the debates and manoeuvrings about how each of the remaining regions should be structured politically, we shall simply review in Table 7.2 the current state of affairs. In all cases, voters (rather than lower-tier councils) elect all regional councillors; similarly, mayors of all lower-tier municipalities are members of their respective regional councils. But the table shows that in Waterloo and Niagara the mayors are the only lower-tier elected officials serving at the regional level; in the other four regional municipalities most mayors are joined by members of their own councils. In Waterloo, Halton, and Durham the regional chairs (who are best understood as regional mayors) are directly elected. Elsewhere, regional chairs are elected by members of regional council. If a person elected chair is a member of regional council, he or she gives up whatever other position to which elected.

The table also shows that, except in Durham, the largest municipality in each region is generally under-represented on the basis of their respective shares of each region's population. This is in part caused by the fact that even the smallest municipality always gets at least one rep-resentative, however small its population. But there is also a general bias against giving any one municipality too much power within the region. This has been especially true with respect to Mississauga within Peel, and the issue has been the cause of one of the most serious challenges this century to an Ontario regional municipality.

Mississauga and the Regional Municipality of Peel

The creation of most regional governments in Ontario was preceded by a "review" conducted by an expert on local government. Thomas J. Plunkett was assigned to review the local government structures in Peel and Halton counties, the fastest-growing areas in the Toronto region. Plunkett's report was the most radical of any of the reviews conducted in the 1960s. He proposed a single-tier "urban county of Mississauga" that would replace all existing municipalities in the southern parts of Peel and Halton counties and another large rural unit covering the northern parts. Although the report made perfect sense in terms of patterns of suburban development, it was opposed by virtually all of the local polit-icians and developers. After much delay and debate, the Ontario govern-ment announced in 1973 that there would be two regional governments in the area—one for Peel and one for Halton.[19]

The boundaries of the old counties were left almost untouched, but the constituent parts were dramatically restructured. The most contro-versial of these was the creation of the new city of Mississauga within Peel. It was formed by the amalgamation of the town of Mississauga (for-merly Toronto township) with the towns of Port Credit and Streetsville. One of the fiercest critics of the amalgamation was the mayor of Streetsville, Hazel McCallion. In 1978, however, she was elected mayor of Mississauga and has held that post until 2014, retiring only when she was 93 years old.[20]

After 2000 (when the constituent parts of Ottawa–Carleton regional municipality were merged together to create the new City of Ottawa), Mississauga became the most populous city in Ontario to be part of a two-tier system. Starting in 2001, McCallion launched a campaign to separate Mississauga from Peel. McCallion's biographer sets the stage with these words:

> The Region of Peel hardly seems like a monster, with its soft-spoken chair, its low-profile bureaucrats, and a lack of controversy over day-to-day operations. But if it is not a monster, it could be portrayed as a monstrosity—a wasteful tier of local government on whose council

Table 7.2 Features of Ontario's Six Regional Municipalities

	Number of Lower-Tier Municipalities	2011 Population	% Population in Largest Municipality	Number of Regional Councillors Excluding Chair	% of Councillors Assigned to Largest Municipality
Waterloo	7	507,096	43.2	15	33.3
Niagara	12	431,346	30.5	30	23.3
Halton	4	501,669	36.4	20	35.0
Peel	3	1,296,814	55.0	24	50.0
York	9	1,032,524	29.2	20	25.0
Durham	8	608,124	24.6	28	28.6

Sources: Statistics Canada, *2011 Census of Canada*; websites of the various regional municipalities.

Mississauga is grossly under-represented. Smaller cities like London, Guelph, and Barrie are "separated" cities. They do not groan under an upper-tier government. Why should Mississauga?[21]

In 2002, a citizens' task force created by McCallion recommended that the Peel regional municipality be phased out over a five-year period to be replaced by a lighter coordinating body for a larger Toronto region. Twenty thousand residents returned a form to Mississauga city hall supporting the mayor's position that Peel region should be abolished.[22] Despite McCallion's strong pressure, the provincial Liberal government (elected in 2003) refused to act, knowing that any move to split up Peel would throw "wide open the debates across the province on all sorts of municipal grievances, separatist aspirations, de-amalgamations, annexationist proposals, and maybe even schemes not hitherto contemplated."[23]

Then McCallion announced her alternative: that Mississauga should at least be fairly represented on the Peel council. At the time, the mayor and all nine councillors comprised Mississauga's representation on the 21-member council, which then elected a chair as a twenty-second member. In April 2006, the Ontario government announced that it would introduce legislation expanding the Mississauga council to 11 members, plus the mayor, and that all would continue to sit on a Peel council of 24 members, who would then elect a chair. McCallion declared victory.[24]

Conclusion to Ontario's Regional Governments

In the early 1970s, two-tier regional governments in Ontario were seen by experts as significant institutional reforms in urban governance. Many expected that they would eventually be established throughout the southern part of the province and that single-tier separated cities would become relics of the past. But the process was halted in the mid-1970s in the wake of much local political opposition.[25] Four were abolished in 2000. Four of the six that that remain (including Peel) are in the immediate orbit of the amalgamated city of Toronto, anomalous survivors of the dramatic municipal amalgamations of the late 1990s. The regional municipalities of Niagara and Waterloo are more removed from Toronto's core but as they are still in the Greater Golden Horseshoe, both exist in complex municipal environments with a number of significant urban municipalities as their reluctant members. Mayor McCallion's efforts to bring change to Peel are likely to be replicated elsewhere.

Urban, Regional, and Metropolitan Communities in Quebec

After the city of Montreal's financially disastrous annexation of Maisonneuve in 1918 (described in Chapter 6), the Quebec government established a Montreal Metropolitan Commission. Its main purpose was to force wealthier suburban municipalities to subsidize poorer ones, which Montreal was no longer willing to annex. Although a few inter-municipal functions were added later, it never became a wide-ranging metropolitan government such as those established later in Toronto and Winnipeg. The same can be said for its successor, the Montreal Metropolitan Corporation, established in 1959.[26]

The Montreal Urban Community

The late 1960s was a time of considerable political instability in many cities in the Western world. Among Canadian cities, Montreal was especially affected by street violence, largely because of linguistic and political tensions between French and English, and separatists and federalists. Between June 1968 and October 1969, two Montreal police officers were killed and more than 250 were injured. Notwithstanding the perils for the Montreal police, they were paid less than those in Metro Toronto. In the aftermath of Expo 67, city officials claimed they could not afford to match Toronto's police salaries. On 7 October 1969, the Montreal police launched an illegal work stoppage that lasted for 16 hours before Quebec's legislature approved a law, obeyed by the police, which forced them back to work. During this brief interval there were 9 armed bank robberies, 30 other armed robberies, and 494 complaints involving almost a million dollars of damage, much of it from looting. Federal troops and Quebec provincial police were moved into the city. Meanwhile, Montreal's suburban municipalities were protected by their own police services, whose members stayed on the job.[27]

Montreal officials soon agreed to meet most of the financial demands from the police union. Their strategy was to convince the provincial government to force the suburbs to help them meet the cost. They pointed out that, because Metro Toronto had a unified police force that covered the relatively peaceful suburbs as well as the downtown, it was able to reduce per capita costs compared to the city of Montreal. One of them stated: "Montreal's police department is effectively the shield which protects all of the Island of Montreal. Justice would almost be restored if the costs of all police services were shared by all citizens of the island."[28] The city's strategy was successful. Starting in 1970, the island of Montreal had a new metropolitan government, the Montreal Urban Community (MUC), the main purpose of which, initially, was to share policing costs.

The legislation establishing the MUC also gave it the authority to take action on such matters as regional planning, air pollution, traffic control on main arteries, public transit, the supply of drinking water, the treatment of sewage, and the disposal of garbage. Over the years it acted on many of these matters, most notably to build a primary sewage treatment plant to stop the practice of releasing the city's untreated sewage directly into the St. Lawrence River. But policing remained its primary focus. In 1970 and 1971, all the municipalities kept their own police services but shared costs on the basis of each municipality's share of total MUC property assessment. Not surprisingly, total police costs rose dramatically. The situation was like a group of 30 diners going to a restaurant and agreeing that they would split the bill in proportion to the value of each diner's home. Even the person with the most expensive home is likely to do better by ordering the most expensive items on the menu, because that is what others—especially the people living in cheap homes—are likely to do. Starting in 1972, all the police forces were unified and the Montreal Urban Community Police Department was created.[29]

The MUC existed from 1970 until 2001, when the 28 municipalities in the MUC were amalgamated. During its existence, battles between the city and the suburbs were constant. The main problem was that the city of Montreal comprised more than half the population of just under two million and the suburbs varied in size from almost 100,000

(Montreal North) to just over 1000 (Senneville). Representatives of the various municipalities on the MUC council were given multiple votes in accordance with population (one vote for each 1000 people represented), and all decisions required a double majority of both city and suburban votes. The system was very complex, and few MUC residents had any idea how their metropolitan government actually worked. Various attempts to restructure the boundaries of the constituent municipal units (similar to what happened in Metro Toronto in the 1960s) foundered on linguistic issues: few politicians wanted to merge French and English municipalities or to create a large English one in the western part of the island. The result was that all boundaries were left alone.[30]

Elsewhere in Quebec

Opposition parties in the Quebec legislature agreed to the speedy passage of the law establishing the MUC. In return, the government also agreed to establish an urban community for the Quebec City area and a regional community for the Outaouais, thereby enabling Quebec City and Hull (now Gatineau) to benefit from the same assistance from their suburbs as did the city of Montreal from theirs. Unlike the MUC, the lower-tier municipalities within these upper-tier institutions were consolidated—from 26 to 13 in Quebec City, and from 32 to 8 in the Outaouais.[31] Like the MUC, these institutions ceased to exist at the end of 2001.

In 1979, provincial legislation was approved that abolished Quebec's 71 upper-tier rural counties (similar to Ontario's) and replaced them with 95 municipal regional counties (MRCs). The main difference between the old counties and the MRCs is that the latter have responsibility for regional planning. For this purpose, separated cities became part of the MRC in which they were located. In some respects, therefore, they are similar to regional governments in Ontario, the main difference being that they are not responsible for nearly as many municipal functions and therefore have much smaller budgets. As shown in Table 1.1, there are now 86 MRCs in Quebec.[32] .

Metropolitan Communities in Montreal and Quebec

There are two *supra-regional authorities* in Quebec. These came into existence in 2002 for areas very similar to the CMAs for both Montreal and Quebec City, meaning that the territories they cover are much larger than their predecessors, the Montreal and Quebec urban communities. But their functional responsibilities are much less. They have nothing to do with policing, but they do have responsibilities relating to regional planning, waste disposal, regional parks, coordination of public transit, economic development, regional infrastructure, and cost-sharing for public housing.[33] An unusual feature of these entities is that the mayors of Montreal and Quebec City are automatically the chairs of the governing councils of their respective metropolitan communities, which means that their leadership functions extend beyond their own municipal boundaries. In 2011 the councils of both metropolitan communities adopted regional plans designed to shape the future development of their territories. However, neither of these supra-regional entities has yet had much impact, and very few residents have any reason to be aware of them.

Some of the territories of these two metropolitan communities are also under the jurisdiction of MRCs. Residents of such areas are faced, therefore, with three tiers of municipal government—the only place in the country where this is the case. As we shall see in the next chapter, the arrangements for municipal government within the former territory of the MUC are even more complex.

Regional Districts in British Columbia[34]

Between 1965 and 1967, the British Columbia government implemented a system of regional districts for the entire province, including those areas not contained within incorporated municipalities. The 27 regional districts in British Columbia differ from regional government in Ontario in the following ways:

- The district's governing body is called a *board of directors* not a *council.*
- Some members have multiple votes, depending on the population of their municipalities, and the number of these votes for each member is adjusted automatically after the most recent federal census.
- Member municipalities can opt out of many district functions, but no districts have any responsibility for police or social services.
- Unincorporated areas are included within the boundaries of regional districts and are known as *electoral areas*, because people living within these areas elect their own representatives directly to the board of directors.
- Districts provide different functions for different areas within their boundaries, especially for electoral areas. Except for the representatives from electoral areas, all municipal representatives on district boards of directors, including the chair, are elected members of municipal councils.

- Districts were created without changing any existing municipal boundaries—that is, no simultaneous lower-tier consolidation took place.

In short, the creation of regional districts was much less disruptive to the traditional pattern of municipal government. Although there have been some calls for direct election to the boards of directors of regional districts,[35] the provincial government has never moved towards implementing such a change, presumably because of the lack of municipal support for such a move and a concern about the jurisdictional conflicts that would likely ensue, as they did in Metro Winnipeg and Metro Toronto.

Metro Vancouver

Until 1967, inter-municipal services in metropolitan Vancouver were handled largely by special-purpose bodies. Two of these were continued as the Greater Vancouver Sewerage and Drainage District, and the Greater Vancouver Water District, but their operations were essentially combined with those of the Greater Vancouver Regional District (GVRD), now known unofficially as Metro Vancouver. Its territory "essentially corresponds"[36] to the Vancouver census metropolitan area (CMA). Unlike two-tier metropolitan and regional governments in Ontario, the GVRD has actually expanded its boundaries since its inception. The fact that peripheral municipalities, prior to their application for full membership, have already been part of the GVRD for a limited number of functions (as Abbotsford is for parks) is no doubt part of the explanation. The governance arrangements for Metro Vancouver are complex, as shown in Table 7.3.

More so than for any other metropolitan area in Canada, planning documents for Metro Vancouver are obsessed, for understandable reasons, with protecting the natural physical environment and with maintaining a "livable region." In the mid-1970s, the GVRD adopted its *Livable Region Plan* (LRP). The plan's main objective was to prevent urban sprawl by minimizing commuting. More jobs would be created in regional town centres so people could live closer to where they worked.[37] The latest version of the area's "regional growth strategy"—*Metro Vancouver 2040*—was adopted unanimously in 2011 by all the municipalities in the region.[38] Unlike regional governments in Ontario, regional districts do not have the authority arbitrarily to impose planning objectives on municipalities; their influence is accomplished by persuasion and, ultimately, by various forms of mediation and arbitration. Probably because many residents of Vancouver seem profoundly worried that continued economic growth might destroy their remarkable natural environment, they seem to have

Table 7.3 Number of Votes for Each Board Member for Each of Three Boards Comprising Metro Vancouver, 2013

Director	RD*	SD†	WD‡
ABBOTSFORD			
Mayor Bruce Banman	4		
Councillor Patricia Ross	3		
ANMORE			
Mayor Heather Anderson	1		1
BELCARRA			
Mayor Ralph Drew	1		1
BOWEN ISLAND			
Councillor Andrew Stone	1		
BURNABY			
Mayor Derek Corrigan	4	4	4
Councillor Sav Dhaliwal	4	4	4
Councillor Colleen Jordan	4	4	4
COQUITLAM			
Mayor Richard Stewart	4	4	4
Councillor Mae Reid	3	3	3
DELTA			
Mayor Lois Jackson	5	5	5
ELECTORAL AREA A			
Director Maria Harris	1	1	1
LANGLEY CITY			
Councillor Gayle Martin	2	2	2
LANGLEY TOWNSHIP			
Mayor Jack Froese	3	3	3
Councillor Bob Long	3	3	3
LIONS BAY			
Mayor Brenda Broughton	1		
MAPLE RIDGE			
Mayor Ernie Daykin	4	4	4
NEW WESTMINSTER			
Mayor Wayne Wright	4	4	4
NORTH VANCOUVER CITY			
Mayor Darrell Mussatto	3	3	3
NORTH VANCOUVER DISTRICT			
Mayor Richard Walton	5	5	5
PITT MEADOWS			
Mayor Deb Walters	1	1	1
PORT COQUITLAM			
Mayor Greg Moore	3	3	3

continued

Table 7.3 continued

Director	RD*	SD†	WD‡
PORT MOODY			
Mayor Mike Clay	2	2	2
RICHMOND			
Mayor Malcolm Brodie	5	5	5
Councillor Harold Steves	5	5	5
SURREY			
Mayor Dianne Watts	5	5	5
Councillor Linda Hepner	5	5	5
Councillor Barinder Rasode	5	5	5
Councillor Judy Villeneuve	5	5	5
Councillor Barbara Steele	4	4	4
TSAWWASSEN			
Chief Bryce Williams	1		1
VANCOUVER			
Mayor Gregor Robertson	5	5	5
Councillor Heather Deal	4	4	4
Councillor Raymond Louie	5	5	5
Councillor Andrea Reimer	5	5	5
Councillor Kerry Jang	4	4	4
Councillor Tim Stevenson	4	4	4
Councillor Geoff Meggs	4	4	4
WEST VANCOUVER			
Mayor Michael Smith	3	3	3
WHITE ROCK			
Mayor Wayne Baldwin	1	1	

Note: (1) The 2013 board consists of 40 directors representing 21 municipalities, one electoral area, one treaty First Nation, and one municipality that is a member of the GVRD for the parks function. These directors are members of municipal or First Nation councils who have been appointed to the board by their respective councils. (2) The number of directors appointed to the board depends on the population of the municipality, electoral area, or First Nation. As well, directors are allowed one vote for every 20,000 people in their municipality, electoral area, or First Nation, up to a total of five votes. The number in each of the three columns refers to the number of votes allocated to each of the directors for each of the three boards.

*RD: Greater Vancouver Regional District; †SD: Greater Vancouver Sewerage and Drainage District; ‡WD: Greater Vancouver Water District

Abbotsford is a member of the GVRD for the parks function only.

Source: Courtesy Metro Vancouver.

injected a greater sense of urgency into their regional planning than residents of other Canadian metropolitan areas. Metro Vancouver might not have much formal authority, but its planning activities spark considerable public involvement.

The Vancouver CMA is Canada's third most populous (2.: in 2011). The population of the city of Vancouver is only 603, suburban city of Surrey is not far behind at 468,000, and the other independent municipalities. In short, at least by Canadi dards, the metropolitan area is municipally fragmented. Nevertheless, looking at Vancouver's governance system as a whole, it is hard to imagine a mechanism that could better combine local self-government with the existence of an institution that can provide a degree of metropolitan leadership as well as a framework in which municipalities can voluntarily co-operate with each other.[39] Metro Vancouver's governance arrangements have lots of problems. For example, a recent judicial inquiry into the response of various area police services to the disappearances of numerous women from Vancouver's Downtown East Side recommended that a single, unified police service be established.[40] The idea is highly controversial, especially in the suburban municipalities. If there is to be a regional police service, it is not at all clear if or how it would relate to Metro Vancouver. Nevertheless, compared to the governance problems found elsewhere in Canada and in other countries, such problems in Vancouver are minimal.

Regional Commissions in New Brunswick

Since 1971 there have been more than 25 official government studies in New Brunswick relating to the organization of municipal government.[41] Few led to any significant changes (except for the creation of the amalgamated municipality of Miramichi, to be briefly discussed in the next chapter). However, in 2012, the Progressive Conservative government led by Premier David Alward sponsored legislation that created 12 regional service commissions in 2013. The commissions replace regional special-purpose bodies for planning and solid-waste management and cover the entire province, including unincorporated areas, residents of which elect their own representatives to their respective commissions. The commissions are also responsible for facilitating police collaboration, planning for emergency measures, and planning and cost-sharing for regional recreational facilities. Each commission can decide to take on additional functions if it wishes. Except for the representatives of unincorporated areas, all members of each commission are the mayors of the constituent municipalities. The provincial minister of the environment and local government has the authority to make regulations allowing for weighted votes and "to ensure that no single member is able to impose decisions on an entire region."[42] With the creation of the regional services commissions, New Brunswick became the fourth Canadian province to implement a two-tier system of municipal government.

Regional Partnerships in Edmonton and Calgary

In the previous chapter we noted the importance of municipal annexations for the recent territorial expansion of both Edmonton and Calgary. More so than Calgary, the Edmonton area faced significant inter-municipal issues, in part because of bad feelings that survived the annexation battles of 1979 and 1980. These issues were exacerbated in the late 1990s after the Alberta government abolished the province's regional planning commissions in 1994 as an economy measure and as a means to promote local economic development by making individual municipalities almost completely responsible for land-use issues.[43] In an effort to address remaining inter-municipal problems in Edmonton, the Alberta government in 1998 appointed a former provincial treasurer, Lou Hyndman, to review the governance arrangements for the entire area.

Edmonton

Hyndman's final report is an important document for local government in Canada because it did not focus on *structural* change and was less consolidationist than any official government report on the subject of municipal organization in metropolitan areas. In his report Hyndman wrote:

> Many different approaches were considered as part of this Review. Of the many options available, partnerships are the best option for this region. Partnerships involve networking, negotiation, and mutual investment for mutual gain. The old style, centralized approach with command and control from the top is not the way to govern our region. . . .
>
> Over the last four decades, this region has developed as a "community of communities," offering a range of residential and business choices that is unusual in comparison to most metropolitan areas in Canada. This is a strength of the region and it should be respected.
>
> A standardized "one size fits all" approach to the delivery of services in the region simply will not work. Citizens and their municipal leaders want choices. Those choices must include being able to choose among the diverse neighbourhoods and communities in the region. . . .
> Choices in how services are delivered in the region must also be considered. These could include municipal collaboration, co-operation or integration, service boards, agencies and commissions, private companies, volunteer associations, or any combination of these options.[44]

Nevertheless, Hyndman did recommend that a *Greater Edmonton Partnership* be established comprising all 21 municipalities in the area, each of which would have voting strength roughly equivalent to its relative share of the total population.[45] Such an institution was essentially the continuation of the Alberta Capital Regional Alliance (ACRA), a voluntary inter-municipal body that had been in existence since 1995. Rather than legislating for the new body, the Alberta government simply encouraged ACRA to continue.[46]

In October 2006, however, the city of Edmonton withdrew from ACRA, claiming that it had proven incapable of addressing important regional land-use issues that had implications for the fair sharing of fiscal resources in the region. In January 2008, provincial legislation replaced ACRA with the Capital Region Board (CRB), a planning body that 24 municipalities in the area were compelled to join. Provincial regulations authorized by the legislation provide that each member municipality has a single representative with one vote. However, any decision must be supported by the representatives of at least 17 municipalities representing at least 75 per cent of the total CRB population. If a municipal representative is absent or abstains from a vote, then the representative's vote is considered to be affirmative. This latter provision prevents members from blocking action by boycotting votes. The CRB approved the *Capital Region Growth Plan: Growing Forward* in April 2009 and now meets regularly to approve planning strategies of member municipalities before they become legally enforceable and to respond to various provincial requirements for regional planning decisions.[47] Although the CRB delivers no real services to residents, it does have significant planning authority with the potential to shape the future of the region. As part of its responsibilities for regional growth, it has become more involved in investigating how to improve the delivery and governance of regional public transit services. However, great tensions remain within the CRB: outer suburban municipalities see no reason why they should be forced to remain members, and all the suburbs resent Edmonton's effective veto power, which results from the fact that it contains about 70 per cent of the region's population. The city's 2013 annexation proposal (discussed in the previous chapter) adds to the inter-municipal acrimony. In any event, developments subsequent to Hyndman's report in 2000 suggest that his faith in voluntary partnerships was misplaced.

Calgary

ACRA served as a model for the Calgary Regional Partnership (CRP) that began operations in 2001. In 2009, it approved a Calgary Metropolitan Plan that is designed to guide regional development. Unlike the CRB's plan, it has no legal standing, unless or until it is enacted by the Alberta legislature. Since 2009, three rural municipalities—Rocky View, Wheatland, and Foothills—have left in protest because they considered that the plan, by concentrating future growth in established urban communities, limits their capacity to grow.[48] In 2013, the town of High River also departed, leaving the CRP with 14 member municipalities, only two of which (Calgary and Chestermere) are contiguous.[49]

The underlying problem is that the city of Calgary contains more than 90 per cent of the population of the census metropolitan area (CMA). If there is to be any democratic decision-making about regional growth, Calgary will be in complete control, and most suburban and rural municipalities will be resentful. To add to its regional dominance, Calgary sells water and wastewater services to the city of Airdrie, the second most populous municipality in the CMA. The town of Cochrane, the fourth most populous municipality, uses Calgary's wastewater treatment services.[50] In late 2013, the Alberta legislature approved the Enabling Regional Growth Boards Act (Bill 28), which provides a statutory base for some CRP (and CRB) activities. Nevertheless, the Act makes clear that municipal participation is strictly voluntary in any organizations such as growth boards or the CRP, so it is hard to see that any real change has occurred.[51] It remains to be seen whether municipalities in the Calgary metropolitan area can work together to achieve common goals voluntarily.

Conclusion

In this chapter we have observed a wide range of two-tier systems. At one extreme is the Corporation of Metropolitan Winnipeg (1961–71), governed by a 10-person council, all of whom were directly elected from districts that included territory from at least two different municipalities. At the other end of the scale is the voluntary regional partnership in Calgary. Metro Winnipeg was abolished primarily because of the intense political conflict between the two levels. The voluntary partnerships in Alberta were plagued by the departure of key members, causing Edmonton's to be replaced by the province and Calgary's to be severely threatened. The record of other two-tier systems has been shaky as well: Metro Toronto could not survive more than 10 years (1988–98) of direct elections to Metro council, and Ontario's other two-tier regional systems have faced both political turmoil and outright abolition. In Quebec, urban and regional communities survived for about 30 years (1970–2001), only to give way to much weaker metropolitan communities.

The only success stories have been the regional districts in British Columbia, including Metro Vancouver. Municipal membership is compulsory, but municipalities can opt in or out of most services that they provide; boundaries are fixed, but territories of particular services are not; all municipalities are represented on the boards of directors, but votes are weighted to account for population differences; regional planning is an important function, but local municipalities retain significant planning autonomy; the province is not afraid to step in on important policy issues (transit, for example), but it does not try to rearrange municipal boundaries. These are the kinds of policies and practices that have enabled regional districts to survive and prosper for a period of more than 40 years. They are Canada's success stories in two-tier metropolitan and regional government.

RESOURCES

Canada's longest-lasting, most successful example of a multi-functional metropolitan government is the Greater Vancouver Regional District, now known as Metro Vancouver. It has an impressive website that is worth thorough exploration. See www.metrovancouver.org/Pages/default.aspx

STUDY QUESTIONS

1. What is "the metropolitan problem"? What are the main differences in how consolidationists and adherents of public choice approach this "problem"?
2. Why and how was the Municipality of Metropolitan Toronto originally created? What were its main successes, and why, in your view, was it less successful in its later years?
3. What, in your view, are the reasons why the Greater Vancouver Regional District (now known as Metro Vancouver) has lasted longer than other two-tier urban governments in Canada?
4. Do inter-municipal problems in Edmonton and Calgary result primarily from the central cities being too populous? If so, what, if anything, can or should be done to fix this problem?

CHAPTER 8

Amalgamations and De-amalgamations

In Chapter 6 we were concerned with the outward expansion of city boundaries, the process usually known as annexation. Chapter 7 was about how some provincial legislatures established two-tier systems of urban government that were usually alternatives to continuous annexation, although the establishment of urban two-tier systems in Ontario was generally accompanied by the consolidation of lower-tier governments as well. This chapter is about the most dramatic form of provincial intervention in urban governmental arrangements: the passage of laws that amalgamate urban (and sometimes adjoining rural) municipalities with each other to create a much larger single-tier urban government. In Western Canada, the most dramatic example of such an amalgamation occurred in Winnipeg in 1971 when a "unicity" replaced the Metropolitan Corporation of Greater Winnipeg.

But most of the Canadian legislated amalgamations occurred in the 1990s and early 2000s. Such action in turn sparked demands for de-amalgamation, a process that in Quebec actually was implemented. Contrary to what is sometimes claimed, there was no worldwide movement for municipal amalgamations during this period, although significant amalgamations took place in parts of Britain, Australia, New Zealand, Greece, and Denmark.[1] Even in Canada, legislated amalgamations were restricted to the eastern provinces. In British Columbia, governments of various political persuasions made it clear they would not force amalgamations. However, Abbotsford and Matsqui were amalgamated in 1995 after voters in both municipalities approved the process in referendums.[2] The first involuntary municipal amalgamation occurred in Windsor, Ontario, and because it was a precedent for all that followed, it deserves our attention.

The Windsor Precedent

The first case in Canada of a municipality being amalgamated with another against the expressed will of its council and residents occurred in Windsor, Ontario, in 1935. The only scholars who have reported on it are Larry Kulisek and Trevor Price, and the following description of the case is based on their account. Kulisek and Price call the Windsor case "a decisive development of provincial policy"[3] and they are absolutely right. They describe the pre-1930 situation in Ontario in these words:

> [M]unicipalities had considerable scope to initiate services, respond to their citizens' needs and to seek authority for changes. While the process recognized the legal authority of the provincial legislature to approve changes, the initiative lay with the municipalities, which were building up their budgets and their administrative capabilities.
>
> In such key issues as the establishment of municipal boundaries and the changing of structures of government, the initiative also lay at the local level. Before amalgamations and annexations could occur it was necessary for local plebiscites to be held and for majority approval of those in the affected areas to be given . . . .[4]

It is startling to turn to the footnote accompanying this last sentence and to see that authority for it is attributed to the 1937 Harvard University master's thesis of Bora Laskin entitled "The Ontario Municipal Board." Laskin was to become one of Canada's most distinguished jurists, eventually serving as Chief Justice of Canada.

In 1917, in the midst of an unprecedented urban development boom in the area, various municipalities, including the city of Windsor, asked the provincial legislature to establish the Essex Border Utilities Commission (EBUC). The province obliged, and the EBUC ended up creating an integrated water supply system for the area, taking over some aspects of area-wide planning, creating a district health board and operating hospitals, and taking over some parks that served district-wide needs.[5] In short, the EBUC seems to have evolved from an inter-municipal special-purpose body to an early variety of a multi-functional metropolitan government. It is important to note, however, that its creation was initiated by the local municipalities, not by the Ontario government. Notwithstanding the existence of the EBUC, local business elites in the 1920s promoted municipal amalgamation but, because it was not approved by referendum in all the affected municipalities, it was not implemented.

The Windsor area was especially hard hit by the Great Depression. By 1933 all municipalities in the area except Walkerville, which had been the most adamantly opposed to annexation, were effectively bankrupt and under the financial supervision of the province. In 1934, a new Liberal government was elected in Ontario. David Croll, a former mayor of Windsor, was appointed as the province's first Minister of Municipal Affairs.[6] He sponsored legislation to establish a Windsor Finance Commission and to amalgamate the four central municipalities, including Walkerville, into a new city of Windsor. The legislation was introduced with no local consultation. It was announced on 11 April 1935 and was approved in its final form on 16 April, there being virtually no debate in the legislature—apparently because it was introduced right at the end of the session.[7]

Walkerville had the most to lose since its debts were less than the others in relation to its tax base and it had not defaulted on interest payments up to 1934. Walkerville feared that its tax assessment would be increased to help pay for the debts of weaker municipalities and that its own services would deteriorate to a lower uniform level once all services had been merged in a new Windsor. Walkerville put great emphasis on pride of place, which had been heightened by the fact that its name was carried worldwide on Canadian Club whisky produced by Hiram Walker Ltd.[8]

Walkerville residents fought the legislation in the courts, all the way to the Judicial Committee of the Privy Council in London, England— at that time Canada's highest court of appeal. The residents advanced the ingenious argument that the amalgamation legislation was really about bankruptcy, a subject under federal jurisdiction. By amalgamating municipalities to stave off bankruptcy, the residents argued, the provincial legislature was somehow invading federal jurisdiction. Everyone knew, however, that the main objective of the Walkerville residents was to protect local autonomy and that the arguments about bankruptcy were the slender legal reed to which they could attach their real concern. They claimed that:

> Quite apart from its many financial inequities both the act itself and the methods used in securing its enactment . . . were so un-British in character that it had become imperative . . . to take action in order to preserve (community) rights, if the long tradition of British justice and fair play is to be maintained in this country.[9]

The residents lost at all levels, with each court declaring that provincial legislatures had the unfettered authority to alter municipal structures in whatever way they wanted. In 1939, the Judicial Committee upheld the amalgamation legislation by stating that, "It is not only the right . . . but it would appear to be the duty of the provincial legislature to provide the necessary remedy, so that the health of the inhabitants and the necessities of organized life should be preserved."[10] As we shall see, recent judicial rulings on related matters in Canada have been remarkably consistent with the rulings made decades before with respect to Windsor, even though the Windsor case has not appeared in the judgments.

If Walkerville had been on the other side of the Detroit River in the United States, it could have appealed to American law and convention respecting the right of many municipalities to "home rule"—that is, the right to determine their own municipal structures and procedures. But home rule, as we saw in Chapter 3, never emerged in Canada, in large part because there are no written provincial constitutions in which its provisions can be embedded. In the absence of home rule, the residents of Walkerville had no legal ammunition with which to fight, especially when the enemy was a former mayor of Windsor backed by a disciplined majority in the provincial legislature.

The effect of the Windsor precedent in Canada is far from clear. The impact on Canadian municipal experts at the time must have been considerable, but whatever it was seems not to have been recorded. In the first major university textbook on Canadian municipal government, published in 1954, K. Grant Crawford wrote only one sentence about the Windsor amalgamation: "On occasion the province may take action [with respect to boundary changes] as was done in Ontario in 1935 when the cities of Windsor and East Windsor and the towns of Walkerville and Sandwich were amalgamated by provincial statute."[11] In any event, by the 1960s, no one seemed to be arguing in Canada, as Bora Laskin was in 1937, that any form of provincial action to change municipal boundaries and structures customarily required local consent; neither did anyone justify unilateral provincial action on the basis of what had happened 30 years before in Windsor.

In 1965 in Quebec, the provincial legislature merged 14 municipalities on Île-Jésus (immediately to the north of the Island of Montreal) to create the new city of Laval, with a population of 170,000. Most of the affected municipalities were opposed, but there were no claims that the provincial legislature was acting beyond its jurisdiction.[12] In 1967, New Brunswick merged the city of Lancaster with the city of Saint John. In 1970, Ontario amalgamated Port William and Fort Arthur to create the new city of Thunder Bay. Much more significant, however, was the creation a year later of Winnipeg's unicity.

Winnipeg's Unicity

The municipal amalgamation in Winnipeg was brought about by a newly elected Manitoba New Democratic Party (NDP) government led by Premier Ed Schreyer. The new government wanted to end inter-municipal bickering, promote fiscal equity, and provide new mechanisms for citizen involvement in municipal government. The general theory was that the administrative operations of Metro Winnipeg and its 12 constituent municipalities could be combined and centralized to create a powerful and effective bureaucratic machine that could be harnessed to solve the city's many problems, especially in the core. Financial resources for this purpose would be generated by the centralization itself and by the fact that the tax bases of the wealthier suburban municipalities would henceforth be shared.

Fortunately for students of municipal reorganization, the NDP government hired consultants to assist them with the process, and these consultants wrote a book about their experience.[13] One of its most fascinating parts is an account of the discussion and conflicts that went on within the Manitoba cabinet about "the relationship between citizens and the proposed new city government."[14] Some ministers advocated radically new mechanisms for citizen involvement and others were more interested in maintaining traditional forms. For a brief period of time, one of the consultants was James Lorimer, a Toronto-based activist and publisher, who submitted a paper calling for local community councils or corporations to be established within the unicity structure. Lorimer's paper proposed four potential responsibilities for such bodies:

1. To draw up and administer a community plan to control land use densities and development within their locality;
2. To influence overall policies regarding other functions of local government;
3. To instruct the elected representatives sitting on the central city council as to what position to take up in that forum; and
4. Limited fiscal power to establish a mill [tax] rate to raise the funds necessary to pay for a limited staff, including social animators whose task would be to reach out into the community for the involvement and participation of a large number of residents in the government of the city.[15]

Sidney Green, a convinced amalgamationist and a member of the cabinet committee developing the policy, rejected the Lorimer proposals. In a letter to a cabinet colleague he wrote:

I believe that any attempt by the provincial government to implement . . . [Lorimer's] proposals will put us further behind relative to the reorganization of municipal government. . . . Specifically, I do not believe that neighbourhood councils should have authority in the area of planning or development, nor do I believe that that they should have a residuary, albeit limited, fiscal power.

It is my view that the process of community involvement is one that must be created by the structure of the government itself and then by the political activities which are inspired as a result of intensified political interest. It is not artificially created by social animators.[16]

Green's position won out, a fact that explains why Lorimer was only briefly a consultant on the project. The conflict between Lorimer and Green was important. It happened in 1970, a time when enthusiasm for direct citizen involvement in government was at its peak. Lorimer was in the process of establishing himself as a prominent spokesperson for increased urban democracy. He was consulting for an NDP government that appeared outwardly sympathetic to his position. If ever there were a chance that Canadian municipal government would take a radically different path, this was it. But in the end, the Manitoba NDP implemented a municipal amalgamation that was hardly radical. As we shall see later in this chapter, it was in Montreal 30 years later that more radical ideas for decentralization in an amalgamated city were actually implemented— and not as a result of an explicit plan to enhance citizen participation.

Unicity started in 1972 with a municipal council having 50 members and a mayor. The idea was that a large council elected from small single-member wards would give a wider variety of people a chance to be elected. But there were many complaints about its unwieldy size, and it has been progressively cut to its current size of 15. Each councillor sits on a community committee with other councillors from his or her area of the city. Initially, the legislation required that there be 13 community committees, but now no such legislative requirements remain. In any event, these committees could never make final decisions, even for their own areas. Still more problematic were the initial legislative requirements that each community committee be advised by a residents' advisory group to be elected annually at community meetings. Because these advisory groups were charged with advising committees that in turn had no decision-making authority, residents soon lost interest. There is very little about Winnipeg's current arrangements for citizen participation in municipal government that makes it different from any other large Canadian city.

A frequent complaint from those concerned with social problems in Winnipeg's core was that the unicity council directed most of its resources to developing the suburbs. This was not surprising since most of the voters in the amalgamated city lived in the suburbs. Fortunately for Winnipeg, its federal politicians, especially Lloyd Axworthy, were adept at attracting federal investment to the core. The tri-level agreement on Winnipeg's "Core Area Initiative," first negotiated in 1981, has been especially important.[17]

When unicity began in 1972, its territory included 99 per cent of the population of the Winnipeg CMA. In 1992, a Progressive Conservative provincial government allowed the rural area of Headingley in the west of the city to secede and establish a new rural municipality.[18] This was just one of many factors that caused the city's share of total the CMA population to decline to 91 per cent by 2011.[19] Municipalities that are economically connected to Winnipeg are growing faster than the city of Winnipeg itself. As a result, in 2005 the Manitoba legislature approved a law to establish the Capital Region Partnership comprising the city of Winnipeg and 15 surrounding municipalities.[20] The organization is now known as the Partnership of the Manitoba Capital Region. Meanwhile, Winnipeg would like to annex land for industrial development from the rural municipality of Rosser, and it is providing sewage treatment for the contiguous municipality of West St. Paul. Even with a unicity, metropolitan Winnipeg experiences inter-municipal issues and problems.

The Early 1990s: Newfoundland, Prince Edward Island, and New Brunswick

The 1990s brought a dramatic increase in legislated municipal amalgamations. The movement was barely noticeable in Newfoundland and Prince Edward Island, picked up steam in New Brunswick, and captured national attention with a huge amalgamation in Halifax in 1993. This activity in Atlantic Canada turned out to be a prelude to later events in Ontario and Quebec.

St. John's, Newfoundland

The St. John's Metropolitan Area Board was in existence between 1963 and 1991. Its main mandates were "to control and administer the [unincorporated] fringe areas" and "to provide a general control of development and growth in the Metropolitan Area."[21] In 1978, it was given control of a provincially owned regional water supply system. At no time, however, did this board have any jurisdiction within the territory of incorporated municipalities. During the 1970s and 1980s various proposals for the establishment of a form of two-tier government in the area emerged, but none was implemented.

Effective 1 January 1992, the provincial government enacted a significant municipal reorganization within the St. John's CMA. Its main effect was to abolish the Metropolitan Area Board and to reduce the number of municipalities from 18 to 13. The city of St. John's absorbed the municipalities of Wedgwood Park and Goulds and most of the area previously under the jurisdiction of the board. For the city, this effort was of dubious benefit. In a 1996 position paper, the city stated:

> The Goulds and Metro Board lands are, for the most part, rural in nature with sprawling lineal urban developments. Upgrading infrastructure in these areas to a standard comparable to that in St. John's will require a major infusion of funding. As the Province did not provide the necessary transition funding for capital works, and with development frozen until adequate infrastructure can be provided, these areas are seen more as a financial responsibility than an asset for the City.[22]

Also effective 1 January 1992, the city was given jurisdiction over the area known as Southlands, previously part of the suburban city of Mount Pearl. It was clear from the beginning that this particular transfer was a form of provincial compensation to the city. Because it was an expanding, serviced, suburban subdivision, tax revenues from it would grow over time. But what makes St. John's especially important is that the 1992 reorganization charged the city with new regional responsibilities. Instead of establishing an upper-tier regional government, the city became responsible for providing the following services outside its boundaries within various parts of the wider region: public transit, solid-waste management, water supply, fire protection, and secondary processing of sewage.[23] The amalgamations were relatively minor, but the increased regional responsibilities for St. John's were significant.

Charlottetown and Summerside

As befits Canada's smallest province, amalgamations in Prince Edward Island were modest. In 1994, the legislature approved the City of Summerside Act and the Charlottetown Area Municipalities Act. To create the new city of Summerside, the province amalgamated five distinct areas, three of which were incorporated as municipalities. In the Charlottetown area, the province created three new or enlarged municipalities (Charlottetown, Stratford, and Cornwall) where there were once 18 municipalities and two unincorporated areas. In 2005, a close observer of PEI politics wrote:

> By creating three municipalities in the Charlottetown urban area, the province left unresolved the issues of effective urban planning and service delivery. Stratford, with a population of fewer than 6,500, and Cornwall, with a population of fewer than 4,500, are relatively small and, therefore, pressure for further rationalization is likely to arise.[24]

So far, nothing has happened. Meanwhile, the populations of the cities of Summerside and Charlottetown in 2011 were 14,751 and 34,562, respectively.

New Brunswick

In 1992, the provincial government in New Brunswick launched what appeared to be an ambitious program of municipal amalgamations. The city of Miramichi was created from 11 communities (including Newcastle and Chatham) in 1995,[25] and four communities were amalgamated with Edmundston in 1998.[26] However, what did *not* happen in New Brunswick's two largest cities, Moncton and Saint John, is more interesting. In the case of Moncton, one of the suburban municipalities, Dieppe, has a French-speaking majority. Merging it with Moncton was seen as an assault on minority rights and was avoided. Because Dieppe was left alone, the English-speaking suburb of Riverview also was left undisturbed, and the three communities then worked on ways to increase inter-municipal co-operation.[27] In Saint John the provincial government at one stage declared itself committed to an amalgamation of almost the entire CMA. But it backed away when it became convinced that spreading the pension plan of the city of Saint John to suburban municipalities would cost taxpayers more than any amalgamation might save. Instead, it reduced the number of suburban municipalities from eight to three.[28] Saint John and area is now covered by the Fundy Regional Services Commission, one of the new upper-tier authorities for New Brunswick described in the previous chapter.

Cape Breton and Halifax

After receiving a report from his Task Force on Local Government, Premier Donald Cameron of Nova Scotia (a Progressive Conservative) announced in late 1992 that municipal amalgamations would go ahead in both Cape Breton and Halifax. But in May 1993, he was replaced as premier by the former mayor of Dartmouth, John Savage (a Liberal), who proclaimed during the election campaign that amalgamation of the four Halifax municipalities was "a crazy idea,"[29] In mid-1994, Savage sponsored legislation to amalgamate eight municipalities in the industrial part of Cape Breton (including Sydney, New Waterford, and Glace Bay) so as to create the single-tier Cape Breton Regional Municipality.[30]

In July 1993, the Savage government received the Interim Report of the Municipal Reform Commissioner for Halifax County, a document commissioned by its predecessor and prepared by C. William Hayward.[31] The report is a landmark document in the history of Canadian municipal government. For the first time ever, a person charged with making recommendations about municipal amalgamation analyzed the budgets of the affected municipalities, and for each item declared how much money would be saved "due to restructuring"—that is, by amalgamation. In the fiscal year 1992–3, Hayward estimated total spending for the four municipalities (Halifax, Dartmouth, Bedford, and Halifax County) to be $439.6 million. Savings resulting from amalgamation were stated as $9.8 million, or 2.2 per cent of the total.

It would be unfair to suggest that the Hayward report paid no attention to non-financial issues. There were claims that a unitary system would be "more responsive, [that] accountability . . . [would] be improved, [that] planning . . . [would] also be more effective, [and that] [s]ounder financial decisions, particularly for capital spending, should also result."

Hayward did acknowledge two potential difficulties. The first was that "[i]n larger municipal units citizens may view their governments as distant and inaccessible." His solution was to provide for a network of "community councils, community committees, community advisory committees and citizen advisory committees." He briefly discussed the Winnipeg experience with such bodies, listing seven different reasons why they had not worked. He concluded the discussion by writing: "The intention is to provide a way for citizens to have a greater say in the way services are provided, in what services are provided, and in the form the community will take. At the same time, whatever advantages can be obtained from a larger unit are kept. The result should be accessible and responsive government at the least cost."

The second problem was the new municipality's sheer territorial size, especially the difficulties posed by the existence of a very large, sparsely populated rural hinterland. Here Hayward made a telling admission:

"Those who look simply at numbers and conclude that the rural areas will be outvoted and ignored are overlooking the way the democratic process works. Councillors, like any other elected persons (absent party discipline), will support the concerns of others in an attempt to generate support for their own pet projects."

Despite Premier Savage's initial declared opposition to amalgamation, he reversed his position in October 1994 as part of an overall strategy to reduce government spending and to promote economic development. The government's new policy caused the four affected municipalities to sponsor their own consultants' study of the proposed amalgamation. The consultants' report generally accepted Hayward's findings about cost savings, but pointed out that they would roughly be cancelled out by increases in expenditures caused by "policy harmonization" and "service levelling."

By May 1995, the legislation establishing the Halifax Regional Municipality was approved. There was relatively little difficulty in the legislature because the main opposition party, the Progressive Conservative Party, was in government when the whole process was started. The Halifax Regional Municipality (HRM) comprises more than one-third of Nova Scotia's population and more than 10 per cent of its territory. Originally the HRM council comprised 24 council members, each of whom was also a member of one of six community committees, which have small budgets and limited authority to make decisions about local matters, including zoning changes, as long as they are consistent with overall HRM policies. However in 2011, after long and bitter debates within the HRM, the Nova Scotia Utilities and Review Board decided that, effective in 2012, there would be only 16 HRM councillors and three community committees.[32] Because the territory of each of the community committees includes both urban and suburban areas and large expanses of rural land, it is not at all clear exactly what type of "community" is being served. In any event, the reductions in the size of the council and in the number of community committees closely parallels the Winnipeg unicity experience.

The Halifax amalgamation took place almost 20 years ago. Unlike the other amalgamations in Atlantic Canada it created a major Canadian municipality. In 2011, there were 390,096 residents of the HRM, making it the fourteenth most populous municipality in the country (between Laval, Quebec, and London, Ontario). Most residents of the urban part of the HRM are no doubt quite reconciled to its existence and can hardly remember the inter-municipal squabbling among the city, the county, Dartmouth, and Bedford. Rural residents still grumble about being overlooked and forgotten by their urban counterparts, even though they are almost certainly better off financially than they would have been without the amalgamation.[33] According to one recent academic observer, urbanites feel "submerged" in the HRM by the combined voting power of rural and suburban residents.[34] Numerous accounts[35] suggest that the HRM has cost more money than it has saved. Transition costs associated with the amalgamation were $26 million; Hayward had predicted $10 million. In a comprehensive study of the effects of amalgamating police services within the HRM, James C. McDavid concluded that costs went up (in real-dollar terms), and that there were fewer total police officers, lower service levels, and no real change in crime rates.[36]

Since amalgamation, the HRM has resolved long-standing disputes about a regional landfill site and established a state-of-the-art composting facility. Benefiting from extensive federal and provincial grants, it has also built a sewage treatment plant to stop the dumping of raw sewage into Halifax harbour. Although the plant has suffered serious operational difficulties, these can hardly be blamed on the amalgamation. Halifax has been relatively prosperous over the past 20 years, but this cannot be attributed to amalgamation either. It seems due much more to the development of offshore natural gas and to the ongoing tendency of large organizations to choose the Maritimes' largest urban area as the location of centralized office functions.

Ontario

The most significant changes in the history of Canadian local government occurred in Ontario in the 1990s. Amalgamations were a major part of the story, but there were also major changes to provincial–municipal funding arrangements and to the operation of the property tax system. The fact that so much was going on at once has made it difficult to analyze the individual effect of any particular change. Some analysts believe that this strategy was part of the government's intention to provoke so much change all at once that "politics as usual" would fundamentally change in some way that could only be better, at least for the provincial government. Others tended to see a more carefully crafted set of changes: the province would download its costs to municipalities; these extra municipal costs would be paid for by savings from amalgamations and/or by a property tax system that was fairer and more conducive to economic growth.

We need not concern ourselves with the inner workings of Ontario's provincial government. We need only to understand that the Progressive Conservative government elected in 1995 and led by Premier Mike

Harris achieved office by tapping into an apparently profound public dissatisfaction with high deficits, high taxes, and perceived government waste.[37] Two-tier governments, with their perceived "overlap and duplication," appeared to be a significant part of the problem. Much more so than the federal Conservative Prime Minister Brian Mulroney, who left office in 1993, Harris was committed to following in the footsteps of Margaret Thatcher in Britain and Ronald Reagan in the United States, both of whom had dramatically reduced the size of government in their respective countries. In the pages that follow, it is important to remember that the actions of the Harris government with respect to municipalities were only a part of its attempt to implement its overall plan, known as the Common Sense Revolution (CSR). But as we shall see, sometimes only a minimum of common sense was evident in what it did.

The Harris government sponsored three major pieces of legislation that caused municipal amalgamations:

- The Savings and Restructuring Act, Schedule M, 1996
- The City of Toronto Act, 1997
- The Fewer Municipal Politicians Act, 1999.

Each will be discussed in turn.

The Savings and Restructuring Act, Schedule M, 1996[38]

Municipal amalgamations did not clearly appear on the Harris government's public agenda until 29 November 1995, the day on which Bill 26, the Savings and Restructuring Act, was first made public. Schedule M of Bill 26 defined municipal restructuring in terms of various forms of annexation and amalgamation; established a procedure for municipalities to arrive at locally agreed restructuring arrangements; and provided for the appointment, in the case of local disagreement, of a commissioner who would have the power to impose new boundaries and structures within the affected area. This innovation had much more to do with the "arbitration" experience in London a few years earlier than with anything contained within the CSR. Significantly, Schedule M did not apply within two-tier regional governments or restructured counties, presumably because they had already been "restructured." In any event, nothing in the CSR prepared the way for all the amalgamations that would follow. By early April 1997, more than a year after the Bill 26 procedures had been in place, relatively little action had been taken with respect to municipal restructuring. The minister had approved 21 plans, which, in total, had reduced the number of municipalities by 50 (out of a total of 815). After this time, the pace of municipal submissions quickened, in large measure because of what had happened when the first commission appointed under the terms of Schedule M ordered the amalgamation of the city of Chatham with all municipalities within Kent County.

Chatham–Kent

The Chatham–Kent case deserves attention not just for its influence on subsequent municipal behaviour but also because it has been the most dramatic and extensive of all the restructurings carried out under the provisions of Schedule M. From April 1996 until January 1997, local politicians in Kent County—located halfway between London and Windsor in southwestern Ontario—debated every conceivable alternative form of structure, from abolishing the county to merging all county municipalities into one. The only option that failed to win any degree of support was the idea that a complete merger should include the city of Chatham. On 22 January 1997, a member died of a heart attack on the floor of the county council while defending the county's continued existence. A week later a majority of members boycotted the next meeting, which was the last opportunity to arrive at a local decision. Seven municipalities had already asked for a commission to be appointed, but the Minister of Municipal Affairs, Al Leach, had postponed action until it was clear that local agreement was not possible.

When he appointed a one-man commission on 6 February 1997, Leach prescribed that the area in question include both the city (population 43,000) and the county (66,000). This was probably the single most important decision in the entire process—and it was clearly taken by the government, not the commissioner. After issuing an initial report in which he had narrowed the choices—to a two-tier system including the city or a one-tier system including the city—the commissioner, Peter Meyboom, reported on 28 April that he had chosen the one-tier option. He acknowledged that only 1 of the 23 affected municipalities, the township of Tilbury East, supported his choice.

The commissioner's decision sparked predictable statements of outrage from various municipal politicians—but after a few days the storm passed. Part of the explanation for the lack of dissent is that both politicians and administrators realized they soon would be jockeying for position in the new structure and no one wanted to diminish his or her chances by arguing that it was illegitimate. Another reason is that the Toronto megacity battle was going on at the same time and, in comparison, Chatham–Kent seemed insignificant. But unlike Toronto, amalgamation in Chatham–Kent did not require an act of the legislature;

it merged entities (the city and the county) that were not previously linked for local government purposes; and it included a city, a large town (Wallaceburg, with a population of 12,000), and various less-populous towns, villages, and rural townships.

The real lesson from Chatham–Kent is that amalgamation was accepted, even though it was not popular. Residents demonstrated remarkably little public concern about the loss of their local governments as a result of one person's decision. It almost appeared that people in the area felt they deserved a form of punishment or strong medicine because their municipalities had behaved badly by not restructuring themselves before a commissioner was brought in. Remarkably, the government's claims that the appointment of a commissioner was a response to local wishes and that it was not responsible for the content of his decision seem to have been accepted. The fact remains, however: never before in Ontario (or in any other liberal democratic jurisdiction, it seems) has one person had the authority—and used it—to so dramatically alter an established system of local government.

"Voluntary" Amalgamations

From April 1997 on, Chatham–Kent became the horrible example that no one else wanted to follow. Counties scurried to get on with restructuring so they could avoid a commissioner telling them what they had to do. For many, the main object was to devise a plan that would not involve becoming linked with a populous urban centre whose residents could dominate the local political process. Ironically, if all the parties involved were convinced that no one in their group would request a commissioner, the urgency to take action was greatly reduced. This probably explains why some areas acted and others did not.

Prior to the passage of Bill 26, there were 815 municipalities in Ontario. Except for the creation of the megacity in Toronto, all of the municipal restructurings approved by the Harris government prior to 1999 were brought about under the provisions of Bill 26. As of 23 August 1999, the Harris Conservatives had caused the number of municipalities in Ontario to be reduced by 229 (28 per cent) and the number of elected municipal officials had shrunk by 1,059 (23 per cent). Some of the amalgamations were clearly defensive: assessment-rich townships merged with each other so that they could avoid pressure to share their assessment with poorer neighbours. The general pattern, however, was that villages or towns merged with neighbouring townships, despite long-standing local views that they were best kept separate due to significantly different needs for municipal services. The basic trade-off was that the village or town shared its richer tax base in return for political dominance (through representation by population on the new council) and for new room for urban expansion. Most of these amalgamations came about as a result of a fear that if they were not done voluntarily, the Ontario government would step in and force amalgamations, possibly with less desirable partners.

Kawartha Lakes[39]

The city of Kawartha Lakes was the result of Commissioner Harry Kitchen's deliberations about the municipal structures of Victoria County, including the town of Lindsay. It came into existence on 1 January 2001 with a population of about 69,000. Unlike the situation in other government-forced Ontario amalgamations, the main citizens' group opposing the merger, Voices of Central Ontario (VOCO), became even more active after the merger. VOCO gathered petitions with 11,000 signatures asking that the merger be undone, and it conducted its own referendum in which 96.5 per cent of 6,209 voters expressed a preference to undo the amalgamation by returning to the previous system of municipal government.

During a visit to Kawartha Lakes in October 2001, Ontario's then opposition leader, Dalton McGuinty, stated that Ontario Liberals believed that past amalgamations could be reversed by a local referendum if there were a substantial demonstration of public support for the holding of such a referendum. He stated that the petition campaign in Victoria County "has clearly met that threshold."

On 15 April 2002, Ernie Eves succeeded Mike Harris as the Conservative Premier of Ontario. On that day, Premier Eves appointed Chris Hodgson, the MPP for Kawartha Lakes, as his new Minister of Municipal Affairs. We do not know whether Eves took into account the fact that Hodgson for two years had been under intense pressure from his constituents to do something about Commissioner Kitchen's decision to create the city of Kawartha Lakes. In any event, as Minister of Municipal Affairs, Hodgson was in a position to act. With little or no publicity outside his own constituency, Hodgson agreed in November 2002 to put a "minister's question" about demerger on the ballot in Kawartha Lakes at the time of the municipal elections in November 2003. He stated that the threshold for success would be the same as in any democratic election: 50 per cent plus one of the ballots cast. After a brief local debate about the wording of the question, Hodgson decided that it would be: "Are you in favour of a return to the previous municipal model of government with an upper-tier municipality and 16 lower-tier municipalities?" A few weeks later—long before the date of the referendum—Chris Hodgson retired from politics.

By the time the referendum actually took place, Dalton McGuinty was premier.

The first and only government-sponsored de-amalgamation referendum in Ontario was held in November 2003. The campaign in Kawartha Lakes was hard fought. Opponents of de-amalgamation warned of new costs and despaired at wiping out all the work that had been done in creating the new municipality. They especially highlighted fears that some of the smallest urban settlements could not afford by themselves to provide water to their residents because of the tightened provincial requirements for public water supply systems. With a turnout of 48 per cent of eligible voters, 16,802 voted Yes and 15,918 voted No. According to the rules of the game, the electors had approved the dismantling of the city of Kawartha Lakes. But nothing would happen unless the McGuinty government took action.

Clear victories for the Yes side were apparent in southern townships closer to Peterborough and Toronto and in the town of Bobcaygeon. Not surprisingly, the No side won by approximately 3,000 to 1,000 votes within the old county seat of Lindsay, the largest urban community in the municipality. Outside Lindsay, the decision to dismantle Kawartha Lakes was clear. The count was close only because voters in Lindsay supported the amalgamation, just as their council had supported the original plan to bring in a commissioner.

At the same time as the referendum, voters in Kawartha Lakes elected a mayor who supported de-amalgamation and a council that was also narrowly in favour. After their election, they attempted to convince the McGuinty government to implement de-amalgamation on the most favourable terms possible. But the process was ended by a letter from the Minister of Municipal Affairs dated 18 February 2004 in which he simply stated that the government "will not be implementing the de-amalgamation of the city of Kawartha Lakes at this time." The minister closed by stating that he would be open to considering other proposals for municipal restructuring. Despite its referendum, Kawartha Lakes was now in the same situation as every other merged municipality in the province: de-amalgamation was theoretically possible, but no one had any idea how it could or should be carried out. As we shall see later in this chapter when discussing amalgamations in Quebec, the de-amalgamation movement there turned out to be much stronger.

The Megacity in Toronto

The largest and best-known municipal amalgamation in Canadian history came into effect on 1 January 1998 when the constituent parts of the

Municipality of Metropolitan Toronto were merged to create a new city of Toronto. The amalgamation was the result of a separate piece of legislation applying only to Toronto. It is absolutely clear that, prior to their election in 1995, the Harris Conservatives had no intention of creating what was to become known as the "megacity." Their original intention was to eliminate the Metro level of government, but in the final analysis they could not figure out what to do with the municipal services for which Metro was responsible. Amalgamation eliminated such a concern because all municipal services within Metro's territory would henceforward be delivered by the same municipality. Other possible reasons for establishing the megacity were to swamp the left-wing voting majority in the old city of Toronto with more right-wing suburban voters in Etobicoke, North York, and Scarborough[40] and/or to enhance Toronto's global competitiveness.

Saving Money[41]

The government itself focused on saving money. On 23 November 1996—about three weeks before first announcing his megacity policy—Municipal Affairs Minister Al Leach commissioned a study to assess the financial implications of the amalgamation. The results were made public on 16 December. The next day, as part of his announcement, Leach made the following statement: "Yesterday, our government released a study prepared by management consultants KPMG. It claimed that over the first three years of its existence, a unified City of Toronto would save $865 million, then $300 million annually from then on." Despite many questions being raised about the validity of the KPMG conclusions, Leach continued to refer to it as justification for the megacity's creation.

As the protracted debate proceeded, government spokespeople tended to make fewer references to the KPMG study, but they kept referring to the elimination of duplication and overlap and the creation of more private-sector jobs. Saving money was supposed to be a result of eliminating duplication and a cause of private-sector job creation. By the government's own standards, savings from megacity were absolutely crucial. This is precisely why so much effort was expended while the provincial Conservatives were still in office (until 2003) to attempt to show that the megacity was indeed saving money.

During 1998, megacity residents noticed very few changes in how municipal services actually were delivered. This was because, except at the management level, nothing much changed. City workers simply carried on as before, without being integrated with respect to their day-to-day operations. It was largely because there were so few changes that most residents seemed to believe at first that amalgamation was a success. Those who had predicted chaos from the megacity were manifestly wrong.[42] In 1999, noticeable change began, but it was gradual and relatively well-managed. In subsequent years, each new annual municipal budget seemed to bring some new financial crisis or other. The usual pattern was for the province to come up with some form of last-minute rescue plan.

In the immediate aftermath of the amalgamation, various attempts were made to demonstrate its beneficial financial effects. More than 15 years later it is clear that the city of Toronto has many financial problems, but it is impossible to trace them all to the amalgamation or to claim that they would have been absent had there been no amalgamation. Probably the most definitive political statement about the financial effects of the amalgamation was made in April 2003 when the Toronto City Summit Alliance (since renamed the Greater Toronto Civic Action Alliance), a coalition of over 40 civic leaders from the private, volunteer, and public sectors in the Toronto region, argued that Toronto needed "a new fiscal deal," in part because "The amalgamation of the City of Toronto has not produced the overall cost savings that were projected. Although there have been savings from staff reductions, the harmonization of wage and service levels has resulted in higher costs for the new City. We will continue to feel these higher costs in the future."[43]

The most useful academic analysis of the effects of amalgamation on Toronto spending has been carried out by Enid Slack and Richard M. Bird. They looked at the per-household costs of four municipal services—fire protection, garbage collection, parks and recreation, and libraries—that were previously administered by the pre-amalgamation lower-tier municipalities. For all four services, the ten-year pre-amalgamation pattern was for per-household costs to decrease over time. Except for libraries, for the first 12 years after amalgamation, the trend was for per-household costs to increase. The increase was particularly dramatic for garbage collection. Bird and Slack have no easy explanation. They state that, "As with fire services, it is not clear to what extent the expenditure increase reflects higher wages and salaries or higher service levels."[44] Whatever the explanation, it is absolutely clear that the creation of the megacity did not save money.

Opposition to the Megacity

Although initial polling by the government suggested that the public supported amalgamation,[45] public opinion quickly turned negative. The Harris government enjoyed significant political support in Metro's suburban municipalities, but residents soon expressed dissatisfaction with the prospect of being joined with the city. Various polls and informal referendums demonstrated considerable levels of discontent.

But the most surprising and flamboyant opposition came from within the city of Toronto, especially from a group called Citizens for Local Democracy (C4LD) led by well-known community activists such as former Toronto Mayor John Sewell and by less well-known ones such as Kathleen Wynne, who became premier of Ontario in 2013. C4LD held open weekly meetings throughout most of 1997, organized street protests, and attempted to form links to amalgamation opponents in the suburbs. But C4LD was primarily committed to defending the central city's "progressive" municipal policies concerned with protecting inner-city neighbourhoods against disruptive development, providing free recreation programs to all residents, and supplementing local social services with additional municipal services for the poor. Suburban opponents of amalgamation had little interest in such objectives; one of the reasons they feared amalgamation was the prospect of having to use their tax contributions to finance what they considered "frills" and "extravagances." But C4LD and suburban opponents could at least agree that forcing the amalgamation was undemocratic in that it denied local citizens the ability to make their own decisions about their local institutions. Such a political agenda could not attract much in the way of support from poor and working-class residents or from Toronto's many recent immigrants, and even C4LD remained primarily a middle-class movement.[46] Nevertheless, the relatively brief existence of C4LD remains hugely important for any student of Canadian urban politics because it dramatically demonstrated that large numbers of citizens can be so committed to their municipality and its policies that they will commit huge amounts of time and resources to defending them. The emergence of C4LD was certainly a big surprise for the Harris government.

C4LD and the lower-tier municipalities of Metro Toronto challenged the amalgamation legislation in the courts, arguing that it violated political rights that were implicit in the Canadian Charter of Rights and Freedoms. Creating a new Yiddish word in the context of the Toronto debate, Justice Stephen Borins of the Ontario Court's General Division ruled that the provincial legislature was fully entitled to enact municipal amalgamations. He stated that the arguments he had heard in his court were political, not legal. "It may be" he wrote in his decision, "that the government displayed *megachutzpah* in proceeding as it did, and in believing that the inhabitants of Metro Toronto would submit . . . without being given an opportunity to have a real say in how they were to live and be governed." Nonetheless, "the *Charter* does not guarantee the individual the right to live his or her life free from government *chutz-pah* or imperiousness."[47] The Ontario Court of Appeal upheld Borins's decision.

Community Councils

During the legislative debates and the court case, the government placed considerable emphasis on the fact that the ward boundaries for the new council would not cross the old municipal boundaries and that the territory of each of the old municipalities would be served by a "community council" comprising the members of the city council for that territory. Although the community councils were given no decision-making authority, the government claimed they would be important mechanisms for local views to be channelled to the new amalgamated municipality. In many important respects this was true. The new council ended up with such large agendas that almost all recommendations from community councils about local zoning changes were accepted without debate. One of the operational problems was that the community council of East York was responsible for only about one-sixth as many people as the one for the old city of Toronto. After the passage of the Fewer Municipal Politicians Act in 1999 (to be discussed in the next section), the number of community councils was reduced to four (Toronto and East York, Etobicoke York, North York, and Scarborough). But they can hardly be considered as particularly "local" because the number of residents that each covers is larger than the number of residents in all but a handful of the most populous Canadian municipalities. More important than the boundary changes was a legislative change in 2006 that allowed the Toronto city council to delegate some decision-making authority to community councils. Significantly, however, community councils still cannot make final decisions on zoning changes; nor can they levy any form of local tax.

Political Developments in the Megacity

The megacity's first municipal election was in the autumn of 1997. The mayor of North York, Mel Lastman, an apparent political ally of the Harris Conservatives, defeated Barbara Hall, the mayor of the old city of Toronto, to become the first mayor of the megacity. Most of the newly elected councillors supported Lastman, who did a good job in steering the new institution towards stability and acceptance but a bad job in making the kind of drastic changes that would have been needed to capture dramatic cost savings. Lastman was re-elected in 2000, but in 2003, David Miller, a left-leaning councillor from the central city, won

Mayoral Winners by Ward ■ Ford   ■ Smitherman

Figure 8.1 Toronto Mayoral Voting by Ward, 2010

Source: © NATIONAL POST / Richard Johnson.

the mayor's job after Lastman retired. Like Lastman, Miller was generally supported by a majority of councillors and he too was re-elected (to
a four-year term) in 2006. The great irony, of course, was that from 2003
to 2010, the amalgamated city of Toronto was governed by a left-leaning
mayor and council, a prospect that had seemed impossible to the many
supporters of C4LD in 1997. Not only did the megacity policy not save
money, it was not even successful in producing a permanent conservative
majority on the new city council.

With the election of Rob Ford as mayor in 2010, conservatives did
once again dominate. But the most significant feature of the 2010 election was the obvious split in mayoral preferences between residents in
the old city of Toronto and those in the Metro suburbs. Figure 8.1 shows
that Ford won a plurality of the votes in all the suburban wards while his
main opponent, former provincial cabinet minister George Smitherman,
won a plurality in all of the wards within the pre-amalgamation city of
Toronto. After 15 years of municipal amalgamation in Toronto, it appears
that central-city and suburban differences are just as strong as ever.

The Fewer Municipal Politicians Act

After the passage of Toronto's amalgamation legislation in 1997, the
Ontario government still faced some difficult municipal issues. There

was much dissatisfaction with two-tier regional government. After receiving reports from four "special advisers" (who were like the commissioners in Chatham–Kent and Kawartha Lakes but without final decision-making authority), the Minister of Municipal Affairs announced that each of the regional municipalities of Ottawa–Carleton, Hamilton–Wentworth, and Sudbury would be amalgamated on 1 January 2001 into one new city each: Ottawa, Hamilton, and Greater Sudbury, respectively. The Regional Municipality of Haldimand–Norfolk, comprising six lower-tier municipalities, was to be reorganized at the same time into two single-tier counties, Haldimand and Norfolk. The same legislation reduced the size of the Toronto city council to 45. The government could rightly claim that the various components of the legislation eliminated the positions of 203 municipal politicians, an accomplishment that was designed to appeal to the notion that any reduction in the number of elected politicians must be beneficial.[48]

Unlike the amalgamation in Toronto, the creation of the new cities in Ottawa, Hamilton, and Greater Sudbury meant that many small villages and large tracts of rural and sparsely populated land became united with densely populated urban areas, resulting in significant political tensions. The rural residents have successfully argued for more representation on the new councils than their numbers warrant so that their political influence will not be completely swamped by the urbanites. The granting of such extra representation means that urban votes are worth less than rural votes within the same municipality. Nevertheless, a recent study of voting blocs within the Hamilton city council shows that, as time has gone on, the tendency for councillors from outside the old city of Hamilton to vote together has decreased.[49] Amalgamation remains a salient political issue, but this analysis suggests that, in Hamilton at least, some element of political integration within the amalgamated municipality might well be occurring.

Conclusions from the Ontario Experience

Between 1996 and 2001, the number of municipalities in Ontario was reduced from 850 to 445.[50] After 2001, neither the Conservative government nor its Liberal successor has had any interest in pursuing municipal reorganization in any form. The relatively brief frenzy of amalgamations at the end of the 1990s has had a profound influence on Ontario municipal government, but it is difficult to point to any significant improvements. One of the most sympathetic assessments comes from David Siegel:

The new municipalities cover larger areas, thus improving fiscal equity across the entire area and improving the ability to deliver certain services such as land-use planning, public transit, streets and roads, and economic development. Hardly anyone believes that the new system saves money as was hoped, but the larger municipalities have larger budgets and are therefore able to hire more highly qualified people. Surveys in some municipalities, though, have indicated that citizens have seen no change in the quality of service delivery.[51]

But the lack of any positive achievements from municipal amalgamations in Ontario did not stop Quebec from pursuing the same course of action in the early 2000s.

Quebec

Municipal amalgamations have been on the political agenda in Quebec since the mid-1960s. Between 1961 and 2000, the number of municipalities in the province was reduced from about 1,750 to just over 1,300.[52] But the biggest changes took effect in 2001 and 2002. Unlike Ontario, they were initiated in large measure by the mayors of larger cities, especially Pierre Bourque of Montreal, who urged the provincial government to follow Ontario's example and legislate the amalgamation of suburban municipalities to the central city. The central-city mayors were convinced that such amalgamations would be financially beneficial to their residents in that suburbanites would be required to pay a greater share of central-city costs. The amalgamations resulted from two laws approved by Quebec's National Assembly in 2000. The first, Bill 124, authorized the Minister of Municipal Affairs to amalgamate municipalities not contained within the census metropolitan areas of Montreal, Quebec City, and the Quebec portion of the Ottawa CMA. The second, Bill 170, specified amalgamations within these CMAs and established metropolitan communities for Montreal and Quebec City (discussed briefly in the previous chapter). In addition to Montreal, which is the main focus of this section, the laws also had the effect of amalgamating neighbouring municipalities with Quebec City, Longueuil (on the south shore of the St. Lawrence across from Montreal), Hull, (now known as Gatineau), Chicoutimi (now known as Saguenay), Sherbrooke, and Trois-Rivières. Numerous other amalgamations took place involving rural areas, small towns, and villages.

The Montreal Amalgamation[53]

In 1999, Mayor Pierre Bourque of Montreal was already working hard to accomplish his objective of amalgamating all the municipalities on the Island of Montreal into a new city of Montreal. The suburbs—francophone and anglophone alike—were resisting. The political dynamics were almost identical to what they had been when Mayor Drapeau of Montreal launched his similar campaign in the 1960s. The main difference was that, at the level of the Quebec government and in the anglophone municipalities, there was a heightened sense of the linguistic implications. For the Quebec government the concern was that an amalgamated city of Montreal would have only a razor-thin francophone majority and could conceivably be captured politically by declared non-sovereignists, even by partitionists who could threaten to have Montreal separate from a newly independent Quebec. For the anglophone suburbs, the concern was that, under the provisions of Quebec's Charter of the French Language, their territories would lose their bilingual status if they were absorbed by a city whose majority was French-speaking. In the mid-1960s, sovereignty, partition, and language laws were not serious political issues. In the late 1990s they were.

But these issues could not be raised by mainstream politicians, francophone or anglophone, provincial or local. This is why they do not appear in any official reports, including the Bédard Report on municipal fiscal issues,[54] a report that favoured a drastic reduction of municipalities on the Island of Montreal, but not total amalgamation. The unspoken linguistic problem with any such proposal is that it involved, at a minimum, the merger of some francophone-majority municipalities on the West Island into a new and populous anglophone-majority municipality. In practical political terms, this simply was not possible.

The point, of course, is that total amalgamation seemed equally impossible. This was confirmed in June 1999 when both Premier Lucien Bouchard and Louise Harel, the Minister of Municipal Affairs, explicitly rejected the plan espoused by Mayor Bourque. Premier Bouchard was quoted as saying, "One island, one city—that's not in the picture for us. But one knows, meanwhile, that one cannot leave the situation just as it is."[55] A modest reorganization, such as one that would bring the inner suburbs of Westmount and Outremont into the city of Montreal, might have made sense to those who wanted to bolster the social and economic strength of the central city, but it would have been seen by many as an arbitrary and stopgap measure that could be achieved only at a huge political cost.

By September 1999, the option of complete amalgamation was back on the table. As with Premier Harris in Ontario when he had promised to do something about municipal structures in the Toronto area, the option of amalgamation re-emerged for Premier Bouchard after his own outer suburban MNAs rejected the option of a strong, directly elected authority for the entire Montreal region. In April 2000, at the same time as it released its white paper on municipal reform,[56] the government appointed chairs of advisory committees for municipal structures in Montreal, Quebec City, and the Outaouais area. For Montreal, the chair was Louis Bernard.

Bernard's report was made public on 11 October 2000. Although the report called for the creation of a single city of Montreal covering the entire island, it also noted that it was important "to preserve the tie between the citizens and their immediate political environment, to reinforce the feeling of being attached to the place where one lives and to favour the development of social and cultural diversity." Bernard also made reference to the need to "preserve the cultural and historical heritage of diverse communities." Nevertheless, the report made no explicit reference to language.[57] There was no evidence that Bernard consulted anyone other than municipal officials.

The report created a crucial political challenge for Montreal's larger suburban municipalities, especially the anglophone ones, because it went much further to accommodate suburban demands than anyone had predicted. Bernard proposed the creation of 27 boroughs, each to have a council that would have the authority to manage a significant range of local services and to levy a tax on property within the territory of the borough to pay for these services. Boroughs that were formerly autonomous suburbs could even maintain responsibility for negotiating collective agreements with their unions, a provision that enraged the existing unions within the city of Montreal. Never in Canadian municipal history had a serious proposal for an amalgamation been accompanied by such a high degree of political and financial decentralization. Indeed, the most compelling criticism of the Bernard plan was that it effectively involved the creation of a three-tier system of local government for the Island of Montreal: the newly created Montreal Metropolitan Community (MMC) covering the entire metropolitan area (see Chapter 7); the new city of Montreal covering the island; and the 27 boroughs.

The Bernard report caused a split within the Montreal suburban municipalities. Unlike many mayors of francophone-majority suburbs, the mayor of Westmount, Peter Trent, announced that he was completely opposed to the Bernard plan, the main reason being that suburban municipalities would lose their separate corporate existence.[58] He believed that whatever autonomy the proposed boroughs began with would inevitably be eroded as the amalgamated city of Montreal became established. On 15 November 2000, the government announced the content of Bill 170. Boroughs were not given any authority to levy taxes or to enter into collective agreements. It appeared that Premier Bouchard decided he could not take on both union and suburban opposition at the same time.[59] When suburban municipalities such as Westmount objected to the Bernard report just as strenuously as the unions in the city of Montreal, it was not surprising that Premier Bouchard opted to gain at least some significant political support by satisfying the unions and limiting the autonomy of the boroughs. Nevertheless, even without any authority over taxation and collective agreements, the boroughs were given more legal authority over local services than similar bodies that were established after amalgamation in other Canadian cities, including Halifax and Toronto.

The language issue emerged in a much more public way at the same time. The government announced that boroughs formerly within anglophone municipalities would retain their bilingual status under the Charter of the French Language. This policy required in the West Island that the territories of francophone municipalities be grouped together to form a single borough, even though their territories were not contiguous. Furthermore, the section of Bill 170 concerning Montreal opened with the declaration that "Montreal is a French-speaking city." Taken together, these various provisions indicated how carefully the government had balanced the various linguistic imperatives it faced, both from within the Parti Québécois and from the anglophone minority.

The government's careful handling of the language issue demonstrated that its imperatives were actually more important than the amalgamation itself. In many respects the very existence of the boroughs is merely a mechanism to work around the language issues that the amalgamation created. But why did the Bouchard government choose the amalgamation option in the first place? One answer, as we have seen, is that the alternative of creating a new, stronger metropolitan authority was not acceptable to its own core supporters in the outer suburbs. Just as Harris amalgamated Toronto in order to be shown to be doing something to address an apparent crisis of governance in the province's largest city, so did Bouchard amalgamate Montreal. Bouchard had the added justification that he was merely following Ontario's example.[60] Unlike Harris in Ontario, Bouchard and his colleagues pointed to the desirability of equalizing taxes and services across the new city.

The first elections for the new council of the amalgamated city of Montreal were held in November 2001. Notwithstanding his great success in promoting the amalgamation, Mayor Bourque lost his bid for re-election to Gérald Tremblay, a former provincial Liberal cabinet minister whose support was based mostly in the amalgamated suburbs.

The De-amalgamation Movement[61]

In October 2000, during the time when the legislation for amalgamation was dominating Quebec's political agenda, the opposition Liberal Party held a policy convention. One of the resolutions, approved with little deliberation or fanfare, committed the party to a policy of allowing referendums in the territories of amalgamated municipalities so that residents could de-amalgamate and re-establish their former municipalities. A few weeks later, party leader Jean Charest was wildly cheered at a large anti-amalgamation rally in the Montreal suburb of Pointe Claire when he restated his party's commitment to implementing a de-amalgamation process.

From December 2000 until March 2003, de-amalgamation was not on the agenda of Quebec politics. At one point, the Liberal critic for municipal affairs was quoted as saying that his party "would not be unhappy" if the issue went away. Unnamed aides to Mayor Tremblay stated that "senior Liberals have told them privately any provincial demerger framework law would either exclude Montreal or fix the details so as to make demergers highly unlikely."[62] There was no mention of de-amalgamation in the official Liberal platform released in September 2002. Focus instead was on the myriad complications of merging multiple bureaucracies. In many ways the Montreal amalgamation was far more difficult than Toronto's. In Montreal more than four times as many municipalities were involved. More important still was the fact that, within the borders of the old city of Montreal, the amalgamation involved decentralization to boroughs that had never existed before,[63] a factor that was totally absent from the Toronto restructuring.

Most former suburban politicians either had withdrawn from local politics completely or had become part of the power structure of the amalgamated municipality. The main exception was Peter Trent, the former mayor of Westmount. Because de-amalgamation was the only mechanism for restoring Westmount's corporate existence, he had become a fervent advocate. In mid-January 2003, he took the initiative on behalf of various anti-amalgamation citizens' groups across the province to hire a retired judge, Lawrence Poitras, to write a report about the feasibility of demergers. The report was released on 17 March 2003, five days after the beginning of the provincial election campaign that brought Jean Charest to power. On the first day of the campaign Premier Bernard Landry had attacked the Liberal position by stating that, "Just having such an idea disqualifies them from having the ambition to govern Quebec."[64] The combination of the unprovoked attack by the PQ on the idea of municipal de-amalgamation and the release of the Poitras report ensured that de-amalgamation would be an important issue during the campaign.

The Poitras report said little that was new. It did point out that, unlike Ontario, Quebec had actually experienced a few cases of de-amalgamations, notably affecting Buckingham in 1974, Gatineau in 1988, Côte-Nord-du-Golfe du Saint-Laurent in 1989, and Bonne-Espérance in 1993.[65] It claimed that inter-municipal services for de-amalgamated municipalities could be provided by a combination of special-purpose agencies and inter-municipal agreements.[66] The combination of Landry's initial attacks and the release of the Poitras report forced Charest to take a position. The same day that the Poitras report was made public, Charest stated that he was still committed, during the first year of his mandate as premier, to providing a mechanism for citizens to decide on de-amalgamation, even though he personally would not campaign for or against. Charest won the election. De-amalgamation was clearly an important issue as the Liberals unexpectedly won seats in areas where opposition to amalgamation was strong, such as in Saguenay.

Making De-amalgamation Possible

Once Mayor Tremblay of Montreal became convinced that the new Charest government was going to provide for de-amalgamation referendums, he decided he had to be able to present a viable case for keeping the amalgamated city together, so he requested that the Quebec National Assembly approve legislation (Bill 33) to allocate still more authority to the boroughs and to have their mayors (i.e., the chairs of the borough councils) directly elected. Defenders of the original amalgamation, such as the former mayor of Montreal, Pierre Bourque, objected on the grounds that borough decentralization had gone so far that the original purposes of the amalgamation were being undermined. Nevertheless, the Charest government effectively gave Tremblay what he asked for.

Formulating its legislation for the de-amalgamation process proved much more difficult. The decisions that had to be made were numerous. What would trigger a de-amalgamation referendum? How much support for de-amalgamation at the referendum would be necessary for it to be implemented? How would it be implemented? Who would pay for what?

The most important and difficult set of questions involved the nature of the subsequent relationship between any de-amalgamated municipality and the municipality from which it separated. The government decided that many common services, including firefighting, would be under the jurisdiction of an "urban agglomeration council" that would bring together representatives of both the central municipality and the de-amalgamated ones. Exactly how such a council would work was not determined until long after the de-amalgamation referendums took place.

The government's legislation stated that, for a de-amalgamation referendum to take place, 10 per cent of eligible voters within the territory of a former municipality would have to sign a petition requesting such a referendum. This happened within 87 former municipalities that formed parts of 29 amalgamated municipalities. The referendums were held on 20 June 2004.[67] For a de-amalgamation to be approved, 50 per cent of the votes cast, representing 35 per cent of the total eligible voters, had to be affirmative. This threshold was met in 31 former municipalities that were part of 12 different amalgamated municipalities. Fifteen of the affirmative decisions for demerger were within the amalgamated city of Montreal. The de-amalgamated municipalities regained their corporate identity on 1 January 2006.

Municipal Complexity in De-amalgamated Montreal

Montreal's 15 de-amalgamated municipalities have roughly the same functions and structures as they did prior to 2002, with the important exception that they are no longer responsible for firefighting. The city of Montreal, however, is now quite radically different than it was prior to 2002. The most important difference is that it now comprises 19 boroughs. These boroughs are *not* distinct corporate entities; they remain part of the municipal corporation of the city. The territory of each borough comprises one or more electoral districts of the city, each of which has a directly elected mayor who also sits on city council. All but one (Outremont) of the boroughs has at least one other city councillor on its borough council, and some have four. Because each borough council must have a minimum of five members, 40 borough councillors also are elected to serve only at that level. In total there are 64 members of the Montreal city council, including the mayor of Montreal, who also serves as the mayor of the downtown borough of Ville-Marie, and the 18 mayors of the other boroughs.[68] The borough councils have the same functional responsibilities as the de-amalgamated municipalities, but they cannot levy their own taxes without the agreement of the city council. In actual practice, boroughs rely on city council for an annual grant of funds. There are major problems with these grants because, more than 10 years after the original amalgamation, they still largely reflect patterns of expenditure at the time of amalgamation, which varied considerably especially among municipalities that were amalgamated and remained amalgamated after 2006.[69] Boroughs can hire personnel, but such personnel are employees of the city and are subject to the city's collective agreements.

Municipal functions within the city that are not the responsibility of the boroughs are the corporate responsibility of Montreal and are administered by its employees. However, decision-making with respect to these functions is the responsibility not of the Montreal city council but of the agglomeration council. The only remaining functions of the Montreal city council are to allocate funds to the boroughs and to make decisions about the position the city will take with respect to issues coming before the agglomeration council. The mayor of Montreal appoints 15 of Montreal's city councillors to the agglomeration council and 15 representatives come from the de-amalgamated municipalities. Votes are weighted according to population, so city representatives have 87 per cent of the total votes.[70] The result is that de-amalgamated municipalities have virtually no power with respect to functions under the control of the agglomeration council. They simply have to pay their share of the costs based on their relative share of property assessment within the agglomeration. Using a careful and detailed set of calculations, Peter Trent has calculated that the additional cost in Montreal resulting directly from the amalgamation is $400 million annually.[71]

Conclusions from the Quebec Experience

In the aftermath of the amalgamations and de-amalgamations of the early 2000s, there were 1,139 municipalities in Quebec,[72] down only marginally from the number at the beginning of the millennium. In 2003, when the Charest government took office, the MMC was in place, anchored at the centre by the city of Montreal, which included all of the Island of Montreal, comprising 27 boroughs having significant local authority. The MMC is still there, but 15 municipalities have de-amalgamated from the city, and the political authority of the Montreal city council has been fragmented both by the establishment of the agglomeration council and by the strengthening of the remaining 19 boroughs. How are we to assess these changes? The easiest response is to conclude that what has happened is a complete disaster. De-amalgamation has meant nothing in practice: amalgamated municipalities have been needlessly dismembered and the resulting system of inter-municipal relationships is both incomprehensible and hopelessly undemocratic. But there are other possible interpretations.

First, it is no small accomplishment that the Charest government, unlike the McGuinty government in Ontario, followed through on its promise to create a mechanism for de-amalgamation. The process was accepted as legitimate by the de-amalgamation activists who worked hard to collect signatures to trigger referendums and then, in some cases at least, to win them. Second, the government did absolutely nothing to harm the post-amalgamation fiscal position of the central cities, including the city of Montreal. De-amalgamated municipalities escaped neither old nor new fiscal burdens. What they regained was the undisputed authority to tax their property-owners to pay for local services at whatever rate they desired.

With respect to arrangements for the agglomeration council and the strengthened role for the boroughs, we can at least conclude that the Charest government was innovative. Who would have thought 10 years ago that a single Canadian municipal corporation could have three distinct levels of political decision-making authority (borough, city, agglomeration), including 19 directly elected mayors? And that superimposed on all this would be another layer of metropolitan government? Such a system exists not only in Montreal, but in Quebec City and Longueuil, as well.

Conclusion

Provincially imposed municipal amalgamations in Canada seem to have come in waves. The precedent was set in Windsor in 1935; more followed from the mid-1960s to the early 1970s, the most important being the creation of the Winnipeg unicity in 1971. From the early 1990s to the early 2000s, the eastern Canadian provinces experienced an intense period of amalgamations, with Toronto and Montreal being the most important examples. But since 2002, there have been no forced amalgamations, and Quebec has experienced de-amalgamations. What can we learn from this strange chronology?

Odd as it may seem, waves of imposed municipal amalgamations are probably best thought of as fads. One jurisdiction starts, for reasons peculiar to its own particular circumstances. Then others follow, fearing that they might somehow be falling behind. In Canada, this particular fad has been weak in the provinces west of Manitoba, although some have argued that both rural Saskatchewan and rural Manitoba are in dire need of municipal consolidation.[73] British Columbia seems to have escaped the fad altogether, perhaps because its regional districts have dealt effectively with inter-municipal services and disputes since the late 1960s. In any event, it would surely be difficult to demonstrate that the people of British Columbia are somehow worse off than other Canadians because their provincial legislature has not imposed municipal amalgamations.

At some point in the future, when a new generation of politicians knows little about our last wave of municipal amalgamations, some will trot out arguments about the need to save money, enhance economic competitiveness, or ensure equality in urban tax levels and services. They will propose municipal amalgamations as a solution. Hopefully, citizens will demand to examine carefully the experience of the 1990s and 2000s. What will the policy-makers of the future conclude?

RESOURCES

For an entertaining and instructive video by Ryan Young about how citizens of Sainte-Anne-de-Bellevue reacted to their village's forced amalgamation with the city of Montreal and how they were successful in the de-amalgamation referendum, see *The Village Resists*. The video can be downloaded from YouTube at www.youtube.com/watch?v=1KlNzgnuwpk

STUDY QUESTIONS

1. What is the significance of the Windsor amalgamation in 1935?
2. Is it possible to combine a large, amalgamated city with increased opportunities for small-scale decision-making and citizen participation? Explain your reasoning.
3. In what ways, if any, do you think amalgamation makes a city better able to compete for new economic development?
4. Do you think Premier Charest of Quebec was wise to have kept his promise to allow for a form of municipal de-amalgamation? Do you think Premier McGuinty of Ontario should have done the same thing? Explain your reasoning.

PART III

POLITICS AND MANAGEMENT IN CANADIAN URBAN GOVERNMENT

CHAPTER 9

Municipal Politics, Councils, and Elections

M uch of the material in previous chapters has been about the structures of local government: why they exist; what they do; how they have changed. Because Canada's Constitution places "municipal institutions" under provincial jurisdiction, any student of the structures of Canadian local government has to know a great deal about decisions made by provincial legislatures. So far, we have paid more attention to what provinces have decided than to how municipal councils work. In this part of the book we change our focus and begin to look at what actually goes on within municipal politics. We shall not be able to ignore provinces altogether, however, because they are responsible not just for deciding about the functions and boundaries of municipal governments, but also for making the basic rules of the game for municipal politics. We need to know about these rules in order to understand Canadian municipal politics. But understanding politics at any level involves far more than understanding formal rules. We have to understand informal rules and conventions and, more important still, we have to understand how certain people acquire power to get things done or to prevent other people from doing what they want to do. This part of the book, therefore, is primarily about power in Canadian municipal government. Chapter 9 is introductory as it outlines some of the important factors involved in understanding Canadian municipal politics, councils, and elections.

Municipal Politics and Political Parties

The formal source of power in municipal government is the municipal council, the members of which are elected. Later in this chapter we shall be examining how these elections actually work in Canada. But before getting caught up in these important details, we need to know something about how Canadians (and people in other democratic countries) have conceptualized municipal politics over time.

Municipal Politics as a Reflection of Social Elites

Anyone who has ever lived in a small town knows that many community decisions are made not in open meetings of official organizations such as municipal councils but in private, informal get-togethers of a few local notables. To the extent that this really is the case in whatever size of town we might be studying, the formal rules of municipal government are of very little importance, because everyone understands that what happens in municipal councils is a mere rubber-stamping of decisions that have already been made elsewhere. Often, the really powerful people in small towns are elected to municipal councils. If they are, their power in the community does not derive from being a municipal councillor but from being part of the small informal group that decides things. If they do not run for local office, they are not any less powerful, because real decisions are not made in the municipal council anyway.

This way of viewing power in local communities was given considerable credence in the mid-twentieth century by various American sociologists who studied *community power*. One of the most famous of these studies looked at how local decisions were made in Atlanta, Georgia. The author discovered a small and powerful elite that, indeed, effectively made most of the important local decisions, whether such decisions were formally within the purview of the municipal council or not.[1] Community power studies generated significant controversies in American political science,[2] some of which we shall address in Chapter 11.

The most comprehensive study of power in a single Canadian small town was written by David M. Rayside in 1991. It focused on Alexandria, in eastern Ontario. This is what Rayside had to say about community power in Alexandria:

> Because Alexandria's town council is preoccupied with avoiding controversy, and because initiatives for change often come from outside municipal government circles, understanding power and influence over community affairs requires complex analysis. Earlier in the area's history, political, social, and economic hierarchies coincided more clearly, and locating a single set of notable figures with influence in a variety of domains would have been relatively straightforward. . . . In late twentieth-century Alexandria, influence over community affairs in some ways still seems concentrated in a small and relatively cohesive

circle of associates, in ways that parallel the findings of much of the community power literature. In other ways, though, influence seems dispersed, hardly located within the town at all, let alone within a small circle of notables.[3]

Much of Rayside's book is aimed at showing how governmental and corporate institutions outside Alexandria were increasingly making the most important decisions for the community. This is a theme largely neglected in the American literature, in part because it was written decades earlier before such centralizing forces gained so much strength, and perhaps because American state governments have been more careful about intruding on local decisions. In any event, Rayside gives us few reasons to study small-town politics in Canada: no one wants to launch local political conflict—and important decisions for the town are made somewhere else besides.

In the early days of major Canadian cities, provincial governments established municipalities and left them relatively free to decide local issues for themselves. But cursory glances into the backgrounds of the kinds of people who tended to get elected to municipal councils suggest that service on a municipal council for a community's elite was not unlike service today on the board of a local art gallery or symphony orchestra. Election to municipal councils was "arranged" for the right people; being a member was very much part-time and continuing with one's regular business activities was completely normal. For such people, making decisions about city business was in large measure simply an extension of their other business activities.

In Canada's major cities today, membership on municipal councils is most assuredly not dominated by social and/or economic elites. The presidents of the big banks are unlikely to appear as participants in Toronto's municipal election campaigns; the same is true in Calgary of the big energy companies. Sociologists would say that this is a sign of functional specialization and role differentiation, a characteristic of all complex urban societies. But Marxist sociologists (and political scientists) would be quick to point out that such specialization and differentiation do not prevent the major economic forces in society from *controlling* decisions apparently made by democratically elected politicians. In the next chapter, we shall examine a variant of this general claim: that because the main economic role of Canadian urban municipal governments is to control urban development, these governments are really controlled by urban developers. But, whatever we might think of the general validity of Marxist analysis in the early twenty-first century, we must, in our analyses of municipal decision-making, keep in mind the possibility that governmental structures and elections might not be very important, because economic forces—some difficult to observe and to understand—might be the key determinants of local political outcomes. A related possibility, explicitly stated by Rayside, is that important decisions for most local communities are made somewhere else by big corporations or by central (provincial or federal) governments.

Municipal Politics and National Parties

By the mid- to late nineteenth century, a larger proportion of adult males had been granted the vote and political parties had become increasingly important in mobilizing voters. In Europe, working-class voters were mobilized primarily by parties on the left: Marxist or social democratic. In North American cities, where there were usually many recent immigrants, parties often mobilized votes through "urban political machines."[4] The key characteristic of such machines was that their organizers (or "bosses") promised material rewards—often, jobs—in return for votes. In the United States, a huge amount of literature is devoted to these urban political machines, much of it attempting to determine whether their levels of obvious corruption were justified by the great social gains experienced by the ethnic groups (especially the Irish) who benefited from their newly found political power.

Bosses of American urban political machines were key figures in national political parties—usually the Democrats, but not always. As recently as 1960, the boss of Chicago's Democratic machine played a key role in the election of John F. Kennedy to the presidency of the United States, perhaps by dumping a few crucial ballot boxes into Lake Michigan instead of having them tilt Illinois towards Kennedy's opponent, Richard Nixon. By promising electoral support for state and national political candidates, urban bosses could gain more resources (jobs, contracts, projects) for their own supporters. Regardless of their national importance, these bosses maintained considerable local autonomy. In Europe, however, socialist parties tended to run candidates at all levels of government, and candidates for local office often had little room to manoeuvre in addressing local issues.

Some examples of urban political machines and of socialist parties in local politics crop up in Canada but, compared to elsewhere, they have been minimal. On the other hand, and more so than perhaps in any other democratic country, Canadian municipal politics is generally not influenced by national political parties. Again, unlike most federations, Canada has political parties at the federal and provincial levels that—except for the

New Democratic Party (NDP)—are structurally separate from each other. Because municipalities are under provincial jurisdiction, we might at least expect *provincial* parties to be involved in municipal politics, but little evidence suggests that is the case. To understand why, we must know about the reform movement that transformed the politics of North American cities over a hundred years ago.

The Era of Municipal Reform

By the second half of the nineteenth century, large cities in North America had become unhealthy, dirty, and corrupt. The urban reform (or Progressive) movement was about cleansing cities, in every sense of the word. The movement marked the beginning of professional social work, urban planning, public health, public libraries, and serious attempts to promote temperance and honest and efficient municipal government. This last concern is most relevant to our focus. With regard to municipal government, reformers wanted to rid the cities of political machines, most obviously by minimizing the role of political parties in municipal politics. They proposed various institutional reforms to achieve this objective, some of which will be examined later. For the current discussion, we need only consider their desire to have small city councils composed of members elected not for their party qualifications but for their potential to make policy decisions based on the overall best interests of the city. Reformers wanted the administrative apparatus of the city to be taken from party hacks and turned over to trained professionals headed by a city manager, someone with special skills in coordinating and controlling a wide range of city services in accordance with modern administrative practices.

The North American reform movement had strong support in Canada, especially in the largest cities, Montreal and Toronto.[5] As other cities grew larger, especially in Western Canada, reform influence spread there as well. For our purposes in this section, the most important effect of the reform movement was to convince most Canadian urban municipal voters that political parties served no purpose in municipal politics because they introduced political factors into decisions that should be based only on sound business-like and technical principles. One of the best-known reform maxims was that "There is no political way to pave a road." In pre-reform times, road-building was assumed to be the lucrative privilege of the supporters of whoever was in power. One of the great reform accomplishments was to convince most people that contracts for roadwork (and other municipal activities) should go only to those who can best balance quality and price. A hundred years ago, decisions to build particular roads were generally assumed to be good decisions; now decisions about building particular roads are almost always subject to genuine political debate. In short, it remains the case that there is no political way to pave a road; the only way to get approval to build a road is through a political process, usually in a municipality.

Because of the ongoing influence of the reform movement, most candidates and voters in municipal politics seem to value the non-partisan approach. They do not want political parties of any kind to be overtly involved in municipal elections, even though parties often play important roles that are generally invisible, except to the most careful of observers. Especially in smaller cities, it is common for successful candidates to proclaim their independence from all parties and their attachment to making decisions in accordance with "sound business principles." Few of the candidates who make such declarations are aware that they are in fact parroting the talk of anti-party reformers from over a hundred years ago.

Local Political Parties in Canada

An important student of American urban politics, Paul Peterson, has suggested that political parties that exist solely at the municipal level cannot be sustained because the issues are not sufficiently important.[6] In national politics, parties are formed and sustained around major political issues such as war and peace, free trade, and social class. The media pay close attention to what the parties do, and individual voters form relatively long-lasting party attachments of varying degrees of intensity. Such factors generally do not exist at the municipal level. The main political cleavage in municipal politics is often between pro-development and anti-development groups, but such a division seems incapable of generating ongoing party allegiances, perhaps because people's attitudes to development tend to be affected by where it is taking place (near or far from home) or the state of the local economy at any particular point in time. In any event, two major Canadian cities—Vancouver and Montreal—provide evidence to suggest that, in the Canadian context at least, Peterson might be wrong.

Vancouver

In the 1936 Vancouver municipal election, candidates from the Co-operative Commonwealth Federation (CCF, predecessor of the current NDP) won three of eight seats on the city council. As we have seen, the idea of socialists running for municipal office was not unusual, especially during the Depression. But their success caused local Liberals, Conservatives, and business people to come together in 1937 to form the Non-Partisan Association (NPA). By the end of the decade the CCF "was spent as a municipal force."[7] The NPA—a political group that runs candidates in municipal elections and that is committed to keeping party politics out of municipal government—has been a dominant force in Vancouver politics ever since.

In the late 1960s, two other local parties formed: the Committee of Progressive Electors (COPE) and The Electors Action Movement (TEAM). COPE was clearly on the left of the political spectrum; TEAM was in the centre. In 1972, TEAM's candidate for mayor, Art Phillips, won the election. When Mike Harcourt was mayor as an independent between 1980 and 1986, he was generally supported on council by TEAM. Harcourt later became leader of the provincial NDP and premier of British Columbia, but TEAM faded away. Gordon Campbell was the NPA mayor of Vancouver from 1986 to 1993 and the province's Liberal premier from 2001 until 2011. COPE controlled the Vancouver city council from 2002 to 2005, with its leader, Larry Campbell (whose previous work as city coroner inspired a TV show, *Da Vinci's Inquest*), as mayor.[8] But COPE could not survive the stresses of governing. Larry Campbell decided not to run again and was appointed to the Senate in Ottawa as a Liberal. Politically moderate members of COPE split away to form Vision Vancouver, which took control of the Vancouver city council in 2008 when its leader, Gregor Robertson, became mayor. The most recent NPA mayor of Vancouver was Sam Sullivan, who governed the city from 2005 to 2008.

Montreal

In 1954, the Civic Action League, a citizens' group committed to cleaning up corruption in Montreal, decided to run candidates for municipal office. Its mayoral candidate was Jean Drapeau. To everyone's surprise, Drapeau won his election, but the League did not win control of the council. In 1957, Drapeau was defeated by Sarto Fournier, a Liberal senator who also had the support of Premier Maurice Duplessis. When Drapeau ran again in 1960, he created his own Civic Party, which was totally under his personal control. With Drapeau as mayor, it controlled Montreal city council for 26 years, thereby becoming the most successful municipal political party in Canadian history. During that time Montreal built its subway system (the Métro) and hosted Expo 67 and the 1976 Olympic Games. The Civic Party effectively ceased to exist when Drapeau decided not to seek re-election in 1986.

Since that time, three separate municipal parties have held majorities on the Montreal city council: the Montreal Citizens' Movement (MCM) led by Mayor Jean Doré (1986–93);[9] Vision Montreal, with Mayor Pierre Bourque (1994–2001); and the Montreal Island Citizens' Union, which became Union Montreal in 2007, with Mayor Gérald Tremblay (2002–13). The MCM was a left-leaning party that had opposed Mayor Drapeau for many years. After losing the 1993 municipal election, it went into a period of decline before merging with Tremblay's party in 2001. Mayors Drapeau, Bourque, and Tremblay constructed their own parties in order to win the mayor's office and a majority on city council. In 2009, Vision Montreal chose a new leader and candidate for mayor, Louise Harel, the former Parti Québécois Minister of Municipal Affairs who had sponsored the legislation for amalgamation in Montreal. Although she failed to defeat Mayor Tremblay, she certainly perpetuated Vision Montreal as a strong opposition party and as a defender of a strong and centralized city of Montreal. Union Montreal, on the other hand, supported the decentralized borough system that Mayor Tremblay implemented in a fruitless attempt to prevent de-amalgamation in 2004. Union Montreal collapsed in 2013 when it became apparent that some of its members were involved in widespread corruption involving construction contracts in Montreal.[10] Vision Montreal changed its name in 2013, and in the elections of that year, Louise Harel lost her seat, and her candidate for mayor finished fourth. The victor was former federal Liberal cabinet minister Denis Coderre, but he obtained only 32 per cent of the mayoral vote and his "party," Team Denis Coderre for Montreal, won only 27 of 65 council seats. The main opposition party, Projet Montréal, which is primarily interested in environmental issues, won 20.[11] All these developments suggest that Montreal's municipal party system could well be in the process of breaking down.

Provincial Support for Municipal Parties

Quebec and British Columbia are the only provinces in which municipal election laws provide for the existence of municipal parties, although in the latter they are referred to as "elector organizations" or "slates." The BC law even governs contests to seek nominations from elector organizations or slates, and the Quebec law provides that party candidates rely exclusively on party fundraising and expenditures, half of which is refunded by the municipality for all candidates (including independents) who receive more than 15 per cent of the total vote.[12] Quebec law also provides that both government and opposition parties in municipal councils of cities with populations over 50,000 receive municipal funding for staff and research.

But as we have seen, even such provincial support does not guarantee the stability of municipal political parties. If anything, all it guarantees is that different municipal politicians at different elections will try to create their own temporary parties in order to benefit from various provisions of the law, such as getting the party name on the ballot or (in Quebec) receiving public subsidies for election campaigns. The most stable municipal political parties in Canada have been the NPA in Vancouver, which is committed to keeping political parties out of municipal politics, and the Civic Party in Montreal, which lasted no longer than its founder's career as mayor. Arguably the NPA is stable because its members share ideological interests in defeating attempts by NDP supporters to control the Vancouver city council. Perhaps Vision Vancouver will be more successful in unifying such people into a cohesive local party on the left of the political spectrum.

Whether or not there are political parties in municipal councils is a key question in the governance of our major cities. Many (including, no doubt, those in the NPA in Vancouver) will agree with the reformers of more than a hundred years ago that parties have no place in municipal government and that municipal councils should be more like boards of directors of large businesses than like provincial or federal legislatures. Others look enviously at the political coherence and predictability provided by a prime minister or premier backed by a disciplined majority party, and wish that such a state of affairs could be replicated in municipal government, as it has been for much of Montreal's recent history.[13] But the problem here, of course, is that many citizens do not want city governments that seem as remote and centralized as a majority government in a parliamentary system. How could ordinary citizens mobilize to convince such a government to change its mind on important issues about local development, for example? Some would point to Mayor Drapeau's Montreal as the horrible example of how strong local parties eliminate meaningful local participation. Others will point to Drapeau's accomplishments and conclude that we need parties such as his to enable municipal leaders to achieve ambitious goals. As we confront various issues in this and later chapters relating to city governance, the desirability or undesirability of municipal political parties will never be far from the surface.

Size and Structure of Municipal Councils

Councils are the formal decision-making mechanisms for municipalities. How they are structured is important both for municipal elections and for the process of decision-making. Provincial legislation ultimately determines how municipal councils are structured, but this same legislation often allows municipal councils to make some structural decisions themselves. In this section we shall be less concerned with the sources of legal authority for structural decisions and more concerned with the nature and implications of the various structural alternatives. There are three main variables in studying council structures:

- size;
- representation by wards or at-large, or some combination of both; and
- committee system.

It is important to realize that these three variables are connected with each other and, to a lesser extent, with the existence or not of municipal political parties. In the *parliamentary* model of municipal councils, which has historically been present in Britain and other European countries, we expect to find political parties in large councils where members are elected by wards (i.e., electoral districts) and in which much important business is carried out by council committees. In the *reformed* or *council-manager* model found in many American smaller towns and suburbs and in some Canadian ones, we find the absence of political parties, small councils elected at-large (i.e., all members elected from the entire municipal territory), and no committees. As we shall see, however, municipal councils in most major Canadian cities do not fit neatly into one model or the other.

Council Size

When we consider the universe of municipal councils in Canada, we must not forget that there are not only single-tier municipalities but also the 2 supra-regional authorities and 86 regional or upper-tier municipalities in Quebec, 30 in Ontario, 27 in British Columbia, and 12 in New Brunswick. Listed in Table 9.1 are the populations and sizes of the councils for the 2 supra-regional authorities, the 2 largest regional ones, and the 10 largest single- or lower-tier ones (all numbers include the mayor and/or presiding officer).

There are two ways to assess council size. The first has to do with the number of residents per councillor. By this measure, the supra-regional and regional authorities listed here are irrelevant, because all of their members are elected to serve also at the lower tier. In other words, the existence of these authorities adds nothing to the total number of councillors in the area. For those concerned only with the costs of having councillors, it would seem that, in theory at least, it would be better to have more people per councillor than fewer. In this regard, Calgary is the most efficient council in the country, with each member serving an average of about 73,000 people. Although Ontario's Progressive Conservative government in the 1990s led by Mike Harris took great pride in reducing the total number of municipal politicians in the province, there is no inherent virtue in having fewer elected municipal politicians rather than more. Even if cost is the only criterion—and it surely cannot be in a democratic society—it is likely that individual councillors serving large numbers of residents (as in Calgary) will require more support staff to do their job, thereby limiting the savings associated with having fewer councillors. The exact cost of councils in various municipalities can be empirically investigated, but obtaining comparable data across municipalities is difficult.[14] In any event, contrary to common public perceptions, the costs attributed to councils are never more than 1 per cent of municipal operating budgets, and are usually considerably less, so whenever concerns about such costs are expressed, they are inevitably exaggerated.

The issue of council size was debated in Halifax from 2009 to 2011. From its creation in 1996 (see Chapter 8), the Halifax Regional Municipality (HRM) was governed by a mayor and 23 councillors. The provincial law governing HRM (the Halifax Regional Municipality Charter) requires the HRM council to review the size of the council and the ward boundaries (called *polling districts* in Nova Scotia) every eight years. After a long and complex discussion in 2010, the council decided to maintain 23 councillors for the 2012 election. As required by the HRM Charter, this decision was reviewed by three members of the Nova Scotia Utility and Review Board. The issue was controversial because HRM council had rejected various pleas from citizens to reduce the size of the council. The board held hearings on the matter in 2011. Witnesses included HRM staff, interested citizens and, of special interest for our purposes, two political scientists with expertise on Canadian local government. Jack Novack of Dalhousie University was one of the witnesses "on behalf of the municipality," and Robert Williams, retired from the University of Waterloo, provided expert advice direct to the board. Novack cautioned board members against "changing the size of council under the guise of more efficient and effective decision making." He went on:

Notwithstanding, over the past 16 years since amalgamation, HRM councillors have tried to make amalgamation work by making decisions that balanced the array of divergent interests that naturally reside within this political entity. This is a large and difficult challenge given the size and complexity of the HRM. Assuming that these difficulties can be addressed and overcome by an arbitrary reduction in the number of councillors is to unnecessarily simplify the nature of the debate.[15]

The board noted in its decision, however, that Novack acknowledged "that he had not done any research to support any particular number"[16] for the ideal size of a municipal council.

Much of Williams' testimony was related to the inadequacies of the review process carried out by the HRM council. Like Novack, Williams acknowledged that there was no evidence to support a case that one size of council was better than another. He did, however, caution that cutting the council by one-third (to 16), as had been suggested by some, was "inviting consequences that really haven't been thought through."[17] Despite Williams's warning, the board did exactly that: it decided that, starting with the 2012 municipal election, the HRM council would comprise a mayor and 16 councillors. It justified its position by stating that it was responding to the demonstrated preferences of the citizens who expressed their views at various stages in the process, and by stating that the reduction was needed to bring HRM closer to other Canadian municipalities of similar size in terms of the ratio of councillors to population. HRM is not included in Table 9.1 because it is only the fourteenth most populous municipality in Canada. With a 2011 population of 390,096 and with 17 members of council, its number of residents per councillor is 22,947.

Most Canadian councils have memberships between about 7 and 25. Councillors sit around a table, often shaped like a horseshoe, with the mayor presiding. In this setting they interact directly with each other and occasionally convince their colleagues to change their minds on the basis of new information and new arguments. Although there might be factions on the council, voting alliances usually shift from issue to issue. Such meetings can be very messy, with much confusion about wording of motions and the implications of various courses of action. But decisions get made, and some get reported in the local media. More than any other venue in the Canadian governmental system, a relatively small non-partisan municipal council is a place to watch representative democracy in action. Much of what goes on in public in federal and provincial legislatures is political theatre and has little to do with decision-making. In

Table 9.1 Sizes of Canadian Municipal Councils

	Population	Number of Councillors	Residents per Councillor
Supra-regional			
Montreal Metropolitan Community	3,700,000	28	
Quebec Metropolitan Community	760,000	17	
Regional			
Metro Vancouver	2,313,328	40	
Regional Municipality of Peel	1,296,814	25	
Single- or lower-tier			
Toronto	2,615,060	45	58,112
Montreal[a]	1,649,519	65	25,377
Calgary	1,096,833	15	73,122
Ottawa	883,391	24	36,808
Edmonton	812,201	13	26,477
Mississauga[b]	713,443	12	59,454
Winnipeg	663,617	16	41,476
Vancouver[b]	603,502	11	54,864
Brampton[b]	523,991	11	47,635
Hamilton	519,949	16	32,497

[a] Indicates the municipality is part of a supra-regional authority. Number of council members does not include councillors serving only at the borough level.

[b] Indicates municipality is a lower-tier municipality in a two-tier system.

Sources: Websites of the relevant municipalities, and the 2011 Census of Canada.

these systems, real decisions get made in party caucuses and in cabinets, but such meetings are not open to the public or the media. Openness of municipal council meetings is an important issue and will be discussed below.

Wards versus At-Large Elections

It generally is agreed in democratic societies that elections should determine who holds public office, but much disagreement prevails about how the electoral systems should work. For example, in Canadian federal and provincial politics, numerous proposals are put forward to switch from a system in which legislatures are composed of individuals who obtain the most votes in particular electoral districts to one in which multiple members are elected from much larger districts in accordance with the relative strength of the various parties. The problem with the current system is that, if a Liberal wins each district with 51 per cent of the vote, Liberals will occupy all the seats in the legislature. The problems with the alternative system are that there are no longer distinct local members, and party organizations attain considerable power in determining who gets elected. In the general absence of parties in municipal politics in Canada, there is no way that the second system—proportional representation—could be implemented. But that has not stopped frequent searches for better systems.

In Canadian municipal government, electoral districts are generally known as wards. Most large municipalities (except in BC) are divided into wards, and in most cases the one candidate at an election who gets the most votes is declared the councillor for that ward. But in some municipalities, more than one member is elected from each ward. In these cases, voters in each ward have as many votes as there are councillors to be elected. If two are to be elected, the top two vote-getters are the winners.

Three main questions associated with drawing ward boundaries are:

- Should they be relatively equal in population?
- Should they attempt to encompass particular "communities of interest" and, if so, which ones?
- Who draws the boundaries and when?

Population

The idea that wards should have roughly equal population would appear to be self-evident in a democracy where the objective, presumably, is to make everyone's vote in a given municipality roughly equal in weight. There can be debates about whether the measure of ward size should be based on population or on the number of eligible voters. Some parts of particular municipalities might contain relatively higher numbers of people too young to vote, or recent immigrants who are non-citizens.[18] In most cases, population is the measure, justified on the grounds that the person who is elected has to represent all residents, not just those who are eligible to vote.

In the last decade in Ontario, however, the effects of some municipal amalgamations have caused the issue of equal populations of wards to be revisited. The problem is that some amalgamated municipalities have large areas of rural land in which relatively few people live. Prior to amalgamation, such people were used to governing themselves in their own rural-based municipalities. After amalgamation, they found themselves swamped by urban voters with little interest in rural issues. The rural people felt the least that could be done for them was to establish rural wards with smaller populations. When Ottawa refused to do this in the early 2000s, rural residents appealed to the Ontario Municipal Board. In a 2003 decision, the OMB overturned a city bylaw establishing wards that generally mixed rural and suburban areas. In the decision, the OMB stated:

> The evidence supports the contention that the City of Ottawa does contain rural communities with historical economic and social differences. Rural concerns are not always understood in the context of urban policy and rural concerns often require a special understanding of rural issues. Members of council elected by urban voters may not always have the experience or the willingness to represent rural points of view. One-dimensional representation will eventually be harmful to the local economy.[19]

The end result was the establishment of three rural wards whose average population was 34 per cent lower than the average for the city as a whole.[20] Such an arrangement would have been illegal in Quebec because legislation relating to municipal elections provides that "the number of electors in an electoral district must not deviate by more than 25 per cent from the average for municipalities with less than 20,000 inhabitants. This percentage is 15 per cent for municipalities with over 20,000 inhabitants."[21] In Halifax, following its decision to reduce the size of the HRM council to 16, the Nova Scotia Utilities and Review Board approved new ward boundaries in which the least populous of the wards was only 18.8 per cent lower than the average,[22] notwithstanding the fact that the territory of the HRM is about twice that of the City of Ottawa.

Communities of Interest

The OMB decision on the Ottawa wards recognized that rural areas comprise communities of interest that should have their own wards. But how are communities of interest determined in urban areas? First, it should be recognized that, however they are defined, urban communities of interest are unlikely to have populations of similar size, so it is unlikely that each could ever have its own ward. If different neighbourhoods have to be put together or split, how should it be done? One way is to build wards along major arteries leading into the core area, thereby creating "pie-shaped" wards. Another way is to unite areas of similar social class or ethnic backgrounds. The latter approach is more commonly accepted. In a 2003 decision about wards in London, Ontario, the OMB stated:

> It seems obvious to the Board that a pie-shaped Ward system could be inequitable based upon "communities of interest" because in each Ward there are more votes in the outer suburban areas. A possible result could be that suburban "communities of interest" are overprotected by City Council to the detriment of other "communities of interest."[23]

Who Decides and When?

Municipal councils generally are responsible for drawing ward boundaries, but, as we have seen above with respect to Ontario, some form of appeal from council decisions usually exists—which is entirely appropriate because incumbent councillors do have a special interest in how the boundaries are drawn. In Quebec, municipal councils are required to review the boundaries every four years prior to a municipal election. In other provinces, including Ontario, councils are not required to regularly review boundaries. As a result, wards can become quite unequal in population over time without the council taking any action at all.[24] Ontario citizens can appeal to the OMB to take action, but such appeals are rare.

At-Large Elections—Vancouver

Reformers a hundred years ago wanted to get rid of wards. They thought that ward councillors were largely incapable of looking at the interests of the city as a whole and meddled too much in administrative matters affecting their wards. Similar criticisms are made today,[25] which explains why some continue to extol the virtues of at-large municipal elections in which all councillors are elected by all voters in the entire municipality. There is no reason why ward and at-large elections cannot coexist. Indeed, this is exactly what happens in Thunder Bay, Ontario, where five councillors (and the mayor) are elected at-large and seven more are elected from each of seven wards.

A strong case can be made against at-large elections. Indeed, the United States Supreme Court has struck down local at-large electoral systems on the grounds that they can submerge the electoral strength of racial minorities. If a racial minority made up 40 per cent of the population of a city and if they were concentrated in a particular area (which is usually the case), they could easily end up with no council representatives if the majority voted as a bloc against minority candidates. But such a

possibility has not prevented British Columbia from legislating a municipal electoral system in which at-large elections are the default option for
all municipalities. No municipality has opted for wards.[26] The issue has
been particularly controversial in Vancouver, and it merits our attention.

Vancouver's history with at-large elections is a fascinating story, told
well by Thomas R. Berger in the opening pages of his 2004 report on
electoral reform in Vancouver. The following account closely follows
Berger's.[27] After incorporation in 1886, Vancouver voters elected a mayor
and 10 councillors, all at-large. But the third bylaw passed by the council
established a five-ward system for the next election in which two councillors were elected from each ward. Except for a brief "interregnum" from
1920 to 1923 when the city experimented with a form of proportional representation, Vancouver operated with a ward system until 1936, although
the number of wards was occasionally increased. Starting in 1916, only
one member was elected from each ward. In 1935 both business groups
and the CCF (not an unusual alliance among reformers) convinced the
provincial government to hold a referendum on an at-large system for
Vancouver. With only a 19 per cent turnout, 69 per cent of voters supported the change and the city has had an at-large system ever since.

After World War II, the at-large system became deeply unpopular
with left-leaning citizens who watched the NPA dominate elections and
saw few residents of the poorer east side of the city get elected to city
council. In a referendum in 1973, 58.9 per cent of voters rejected a return
to a ward system. In 1978, 51.7 per cent approved such a change but the
commission charged with implementation designed such a complex new
system that the council refused to approve it. Not surprisingly, the city
held another referendum in 1983, and a ward system was approved by
57 per cent of the voters. By this time, the issue had become extremely
polarized between left and right, with conservatives seeming to believe
that wards were a kind of Communist plot. In any event, the (conservative) Social Credit premier, Bill Bennett, decided that he would only
approve of a ward system if 60 per cent voted in favour, and this requirement was written into law. In a referendum in 1988, 56 per cent voted in
favour of wards but, in accordance with the law, nothing happened. By
1996, the 60 per cent rule had been repealed, but Vancouver city council
drafted "a confusing multi-question referendum that produced a 59 per
cent majority in favour of retaining the at-large system, with a 54 per cent
margin favouring wards if the existing system were to be changed."[28]
Once again, nothing happened.

In his 2004 report (p. 40), Berger recommended a 14-ward system with one councillor from each ward. He pointed out that west-side

residents were much more likely to vote than east-side residents (39.2 per cent and 31.5 per cent respectively in 2002). With a ward system, a lower turnout rate would not affect the ability of east-siders to obtain their own representation, but with an at-large system it did. Another referendum was held in October 2004, and this time there was a 54 per cent majority in favour of retaining the at-large system. Analysis of results by polling district suggests, not surprisingly, that the wealthier west side voted in favour of the at-large system and the poorer east side voted for wards. Polls near the centre of the Indo-Canadian community supported wards (as one would expect from a geographically concentrated minority group), but polls where many Chinese Canadians lived were against.[29] Wards remain an important issue for some voters but most elected officials, including the Vision Vancouver members who control the council in 2014, do not seem enthusiastic about taking it up yet again. In no other Canadian city—and possibly in no other major world city—have issues about the nature of the municipal voting system been so important in local politics.

Committee Systems

Most municipal councils, especially larger ones, establish a network of council committees to facilitate their work. Council committees are different from special-purpose bodies because the former are made up exclusively of councillors and they have no legal authority to make any decisions unless they have explicitly received delegated authority from the council as a whole. They also must be distinguished from citizens' advisory committees, whose members usually are appointed by council from among ordinary citizens to advise on particular topics. Council committees are usually one of two types: *standing* and *special*. Standing committees are permanent, although membership might change relatively frequently. They are charged with reviewing particular kinds of agenda items (roads, land-use planning, corporate services, etc.) before those items are decided on by council as a whole. In larger municipalities, standing committees are especially suitable as a mechanism to hear delegations from the general public prior to decision-making. As the name implies, special committees are established for a particular purpose and cease to exist when the purpose has been accomplished.

Some councils establish executive committees that, because of their leadership responsibilities, will be discussed in Chapter 11. At the opposite extreme is a *committee of the whole*, which is nothing more than the whole council meeting under relaxed rules of order. Committees of the whole are used by many councils whenever they want to engage in extended and informal discussions of a particular topic. They are also often used by councils—especially by councils that do not have standing committees—as a mechanism for hearing delegations from citizens. Because all committees must report formally to the council, committees of the whole present the unusual spectacle of a group of people reporting to itself.

Strange as it may seem to some, committee systems can be controversial. Experience with committees in some municipalities in the past suggests that, if councillors stay on particular standing committees for a long time, they can come to think that they (rather than staff) are actually meant to be administering the service or function, rather than advising the council as a whole about policy decisions that need to be taken. This has been a particular concern in rural areas, such as in Ontario counties, where councils can sometimes be large and administrative staff relatively weak. Sometimes councillors can get so wrapped up in the business of their particular committee that they simply do not pay much attention to other issues facing the council, assuming that members of other committees are looking after other business. To the extent that this pattern exists, no one is looking after the interests of the municipality as a whole.

Reformers in the early twentieth century were particularly concerned about the toxic combination of powerful standing committees and ward councillors whose sole focus was on their own wards. For such people, membership on the roads committee, for example, was simply a mechanism for getting better roads in their own wards. This problem is just one of many reasons why reformers favoured small councils, at-large elections, weak committees, and highly qualified staff. As we have seen, the city of Vancouver fits this model. Its council does have standing committees, but all members are on all committees. The committees serve mainly as mechanisms to hear delegations from the public, not as potentially independent sources of decision-making power.

In large cities with large city councils, such as Toronto, committees are essential. Without them, items of municipal business would never be properly considered because each of the thousands of items before council each year could not possibly be fully debated by the entire council. As it is, agendas are filled because all recommendations from standing committees need to be approved by the full council before being implemented. At least council members with minimal interest in particular items know that the items likely have been properly reviewed in the appropriate committee.

Openness of Meetings and of Votes in Municipal Councils

Unless provincial statutes state otherwise, municipal councils can make their own rules about the extent to which their meetings will be open or closed to the media and the public.[30] Many provincial statutes originally included provisions stating that regular council meetings were to be open to the public but that the council could decide to go *in camera* (into a closed meeting) at its discretion. Such discretion was necessary. If, for example, the council were deliberating about how much money it would be willing to pay for a parcel of land, a public discussion would disadvantage the municipality in any negotiations with the seller. In extreme cases, however, some councils used their discretion to form a committee of the whole, discuss virtually all items of business *in camera*, and then rubber-stamp the decisions after the committee reports to the open council meeting. Such action caused much media and public discontent, causing provincial legislatures to approve various laws to tighten the rules. Ironically, any provincial cabinet that formulated such legislation prior to its introduction in the legislature would meet in private, so the public would not know the original positions of the various ministers on such matters. Legislatures have little difficulty meeting in public because, prior to debates, the government and even the opposition have already worked out their positions. Unlike municipal councils, legislatures rarely have to make decisions about ongoing negotiations with private bodies or individuals.

In most provinces it is now extremely difficult for councils to meet in private unless they explicitly declare that they are dealing with such matters as commercial transactions, labour relations, personnel issues affecting identifiable individuals, or the receipt of legal advice. Laws about open meetings generally extend to informal meetings or to "retreats" at which councillors might be expected to plot long-term strategy in a relaxed atmosphere away from the media and the public.[31] In short, municipal councils are required to carry out their public business in public. Although enforcement mechanisms vary from province to province, there must now be very few municipal councillors in Canada who are not aware of the legal requirements for openness.

Recent disputes about open meetings, especially in Ontario, have involved informal gatherings of municipal councillors—or telephone conversations—during which municipal business is discussed. The Ontario ombudsman, who has jurisdiction to act as a *closed meeting investigator* when a municipality has not appointed someone else to do the job, claims that a meeting takes place when members come together "for the purpose of doing the groundwork necessary to exercise" their power or authority.[32] Such a broad definition—apparently not based in any Ontario law or relevant jurisprudence—has caused considerable concern among many members of Ontario municipal councils. Any informal discussion among councillors about municipal business is potentially a "meeting." Must all their discussions about municipal business take place within the confines of formal meetings? If so, is this not a recipe for the holding of even more confused and lengthy meetings than are held already? Why should municipal politicians be at such a disadvantage in relation to federal and provincial politicians? Who will want to be elected to a municipal council if their capacity to talk informally with their colleagues is so limited?

The British Columbia ombudsperson has been more flexible. She has issued a document that, while not clear about the definition of a *meeting*, at least provides some useful guidance.

A gathering is less likely a meeting if:

- there is no quorum of board, council, or committee members present;
- the gathering takes place in a location not under the control of the council or board members;
- it is not a regularly scheduled event;
- it does not follow formal procedures;
- no voting occurs; and/or
- those in attendance are gathered strictly to receive information or to receive or provide training.

A gathering is more likely a meeting if:

- a quorum of council, board, or committee members are present;
- it takes place at the council or board's normal meeting place or in an area completely under the control of the council or board;
- it is a regularly scheduled event;
- formal procedures are followed;
- the attendees hold a vote; and/or
- the attendees are discussing matters that would normally form the basis of the council's business, and dealing with the matters in a way that moves them toward the possible application of the council's authority.[33]

Curiously, the BC ombudsperson makes no reference to *electoral organizations* or *slates*. To what extent do municipal councillors elected on the same slate in BC consult with each other about municipal business? To what extent is such consultation acceptable under the ombudsman's guidelines? If councillors in Ontario were elected on a slate, could they consult with each other about what they wanted to accomplish within particular council meetings? According to the Ontario ombudsman, it would appear not. Writing for a provincial commission on freedom of information in 1979, one of Canada's foremost municipal lawyers, Stanley M. Makuch, addressed this exact issue:

> Some members of a municipal council may decide that they have a common political perspective and may wish to meet together to discuss positions they should take on particular issues and to formulate policy proposals and strategies for having these proposals passed. . . . In effect, these groupings are similar to the political parties found at the federal and provincial levels of government and should be allowed to caucus in private under the open meetings provisions.[34]

According to the Ontario ombudsman, something has apparently changed since 1979 that would make it all but impossible for groups of councillors in Ontario to form municipal political parties. But he has never explained what that change might be.

Open meetings imply that the voting decisions of individual members of council on items of council business also are public. Sometimes, tracking down councillors' voting records is difficult. Most decisions in most councils are made without any vote—they are deemed to be approved because no one objects. If all such items were included in any analysis of council votes, there would be little variation among members because the vast majority of all votes cast would be affirmative. For other matters, however, votes in many councils are taken by an informal show of hands, and no record is kept unless a councillor requests a recorded vote. If the recorded vote is taken orally, then members at the end of the roll call can take account of others' votes as they decide what to do. Electronic voting prevents such a problem and leaves a clear record about who has voted for what on every issue about which there is disagreement. Municipal decision-making will be more transparent and open when all councils have adopted such technology.

Is Being a Municipal Councillor a Full-Time Job?[35]

In principle, every municipal councillor can decide how he or she wants to do the job. In a small municipality, where remuneration is negligible, a councillor with lots of time and independent financial resources could work on municipal business all the time. In large municipalities, where councillors might get paid around $100,000 annually (not counting budgets for office supplies and staff support), a councillor could still carry on a private business, only showing up for the occasional meeting at city hall. Re-election, of course, would be unlikely because attentive media would soon note the slacking off. The point here is that there is really no job description for a municipal councillor. Even within the same municipality, councillors take radically different approaches to their jobs, which is not necessarily a problem—variety among democratic representatives is not wrong.

But councils do have to make decisions that affect the nature of the job and, therefore, the kind of people who run for municipal office. Such decisions are of particular importance in mid-sized cities, where expectations of municipal councillors might be ambiguous. One such decision seems very simple on the surface: when to schedule official meetings of council and its committees. If meetings are regularly held in the daytime, the implication is that being a councillor prevents regular full-time employment. The attendant implication is that remuneration should be relatively high, unless the assumption is that council membership really is being reserved for retirees, autonomous professionals (e.g., lawyers in private practice), or people with independent incomes. But what does a "relatively high" income mean? For a recent university graduate, the prospect of earning $80,000 a year as a councillor might seem enormously attractive; the attraction might be considerably less for a 40-year-old accountant with three children and a mortgage.

For reformers who wanted to minimize the role of traditional politics in municipal government, the favoured policy would be to hold evening meetings and pay councillors relatively little. The expectation would be that councillors would stay clear of details and show up at council meetings only to make decisions on matters presented to them by their highly qualified staff of municipal professionals. Attractive as such a model might seem, it runs into difficulty when residents expect councillors to respond immediately to requests for help with neighbourhood issues or when the local media uncover improper actions by trusted municipal staff. In fact, the pressure in municipal government is towards making the position of councillor closer to full-time rather than to part-time. In many cities, councillors are expected to attend meetings at city hall in the day and meetings with residents in the evenings. The job becomes more than full-time and not suitable for people with young families, even if remuneration is exceptionally high.

As the job of councillor becomes closer to full-time, municipalities as organizations become much more complex. The old reform-style model of a professional staff working in isolation from politicians—except at times of formal meetings—becomes totally out of touch with reality. In our major cities today, councillors are interacting with staff at all levels all the time. In places like Toronto, members of councillors' personal staff are interacting with municipal staff, often asking officials to bend normal practices to meet the needs of particular constituents.[36] Thus the management function in municipalities often becomes more difficult than in private companies—where members of boards of directors have nothing to do with mid-level managers; or in federal or provincial governments—where individual legislators hardly have more influence on public servants than members of the general public. We shall return to this issue in Chapter 13.

Conflicts of Interest

Whether full-time or part-time, municipal councillors must pay close attention to increasingly stringent rules about conflicts of interest. In general, they must not participate in decision-making concerning any matters in which they or their immediate families have a pecuniary interest. From 2009 until 2011, a judicial inquiry investigated allegations that Mayor Hazel McCallion of Mississauga acted improperly because she acted as mayor to promote development on land in which her son had a significant financial interest. The report of the inquiry makes interesting reading for anyone wanting to find out how business was conducted in this particular large municipality. However, for our purposes, the important point is that the judge concluded that Mayor McCallion did have a conflict of interest but that she had not violated the Ontario law on the subject. Such law only applies to voting in council and to participating in council debates, but the mayor's actions took place quite outside the council chamber while she was negotiating on the city's behalf with interested parties. Not surprisingly, the judge recommended that "the statute should be amended so that it clearly applies to all meetings attended by members of council in their official capacities."[37]

In 2013 the mayor of Cambridge and member of the council of the Regional Municipality of Waterloo, Ontario, asked the Ontario Superior Court of Justice to determine if he had a conflict of interest in relation to a regional mass transit system for which one station was proposed to be "in close proximity" to property owned by his son. Official reports suggested that the building of such stations would cause a "land value uplift" to nearby properties. The judge ruled that there was no conflict of interest under Ontario law: "In my view, a reasonable elector, apprised of all the circumstances, would regard the deemed pecuniary interest of Mayor Craig, by virtue of his son's ownership interest in the condominium in proximity to a transit station, to be unlikely to influence his actions or decisions on mass transit issues in his role as a Regional Councillor."[38] Few members of council would ever be likely to take the trouble to go to court to get such a ruling. In this mayor's case, however, he considered his vote on this important regional issue to be a valuable resource for his community and he did not want to lose it on what could be considered a technicality.

In small communities especially, public-spirited citizens can have a personal interest in just about anything. A recent court decision in British Columbia found that members of a small local council had a conflict of interest when they voted on granting money to other local non-profit organizations on whose boards of directors they were also members. These kinds of rulings cause some citizens to find the idea of being a municipal councillor unappealing. This observation is not to suggest that we should tolerate conflicts of interest. Rather it attempts partly to explain why we get the kind of councillors that we do. Not only is the job of municipal councillor becoming increasingly full-time in some places, it also is becoming increasingly a lifelong, full-time career. Municipal elections are of crucial importance.

Municipal Elections: Terms of Office, Turnout, and Minority Representation

Municipal election dates and terms of office are set by provincial law. Unlike parliamentary systems, municipal leaders cannot call elections when it suits them or when the majority of council disagrees with the mayor (as in a vote of no confidence). Even when a member of council dies or resigns, councils often appoint a replacement rather than go through the trouble and expense of holding a special election. Provincial legislatures frequently make adjustments to laws for municipal elections. In recent years a general trend has been to lengthen municipal terms of office, usually on the principle that, if federal and provincial legislatures are normally supposed to be elected for four-year terms, a similar term should be appropriate for municipalities. In the past, terms have been as short as two years, leading to claims that municipal councillors could never focus on the long term because they were always either preparing for an election or recovering from one. Terms of office for municipal councils are now four years in all provinces.[39]

Despite much wringing of hands and increasingly visible advertising campaigns to convince people to vote, turnouts at municipal elections generally are low. Occasionally, when a particularly contentious issue is at hand or when a mayoral campaign involves well-known opponents, turnout of eligible voters in cities is over 50 per cent, but 30 to 40 per cent is much more the norm. Evidence from Ontario in the 1980s and 1990s suggests that the smaller the municipality, the higher the turnout is likely to be.[40] A telephone survey conducted shortly after the municipal election in St. Catharines, Ontario, confirmed what most observers of Canadian municipal elections have always assumed: older people claim to have voted at a higher rate than younger people and homeowners are more likely to claim to have voted than tenants.[41] More surprisingly, the same survey found that levels of education were not a factor affecting voter turnout (although the authors of the study apparently did not control this factor for age, and we know that younger people generally are better-educated than their elders) and that people not born in Canada are more likely to claim to have voted than those born in the country. However, these data are questionable because 63 per cent of respondents in the supposedly random survey claimed to have voted in the 2003 election, but the actual turnout was only 30 per cent.

The harsh reality is that we know very little about municipal voting behaviour in Canada. One of the few things we do know, however, is that in non-partisan elections, incumbents have a huge initial advantage because, at least, voters tend to know who they are.[42] Unless they have behaved badly, incumbents tend to get re-elected, a factor that greatly encourages the phenomenon of the career municipal politician described above. When an incumbent decides not to run, competition for the vacant position can be fierce, although in Toronto a practice seems to be developing whereby retiring councillors attempt to pass on their seats to the most senior members of their respective personal staffs, a factor that goes even further to suggest that paid involvement in municipal politics in major Canadian cities can last throughout an entire working life.

Many people are rightly concerned about the representation of women and minorities on municipal councils. Ample evidence shows that women and minorities are under-represented.[43] The most important question for students of municipal government is whether women and minorities are better represented on municipal councils than they are in federal and provincial legislatures. Fortunately, a recent study has addressed precisely this question, at least as far as women's representation is concerned. Looking at election results in almost all of Canada's municipalities, the author concludes that women are no better represented at the municipal level than at the federal and provincial levels. This contradicts long held assumptions that, for a variety of reasons, women did relatively better at the local level. Data for 2009 suggested that women were best represented at the provinces but that there was little difference among the three levels. In each case, women held between 20 and 25 percent of the elected positions. At the municipal level, there was little difference in levels of women's representation between municipalities with populations more than 10,000 and those with less than 10,000. The big question of course is: Why do women in Canada seem stuck at 25 per cent?[44] Answering this question would take us far beyond the subject of local government.

The only recent study about the electoral success of visible minorities at the local level relates to the Greater Toronto Area. It shows that such minorities do significantly less well in getting elected locally than they do provincially and federally. In 2010 visible minorities made up 40.2 per cent of the GTA population but they held only 7.1 per cent of the seats on municipal councils. The study's author attributed this lack of success to the absence of political parties (which have been pro-active in attracting minority candidates at the provincial and federal levels) and to the difficulty of newcomers in defeating incumbents, who benefit from name recognition and greater fundraising opportunities.[45]

Financing Municipal Campaigns

Running a serious campaign for municipal elected office in cities costs money. Office space and equipment need to be rented; lawn signs and brochures printed; media spots purchased; pizza delivered to volunteers. Sometimes candidates also will pay for public-opinion polling and engage in other sophisticated campaign operations. In past decades no one seemed to care much where the money for such expenses came from, although it always has been against the law to offer outright bribes to councillors to buy their support for council votes. As we shall see in the next chapter, many have been concerned since the 1960s that people who are reliant on municipal policy decisions to make a living—developers, builders, contractors, owners of taxicab licences, and the like—can become too powerful if they can spend sufficient sums of money to get some candidates for municipal councils elected and to prevent the election of others.

Rules about election financing have changed significantly in recent years. Alberta, Manitoba, Quebec, Ontario, Nova Scotia, and Newfoundland and Labrador require some form of disclosure of campaign contributions, and often expenses as well, though only Ontario and Quebec also have expense limits. After a lengthy review, the rules for British Columbia are in the process of being changed and there will likely be tougher provincial rules in place for the 2018 municipal election. In the remaining provinces there are opportunities for local municipalities to make their own rules.[46] It is important to note that Quebec provides tax credits for contributions to municipal election campaigns and requires municipalities to reimburse 50 per cent of the electoral expenses of a party or a candidate who receives at least 15 per cent of the vote. Manitoba and Ontario allow municipalities to provide rebates to people who make contributions to municipal election campaigns. Quebec and the city of Toronto[47] prohibit contributions from corporations and trade unions.[48]

Research by Robert MacDermid at York University on campaign funding in Toronto-area municipalities during the 2006 elections has demonstrated the importance of contributions from the development industry. In 2006, one-third of the amount of money donated to candidates who were elected to the Vaughan city council came from development companies. One-quarter came from individuals associated with the development industry.[49] Starting in 2010, contributions from corporations and trade unions were illegal in Toronto. Presumably some of their funds will be replaced by increased donations from related individuals, although limits on individual donations remain at $750 for each candidate and $5,000 in total for each municipality. This still provides development interests with considerable opportunity, even in Toronto, to fund municipal elections. Opportunities elsewhere, except in Quebec, remain much greater. Reasons for their intense concern with municipal politics will be explored in detail in the next chapter.

Conclusion

Municipal councils in Canada are where municipal issues are decided. More so than any other decision-making body in Canada, their work is done in public. Their public meetings generally provide much evidence to citizens that councillors are divided, that they are influenced by powerful groups, that they are highly reliant on staff advice, and that sometimes they do not even fully understand what they are doing. People often think that changing municipal structures and procedures will bring about miraculous cures: smaller councils or larger ones; ward systems or at-large elections; stronger or weaker committees; higher salaries or lower salaries for councillors; shorter or longer terms of office; public subsidies for municipal campaigns or more emphasis on individual contributions. Unfortunately, little, if any, evidence suggests that one alternative or the other leads to better outcomes. This is because no one can agree on what constitutes a better outcome. One person's idea of a success story is another person's disaster.

Nowhere is this more evident in municipal politics than in relation to land development, the key item of municipal business everywhere in Canada. For developers, municipal councils are doing a good job when they approve developments quickly and predictably so as to enhance employment and provide housing and commercial building that enables various local economies to prosper. For many others, especially environmentalists, councils that routinely approve development proposals are pathological in the extreme. Such battles are what municipal politics is largely about. Rather than pursuing further the various issues relating to the structure of municipal councils, it is important that we turn to the politics of urban land development.

RESOURCES

By consulting the website of the municipality in which you reside (or the website of the provincial Directeur général des élections if you are in Quebec), find out who the candidates were for each elected office, what the turnout for the election was, whether incumbents generally were re-elected, and whether a connection appears to exist between campaign expenditures and votes received.

STUDY QUESTIONS

1. Should there be political parties in Canadian municipal elections? If so, what kind of parties?
2. What are the arguments for having small councils elected at large, on the one hand, and having large councils elected by wards, on the other?
3. Should groups of municipal councillors be allowed to meet together in private to plot strategy? Why or why not?
4. What are the advantages and disadvantages of having full-time municipal councillors who attempt to make a career in this line of work?

CHAPTER 10

Developers, Councillors, and Citizens

In Chapter 2 we learned that, unlike in many other democratic countries, municipal governments in Canada and the United States are concerned mostly with the built environment. In Canada, people concerned with the quality of local schools or of services for developmentally disabled adults have little need to be concerned with the actions of municipal governments. People who make a living from converting rural land into urban development are hugely interested in what municipalities do, because municipalities make many of the rules that affect their livelihoods. To a lesser degree this interest also applies to ordinary homeowners, because for many people their home is their major asset, and municipal action (or inaction) in their neighbourhoods can have a significant impact on its value. In theory, municipal policy about land development is equally important for renters who hope one day to own their own homes at a reasonable cost in a pleasing environment, but because these people do not organize themselves in municipal politics the same way that developers and homeowners do, their interests are not so often taken into account.

In this chapter we begin by examining different processes that have been used to convert rural land into urban land. Ontario—in particular, London[1]—will serve as a case study. The evolution of the process has been roughly similar in all major Canadian urban areas except, arguably, in Quebec, where developers have generally not played such a major role in financing urban development. Later in the chapter we look at other issues relating to the role of developers and of citizens' groups in urban politics.

How Rural Land Has Become Urban in Ontario

Creating new urban land usually requires that a large rural property be *subdivided* into smaller lots. For this to happen, there has to be, at a minimum, a governmental system for keeping track of who owns what land. In Canada such systems for *registering* landownership are usually administered by provincial governments. In theory, original grants of land could be registered in such an office and the owner could then proceed to make purely private arrangements—including outright sale—for its disposition. Subsequent owners would rely on proof of purchase to trace their ownership back to the original grant. Such a system is fraught with uncertainty, both for owners and for governments. A prominent scholar of Canadian land-use law has pointed out that, "Because of the failure to register plans consequent upon subdivision of land for sale and because of the confusion arising in land registration, title certification and municipal administration in general, it became, over a century ago in Ontario, mandatory to register such plans in the registry office."[2] The key point seems to be, however, that originally no attempt was made at substantive regulation. Anyone who went through the correct administrative process at the registry office could subdivide his or her land.

Because the subdivision of land, particularly in urban areas, inevitably led to new demands for such local public services as sewers and roads, municipalities were seen to have a direct interest in the subdivision process. The 1910 Ontario Registry Act "provided that the Registrar should not register a plan of subdivision unless accompanied by the approval of the municipal council or order of a judge approving such a plan."[3] Judges could hear appeals from negative municipal decisions. In 1918, the Ontario Planning and Development Act provided that cities, towns, and villages could declare *urban zones* in areas up to five miles outside their boundaries and that, for such zones, they would have to approve any new subdivision. Under the same law, the Ontario Railway and Municipal Board (now the OMB) became the agency for appeals of municipal subdivision decisions.

Unfortunately for many builders and homeowners in the early twentieth century, the requirement that municipalities approve new subdivisions did not guarantee that municipalities would actually provide the necessary infrastructure at the time new homes were built. If municipalities built roads, sewers, and water supply systems before homes were built, they sometimes found that the infrastructure was unused for long periods until economic circumstances caused the home-building to happen. But if builders gambled and went ahead without the infrastructure in place, municipalities would sometimes claim that they had insufficient funds to proceed, leaving new homeowners having to access their properties through mud trails and having to make do with primitive sanitation arrangements.

Local Improvement Taxes

The Ontario Local Improvement Act of 1914 established a system whereby urban municipalities could construct new installations such as water mains, sewers, curbs, gutters, sidewalks, and paved streets and pass on the cost through a special local improvement tax levied on property owners of abutting land. Local improvements could be initiated either by the municipal council or by property owners. If a council supported residential development in a particular area, it would initiate the local improvement process. Property owners could initiate local improvements by petitioning the local council. If two-thirds of owners, representing half the value of the properties liable to be assessed, directed the city to act, council was forced to comply. Regardless of how local improvements were initiated, borrowing was the responsibility of the municipality. When the work was finished, property owners were required to pay back the loan through an additional charge on their property taxes. If, in any year, insufficient funds were raised to pay the property owners' portion of the loan repayment, the municipality was liable to make up the shortfall. To do so, the council could increase each owner's assessment in the remaining years. The main features of this system for local improvements are still in place in Ontario to this day. New arrangements for financing infrastructure in residential subdivisions have been added, but the older ones have not been repealed. In most major municipalities, however, only relatively minor installations in established areas are financed through local improvement taxes. A typical example might be the building of a sidewalk where one had not existed before. Affected property owners present the required petition; the city builds the sidewalk; and, for 20 years, the property owners' taxes are increased accordingly.

From the municipality's point of view there was one major flaw in financing infrastructure in new subdivisions by local improvement taxes: if the properties did not sell, the developer would likely be bankrupt and the taxes would not be paid. The municipality would end up owning, at best, some vacant houses or, at worst, an entire partially completed subdivision, with roads, sewers, and water mains leading nowhere. The tax burden for financing the useless installations would shift to the taxpayers of the city as a whole. In exceptionally difficult economic circumstances, such as those experienced in the 1930s, financial disasters of this kind could push the municipality to the edge of bankruptcy and beyond.

Subdivision Agreements

The aftermath of World War II brought great pressure on municipalities to provide new housing. Notwithstanding their experiences in the Great Depression, most were willing, with federal and provincial help, to finance major expansions in trunk sewers, water mains, and major roads. In so doing, their debt levels shot upward. In such circumstances, how were the more local installations normally associated with local improvement taxes to be financed? The private developers came to the rescue. Knowing that their new houses were certain to be purchased, they (initially, at least) had few reservations about entering into *subdivision agreements* with municipalities, under which they obligated themselves to build the public infrastructure for the subdivisions according to municipal specifications and then turned them over to the municipality when the project was complete. Their costs would normally be passed on to the purchaser, who would then face higher mortgage payments instead of local improvement taxes. As residential mortgage rates are generally higher than interest rates paid on municipal borrowing, total financing costs under this system were higher. The perceived societal benefit was the removal of the constraints on subdivision production caused by real or apparent limitations on municipal borrowing capacities. The Ontario Committee on Taxation described the historical origin of subdivision agreements as follows:

> The early development of direct financing of municipal service installations has not been well documented. But it is clear that the practice of requiring developers to agree to take responsibility for providing certain services or meeting certain costs which would otherwise fall upon the municipality first gained importance in the years immediately following World War II. Among the earliest municipalities to impose such conditions were the three major recipients of Toronto's metropolitan expansion—the large townships of Etobicoke, North York, and Scarborough. Initially, the legality of subdivision agreements . . . was in doubt. These agreements none the less multiplied in a setting where, given the pace of urban growth and the demand for housing, neither developers nor municipalities were overly concerned with legal refinements.[4]

By the time the legal status of subdivision agreements was clarified in the late 1950s and early 1960s, they were being used for all major residential subdivisions throughout the province. Under this new system, there could be no approved subdivision unless the applicant had access to sufficient capital resources to finance and build the infrastructure. The result was that local speculators and small building companies were forced out by larger concerns, usually major construction companies that had begun acquiring farmland for eventual subdivision so as to ensure their own supply of developable land.

Many subdivision agreements contained provisions obliging the developer to pay *cash imposts*, *lot levies*, or *development charges* (the term used varies by jurisdiction, but they are all essentially the same) for infrastructure costs associated with the new subdivision. Such monies could pay for improvements to major installations outside the subdivision that were shown to be needed as a direct or indirect result of the subdivision's being built. As time went on, municipalities increasingly extended the scope of these charges so that they are now often used to help finance extensions to public transit, fire and police stations, libraries, and schools—in addition to roads and parks and such hidden infrastructure as systems for water supply and sewage treatment and removal. The important point to note here is that, even more so than subdivision agreements, they have the effect of requiring that development companies be large and financially strong so that they can absorb the costs, at least until they can sell their new homes.

In the early twentieth century, a key role for any urban municipal government was to plan, build, and finance the infrastructure that makes urban life possible. In the early twenty-first century, municipalities still plan this infrastructure. Within new subdivisions, however, infrastructure is now generally built and paid for by developers. Outside new subdivisions, the required new infrastructure is often paid for by these same developers through development charges. Buyers of new homes, therefore, are not just paying for their houses. They are paying for the infrastructure within their subdivision and some of it that is outside, which is one of the reasons new houses are expensive. Prices of new houses help to drive up prices of older ones. Many people claim that this situation is good public policy because "growth should pay for growth."[5] But there is a case to be made that, if we want it, we all should pay for infrastructure costs associated with growth, and if we do not want it, we should use our municipalities to prohibit it. Such an argument generally gets nowhere in the real world, however, because few municipal politicians would ever contemplate limiting growth. As long as developers are willing to pay, municipalities are willing to charge. It is no accident that development charges are low or non-existent in slow-growing areas of the country.

Subdivision agreements and development charges essentially allow developers the right to purchase growth from the municipalities that are charged with regulating it. However, they must do so within the formal land-use planning arrangements that have been legislated by the various provinces. In Ontario, the council-approved municipal document that specifies where new development is to take place is called the *official plan*. In other provinces, equivalent documents are known by such names as *development plan* (Alberta and Manitoba), and *municipal planning strategy* (Nova Scotia).[6]

Stoneybrook: The Creation of a Residential Subdivision in London in the 1980s

The 69 hectares of farmland at the extreme northern periphery of the city on which Stoneybrook was built became part of London as a result of the massive annexation of 1961 (see Chapter 6). By 1974 it had been acquired by the Matthews Group, one of London's two major residential developers. In that year, Matthews applied for permission to subdivide the land in order to build approximately 570 single-family houses and 200 units of row housing.

London's planning department recommended approval, but the city received dozens of complaints from existing residents on the other side of the area's major east–west arterial road. The complainants argued that the developer's plans to build three-storey row housing along the road would reduce property values in the area. Townhouses of this kind were called "monstrosities." It was alleged that their occupation by families with young children would lead to traffic congestion and safety problems, as well as overcrowding in the local schools. Local councillors argued that such high-density development was too expensive because it would mean increased costs for sewers, water mains, and streets.

The developer's response was that the main reason for including the row housing was so that it could act as a sound barrier for the single-family houses against the noise coming from the main road. Despite such a telling admission, the developer backed down in the face of continued local opposition. The plans were changed to provide for only 635 single-family houses. Final approval of Stoneybrook's first phase did not take place until 1979, five years after the original application. Delays were caused by the need to upgrade the nearby sewage treatment plant, to rezone the land from farmland to residential to bring it into accord with the city's official plan, to acquire the necessary approval from various provincial agencies, and to work out all the details of the servicing arrangements. However, after 1979 it was the developer who wanted to delay, because of a slowdown in the economy. During the 1980s, city council granted various extensions to its original approvals. The plan of subdivision for the first phase was registered in 1982; the plan for the fifth and final phase in 1987.

Subdivision agreements between the city of London and the Matthews Group were signed for each of Stoneybrook's five phases. The agreements set out the standards for all infrastructure construction. They also specified the land that would be transferred to the city on completion, as well as the various utility easements (passageways) that would be required. While construction was underway, city engineers had the authority to make periodic inspections to ensure that work was being carried out as provided in the agreement. It would be incorrect to suggest that the developer made all the important decisions. The city's regulations for subdivisions assured that surface water would drain to some approved, predetermined location; that roads would be suitable for use by garbage trucks, snowploughs, and buses; that underground utilities would be accessible for repair; and that at least some land would be made available for such public facilities as schools and parks.

The early advocates of land-use planning expected more. They argued that the *community master plan*, as enforced by comprehensive zoning, could shape urban development in accordance with some agreed-upon notion of an overriding public or city interest. In this sense the complex planning apparatus of London, Ontario—and other Canadian cities—falls short. Even most planners recognize that their real task in municipal government is to facilitate the cost-effective development of our cities by major companies rather than to inspire new visions for our built environment.

The financing of infrastructure for new residential subdivisions has progressed from local improvement taxes to subdivision agreements and development charges. Whatever the virtues of the modern arrangements might be, they are not a mechanism for increased municipal control of the development process. They have been supported by the development industry—in London at least—precisely because they help free developers from municipal financial constraints. Such constraints derive from the limitations—either self-imposed or as determined by the province and/or the financial marketplace—on a given municipality's capacity to incur long-term debt. As a municipality approaches its upper limit for debt, it must begin to make difficult decisions about allocating scarce resources—in this case, funds for the building of new infrastructure. In such circumstances, the need to make these decisions empowers the municipality to shape the nature of its outward physical expansion. Such empowerment is precisely what private developers wish to avoid; hence their support for a mechanism enabling them effectively to purchase the necessary infrastructure for their own projects by paying some specified per-unit charge in advance.

Apart from the developer, the Stoneybrook case underlines the role of one other important set of actors in the creation of new subdivisions: neighbouring residents. They caused the developer to eliminate row housing from the plans and make the development exclusively single-family dwellings, thereby nullifying an apparent attempt by the developer to follow provincial policy about the provision of new housing for people with moderate incomes. Local councillors appeared to do little more than pass on residents' complaints to the developer.

Nevertheless, the alignment of interests is clear. The province and the development industry favour dense development, the former because it provides more moderately priced housing, the latter because it increases profit on a given amount of land. Local residents usually oppose dense development, and their position is reflected often by their councillors, which in turn becomes the official position of the municipality. For local residents, dense development is seen as causing more noise and congestion as well as lower property values for the area as a whole. Neighbouring residents effectively want lower-income people located anywhere except near them; municipalities (especially in Ontario where municipalities are responsible for sharing the financial costs of various welfare-related services) want the same people located anywhere except within their boundaries. In order to win quick approval, developers seem quite willing to make whatever concessions are required to the municipality and neighbouring residents. This certainly seems to have been the case in Stoneybrook.

Under these arrangements, the municipality and the residents' groups advance their own financial interests while being seen at the same time to be beating down the rapacious developer. The development company still makes money; indeed, if there is a strong market for new single-family homes, it simply passes on its increased unit costs to the purchaser. Low-income people never understand the opportunities they have lost. Only the province comes out an obvious loser, a fact that no doubt explains various provincial efforts to require moderate-income housing in all new developments.

The Stoneybrook case is presented here as a typical example of subdivision development on land that the municipality had already designated for this purpose. In British Columbia, Quebec, and within the Greater Golden Horseshoe in Ontario, provincial governments are implementing quite aggressive policies to preserve agricultural land and to help prevent urban sprawl. In these places it is very difficult indeed for owners to subdivide their land for urban development. Where such provincial policies are in place we can expect conflicts about the creation of new urban land to become even more intense and to involve both provincial and municipal levels of government. Pressure for intense development on new urban land will be greater because provincial policies have caused it to become a scarcer resource. The kinds of people in Stoneybrook who successfully resisted the development of row housing across a main arterial from their own houses will not likely take kindly to being told that dense development will be coming and that there is little they can do about it.[7] Of course, if they live near a greenbelt or agricultural land reserve they have little to worry about except the very real possibility that their pleasant suburban lifestyles will occasionally be disturbed by noxious agricultural odours.

Shopping Malls versus Downtowns

When new residential land is created on the peripheries of urban areas, developers inevitably want to provide new shopping areas, not just for the new nearby residents but for urban and rural shoppers as well. Such is the purpose of a *regional shopping mall* or its apparent successor, the *power centre*. Through their land-use planning policies, municipalities play a key role in deciding where these new commercial facilities are to be located and how big they can be. These decisions are extremely important both for owners of downtown commercial property and for suburban developers of commercial property. In the absence of municipal regulation, we would doubtless have many more failed shopping centres dotting our urban landscapes. This means that owners whose land is designated for major commercial development have received a major financial benefit. Some would say it is like winning the lottery; successful developers would say that skill in understanding the details of a particular city's outward physical development is a much more important factor than luck. As we did in the last section, we shall illustrate the politics of shopping malls and downtowns by looking at a brief case study from London, Ontario. What happened in London also happened in dozens of other mid-sized Canadian cities.

Store Wars in London, Ontario

The authors of a major study of Londoners' shopping habits in 1983–4 noted that London's planning policies had always been protective of downtown interests. The central business district (CBD) was supposed to remain the dominant retail area in London, and competition among shopping centres throughout the city was supposed to be balanced so that each district was well served and no single shopping centre was able to achieve dominance. This policy, generally adhered to, meant London had relatively more but smaller shopping centres per capita than most other North American cities and had apparently avoided the problem of downtown deterioration in favour of regional malls located in the suburbs.

By just about every conceivable measure, the study clearly demonstrated the dominance of the downtown shopping area in relation to other areas and malls within the city. Nevertheless, the study's authors found many reasons for concern. Respondents to their survey expressed dissatisfaction with parking, lack of protection from the weather, and various other matters related to convenience. The downtown attracted old and young shoppers, rich and poor, but, predictably, it was not so effective in attracting middle-aged, middle-income families with children.

The authors' main policy recommendations were based not so much on their survey data as on their interpretations of possible future developments. They note that "while estimates vary somewhat as to exactly how much space is actually coming into the London market over the next five years, we believe the order of magnitude of all reasonable estimates is far beyond what London can support through growth in population or buying power."[8] This reason was mainly why they concluded that the downtown "is faced with a crucial testing period which we believe will determine the long-term viability of the central business district in London."[9] Much of the rest of this section is about what happened during this "crucial testing period." First, however, we must examine why and how so much additional suburban shopping space was approved in the early and mid-1980s.

The first approval for mall expansion in the 1980s involved a major Canadian development company, Cadillac-Fairview, which proposed a new shopping centre at Masonville, located at the extreme northerly edge of the city's territory and near the new Stoneybrook residential subdivision. Apart from the usual neighbouring residents' concerns about increased traffic, the proposal was relatively non-controversial. It was understood, however, that because this was to be the first major shopping centre to serve the relatively affluent northwest area of the city, its existence would likely be a considerable challenge for downtown retailers. When originally approved in 1980, Masonville was supposed to be built in 1983. Mainly because of the recession in the early 1980s, the opening was delayed until 1985, well after the 1983–4 study of Londoners' shopping habits.

While Masonville was being approved in the north, the owners of two large shopping centres in south London announced major expansion plans, and another developer proposed building a new one in the same general area. The city council approved one of the major expansions and the other ones were approved in 1982, after a significant intervention by the provincial government. When all this new suburban shopping space came on stream, the downtown was effectively finished as a major shopping destination, notwithstanding an ultimately unsuccessful effort in the late 1980s by another major developer, the Campeau Corporation, to build and operate a major downtown shopping mall. After becoming almost totally empty, this mall is now home to the main branch of the city's public library (where a major department store used to be), a call centre, the extension department of the University of Western Ontario, and various other non-retail operations. Despite significant municipal investment in the downtown in recent years, it still struggles, although new high-rise apartment buildings downtown indicate that things might finally be turning around. But the days of the downtown being a major shopping destination will surely never return.

No mass movement of citizens in the 1980s defended the downtown against suburban shopping malls. The fight was mainly among major commercial property owners, and the ones downtown did not openly make their case in the political arena. Presumably committed to principles of open free-market competition for the retail dollar, they naively believed that stores downtown could compete with the new major regional malls. They were wrong. A major question for any student of the politics of urban development is this: Could the municipal council have prevented the decline of the downtown by refusing to approve the building of suburban shopping malls? We cannot learn the answer to this question because there are suburban shopping malls in every major Canadian urban centre and, except for the very largest of our cities, most have seen the virtual disappearance of the downtown commercial core. For many who now look back nostalgically at such downtown cores, the harsh truth is probably that they have disappeared because most Canadian urban residents decided they would rather shop in the suburbs. If this is true, we can conclude that the marketplace, as represented by developers, and local democratic politics, as represented by decisions made by elected politicians, combined to give the people what they want.

The great irony is that even the largest of regional shopping malls now are threatened by the power centres anchored by *big-box stores*, each surrounded by its own massive parking lots. The marketplace seems to have shifted again, and municipal councillors have done little, if anything, to shape it. There are even fewer citizens rallying to "save our mall" than there were to save our downtowns.[10]

Old Buildings versus New Buildings

Developers do not restrict their attempts to make money to the suburbs. In central city areas that have any potential for increased economic activity, developers try to turn old buildings into new buildings. Sometimes this is a long process, with the relevant land serving for many years as a parking lot. Municipal councils can regulate both demolition and building and therefore have an important role in this process. The most important form of municipal regulations relating to individual buildings are generally called *zoning bylaws* (*land-use bylaws* in Alberta). Because zoning bylaws apply to individual properties and, therefore, directly affect the value of assets held by particular people and corporations, provinces have generally required municipal councils to demonstrate that they have acted fairly when they make a zoning change. At a minimum, this means that affected property owners get a chance formally to express their views before the council takes action. In Ontario, property owners can appeal any municipal zoning change to the Ontario Municipal Board (discussed in Chapter 3), and the OMB has a particular obligation to provide a fair and impartial hearing.

Municipal councillors generally want to encourage new development because it leads to higher municipal tax revenues and provides immediate employment in the construction industry. But many are also concerned about preserving old buildings, especially in places where there is great pressure for new development. The preservation of older buildings is often an important local issue. Jane Jacobs, an important writer in the twentieth century on the subject of cities, famously argues that cities need old buildings for economic growth. She notes that economic and creative innovators seldom got their start in shiny new glass and steel high-rises. Instead, Jacobs claims, their biggest breakthroughs inevitably are born in low-rent, old buildings that are affordable and convenient to other central city services.[11] One of Jacobs's greatest admirers has pointed out, however, that this is no justification for always preserving all old buildings everywhere in the city. The Harvard economist Edward Glaeser points out that, "Preserving an older one-story building instead of replacing it with a forty-story building does not preserve affordability. Indeed, opposing new buildings is the surest way to make a popular area unaffordable."[12]

A different kind of economic argument relates to the need for downtown areas to have distinct visual identities. Although it is not impossible for new buildings to provide such identities (the Sydney Opera House in Australia is probably the world's best example), it is usually older buildings that provide a distinct sense of place. As the economic function of downtowns turns more to tourism and leisure activities and away from shopping and routine office functions, it is increasingly important that potential visitors have a reason to go to one place rather than to another. The atmosphere provided by older buildings can provide just such a reason. It is important to remember that both of these arguments for protecting older buildings—as incubators for innovation and as providers of visual identity—are based in a desire to enhance a city's economic well-being. The argument is that new development sometimes harms a city's economic prospects. When faced with proposals to demolish old buildings in favour of new development, municipal councillors are often faced with difficult judgment calls about the best course for their city's economy.

Many citizens wish to preserve old buildings for primarily non-economic reasons. They simply believe that our communities must retain links to the past so that we better understand the historical legacies left to us by earlier generations. Such people are likely to argue that preserving important old buildings trumps short-term economic concerns, but, not surprisingly, they also increasingly make use of the economic arguments referred to above. Many developers today understand that preserving older buildings is often very much in their own best interests, so there are fewer battles in Canada around this issue than there were 30 or 40 years ago. For example, neither the Montreal Forum nor Maple Leaf Gardens was demolished after the Canadiens and Maple Leafs departed these hallowed grounds for newer buildings. Both have been recycled for other urban uses, although Maple Leaf Gardens retains a rink that is used by Ryerson University.

Conflicts today about older buildings tend to focus on ones that are much less famous and usually badly run down. Citizens' groups concerned with preservation often argue that developers should be compelled to fix up such buildings rather than be allowed to tear them down. Much of the dispute is about the cost of repairs and who should pay. While the battles go on, buildings get more run down, a fact that strengthens the developer's case. Sometimes such buildings even burn down or get flooded, thereby ending the debate altogether. Difficult legal issues often emerge in such conflicts. How they are settled depends on the details of municipal bylaws or provincial legislation. The developers' claim usually is that property owners should be able to do what they want with their property, especially if it is not designated as a heritage property prior to a requested demolition. They argue that, if a municipality wants to save a building, it should be willing to purchase it at fair market value. Municipalities seldom agree, and search instead for compromise solutions involving the use of old facades on new buildings or even the approval of totally new buildings designed to look like old ones (the Disneyland solution).

Neighbourhoods versus "Cataclysmic Change"

Many of the defining events in Canadian urban politics in the past 50 years have involved battles between governments or private developers intent on building major projects and neighbourhood groups that have resisted them, sometimes successfully, sometimes not. The origins of these battles go back to conflicting visions about the ideal city. Jane Jacobs articulated the conflict best in her book *The Death and Life of Great American Cities* (1961). She began by attacking "modernist" visions of the city that she claimed destroyed its very essence. Such visions involved central cities composed mainly of high-rise buildings and expressways that connected the centre to a ring of planned suburbs. In the mid-twentieth century, these modernist approaches to city-building were at the heart of policies aimed at *slum clearance*, whereby poor and working-class neighbourhoods would be bulldozed and replaced by high-rises or by new expressways. In the 1950s in New York, Jacobs successfully fought to protect her own neighbourhood in SoHo against plans to build an expressway that would have effectively destroyed it. Her famous book was a direct result of her experience. In *Death and Life* she articulates an anti-modernist vision of the city, in which what she calls "cataclysmic" changes are eschewed for cautious, gradual policies aimed at preserving and upgrading neighbourhoods rather than destroying them. Contrary to conventional modernist land-use planning ideas at the time, she extolled the virtues of mixed commercial and residential uses. She explained why both high-rise apartments and sprawling single-family homes were inappropriate for cities, turning instead to the kind of structures that had been at the heart of cities for ages: rows of low-rise mixed use structures built close to the street, often with stores at the street level and apartments above.

During the Vietnam War in the 1960s, Jacobs and her family moved to Toronto. Ironically, she settled in a part of central Toronto directly in the path of an expressway planned by Metro Toronto that would cut right through the neighbourhood. Not surprisingly, she quickly became prominent in the successful citizens' movement to stop the Spadina

Expressway (see Chapter 7). Jacobs's influence was felt in cities throughout the Western world.[13] Citizens' groups felt empowered to challenge so-called experts (such as traffic engineers who designed comprehensive expressway systems for cities), and soon the experts changed their view to incorporate much of Jacobs's thinking. This change is nowhere more evident than among professional land-use planners who now learn in their university courses about the virtues of mixed uses and stabilizing and preserving traditional neighbourhoods.

Battles about expressways have taken place in almost all major Canadian cities.[14] In Montreal, a conflict currently boils about the reconstruction of an expressway interchange originally built in the 1960s.[15] Just as plans to bulldoze entire neighbourhoods are no longer seriously advanced, few, if any, governments plan to build major new expressways in established urban areas. In fact, in Toronto, debates continue about the possible dismantling of the Gardiner Expressway that separates downtown Toronto from the shores of Lake Ontario. Government plans for slum clearance and expressways have not been the only threats to stability in traditional urban neighbourhoods. Private-sector developers have been important as well, and remain today as forces against which neighbourhood associations are always on guard.

In the 1950s and 1960s, developers frequently engaged in what was known as *blockbusting*. They would surreptitiously buy a few houses in a particular city block where they planned to build a new high-rise apartment building. They would then deliberately rent these properties to people whom the neighbours would consider undesirables. This would cause more people to think of selling—and the developers' agents would be right there to buy. The process would be repeated until the development company had enough land for the building, at which time it would go to the city council and ask for the land to be rezoned to allow a high-rise apartment. A justification for the request was that the neighbourhood was no longer stable!

Still, in many older commercial areas of cities, developers buy properties in the expectation that one day they will make money by building new buildings. How big those buildings will be will depends on decisions taken by the municipal council, so developers have a huge interest in who is elected as councillor. However, blockbusting in residential areas is a strategy that is unlikely to work anymore. Most city councils have made it very clear in their land-use planning policies that existing inner-city residential neighbourhoods will never be rezoned to accommodate larger buildings. Developers generally believe them—and citizens' groups act vigilantly to ensure that councillors make few, if any, concessions.

Many new high-rises, especially condominiums, are still being built in our more prosperous cities. How is this possible? The answer is that, due to shifts in shopping patterns that we have already discussed, and even more importantly, due to the move of inner-city manufacturing jobs to the suburbs and to other countries (such as China), our cities in recent decades have found themselves with huge expanses of under-used land. Residential developers have been quick to move in and to create new high-income neighbourhoods where dilapidated factories used to be. One result is that central parts of cities now have more residents and fewer jobs, so much so that commuting flows out of the city to suburban jobs are as great in some places as the more traditional suburb-to-city commute.

Another result is that poorer people are being pushed out of the centres of our more prosperous cities, especially Toronto, Montreal, and Vancouver. Contributing to this process is the *gentrification* of inner-city neighbourhoods. When high-income people are convinced that block-busting will no longer occur and that neighbourhoods are being genuinely protected by municipal governments, they have every incentive to buy houses in such neighbourhoods, even if the houses require extensive renovation. In many respects this process is a sign that things are going well for a city or a neighbourhood. Slow change in this direction fits Jacobs's prescriptions for saving cities. The problem, of course, is that over time (instead of quickly, as in slum clearance) poor people are driven from their own neighbourhoods.[16] This is especially damaging for renters, arguably less so for owners of modest homes who find themselves receiving unimaginably high prices when they decide to sell and move away.

"New Reformers" and the Development Industry

During the 1960s and 1970s, opposition to slum clearance, expressways, and uncontrolled development of high-rise buildings created a new urban reform movement. In the previous chapter we examined some of the features of the "old" reform movement: emphasis on management by experts; diminished role for politicians; at-large elections. In many ways the new reform movement was a direct repudiation of the main positions of the old one. The new reformers looked at municipal government and saw councillors who always favoured new development and municipal staff who thought that their main role was to facilitate it. In most respects these observations were accurate. Councils might comprise representatives of both business and labour, and they would often disagree about tax levels and the distribution of municipal resources, but both sides almost always agreed that new buildings of just about any kind were good for business and good for workers (especially construction workers). With respect to municipal staff, there was nothing in the professional training of engineers, lawyers, and accountants to cause them to question the need for expressways and new buildings. Prior to the general acceptance of Jane Jacobs's vision for cities, the same was true for professional land-use planners.

New reformers began to be elected in Canadian cities in the late 1960s. Like the old reformers, they generally rejected the introduction of federal and provincial parties into municipal government. New reformers, however, accepted the notion that municipal decision-making was political. But rather than being committed to following a party line, most new reformers believed that their greatest obligation was to open the doors of city hall to citizen participation and to reflect citizens' views in their council decision-making. As we have seen, citizens, especially in the inner city, were increasingly likely to reject expert opinion. Wherever new reformers gained a toehold on municipal councils, they caused great frustration for municipal staff, business people, and labour unions because it looked like they were opposed to "progress." In fact, like Jane Jacobs, whom they universally admired (especially in Toronto), they changed the definition of *progress* from a belief in building new roads and buildings to preserving viable and diverse inner-city neighbourhoods.

New reformers were not a coherent group. They split into two broadly different camps: urban conservatives and populist radicals.[17] In Toronto, David Crombie (mayor from 1972–8) and John Sewell (mayor, 1978–80) represented each of the two groups, respectively. Crombie, known as "the tiny perfect mayor" because of his popularity and shortness of stature, emphasized the preservation of neighbourhoods; Sewell emphasized the need for citizens constantly to challenge existing power structures. Crombie went on to become a cabinet minister in the Progressive Conservative federal government of Brian Mulroney, while Sewell has remained steadily a critic and outsider. While Crombie ended up supporting the amalgamation of Metro Toronto in 1998, Sewell, as we have seen in Chapter 8, was the main leader of C4LD, the primary citizens' group in opposition.

In Vancouver, the local political party known as TEAM represented the more moderate new reformers, while COPE was the more radical faction. In Montreal, both tendencies were contained within the Montreal Citizens' Movement (MCM), which is one reason that group often seemed so internally divided. Both COPE and the MCM also received strong support from labour unions, which added another complication given that labour unions generally desire jobs for construction workers. Recent Canadian mayors such as Glen Murray (Winnipeg), David Miller (Toronto), and Gregor Robertson (Vancouver) owe a great deal to the new reformers, but they—and other contemporary left-leaning municipal politicians—have been shaped by other forces as well.

The new reformers emerged from a general radicalism of the 1960s during which all power structures were placed under great pressure. What followed was a series of new social movements, each with its own cause: feminism, environmentalism, gay liberation, the anti-globalization movement. Each of these has had its effect on municipal politics in general and new reformers in particular. Because municipal government is especially concerned with the built environment in cities, it is not surprising that environmentalism has been of special importance. In fact, it is now extremely difficult to distinguish between the influence of the new reform movement and the influence of environmentalism on today's municipal activists. If someone opposes urban expressways, is it because of their vision of the quality of city life or because they are concerned about carbon footprints and global warming? Probably both.

City politics in Canada today still revolves mainly around issues relating to development. Some elected councillors and serious candidates for office have not really been much influenced by the new reform movement (for example, mayors Sam Katz in Winnipeg and Rob Ford in Toronto), but all will say that they favour citizen participation and wish to preserve neighbourhoods. Their real objective is to promote growth and development, even if they sometimes differ from each other about how much they are willing to tax themselves in support of such growth. Councillors and candidates who have been influenced by the new reformers are much more cautious and skeptical about the benefits of development, although such people are hard to find in areas where growth has been slow or non-existent. Not surprisingly, development companies (where they are permitted to do so by law) and individuals associated with development companies will want to contribute to the election campaigns of candidates who generally favour development. Some will want to contribute to their opponents as well, especially if they are likely to be elected. In so doing, the developers are potentially purchasing good will, as well as trying to indicate to the general public that they are fair-minded and not solely intent on purchasing control of municipal councils. Many new reformers will refuse such contributions. Some will argue that no one should be allowed to accept contributions from developers, or that public subsidies for municipal elections should replace developers' subsidies. Whatever happens, as long as Canadian municipalities remain as focused as they have been on making decisions about where and when buildings are to be constructed, developers and municipal politics will never be separated from each other.

Although it is difficult to analyze the overall impact of the new reformers, there is likely to be at least one item of agreement: new reformers have had a profound influence on how municipal governments have approached the issue of citizen participation.

The Development Industry Today in Toronto

New reformers did more than just fight the development industry. They also did a remarkably detailed job of documenting how it actually worked in different Canadian cities. Such documentation culminated in James Lorimer's 1978 book, *The Developers*. Since then, there have unfortunately been no comprehensive studies of the Canadian development industry, academic or otherwise. However, in his 2013 book on *Planning Politics in Toronto*, Aaron A. Moore devotes a chapter to "The Politics of Toronto's Development Industry."[18] Anyone who has even the slightest knowledge about recent developments in Toronto knows that condominium developers are now the key players in Toronto real estate. Major worldwide office developers such as Cadillac-Fairview, Brookfield, and Oxford Properties have their head offices in Toronto, but they are not key players for local condo development. Although some of the local condo developers are foreign-owned, most are focused solely on the Toronto market. North American academic literature on the political role of local developers would lead us to believe that they would be key contributors to the election campaigns of local candidates who were generally supportive of development. Moore points out, however, that because the Ontario Municipal Board (OMB) is the final decision-maker in Toronto on contested development applications, developers have less incentive than in non-Ontario cities to rely on political support from local councillors. Another factor is that corporations, as we have seen in the previous chapter, are now prohibited from donation to municipal election campaigns in Toronto. Individuals (who might, of course, happen to be associated with the development industry) can give no more than $750 to a single candidate and no more than $5000 in total to multiple candidates for a single council.

A great many Toronto condo projects have been built on land near Lake Ontario that was formerly used for manufacturing and related transportation facilities. This has meant that in these places the developers have not had to confront angry neighbours in single-family houses who oppose plans for nearby high-rises. Instead, they face a more generalized concern that the condos are blocking off the lake from the downtown central business district. But whole new neighbourhoods near the downtown are clearly a great benefit for the overall vibrancy of central Toronto.

Controversies have arisen, however, where condo developers have tried to build further north from the lake in or near established neighbourhoods. The best known such battle was about Minto Midtown in the early 2000s. Minto is an Ottawa-based development company that bought land containing a 10-storey office building near a major Toronto intersection (Eglinton and Yonge) in 2000. Later that year it submitted a proposal to the city that its official plan and zoning by-law be amended to permit the building of 50-storey condominium towers on the site. The local councillor expressed opposition from the very beginning, but the city's planning director and a councillor from a nearby ward were more favourable, primarily because of Minto's high design standards and because the project appeared to meet city and provincial policy objectives about the desirability of residential intensification around major transportation nodes, especially subway stations. Local neighbourhood associations vigorously opposed Minto on the grounds that the towers would cause local congestion, including in the subway station, and because they would cast shadows on nearby single-family homes. After a year went by without any decision by the Toronto city council, Minto appealed to the OMB. In April 2002, before the OMB hearing began, city council indicated that it would approve a new proposal from Minto subject to the following conditions:

1. The number of storeys in both towers would be further reduced so as to minimize shadows;
2. Minto would make a contribution of $1 million to the city for seniors' housing;
3. The courtyard between the two towers would be open to the public; and
4. Minto would build direct access from the towers to the subway station and contribute $200,000 toward new pedestrian walkways to the station.[19]

Minto accepted the city's conditions and the revised proposal was approved. In September 2002, the OMB hearings began because the neighbourhood associations still objected. The OMB ruled in favour of Minto and the city. At the next municipal election in 2003, the nearby councillor who had supported the project from the beginning (Anne Johnston) was defeated by a challenger (Karen Stintz) who had opposed the project, which was finally completed in 2008. Contrary to some of the accounts about developer behaviour in Canada in the 1960s and 1970s, Minto appeared reasonable, flexible, and accommodating throughout the entire process. It was not proposing to destroy a neighbourhood to build its new towers; instead it was destroying an old 10-storey office building that no one cared about. It could rightfully claim that it was advancing "good planning" (residential intensification) while it could paint the concerns of the middle- and upper-middle-class residents' associations as selfish and unreasonable. Nevertheless, Minto Midtown's completed towers do dominate the local landscape. Controversies about developments like Minto Midtown that are near single-family neighbourhoods will recur in every Canadian city that is experiencing growth. Canadian developers, however, have learned a great deal about urban politics since the 1970s. They still are committed to making money from investing in property and new buildings, but they pick their spots carefully, remain patient and accommodating, and use all the resources of skilled (and expensive) advisors in public relations and communications to portray themselves as responsible city-builders and good corporate citizens.

Citizen Participation

Prior to the 1960s, ordinary citizens were not much listened to in city government. There was a reason for the aphorism "You can't fight city hall." As we have seen, most agreed that growth was good, that experts knew how to accommodate it, and that the job of municipal councils was to decide how much tax revenue could be wrung from property owners in order to facilitate growth and provide essential services. But new reformers demanded that the citizens challenging these assumptions be heard. Initially, these citizens expressed themselves through raucous public meetings, demonstrations, sit-ins, and blockades, many of which attracted considerable attention from the media. But the more successful they were, the more they were consulted before decisions were made. The most radical of the activists refused such consultations because their real objective was to expose arbitrary state action as a prelude to some form of revolution. But most genuinely wanted less drastic change, and change is what they got.

From the 1970s on, municipalities across Canada introduced a bewildering array of new participatory mechanisms, most notably mandatory public meetings and consultations prior to any zoning changes.[20]

For many land-use planners, a crucially important new skill was the ability to conduct such events so that everyone would feel that he or she had been treated fairly. Depending on the strength of the anti-development forces within a particular municipal council, any substantial opposition to a proposal expressed at these meetings could be its death knell. For developers, therefore, the object of the game was to conduct their own careful and cautious consultations before submitting any formal proposal. From a developer's point of view, the best kind of public meeting was one at which no one showed up. However, as land-use planners and others became more committed to the idea that good planning required extensive public consultation, the fact that the public often seemed uninterested became a problem. Provoking public interest in small proposed changes in a particular neighbourhood was not usually difficult, but the more important and generalized an issue became (the future of downtown, strategies for investment in public transit), the more difficult it was to attract interest. Experience in Canada over the last 20 or 30 years leads to the depressing conclusion that most urban residents do not want to be intensely involved with big issues involving their municipal governments, but that they are concerned about small issues affecting their own neighbourhoods. Opposition to municipal amalgamation was perhaps an exception to this observation, although most such opposition seemed to be based precisely on the assumption that amalgamation would reduce local influence over neighbourhood issues.

Much attention has been paid to the NIMBY—Not In My Back Yard—syndrome. The observed problem here is that many citizen participants in policy-making for land-use issues seem to object to any change that is proposed for the immediate areas in which they live. Sometimes the opposition seems quite irrational. Why do people behave in this way? William Fischel, an American land economist who has also served on a local planning commission, has an answer: what most NIMBY participants are trying to do is simply protect their most valuable financial asset (their home) against possible unanticipated outcomes that would cause a decline in its value. Homeowners buy fire insurance to protect themselves against the unlikely possibility that their house will burn down, but no insurance is available to protect them against the possibility that the value of their home will decline if there is some unanticipated consequence resulting from a modest change nearby. The natural response under these circumstances is to resist almost any change on the grounds that at least current arrangements are fully understood. Fischel suggests that homeowners would be much less resistant to change if they could be provided with some form of insurance to protect the value of their home against possible negative effects of change caused by municipal actions.[21] Unfortunately, it is extremely difficult to see how such insurance would operate in the real world, mainly because it would be almost impossible to isolate the financial effects of such changes from other factors that cause price variations in houses.

As a kind of second-best alternative to such insurance, homeowners often form neighbourhood associations (often called *ratepayers' associations* because members wish to emphasize that they pay property taxes; to be discussed in more detail in Chapter 15). The main purpose of these associations is to do whatever is necessary to protect property values. Often they accentuate the NIMBY syndrome: if only a few members are upset about a proposal for change, they tend to get the support of the entire association so as to maintain loyalty and unity. Instead of a few objectors, the municipality finds itself facing an entire association.

Meanwhile, municipalities will urge people to participate; developers will accommodate concerns of neighbouring property owners as best they can while still maximizing profits; and property owners will remain vigilant. Occasionally, large numbers of people will be mobilized around a particular local issue, but the issues that attract attention are usually related to wider social movements. For example, a municipality trying to find a new landfill site might provoke environmentalists who object in principle to all new landfill sites. Occasions are now quite rare when municipalities attempt to impose changes on a neighbourhood without first making sure that there will be few, if any, objections. But when they make a mistake, they usually are quite quick to back down. The influence of the new reformers is still strong, even if not so visible as it once was.

Conclusion

Knowing about the formal functions and structures of local government is important. Such knowledge by itself is not so important unless we understand how people use these structures to try to get what they want. In Chapter 14, we shall examine the ways in which local governments spend their money, and this will provide considerable information about what makes local government so vital in the real world, especially in cities. But some of the most important things that municipalities are responsible for do not cost money: granting permission to private developers to construct buildings is a prime example. Some municipal decisions about buildings and land development can be appealed (especially in Ontario) to provincial quasi-judicial agencies, but council decisions are still usually the key stage in the approval process. Because municipalities are also responsible for arranging for the provision of the basic infrastructure necessary for new development to be viable, they are of crucial importance for anyone (including homeowners) with financial interests in the built environment. Considerable debate has taken place among social scientists about the extent to which the land-development industry determines the decisions of municipal councils.[22] For our purposes, we need only recognize the close connection between land development and municipal politics, and leave it to others to sort out exactly how these connections work in particular cities at particular times.

As we shall see in the next chapter, citizens usually expect municipal governments to provide leadership in securing the economic development and prosperity of their respective cities. But municipalities have only limited tools that they can use to achieve this objective. This is just one of the many reasons why being a municipal leader, especially a mayor, is such a difficult job. The basic factors needed to create wealth in a city (or anywhere else) are some combination of capital, labour, and land. Municipalities do not control currencies, nor can they regulate how money is moved around or invested. As well, they do not control labour—within a given country, people and workers can migrate as they wish without the permission of any municipality. But municipalities do have a significant level of control over how land is used within their boundaries. This is the main reason that issues having to do with land are so important in municipal politics.[23]

RESOURCES

Explore the downtown area of the community where you live. What actions did the municipal government take to make it lively, interesting, and prosperous? What mistakes did they make? For guidance, you might want to consult Jane Jacobs, *The Death and Life of Great American Cities*.

STUDY QUESTIONS

1. Do you think developers should pay the full cost of all municipal infrastructure associated with new subdivisions? Explain your reasoning.
2. Why, in your view, did municipalities not do more to protect retail business in their downtowns from competition from suburban malls?

3. Would Canadian cities be better off today if there were more inner-city expressways? Why were the original plans of traffic engineers for such expressways not implemented?
4. Have you ever actively participated in a municipal political issue? If not, what kind of an issue would cause you to become involved? What form would your participation take?

CHAPTER 11

Mayors and Local Political Leadership

In the last chapter we focused on the importance of land in municipal politics. The emphasis was on the ways in which land developers and various other interests associated with the industry are able to have considerable influence over what municipal councils actually decide. At the same time, we saw lots of evidence that developers do not always get what they want. This is because municipal councils are not simply passive mechanisms whereby developers' interests are translated into municipal policy. All developers do not share the same interests all the time, and other property-owners, especially homeowners, have their own interests that are usually strongly articulated to municipal councils. At a minimum, municipal councils have to act as referees between different powerful interests. In reality, they usually do more than this. Some council members, especially mayors, want to launch their own independent initiatives and bring about significant change within their cities or towns. This chapter is about how some mayors manage to do this and provide leadership in a complex municipal environment.

First, we need to examine the legal status of Canadian mayors and then look at mechanisms through which they can exert their influence on council. We then turn to some real-world examples of mayoral leadership and consider the extent to which successful municipal leadership in Canada requires the construction of *urban regimes*. We conclude by examining various styles of mayoral leadership, including two contrasting recent cases: Naheed Nenshi in Calgary and Rob Ford in Toronto.

Legal Status of Mayors

Many contradictions appear in the office of mayor in a Canadian city. On the one hand, mayors are directly elected. More people vote directly for the mayor of Toronto than for any other office in Canada, because mayors in Canada, except in many municipalities in Newfoundland and Labrador,[1] are directly elected by all eligible voters. The prime minister of Canada and the premiers of the provinces, on the other hand, are directly elected only by voters in their own electoral districts. They become heads of their respective governments because they lead the party that has the most seats in the legislature. While nothing in the written Constitution mentions the offices of prime minister or premier, the powers of mayors are outlined in every municipal act of every province in the country.

In Ontario, however, the Municipal Act refers to mayors as being *heads of council*, along with the wardens of counties and chairs of regional municipalities (positions that are similar to that of mayors). In Alberta, section 154 of the Municipal Government Act briefly outlines the responsibilities of "chief elected officials," and section 155 states that the council can choose another title (such as *mayor*) if it so desires. In most provinces, including Alberta, the legal duties of the mayor listed in the statute are very limited and include presiding over council meetings. Section 225 of the Ontario Act states that the role of the head of council is "to act as the chief executive officer of the municipality," a grant of authority that seems quite impressive. But section 226.1 circumscribes the role in these words:

> As chief executive officer of a municipality, the head of council shall,
> (a) uphold and promote the purposes of the municipality;
> (b) promote public involvement in the municipality's activities;
> (c) act as the representative of the municipality both within and outside the municipality, and promote the municipality locally, nationally and internationally; and
> (d) participate in and foster activities that enhance the economic, social and environmental well-being of the municipality and its residents.

Compared to the responsibilities of a chief executive officer of a business corporation, these roles are remarkably limited, especially when we consider what section 227 has to say about the role of the "municipal administration":

It is the role of the officers and employees of the municipality,

(a) to implement council's decisions and establish administrative prac-
     tices and procedures to carry out council's decisions;

(b) to undertake research and provide advice to council on the policies
     and programs of the municipality; and

(c) to carry out other duties required under this or any Act and other
     duties assigned by the municipality.

This section suggests that, although the mayor might be the chief executive officer, he or she does not have any direct control over the municipality's administrative apparatus. The usual practice, as we shall see in the
next chapter, is for the council to appoint someone to be the head of the
municipal bureaucracy (usually called a *city manager* or a *chief administrative officer*) and for that person to be responsible to the council as a whole
rather than to the mayor.

The same situation applies to mayors in other provinces. In legal
terms, there are no *strong mayors* in Canada. The strong-mayor system in
the United States is one in which the mayor is directly responsible for the
operation of the city's bureaucracy and, in most cases, has the authority
personally to appoint the senior municipal officers. A strong mayor in
the United States has similar powers in the municipality as has the US
President in relation to the federal government. But just as the president
does not sit in Congress, a strong mayor does not sit in a municipal council. If a strong mayor has political allies in the council, he or she might
be able to control the council, but with no guarantees. The strength of
strong mayors derives from their control over the administration, not
over the council, although sometimes mayors have the authority to veto
council decisions, at least temporarily. In a parliamentary system, on the
other hand, such as we have in Ottawa and in the provincial capitals,
a prime minister or a premier whose party has won a majority of the
legislative seats controls both the legislature and the civil service. Most
mayors in Canada are weak in that they control neither the bureaucracy
nor the council.

In cities with municipal parties (as in Vancouver, Montreal, and
Quebec City), the mayor derives political power from being head of his
or her party. Elsewhere mayors can only approximate such power if they
cultivate groups of councillors to support their position on as many issues
as possible, a time-consuming and often thankless task. Many mayors
in the country are often on the losing sides of important council votes.
Recent data from the last term of the Calgary city council (2010–13)
showed that Mayor Nenshi was on the winning side of 73 important

votes only 60.3 per cent of the time. Only three of the fifteen council members were less likely to be on the winning side than he was.[2]

As was noted above, in most Canadian municipalities, mayors preside over meetings and have a special role in determining the agenda, but this gives them little in the way of special advantage. Presiding over council meetings often puts mayors at a disadvantage. In order to contribute to debates, mayors usually have to leave the chair and ask someone else to take over. In Toronto, Montreal, and Winnipeg, the mayor no longer chairs council meetings; instead a speaker or chair is chosen by the council (often on the nomination of the mayor) to act permanently as the presiding officer. In this way the mayor is freed up to act as a legislative leader on the floor of the council for whatever position he or she wants to advance.

Executive Committees

Prime ministers and premiers choose ministers, usually elected members from their own party, who collectively form the cabinet that is responsible to the legislature for the operation of the government. In Canadian municipalities the council as a whole is collectively responsible for the operation of the municipal government. There is no equivalent to a cabinet in Canadian municipalities. Some councils have executive committees. In their simplest form, such committees result from internal decisions of councils about how to organize the way they do business. An executive committee is simply another standing committee, perhaps with special responsibility for making recommendations to council on matters that relate to the entire municipality, such as human resource policy. Members are chosen by the entire council in the same way as members of other standing committees. The only distinctive feature of such committees is that they usually are presided over by the mayor.

The executive committee for the city of Winnipeg (called the *executive policy committee*) is different. In 1997, a business-oriented mayor, Susan Thompson, undertook to bring significant change to Winnipeg's political and administrative structures. Under her leadership, city council agreed to engage a well-known Canadian municipal consultant, George B. Cuff, to review the city's operations. Much of Cuff's report called for the standard nostrums of the "new public management," which involve trying to adapt the practices of private business to the public sector, but he also addressed structural issues. Probably his most notable recommendation was to abolish the city's board of commissioners. Such a board was a peculiarly western Canadian structure that included a chief commissioner as chair, who was the city's senior staff member; other commissioners who headed different parts of the administration; and the mayor. In addition to acting as a kind of official management team, the board was charged with preparing the council agenda. Cuff concluded that the existence of the board of commissioners caused confusion and delay, and hampered transparency and accountability. As a result of Cuff's report, city council abolished the board and replaced it with both a single chief administrative officer (CAO) and an executive policy committee (EPC) on the council. The mayor chairs the EPC, decides on the number of members (although the number cannot be more than half the size of the council, which is 16), and appoints them. Most simultaneously become chairs of the council's five standing committees. In 2013 there were seven EPC members in total, including the mayor. Although this committee is similar to a parliamentary cabinet in the sense that its members are appointed by the mayor and can be terminated by the mayor at any time, it is important to remember that members have no formal obligation to support or agree with the mayor. Another crucial difference from a cabinet is that most of its business is conducted in public. Nevertheless, the power of the mayor of Winnipeg to control the membership of the EPC makes him or her one of the most powerful mayors in Canada in relation to the operation of his or her municipal political system. Finally, EPC members who are named by the mayor to be either deputy mayor or chair of a standing committee receive an increased salary, a fact that gives the mayor additional leverage over his or her appointees.

Because the mayor of Winnipeg is not clearly and solely responsible for the administrative operations of the municipal government, Winnipeg still cannot be said to have an American-style strong mayor. Neither does Toronto. When the Ontario legislature approved a new City of Toronto Act in 2006, it insisted that the city streamline its political and administrative structures to enhance accountability, especially by strengthening the authority of the mayor. City council decided in June 2006 that, starting in 2007, the mayor would appoint a deputy mayor and the heads of the council's standing committees, who would in turn comprise the majority on a new 13-member executive committee that is supposed to provide policy leadership to the council as a whole. These relatively minor changes met the province's requirements. In 2013, however, in its efforts to rein in the disgraced Rob Ford, the city council withdrew this mayoral authority for the remaining portion of Ford's term.

The strongest municipal executive committees in Canada are in Quebec's major cities, especially the city of Montreal. Ever since the 1960s, Montreal's executive committee has been the main forum for municipal decision-making. Most of its 11 members, who are nominated by the mayor and approved by the council, have special responsibilities for parts of the municipal bureaucracy in the same way that cabinet ministers do. However, many of its former similarities to cabinets at other levels of government have recently disappeared. It no longer meets behind closed doors. Ever since 2010, members have included councillors who are not in the same municipal political party as the mayor. Especially since Mayor Coderre's party does not have a majority on council, Montreal's executive committee is now only a shadow of its former self.

How Mayors Become Powerful

In any political system, the strength of a leader can derive from a number of different sources. Among Canadian mayors, a very few are powerful because they are the leaders of municipal political parties that win a majority of seats on the municipal council; others derive a certain degree of strength from particular institutional powers they have, especially the power to appoint members of an executive committee. The mayor of Montreal has both kinds of powers. But no Canadian mayor is in complete charge of the municipal bureaucracy as in the American strong-mayor system. Some Canadian mayors, however, have managed to become quite powerful within their own municipalities without having any kind of extra formal authority. We need to have some idea of how they did it. We shall look briefly at the mayoral career of Stephen Juba of Winnipeg and in a bit more detail at the career of Hazel McCallion of Mississauga.

Stephen Juba

Allan Levine, a Winnipeg historian, has written that "Stephen Juba ran the city of Winnipeg as his personal fiefdom from 1956 to 1977."[3] Although few mayors in Canada have been as successful with the electorate as Juba, his story is not unlike that of other popular mayors in other places. He seemed to have very few skills other than the ability to get ordinary voters to like him—especially useful for mayoral candidates running city-wide without the declared support of a political party. Astonishingly, he won nine mayoral elections by large margins without spending more than $2,000 in total.[4] Campaigning as an independent "man of the people" at various elections in the early 1950s, he managed to get himself elected in a multi-member constituency in the provincial legislature in 1953. There he became known for fighting for looser liquor laws and coloured margarine, both issues of considerable concern to his Winnipeg supporters. He lost his first two attempts to be elected mayor in

1952 and 1954, railing against both local socialists and the Independent Citizens' Election Committee (the ICEC, similar to Vancouver's NPA). But in 1956 he defeated the ICEC incumbent, a prominent local business person who was a member of all "the right clubs,"[5] and became Winnipeg's first non-Anglo-Saxon mayor. Levine describes Juba's early actions this way:

> As the people's champion, Juba challenged the system at every opportunity. In 1957 he took on the Winnipeg and Central Gas Company and was responsible for a rate reduction. The city's merchants were grateful. The next was the Wolsley Tree Affair, a classic example of Juba's early style and showmanship. The focus of this episode was the fate of a ninety-five-year-old elm tree on Wolsley Street. . . . In the early fall of 1957, the city's public works committee—without notice to the residents of the area—decided to chop the huge tree down because it was a hindrance to traffic. But when the city's engineering department arrived to undertake the job, it was greeted by a band of protesting women who had linked arms around the tree. After one of the workmen started to threaten the women with an ax, the women started to chant for the mayor. On cue, Juba pulled up in his yellow Cadillac. Like a white knight he stopped the workmen and sent away the police, who had arrived to take the women back to the station in a paddy wagon.
>
> Juba believed that he was acting within his authority as the chief executive officer of the city; later the council, by a vote of twelve to six, supported his decision. So the mayor was the neighbourhood hero. But more important, this event received international press coverage and further endeared Juba to the public. It also showed the aldermen [councillors] just how smooth and powerful their mayor had become.[6]

From then on, Juba's power continued to increase. He promoted Winnipeg at every opportunity, both inside and beyond Canada. He fought many battles with the Corporation of Greater Winnipeg and won most of them. When the provincial government was establishing the unicity system in 1971, he fought off its initial efforts to have the mayor indirectly elected by councillors (so as to encourage a parliamentary system at the local level) because he knew that, although the people supported him, most councillors did not, especially the ones from the amalgamated suburbs. Juba easily won two elections in the unicity, but withdrew his candidacy at the last minute in 1977, thereby snookering his main rival from the ICEC who did not want to run against him but who was too late to submit his own nomination papers.[7] The ICEC disbanded six years later. For good or ill, Stephen Juba played a major role in preventing the growth and survival of municipal political parties in Winnipeg.

Hazel McCallion

Hazel McCallion was mayor of Mississauga from 1978 until 2014. During the time she was mayor, Mississauga's population grew from about 300,000 to 713,000 in 2011.[8] It is now Canada's sixth most populous municipality. In theory, Mississauga's authority is limited by the fact that it is a lower-tier unit within the Regional Municipality of Peel, but in practice, as we have seen in Chapter 7, the Mississauga city council largely controls what happens on the Peel regional council. Because Mayor McCallion controlled the Mississauga council, she also was the dominant politician within Peel. How did she manage to be mayor for so long and to build and retain such influence? The question is especially intriguing because she is a woman who was born in 1921. Tom Urbaniak, a political scientist at Cape Breton University who grew up in Mississauga and who has carefully observed her career, has written a compelling biography of McCallion[9] that both provides some answers and helps us better understand municipal politics in Canada's suburbs.

Urbaniak shows that McCallion used many of the same political tactics exploited so successfully by Stephen Juba; for example, she shops at a different supermarket in Mississauga each week in order to meet more people[10] and she is quick to praise. "Many a cleric has been dubbed 'my favourite priest,' many a youth leader labelled 'a future mayor' or future 'prime minister,' many a school given the moniker 'the best school in Mississauga.'"[11] She also benefited from acting decisively and authoritatively soon after she became mayor when a massive train derailment and chemical spill in 1979 caused evacuations and disruptions for thousands of residents in the heart of the municipality. If all that mayors needed to do in Canada to become completely dominant within their own municipalities is simply to copy McCallion, they would do so and reap the rewards. The real strength of Urbaniak's analysis is in explaining what is unique about the political environment in which McCallion has operated.

McCallion was first elected mayor in Mississauga after pro-developer and pro-reform mayors had been discredited—the first by too much disruption and hints of corruption, and the second by hefty tax increases. "What a time it was to step in. The city-wide interest groups were weak. The developers were discredited. And most of the municipality was serviced (with water and sewer) for development. The local leaders need not be beholden to anyone."[12] McCallion managed to keep taxes down by convincing developers to pay development charges (see previous chapter) to fund new infrastructure even before it was clear that such charges were legal. McCallion understood that the developers had little choice because building homes and commercial buildings in Mississauga was a sure way to make money. Urbaniak notes that McCallion's political career prospered because she was working with a large "suburban canvas," which meant that potential sources of conflict concerning land use could be kept isolated from each other. New subdivisions, new industrial parks, and even a new city centre could be built with most existing residents suffering neither inconvenience nor higher taxes. As new residents moved in, the power of older small-town social networks declined. There was little to replace them. Local media were weak, and Toronto's media paid little attention.

McCallion stepped into a political vacuum and used her great personal political skills to fill it. She protected municipal staff against political interference or outside criticism—from everybody except herself. For her, it was quite all right to become involved in administrative details, especially if it was about a matter a resident had brought directly to her attention. About her treatment of councillors, Urbaniak says this:

> Councillors also—if they showed themselves to be deferential—would be allowed to give direction on small matters: a backed-up sewer here, a sidewalk there. Although McCallion was never reluctant to take action directly, she would sometimes hand a file to a councillor and let him or her deal with it and get some credit.[13]

He notes that "In Mississauga, the *de facto* Hazel McCallion Party has held virtually every seat on council. Even if its members had grievances against the mayor, they almost never raised them in public."[14] Her critics outside council received little attention from anybody. To the extent that they sought publicity by making extreme statements, their efforts usually backfired because the end result was that they "drew sympathy to her."[15] To attack Hazel was to attack the entire community, a community so disparate and loosely connected that she was almost the only symbol that held it together.

Tom Urbaniak's analysis of Hazel McCallion and of Mississauga politics provides us with a vivid portrait of a form of local politics that can probably be found only in Canada. In most parts of the democratic world, national political parties dominate local politics almost completely, especially in the larger authorities. Thousands of non-partisan suburban municipalities abound in the United States, but none is more populous than Mississauga, and most have populations of only a few thousand. Urbaniak notes[16] that American urbanists have coined the term *boom-burb* to refer to growing suburbs with populations over 100,000.[17] No American boomburb has a population anywhere near Mississauga's, and most are not as populous as Surrey, Burnaby, and Richmond in suburban Vancouver, or Brampton, Markham, and Vaughan in suburban Toronto. Urbaniak suggests that if Mississauga were in the United States it would probably have a part-time mayor and council, a much more publicly prominent city manager, and frequent plebiscites on tax increases and bond issues that would provoke more citizen interest in municipal political issues.[18] In reality, however, we simply do not know, because there are no municipalities like Mississauga in the United States.

Before leaving Urbaniak's work and beginning a discussion of *urban regimes* in Canada, we should note how Urbaniak thinks Mississauga is relevant to the study of urban regimes. For Urbaniak, the question was, How did McCallion become so powerful that only she could get things done in Mississauga? For regime theorists, the question is, How does anyone get anything done in a municipality? Urbaniak writes:

> Regime theorists, who have come to dominate the urban politics literature of late, see stable local governance as the product of a coalition of organized groups with resources—usually money or votes. In the most-cited case, the Atlanta of political scientist Clarence Stone, it was hard to move anything forward if you were not in with the downtown business elite or the leaders of the African American middle class. They were the coalition. They had fixed resources; they needed each other. But what if the resources were scattered? What if there is no downtown worthy of the designation? What if the voters are in disparate communities and poorly organized and relatively new to the city? What if the city is in the path of development anyway, without requiring grinding efforts to attract it? What if it already has the "empty" space in which to put development? This is not an uncommon suburban dynamic.[19]

The dynamic might not be uncommon around Toronto and Vancouver, but the existence of large suburban municipalities containing "disparate communities" is uncommon in the United States. If one person can be a regime, then Hazel McCallion was a regime. But rather than try to squeeze the Canadian urban political experience into American models, we need to examine American models for their relevance.

Urban Pluralism and Urban Regimes

In Chapters 9 and 10 we saw that one possible conclusion we can make from studying Canadian municipal politics is that all important decisions are determined by economic and social elites, or at least by major development interests. In the United States in the 1960s another significant approach emerged. Robert Dahl, a political scientist at Yale University, studied local decision-making in New Haven, Connecticut, the city in which Yale is located. He discovered that different groups were predominant on different issues and that the municipal council (and other local bodies) acted as a kind of referee in local controversies, making sure that no one group always won or always lost. Politicians who did not carefully weigh all the conflicting interests would likely lose the next election, so the system, in Dahl's view, was self-correcting. Dahl's 1961 book about New Haven, *Who Governs?*,[20] was hugely influential, largely because it presented American urban politics as a model for how democratic decision-making happens in the real world. We might not all participate in all the governmental decisions that affect our daily lives, as some democratic theories would suggest, but for Dahl, as long as our interests are defended by one group or another, and as long as each group is treated fairly and has a chance to win its case every once in a while, then we should all be satisfied. Dahl's version of democracy is called *pluralist* because it works as long as many different interests are involved in the policy-making process. It has been subject to a great deal of criticism, notably that Dahl ignores reality in assuming that all interests in society actually are represented by organized groups and that all such groups are treated fairly when it comes to public decisions that are relevant to their interests. But many have criticized it as simply a defence of "business as usual" in American politics.

Perhaps these criticisms explain why we have had no studies of Canadian urban politics adopting Dahl's methodology (studying how explicit decisions were made on a variety of different subjects) or that have arrived at pluralist conclusions. Instead, we have studies that focus on issues related to land development and that tend to see the decision-making process as one that pits citizens' groups against developers. As Urbaniak suggested, however, it is regime theory, not pluralism that holds sway today among most students of American urban politics. Regime theory has had considerable influence in Canada, so it merits our attention.

Clarence Stone studied urban politics in Atlanta between 1946 and 1988 and discovered neither a decision-making process completely dominated by an economic elite nor a system that was genuinely plural-ist. Instead, he found:

> What makes governance in Atlanta effective is not the formal machin-ery of government, but rather the informal partnership between city hall and the downtown business elite. The informal partnership and the way it operates constitute the city's regime; it is the means through which major policy decisions are made.[21]

Stone notes that all organizations require informal arrangements in order to get things done and that students of any kind of organization need to understand these arrangements. But a regime is "not just any informal group that comes together to make a decision but [is rather] an informal yet relatively stable group with access to institutional resour-ces that enable it to have a sustained role in making governing decisions."[22] The "stable group" that Stone found in Atlanta comprised middle-class African Americans who were able to take control of Atlanta's city government after the passage of the American Civil Rights Act in the 1960s, and the downtown business elite who controlled prime real estate and crucial sources of jobs and wealth. Both groups needed each other to achieve their objectives. Businesses cannot carry on without co-operation and support from municipal governments; municipal govern-ments can accomplish nothing if key businesses decide to leave town.

Stone's analysis of politics in Atlanta has been hugely influential, in no small measure because it suggests that politics is neither subordinate to economics nor simply the result of the particular strengths of particu-lar interests around particular decisions. Instead, according to regime theory, elected politicians, who cannot accomplish what they want at the local level without outside support, make deliberate decisions to enter long-term alliances in order to achieve their goals. For political scientists, following Stone in studying how regimes are formed, how they persist, and how they change is truly an exciting challenge. Nevertheless, students of comparative urban politics have pointed out that regime theory might not be so relevant outside the United States, where political parties are much stronger at the local level and/or where central governments pro-vide much more support and direction to local governments.[23] In these circumstances, local politicians can accomplish their objectives without having to form the kind of regime that Stone discovered in Atlanta. Even within the US, regime analysis seems to have run its course. Douglas W. Rae has pointed out that regimes are most likely to exist within munici-palities that contain both the rich and the poor.[24] Unfortunately however, a large proportion of Americans live within jurisdictions—especially outer suburbs—that are overwhelmingly homogeneous.

There has been considerable academic debate about whether urban regimes exist in Canada.[25] In the final analysis, much depends on exactly how the word *regime* is defined. The more loosely regimes are defined, the more likely we are to find them. If almost any informal interaction among people who are trying to get something done in the political arena constitutes at least the beginning of a regime, then conscientious political scientists are studying regimes all the time. Reading about regimes is a useful reminder that, even if economic conditions *are* extremely important in determining political outcomes, politicians act, at a minimum, to transform economic imperatives into reality and usually do much more. Looking for regimes also prevents us from focusing exclusively on what happens within official institutions, such as municipal councils. This too is good, although hardly innovative in urban politics because the same motivation inspired the original *community power* studies more than half a century ago.

In his work on Atlanta, Clarence Stone provided us with a genuinely innovative analysis of the way in which Atlanta's black middle class (who controlled city hall) worked together with Atlanta's downtown corporate elite (who controlled significant economic resources) over a long period of time to implement policies that benefit both groups. If we can find examples of similar regimes in Canadian municipal politics, our knowledge will be greatly enhanced. Until we do, we still must do the best we can to understand how Canadian municipal leaders, especially mayors, get things done.

Models of Mayoral Leadership

In 1978 in a book provocatively titled *The Ungovernable City*, the American political scientist Douglas Yates suggested that we need to analyze two main variables in order to understand "mayoral leadership style."[26] Such an analysis leads to the labels shown in Table 11.1. We have already seen that most mayors in Canada have a weak power base. Most are not leaders of strong parties; they have little in the way of formal legal power; and we have very limited evidence to suggest that any have been able to construct powerful regimes. Not much evidence exists to suggest most are especially innovative. This means that, according to the table, most can be classified as *brokers*. Mayors who are brokers try to convince people with conflicting interests to compromise with each other so that some kind of policy can be adopted, even if it is nobody's first choice.

Table 11.1 Mayoral Leadership Style

	Innovative	Not Innovative
Strong power base	Entrepreneur	Boss
Weak power base	Crusader	Broker

Source: Adapted from Douglas Yates, *The Ungovernable City: The Politics of Urban Problems and Policy Making* (Cambridge MA.: MIT Press, 1978), 165.

Being a broker in a democratic society is an honourable, if not especially exciting, function. It requires lots of meetings, lots of listening, and lots of patience, much of it in informal settings. Although, as we have seen, informal ways of getting things done are associated with regimes, the art of arranging compromises is especially notable for being at the heart of Dahl's pluralist analysis: a broker has no overriding personal agenda but instead is more interested in balancing competing interests. Much of the day-to-day work of any municipal leader in Canada is about being a broker.

In Ontario, however, it seems that such mayoral work is under threat. As we saw in Chapter 9, Ontario's ombudsman, acting as a closed-meeting investigator for municipal councils, has contended that closed meetings among councillors, including serial one-on-one meetings about the same subject conducted by the mayor, are illegal because they are "doing the groundwork necessary to exercise" the council's power and authority. The ombudsman's position has caused Marianne Matichik, the mayor of Greater Sudbury, to say that she "won't talk to other councillors to try and get their support on any issue because it may break the rules."[27] "I will not go out and lobby people. . . . If that makes me unsuccessful, if that means I may not get a resolution through, you know what? So be it."[28] It is hard for a mayor to be a broker if she or he cannot act behind the scenes to try to ensure that some items get through council and others do not. Occasionally we find mayors who want to bring about great change but are not politically strong enough to do so. *Crusader* is an apt word for such mayors. Because most mayors in large municipalities have a strong appetite for self-preservation, we find few who are crusaders in this sense. John Sewell, the mayor of Toronto from 1978 to 1980, was an example. In the last chapter we noted that he was on the more radical end of Toronto's new reform movement in the 1960s and 1970s. As mayor, he clearly wanted to introduce a much more participatory culture at Toronto city hall, but he spent little time rallying support within the council for his position. Sewell is still active in community causes today. He was defeated in 1980 by Art Eggleton, whose mayoral leadership style clearly fell into the *broker* category. Eggleton is now a Liberal senator in Ottawa.

Stephen Juba and Hazel McCallion both developed strong power bases but were not particularly innovative. However, they were not traditional political bosses whose power depended on being able to deliver jobs, contracts, and favours to their political supporters. The power of a traditional political boss is rooted in a political party, but both Juba and McCallion were strongly opposed to the presence of political parties in municipal politics. They both built their invincible electoral strength by fusing their own political identity with that of the municipality itself. Except for the fact that he led his own personal political party, the mayoralty of Jean Drapeau of Montreal was similar. The main difference perhaps is that he personally sponsored more innovative municipal projects that literally changed the face of Montreal: the subway system, Expo 67, the Olympic Games. In this sense, Drapeau was clearly more entrepreneurial, even if the main sources of funds for his grand projects were the federal and provincial governments.

In recent years, the mayors who seem to have been both powerful and innovative are David Miller in Toronto (2003–10), Glen Murray in Winnipeg (1998–2004), and Larry Campbell in Vancouver (2002–05). None was entrepreneurial in the sense of seeking to bring business-like practices to municipal government, but they all tried hard to use their political capital as mayors of major cities to bring about significant political change. Miller and Murray were committed to a "new deal for cities," and Campbell was a strong advocate for bringing about change in Vancouver's Downtown Eastside. They all had considerable support within their own councils, but to attain their objectives they needed support from other levels of government more than they needed to build a strong regime at home. It is likely, of course, that, had Mayor Miller been part of a regime that included the executive occupants of the top floors of Toronto's bank towers, he would have had more success than he did in convincing the federal government to allocate a share of GST revenues to major municipalities. But why would presidents of national banks want to be involved in such a battle? Unlike the corporate elite in downtown Atlanta, they simply had no reason to seek favour with their local mayor.

Nevertheless, in the mid-2000s, Miller, Murray, and Campbell made significant progress on their respective priorities, especially when Paul Martin was prime minister of Canada. Miller obtained modest new powers for Toronto,[29] but Murray did not get any new taxation authority from the province of Manitoba.[30] Campbell's efforts to aid the Downtown Eastside benefited from Vancouver's bid for the 2010 Winter Olympics.[31] In the final analysis, however, all three mayors might be assigned to the crusader category. Campbell's municipal party (COPE) broke apart and he accepted an offer from Martin in 2005 to become a Liberal senator. Murray resigned as mayor of Winnipeg to run unsuccessfully as a Liberal candidate in the federal general election of 2004 and then moved to Toronto, where he was elected as a Liberal member of the Ontario legislature. In 2014 he became Ontario's minister of the environment and climate change. Elected in Toronto in 2003, David Miller was in office longer than the other two but it already seems that much of his legacy—including the vehicle registration tax and an ambitious plan for renewing public transit called Transit City—has been dismantled by his successor, Rob Ford.

Clarence Stone's book about Atlanta makes scarcely any reference to the Georgia state government. By contrast, it seems highly unlikely that a mayor of a major Canadian municipality could make progress on any significant issue without having considerable support from the relevant provincial government, and sometimes from the federal government as well. To understand how change comes about in Canadian cities we probably need to know more about intergovernmental relations than about municipal links with local businesses.

One of the often overlooked facts about tri-level intergovernmental relations in Canada is that, at any point in time, one of the three levels is preparing for an election, conducting one, or just recovering from one.[32] The times when all three levels can work at a political level on a given project actually are quite limited. More limited still are the times when such elections produce results such that political leaders at all three levels can get along with each other and are committed to some form of significant changes.

For Toronto, one of those magic moments was between late 2003 and late 2005. In 2003, David Miller, Dalton McGuinty, and Paul Martin were elected in Toronto, Ontario, and Canada, respectively. All shared centrist or mildly left political values. All were committed to some form of activist urban agenda and, although their agendas naturally differed given the functional responsibilities of the different levels of government, the agendas were compatible with each other. After the June 2004 federal election, when Martin secured re-election, but only as a minority supported mainly by the NDP, federal support for cities actually increased. But in late 2005, the Martin government was defeated in the House of Commons, and in 2006 Stephen Harper—who did not believe in any new federal initiatives to help city governments—became prime minister. The magic moment was over, but not before municipalities across the country had benefited from new federal policies relieving them of the financial burden of paying the GST themselves and providing for the sharing of the federal gas tax (see Chapter 3).

Ironically, one of candidate Miller's major campaign commitments in 2003 was to prevent the building of a bridge from the city to the Toronto Island airport. The airport is operated by the Toronto Port Authority, an intergovernmental special-purpose body established by federal legislation (see Chapter 4). Prime Minister Martin cancelled the bridge and agreed to compensate private-sector companies that had already been awarded contracts to build it, and in this respect Miller won a major victory. However, Martin refused to take steps to close the airport altogether.[33] Miller hoped that the cancellation of the bridge would cause the airport to wither away, but the port authority bought a new ferry and Porter Airlines, the airport's only commercial client, has been hugely successful operating flights from the island to nearby destinations in Canada and the United States. It appears that the island airport is here to stay. More airplanes are taking off and landing than ever before. Miller won the battle of the bridge, but lost the war about the future of the airport. Now the port authority has built a tunnel to the airport and Porter Airlines is seeking permission to fly a new generation of regional jets in and out of the airport.

Miller and McGuinty each won another election and, as indicated earlier, seemed to work well together until 2010 when Miller announced he would not be running again. Soon after that, Premier McGuinty announced a reappraisal of his government's original decision to help fund Miller's Transit City project, and Mayor Ford later repudiated it. Rob Ford struck the city of Toronto like a hurricane. In a much different way, Naheed Nenshi had a similar effect on Calgary. Both merit our attention.

Rob Ford and Naheed Nenshi

In the autumn of 2010, the cities of Toronto and Calgary each elected a new mayor, both of whom are quite remarkable in their own distinct ways. Rob Ford in Toronto was elected, in accordance with Ontario law, to a four-year term. Naheed Nenshi was elected for a three-year term and re-elected for a four-year term (as a result of a change to Alberta law) in 2013. The mayors discussed in the previous section (Miller, Murray, and Campbell) were significant primarily because of the policies that they advanced. Mayors Ford and Nenshi can both point to strong policy positions, but their significance seems to derive more from who they are than from what they advocate. In this section we examine what their elections might mean for understanding the nature of municipal politics in Canada's large cities.

Much has been written about Ford's various transgressions, especially his admission in 2013 that he had smoked crack cocaine as mayor while he was in a drunken stupor. For our purposes, however, the key questions are, How did he get elected in the first place? How did he remain in office as long as he did? As far as his election is concerned, there are a number of important points to keep in mind:

- Rob Ford's father was a provincial Conservative member of the legislature. Despite humble origins, he started a successful business and launched his short political career from that base. The Ford family is well connected politically.
- As a councillor from 2000 to 2010, Rob Ford built a solid reputation as a local politician who returned telephone calls from ordinary people, even those not in his ward, and who knew how to solve local problems.
- Ford did not build friendships or alliances on council. Even while a councillor, he faced a hostile press and a number of embarrassing incidents, including one where he was accused of drunken behaviour at a Leafs hockey game. He first denied being at the game but, when confronted with proof, apologized for his behaviour.
- Although he was an unlikely candidate for mayor, his campaign was managed by a tough disciplinarian who kept him on message. The main message was that there was much waste at city hall and Ford would clean it up. As we saw in Chapter 8, this message was particularly appealing in the peripheral areas of the amalgamated city of Toronto. Ford won enough votes in these areas to compensate for his lack of support in the central parts of the city, where incomes of residents are generally higher.

To be a leader at the in federal or provincial levels, a politician generally has to win the support of his or her elected colleagues or, at a minimum, the party activists who vote for party leaders. As Rob Ford demonstrated so graphically, a successful mayoral candidate in a major Canadian city does not need such support. Party connections certainly help, but mobilizing large numbers of "ordinary voters" can be a strategy that works, especially if it taps into feelings of bitterness and alienation, feelings that were obviously at the core of "Ford nation." Ford won the 2010 municipal election with 46 per cent of the vote. Voter turnout was high by municipal standards: 51 per cent.[34] This was a convincing win, so much so that councillors who had been skeptical about the desirability of having Rob Ford as mayor were quick to proclaim their support. The important point here is that Ford mobilized council support not before he ran for mayor, but only after polls showed that he had a good chance of winning.

It goes without saying that Ford did not have the support of Toronto's elites: business, media, cultural, or academic. His appeal was to middle-class homeowners in the city's periphery. These people were not organized politically. To the extent that they became a political force, it was because of Rob Ford. This is another way of saying that Ford is not part of any kind of stable coalition; he and his supporters are not a component of an urban regime as originally defined by Clarence Stone. Like Hazel McCallion in Mississauga, Rob Ford created his own source of political power. Unlike McCallion, however, from the moment Ford became mayor, he was under intense media scrutiny. He was mayor of a central city, not a suburban municipality in which the major media outlets are not much interested. It is true, of course, that McCallion's personal life could not possibly have ever been as questionable as Ford's. But how would Toronto media have reacted if the mayor of Toronto had been negotiating with a developer about a major downtown property in which his son had a major financial interest?[35] Would a seasoned developer ever think that such a negotiation was a good idea?

Ford's personal problems were exposed by vigilant mass media, helped along by an American website (Gawker) that specializes in celebrity gossip and scandal. Despite revelation after revelation, he clung to office. There was no legal way to get rid of him. Commentators and councillors urged him to resign, but nothing happened. This too is evidence that there was no urban regime in Toronto. If Ford were part of a regime, its other components would have urged him to leave, if for no other reason than to find another political partner to improve their chances in the next election. Instead of doing anything, leaders in other segments of Toronto life simply looked on in horror as if Ford was quite beyond their control—which he was. He did not need them and they did not need him.[36] Toronto's elites need a municipal government that functions, but the municipality can function quite well without a functioning mayor. City employees still do their jobs; council still makes decisions and allocates funds; the provincial government hovers reassuringly nearby, and makes many of the big regional decisions anyway, especially those relating to transit.

Like Ford, Nenshi was an outsider before he became mayor. He had not even been a member of the Calgary city council. His parents were immigrants and his family had no political connections. While Ford was a university dropout, Nenshi has a master's degree from the Kennedy School of Government at Harvard University. He worked for a well-known consulting company and later accepted a teaching position at Mount Royal University in Calgary. He became known as a commentator on urban affairs but, when he announced his candidacy for mayor in 2010, he was first seen as little more than a fringe candidate. Although he described himself as a "policy wonk" and as someone who shares Jane Jacobs's approach to urban living, his appeal, especially to young people, came from his image as a non-politician and his exceptionally powerful use of social media. On election day, he won just under 40 per cent of the vote and became Calgary's first Muslim mayor. Even more so than Rob Ford, he came to office with no powerful partners. There was no urban regime.

As we saw earlier in this chapter, Nenshi has not been especially successful in convincing his council colleagues to follow all of his initiatives. He alienated some elements of the homebuilding industry by his efforts to rein in urban sprawl. Nevertheless, his personal popularity remained high, especially after his visibly effective leadership following the Calgary flood in the summer of 2013. He was re-elected in 2013 with 74 per cent of the vote. By that time he had 130,000 followers on Twitter. He had tweeted 20,000 times during his first term as mayor.[37]

Ford and Nenshi have been more important for what they symbolize than for what they have actually been able to accomplish. Ford convinced council to contract out some garbage routes, to cut some city services and expenditures, and to tilt future suburban transit expansion toward subways rather than Light Rapid Transit (LRT), a mode of transit that Ford insists are "streetcars." Nenshi has emphasized improved public transit and the revitalization of inner-city neighbourhoods. But what Ford really accomplished was to show that the downtown establishment was not in control. What Nenshi accomplished was to show that Calgary was much more than a collection of sprawling suburban subdivisions held together by energy companies and the Calgary Stampede. Nenshi's symbolic victories were obviously far more positive than Ford's, but whether either of these symbolic victories will be lasting is far from clear.

Political power does not derive from position alone. To exert power to bring about change, politicians either need authority in their own right (such as the authority the US president has with respect to the leadership of the government and the military) or they need the support of a loyal group of followers with authority of their own to enact change (such as a prime minister leading a majority government in a parliamentary system). Canadian mayors have very limited authority of their own. A few—Drapeau and McCallion are perhaps the best examples—have collected sufficient followers on council to be able to get done what they wanted to get done. We should not underestimate the importance of symbolic leaders, however. This is precisely why, in their own very different ways, Rob Ford and Naheed Nenshi are so important to anyone studying the governance of Canadian cities.

Conclusion

The most significant question in political science is, What is the extent to which elected politicians in a democracy can act in a way that is independent of the economic forces that help generate the wealth that enables the system to function? If we are to find any such independent action in Canadian municipalities we would expect it to be led by the mayors. That is why this chapter has focused on their legal and extra-legal powers. We have paid special attention to those few mayors who have managed to overcome legal obstacles and to become relatively powerful within their respective municipalities. We have also reviewed urban regime theory, the dominant approach in the United States to understanding how local elected leaders can shape events within their respective cities.

In order to have any chance of winning elections, democratic politicians must promise to do things that are extremely difficult to implement, if not impossible. Once elected, they operate under severe constraints. This is clearly true even for the most powerful offices in the most powerful countries in the world. How can we possibly expect things to be different for mayors of Canadian cities? Given the immense constraints under which they operate, it is remarkable that we sometimes expect them to single-handedly and substantially change the quality of city life.

Changes in the quality of city life in Canada are rarely caused by dramatic changes in municipal policy. Such changes are ultimately caused by the cumulative impact of years of debate and advocacy about the environment, transportation, recreation, and the desirability of vibrant and diverse neighbourhoods. Although policy objectives relating to these matters are frequently trumpeted in municipal strategic plans and mission statements, it is in the dozens or hundreds of decisions that each urban municipality makes each year about sewage treatment, bus routes, and zoning that these matters really are decided. The municipal political process is important because these decisions are important. Mayors who use whatever resources and leadership skills they can muster to nudge decisions one way or another play a significant role in determining the kinds of cities we shall live in.

RESOURCES

Good biographies of politicians are fascinating because they enable readers to see how politicians' public actions relate to their personal background and experience. Tom Urbaniak's biography of Mayor Hazel McCallion of Mississauga is a fine example. To learn about the personal and political life of Hazel—and to learn a lot about local politics at the same time—read *Her Worship: Hazel McCallion and the Development of Mississauga* (Toronto: University of Toronto Press, 2009). For shorter biographical essays about other mayors—Gerry McGeer (Vancouver), Bill Hawrelak (Edmonton), Grant MacEwan (Calgary), Stephen Juba (Winnipeg), David Crombie (Toronto), Charlotte Whitton (Ottawa), Jean Drapeau (Montreal), and Allan O'Brien (Halifax)—see Allan Levine, ed., *Your Worship: The Lives of Eight of Canada's Most Unforgettable Mayors* (Toronto: James Lorimer, 1989).

STUDY QUESTIONS

1. With regard to the political institutions in which they operate, what makes the role of mayor in a Canadian city different from the roles of the federal prime minister and provincial premiers?
2. What is a *strong-mayor* system? Would you favour it for municipalities with which you are familiar? Explain your reasoning.
3. Explain how the concept of *urban regimes* might be helpful in explaining how political power is exercised within Canadian cities. Describe the components of an urban regime with which you might be familiar.
4. Compare and contrast the political origins, political appeal, and political accomplishments of Naheed Nenshi and Rob Ford.
5. What, if anything, do you know about the mayor of the municipality in which you live? What do you think is the basis of his or her political support? How would you characterize his or her mayoral leadership style?

CHAPTER 12

Policy-making

In previous chapters in Part III of this book we have looked at political and managerial issues in Canadian municipal government. We have also focused on issues relating to land development, because such issues are at the core of Canadian urban politics. But, as we saw in Chapter 2, local governments in general are involved in many other functional activities. In some of these, not much policy-making is involved. For example, once a road has been built, a municipality has little choice but to maintain it. To do so, funds need to be allocated (through the budgetary process to be described in the next chapter) and managers have to be in place to ensure that the work is done either by municipal employees or by contractors. But for many other functions, municipal councils have to make some kind of policy decision about what to do.[1] Analyzing the factors involved in such decision-making is the main subject of this chapter.

There is no shortage of general academic literature about policy-making.[2] But much of it is ill-suited to helping us understand policy-making within Canadian local governments. This is not because the local policy-making process is less complex than that of the federal or provincial governments. In many respects it is more so, because a mayor of a Canadian city has much less power to make policy than a prime minister or a premier in a majority federal or provincial government. Canadian municipal councils generally operate under far more legal constraints than federal or provincial legislatures do. The object of this chapter is not to analyze policy-making in general but rather to focus on the special and sometimes unique features of policy-making within Canadian local governments, especially cities. Before doing so, however, we should address the question: Who makes municipal policy?

In legal terms, municipal councils make policy and municipal staff implement councils' decisions. Knowing the legal framework is important, but that knowledge provides only part of the story.[3] In reality, most items on the agendas of municipal councils include reports written by municipal staff. These reports usually recommend a course of action for council to follow, and they are often backed up by quite detailed reasons, many of which are sometimes highly technical and specialized. Councils frequently approve such reports with little or no debate, leading close observers occasionally to wonder whether council members actually read the reports that are in front of them. Evidence for such skepticism is sometimes derived from councillors asking questions to staff members, the answers to which are clearly stated in the report. Such questions, however, are not always a sign of ignorance: councillors occasionally want staff to repeat in public a fact that is embedded in the report and which council observers might not have noticed. The staff answer can then be used to justify the councillor's vote on the matter.

Such interplay suggests that municipal staff often play a major role in municipal policy-making. The more technical and specialized the issue, the greater their role is likely to be. But many policy issues facing municipal councils combine both technical issues and fundamental issues relating to the nature of urban development. Deciding how big a sewer pipe should be to service a growing area of a city might seem to be an issue solely for engineers, but what if the size of the pipe determines future development options for decades to come? In reality, it is impossible to determine the exact policy roles of staff and politicians. We might expect staff to be focused on longer-term issues and councillors on matters that need to be addressed before the next election. However, little serious research has taken place on Canadian municipal policy-making. All we know for sure is that, when there is conflict between staff and council, the majority on the council has the legal authority to make the final decision. As we discuss different types of municipal policy-making in the sections that follow, we shall also consider the role of staff and councillors with respect to each of the different types.

One of the great debates in the general literature on public policy-making is the extent to which governments at any level make policy "autonomously." Students of local government tend usually to think of *autonomy* in relation to the relevant central government. But autonomy in this other context refers to the capacity of a government to act in ways that are not congruent with the general societal preferences within the territory that it governs.[4] In this sense, a government is autonomous from its society if it adopts a policy that people in general do not want.

Because we usually think that political systems are undemocratic if they behave in this way, it seems on the surface that this form of autonomy might not be desirable. But democratic governments are also often accused of responding only to short-term electoral imperatives, of being incapable of acting to secure our long-term interests by taking decisions that appear to be objectively necessary but which are politically unpopular. Such decisions can be thought of as autonomous. One of the main assumptions of this chapter is that local policy-making (in Canada at least, and probably elsewhere) is generally not autonomous in this sense. In other words, Canadian local governments generally make policy by responding to some kind of external pressure to do something. As will be explained in this chapter, such external pressure usually comes from federal or provincial governments, local developers and business people, and community activists of one kind or another. In some senses, however, municipalities cannot respond to external pressures; their actions are restricted by their own prior decisions and policies. These types of municipal policies will also be discussed. Finally, we shall look at some of the special features of policy implementation in Canadian municipal government.

Responding to Federal and Provincial Governments

Some public-policy analysts might think that municipalities never really make policy; all they do is implement policy that is made by other levels of government. However, we have already seen in Chapter 1 that the Supreme Court of Canada has ruled that municipalities are *governmental entities* because they do what governments do (make rules and regulations, levy taxes, and provide public services). The commonly accepted definition of a public policy is "a course of action or inaction chosen by public authorities [governments] to address a given problem or inter-related set of problems."[5] In other words, it is about making choices about what to do in a given set of circumstances. Usually the choices that need to be made relate to prior decisions and/or overall strategies and priorities. It is very rare that a policy decision is made that is totally unconnected from other decisions.

By any definition, Canadian local governments undoubtedly make policy. At the same time, however, they are *policy-takers*; they operate within policy frameworks that are imposed by other governments, usually the relevant provincial government. Chapter 3 enumerated and explained the various ways in which central governments (mostly provincial governments) establish and control important aspects of the institutional structures and operational procedures of local governments. In this section of the chapter we look at the circumstances in which local governments make their own policies by responding to policies that originate at the federal and provincial levels of government.

The first point to note is that, if federal or provincial policies require local governments to do certain things, then local governments are not making policy when they are simply following such centrally imposed requirements. There are all kinds of federal and provincial rules and regulations that fall into this category. Like business corporations and individuals, local governments have to obey the laws of the land. One of the important jobs of municipal staff in the policy-making process is to report to municipal councils about what those councils are required to do and what they cannot do. According to the City of Toronto Act, the Toronto municipal council *must* establish the offices of municipal ombudsman, integrity commissioner, and auditor general. For Toronto, the policy decision about whether to have such offices is a provincial policy decision. But for other Ontario municipalities, amendments to the Municipal Act adopted in 2006 provided that municipalities have the option of establishing such positions. The result has been that in most Ontario municipalities, certainly the larger ones, at least one councillor has proposed that some or all of these positions be established in his or her municipality. Once a council decides to accept or reject the proposal, it has made a policy decision, even if the decision has been to do nothing. After the decision has been made, there is nothing to stop a councillor in subsequent years from revisiting the issue. This then is an example of a provincial policy decision that gives municipalities an option about following one course of action or another. The policy decision that the municipality takes is a decision that is in response to a provincial policy.

Sometimes provincial governments *require* that local governments adopt a policy on a particular matter. In such cases municipalities are still engaged in policy-making even if they are obligated to do so by the province. They are making policy because they are making choices about what to do. Usually the approval of the province is required before the municipality is considered to have met its obligations; without the requirement of such approval, municipalities could do whatever they wanted and claim that it met the provincial requirements. Examples of this type of provincially required municipal policy-making are the local emergency management programs required by Ontario's Emergency Management Act (2002). The Act lays down minimum standards for such programs but encourages municipalities to do more. Provincial public servants are charged with ensuring that municipalities meet the minimum standards, but local implementation varies significantly from place to place, reflecting the different policy decisions of the various municipalities.[6]

The federal government owns a great deal of land in Canadian cities and towns. Over the last few decades it has been quite aggressive in divesting itself of some of this land, especially land that had previously been used by the military. In New Brunswick, for example, the provincial government helped the city of Miramichi recover from the closure of the major air force base at Chatham by creating an industrial park that helped ease the effects of some of the military job losses. In Moncton, the municipal government converted federal land that had formerly been a railway yard "into a massive public commons space, incorporating over a dozen soccer and ball fields and a four-plex ice rink."[7] Such stories are replicated across the country, although few have involved as much contaminated land as in Moncton, and few have involved such successful co-operative federal-provincial policy-making.

Perhaps the most common form of local response to central government policy involves federal or provincial policy that offers grants to local governments that meet certain conditions. Such conditional grants might go to all municipalities that meet the minimum requirements or only to a limited number whose applications are judged superior to the others. In any event, the initial decision about whether to apply for such a grant is an example of a local policy decision. Keeping track of such programs and advising their councils about the grants for which they qualify is a crucial job for municipal staff. The success of these applications sometimes depends on judgments made at the central level about how well the local policy proposal responds to a documented local need. In other words, municipalities can benefit from having staff members who can skillfully translate the desires of municipal councils into the language required by central government granting programs. Having effective local members of the federal or provincial legislatures who are able to use their political influence to help ensure that their municipalities receive fair (or even preferential) treatment from the program administrators is also beneficial. Here the political connections of local councillors are likely to be more valuable than the technical expertise of staff.

Federal and provincial programs aimed at renewing Canada's urban infrastructure are probably the best-known central initiatives to which municipalities have responded in recent years. Billions of dollars have been made available for new roads, transit lines, buses, water and wastewater treatment plants, and energy-from-waste plants. In many cases, municipal long-term capital spending plans already included provisions for such new investments. But the availability of funds from elsewhere has enabled municipalities to accelerate their plans. Indeed, municipalities with the most comprehensive policies for new capital investment were the ones best positioned to benefit from the federal and provincial funds. The intergovernmental policy process relating to major new investments in public transit facilities has been extremely complex, especially in Toronto and Vancouver. In both these cases, the cities of Toronto and Vancouver (like other major urban municipalities) lobbied hard for new federal and provincial programs that would help fund transit investment. To the extent that they have been successful, they have had to ensure support from both the federal and the provincial governments, from their suburban neighbours, and from Metrolinx and TransLink respectively.[8]

As far as policy-making for infrastructure is concerned, it is misleading to think of municipalities as being passive responders to federal and provincial initiatives. As indicated above, in many cases municipalities had already adopted their own policies about infrastructure investment and would have proceeded, albeit more slowly, without outside financial assistance. But it is also important to emphasize that in many respects the federal and provincial initiatives to which they were responding were themselves heavily influenced by municipal lobbying—not just from major cities like Toronto and Vancouver, but also by provincial associations of municipalities and the Federation of Canadian Municipalities. As will be discussed in Chapter 15, municipalities would ideally like to have direct access themselves to all the financial resources needed to fund their own infrastructure. Responding to federal and provincial programs for funding local infrastructure is a better alternative than having to provide all the funding themselves from their currently limited resources.

Responding to Pressures for Economic Growth

There are huge pressures on municipal politicians to promote growth, both in the local economy in general and for the value of local real estate in particular. Explaining why this is so has always preoccupied most serious students of North American local politics. Municipal councils are constantly faced with proposals of one sort or another that are defended on the grounds that they will promote the local economy. Debate is almost never about whether growth is desirable; it is about which policy among a number of alternatives is most likely to promote the most growth benefiting the most residents.[9] In this part of the chapter we examine competing explanations about why local growth is so important in local politics, and we examine the kinds of policies municipal governments have adopted in order to advance it.

The first set of explanations involves claims that local business elites are invariably successful in dominating municipal councils in one way or another. Because they make money from growth, they ensure that councils adopt pro-growth policies. A crude version of this explanation is that successful business people have the deepest pockets and they can control local electoral outcomes through their campaign contributions. If this explanation were true, we would expect to see significant variation in local policies towards growth depending on the local rules about campaign contributions. But pro-growth policies in Canadian municipalities are ubiquitous even though, as we have seen in Chapter 9, there is a wide variation in Canadian provinces about local election financing. A more sophisticated version of this argument is that land-owning and development-industry interests control local politics. These interests, the argument goes, are so dependent on municipal decisions about land use that they will do everything they possibly can to control the content of municipal decisions about land-use issues.[10] Although there are times and places when developers seem always to get their way, the problem with this kind of analysis is that there are also lots of examples of situations where municipal councils stand up to individual local developers and refuse to permit proposed developments.

More sophisticated explanations for business dominance argue that many municipalities promote growth because they are more like business firms than they are like national governments. According to this view, municipalities, unlike national governments, have little control over economic activity within their territories and are therefore forced to compete with other municipalities to attract new desirable businesses and/or high-end home buyers. If a particular municipality is successful, most of its property-owners benefit from the resulting economic growth.[11] If it is not, property values eventually decline and property-owners lose. This kind of analysis applies especially well to municipal governments that cover all or most of a single *population centre*, as defined in Chapter 5. But, in multi-municipal urban or metropolitan areas, it is not uncommon, especially in the United States, for municipalities to specialize. Some deliberately refuse to approve any form of new growth because their residents like things as they are; new growth is seen as a potential threat to property values.[12] There are a few areas in Canada, especially near the cities of Vancouver, Victoria, and Montreal where such municipalities still exist. The town of Hampstead, an inner suburb of Montreal, has a zoning by-law that prohibits all commercial and industrial development within its borders.[13]

But most municipalities are constantly searching for new economic development that will bring more jobs, more people, and more buildings to their respective territories. Higher real-estate values are a desirable outcome as well, but not so high that they cause some potential new development to go elsewhere. Most mayors and municipal councillors are always looking for some new scheme to attract new investors. In his recent book *Cities of Oil: Municipalities and Petroleum Manufacturing in Southern Ontario, 1860–1960*, Timothy W. Cobban describes how nineteenth-century municipal councils could genuinely be considered to have their own industrial policies.[14] In the almost complete absence of any kind of specialized staff advice, they offered grants and tax concessions to industries and railways, and some of these decisions had significant impacts on private-sector decisions about industrial location. Canadian provinces (but not all American states) have now generally made it impossible for their municipalities to subsidize industry in this way, the objective being to prevent a "race to the bottom" in which almost all industries everywhere end up with some kind of local tax holiday.

If municipal tax breaks and subsidies are illegal, the obvious question is, What can municipalities do to attract new jobs and businesses? A great many people in municipal government would like to have a clear answer to this question. Unfortunately, there is no clear answer. Mario Polèse, a professor of urban geography with long experience in urban economic development, has recently recounted various "urban-development legends" that have been popular in municipal circles over the last 50 years:[15]

1. In the 1960s, it was thought that luring *strategic industries* was the key to local growth. There was supposed to be spin-off economic growth, but it rarely materialized, in part because the new industry often drove up local labour costs thereby discouraging other employers from locating nearby. Polèse cites the steel complex in Sorel near Montreal as an example of this phenomenon.
2. The next fad was *industrial parks*. Every region in North America seemed to want to replicate North Carolina's Research Triangle.[16] But as many Canadian municipalities and universities came to realize, just because the idea worked in one place did not mean it would work everywhere.
3. Then came *industrial clusters*. Every region wanted one, probably the most successful one in Canada being the high-tech cluster in and around Waterloo, Ontario. There is not much evidence, however, that municipalities did anything significant to promote the cluster.[17] With the apparent decline in the fortunes of BlackBerry

(formerly RIM), perhaps its future is less clear. Polèse points to Montreal's "Multimedia City" as another example of a failed cluster.

4. In the 1980s, *community economic development* became popular. It was thought that local economies could best be grown by focusing on helping businesses that were already present in a community rather than chasing new ones. Polèse claims that this strategy remains popular because it appeals to people of widely different political ideologies and because no one can really determine if it works or not.

5. *Branding* of cities and their regions has also been popular recently.[18] Some brands seem to work ("Keep Austin Weird" for the capital city of Texas); others not ("Toronto Unlimited" a failed branding effort in 2005[19]). Branding is not just about slogans. Every city that bids for the Olympic Games is willing to pay for the privilege by projecting its "brand" on the world stage.

6. The latest fad has been associated with the name of Richard Florida, now at the University of Toronto. Florida believes that if a city is able to attract creative people as residents jobs for them will follow.[20] Because jobs for the *creative class* pay more than jobs for non-creative people, local economic growth will follow. Following this strategy, municipalities should be chasing creative people, not conventional capitalist investors. Not surprisingly, this strategy remains controversial. The main issue relates to causality. Everyone concedes that the presence of creative people (as Florida defines them) is associated with high levels of local economic growth, but it is not at all clear what came first: the growth or the creative people.[21]

Municipalities are always looking for the next big thought or proposal that might give them the edge in the competition for economic growth. They will spend money on consultants, reports, and advertising campaigns even without much evidence that any of this activity makes a difference.[22] It has been long ago explained that the failure to do anything about economic development is politically disastrous: better to spend modest amounts of money on economic promotion than be accused by your political opponents of doing nothing.[23] The likely truth, however, is best expressed in the words of Mario Polèse:

> The conclusion to draw from all this isn't that cities can do nothing to promote economic development. It's that they should avoid academic fads and quick fixes, which are no substitute for obvious policy goals

like competently providing mandated services at reasonable cost, keeping streets safe, and not taxing and regulating away businesses—good governance, in sum, and even that comes with no guarantee to work.[24]

Responding to Pressures from Citizens

In Chapter 10 we briefly considered the role of citizens in relation to controversies about urban development, pointing out that often citizens were simply arguing that proposed developments should be "not in my back yard" (NIMBY). This section is about something different: the more positive role that citizens can play in bringing about policy changes at the local level. In almost every community at any given time, various groups, old and new, are trying to influence their local councils to do something different. It could be something as simple as improving the playground equipment in the local park or as complex and controversial as prohibiting smoking in local buildings or providing public support for a Gay Pride parade.

It is impossible to describe all the various forms that local citizen engagement might take.[25] Much depends on the size of the community, the nature of the issue, and the particular political practices of the municipality in question. What will become evident in the discussion that follows is that organized groups of citizens can be remarkably successful in bringing about local change, especially if what they are advocating does not cost a large amount of money. Because of the difficulties in making generalizations, we shall focus here on two kinds of policy issues that result from the articulation of citizen demands at the local level: (1) issues that transcend individual municipalities and that become part of a process of policy diffusion; and (2) issues that are difficult or impossible to deal with locally and are responded to with policy decisions that are primarily symbolic.

Issues Subject to Diffusion

Let us assume for a minute that one night over a few beers and barbecued burgers a group of neighbours decided that outdoor cats are a menace, that it is cruel to keep cats indoors, and that, therefore, they were going to do whatever they could to make it illegal for people to keep cats as pets. The first question we might want to ask is, Where did this idea come from? This is a question about *agenda-setting* in public policy that goes far beyond the scope of this book. The quick answer is that there must have been some kind of media report—perhaps picking up on academic studies of kind or another—that pointed to the problems with outdoor cats (killing too many birds?) and/or the pathological behaviours of indoor cats. In any event, the problem was seen by this group of people as something that they needed to act on. But what to do? In Canada, they could try to contact their local federal member of Parliament (MP) in the hopes that harbouring cats could be made a criminal offence. Or they could contact their representative in the provincial legislature so as to press for provincial legislation regulating cats. Much more likely, however, would be an attempt at local regulation. Many municipalities already require that outdoor cats be licensed, so an outright prohibition on urban cats might not be too much of a stretch. However, cat-lovers would inevitably argue that preventing residents from having cats at all, even in the privacy of their own homes, could well be beyond the legal authority of municipalities.

If the proponents of a municipal cat prohibition made some initial headway, the council would almost inevitably hold some kind of public forum to gauge public opinion on the matter. It is not hard to imagine the emotional atmosphere at such a meeting: cat-lovers, bird-lovers, veterinarians, disgruntled neighbours of cat-owners, pet-food store owners and employees, libertarians—they would all be out in force, all pleading for the municipal council to do the right thing. Even if municipal councillors were convinced that there was indeed a real problem with cats, they might well conclude that outright municipal prohibition was illegal and/or unwise. So they would look for alternatives; they would be looking for an appropriate *policy instrument*. There would be many options: increased licensing costs; increased enforcement; required annual health checks by veterinarians; a publicity campaign aimed at cat-owners that demonstrates the harm cats can cause. Whatever option they chose would be subject to almost constant review and debate. Municipal staff would doubtless write reports on all these different possibilities, but because there is not much in the way of technical or specialized knowledge about controlling cats in urban environments, municipal councillors would likely trust their own political interests and preferences rather than what they might read in the reports.

The process described above for cats is very close to what actually happened in many places concerning smoking in public buildings, recycling of solid waste, and the use of cosmetic pesticides on private lawns. The cities of Ottawa and Toronto passed the first Canadian municipal bylaws about smoking in public buildings in 1976 and 1977 respectively.[26] In 1983, the city of Kitchener, Ontario, began the first blue-box recycling program.[27] In 1991, the town of Hudson, Quebec, approved a bylaw "prohibiting nonessential uses of lawn and garden pesticides on public and private property, except under specific circumstances and in certain locations."[28] The legality of the Hudson bylaw was challenged. In 2001 the Supreme Court of Canada ruled that Hudson's action was legal in relation to the laws that governed Quebec's municipalities.

Municipal policies about smoking, recycling, and pesticides spread from one place to another through a process known as *policy diffusion*,[29] or in more common language *policy copying*. All governments engage in this activity—they watch what others are doing to solve a problem and, if the solution seems to work, they copy the general policy, perhaps changing the details to suit their own particular circumstances. But with so many municipalities (compared to national and provincial governments), policy diffusion is particularly prevalent at the local level. Indeed, it is sometimes said, only half-jokingly, that the process of municipal policy-making mostly involves staff finding out what their neighbouring municipalities are doing right and then recommending it to council for their own municipality. Regarding matters that were originally controversial, such as the local regulation of smoking and pesticides, once some municipalities have taken the initial steps, it becomes much more likely that others will follow.

Ironically, policy diffusion can become so extensive at the municipal level that provincial governments often move in to occupy the policy field themselves. This has certainly happened with respect to smoking in public buildings. But such provincial action only causes local non-smoking activists to push harder at the municipal level. In recent years, some municipalities have passed bylaws restricting outdoor smoking in parks and in areas near schools and other places where children congregate. In some places, non-smoking activists are now pushing for municipal restrictions on the number of retail outlets that can sell cigarettes. With respect to recycling, most provinces have acted to compel municipalities to recycle and to meet various provincially imposed targets. In Ontario, after lawn-care companies lost their pesticide battle in dozens of important municipalities, they reached a deal in 2009 with the provincial government: in return for reluctantly accepting a province-wide ban on cosmetic lawn pesticides, the companies would not have to tolerate more intense levels of municipal regulation.[30] Under Ontario law, municipalities no longer have the authority to regulate pesticides. There can be no *legal* argument that municipalities should have this authority because provincial control over municipal jurisdiction is absolute.

Issues that Are Responded to Symbolically

Most of our society's significant social and economic problems—poverty, drug abuse, homelessness, and others—are manifested within the territories of our major cities. It is therefore not surprising that many residents of these cities expect their municipal governments to act on these problems. Sometimes the demand is simply that the problems be made to disappear, that the homeless, for example, be moved somewhere else where they might be less visible.[31] More often though, groups of concerned citizens and activists genuinely want the municipal government to do something constructive. The problem is that municipalities rarely have the resources on their own to tackle big social problems. If any particular municipality ever somehow managed to develop its own expensive set of programs, how could it possibly prevent non-residents from moving in to take advantage of the program? Unlike sovereign national governments, municipalities cannot operate their own immigration policies so as to ensure that their own social programs are economically sustainable over the long term. Nor do they have access to a wide array of taxation choices. The American political scientist Paul Peterson, who is well known for articulating this position about the limited redistributive policy capacity of municipal governments (i.e., the limited capacity to tax the rich to provide services for people), points out that the municipal response to redistributive demands is often aimed at making it look like there is action when in fact there is very little. Peterson refers to such responses as "symbolic manipulation" and carefully lists a wide range of tactics that have been employed by municipal officials to make it look like they are responding to redistributive demands. One such example is a program that covers a small area for a short period of time: the program is called "experimental," but officials know in advance that, even if it is a great success, there will be no funds to implement it for a longer period of time over a wider area.[32]

Another possible version of "symbolic manipulation" is for a municipality to adopt a grand strategy for addressing a problem (poverty, homelessness, drug addiction, unemployment) while not committing any of its own resources to the solution. Such strategies are often notable for their reliance on other governments and/or non-profit agencies to actually provide the funds and do the work. Staff are relied on heavily to write such documents, but because they often lack the required expertise, outside consultants are often engaged as well.[33] The result is the production of documents that refer to municipalities as "catalysts for leveraging funds," as "coordinators," and as "links" in complex service-providing systems. Councillors sometimes see little need to pay attention because they understand that few, if any municipal resources are being committed. Not all municipal documents that address these types of problems are manipulative. Some might well help bring about real change.[34] The problem is that we have very little real research about the impact of many of these initiatives. The grand strategies are forgotten soon after the press conferences that announce them.

Municipalities and Precommitment

Precommitment is a form of self-restraint.[35] It involves deciding in advance what to do and sticking to that decision regardless of what might happen in the future. For governments, entrenched constitutions are a form of precommitment because the government itself cannot change the constitution by using its normal policy- (or law-) making processes. Municipal governments in Canada do not generally have to worry about their own constitutions because these are decided by provincial legislatures when approving the laws that establish and govern municipalities. There are at least two senses, however, in which Canadian municipalities precommit themselves to particular policies. Each will be examined in turn.

Precommitment in Land-Use Planning

Most provincial legislation about land-use planning enables or requires municipalities to approve some form of "official" or "comprehensive" plan (the term varies from province to province) to act as a framework for future development. The justification for such plans is that they provide an element of certainty for residents and landowners about what is to happen to the built environment over some specified period of time. While most municipalities adopt such plans because they are required to do so, providing such certainty would be a perfectly rational objective for municipalities even in the absence of legislative requirements; arguably it could even be a tool for enhancing economic growth because potential investors would be given a clear idea of the community's future. But what if circumstances change and the municipality wants to alter its plan? It usually has to go through some kind of special procedure involving the province in order to do so—and it becomes a matter for provincial policy to determine how strictly the municipality's precommitment will be respected. In Ontario, the Ontario Municipal Board approves thousands of official plan amendments each year. In Georgia, however, "the state limits major comprehensive plan amendments to one every five years."[36] In Georgia, municipalities are seriously precommitting themselves when they adopt a comprehensive plan. In Canada, such precommitment exists in theory but is not much honoured in practice. Indeed, it is a common complaint that municipalities often have great difficulty taking a land-use decision and sticking with it. When thinking about planning, it is relatively easy for municipal councils to precommit to various restrictions on growth. But when a developer comes along with a seemingly attractive proposal that will generate jobs and tax revenue, the original commitment often looks less important. Anyone who has precommitted to reducing weight through dieting will understand this phenomenon.

Precommitment and Infrastructure

As we have seen, the concept of precommitment was initially developed in relation to constitutions. According to Canada's constitution, we cannot get rid of the monarchy unless Parliament and every provincial legislature agree. The obstacles to change are huge, even if a majority of the Canadian population is clearly in favour. While it is true that municipalities in Canada generally control the built environment, it is not true that a municipal majority can shape the built environment as it wishes. The obstacle is not a constitution or even a provincial law; it is the very practical consideration that the built environment consists of physical structures, and they generally cannot practically be torn down and built somewhere else. So when citizens are asked by a municipality to participate in thinking about a municipality's future, it is always understood (although not usually advertised) that the exercise is about new development, not about what is already there.

It is true, of course, that the federal and provincial governments build infrastructure as well. The federal government builds (and abandons) military bases; the provinces build highways. But as a proportion of their overall activities and resources, the building of infrastructure is much less important to them than it is to municipalities. As of 2011, municipalities owned more than half of all non-financial assets owned by governments in Canada.[37] When a municipality builds a major arterial road, a track for an LRT, a subway line, a new treatment plant for water supply or sewage, or even a new concert hall, it is making a financial commitment over decades and it is locking in place particular limitations and opportunities for future urban development. This is precisely why municipal policy decisions about such matters are so important and why they often generate a great deal of local controversy. The commitment is not just until the next municipal budget is adopted; it will likely be for decades.

Annual municipal budgets are rarely subject to dramatic change from one year to the next, in part because a high proportion of the annual operating budget is committed to the maintenance of infrastructure projects that have previously been built. In one sense, such routine expenditures make municipal budgets seem boring, predictable, and not easily subject to changing citizen preferences, regardless of how conscientiously those citizens might be consulted. In another sense, however, the fact that a decision to build a new arena today could be a major determinant of the budget 20 years from now should at least cause us all to pay more attention to the original decision. This reasoning applies especially to new municipal infrastructure whose capital costs are subsidized by other levels of government. By responding to certain federal and provincial infrastructure programs, municipalities might only have to spend "fifty-cent dollars" to obtain a new project, but they invariably have to pay "hundred-cent dollars" to maintain it.

Implementing Municipal Policy Decisions

If a policy does not get implemented, or if it is implemented differently from the council's original intentions, then the actual decision-making process is not very meaningful. This is why implementation is a crucial part of the policy process. As we shall see in the next chapter, it is the senior management of a municipality that is charged with ensuring that implementation takes place in accordance with decisions that its council has made. But like most aspects of government, the real-world distinction between the decision and its implementation is often not so simple.

The best-known problems with policy implementation involve more than one level of government.[38] Imagine that a federal government decides to pursue a particular course of action but requires state/provincial and local co-operation to get it done. The problem is that each independent level of government bends the program to meet its own needs such that what comes out in various localities can vary a great deal and be almost unrecognizable from what the federal government intended. If the program involved requires that individual municipal employees use their own discretion in implementing a policy that ultimately comes from other levels of government, then the possibilities grow even greater that implementation difficulties distort the objectives of the original program.[39]

Implementing municipal policies within a single municipality should be easier. It surely is easier in very small municipalities, where councillors can easily keep a close eye on what their staff is doing—perhaps too close in the view of staff who would like clear distinctions to be established and respected between policy-making and implementation. But even in small places, the superintendent of roads gets to apply her own interpretations of council policy as she contemplates how to repair a deteriorating section of road, unless of course the mayor is riding along with her on the inspection tour, a not-unheard-of situation in many small municipalities. Until recently, however, we have had no major studies of policy implementation in any Canadian municipalities, large or small.

Now we do have such a study, albeit a quirky and rather unsystematic one. Mariana Valverde's recent book on policy implementation in Canada's largest municipality[40] deserves our attention. Valverde shows that there is wide variation in the city of Toronto concerning how different bylaws are enforced, often depending on the ethnicity or social class of the person or area in question. What is especially interesting about her findings is that much of the variation in implementation and enforcement stems from the involvement of local councillors in micro-level issues in their wards. Most studies of policy implementation point to bureaucrats as the source of implementation failures and inconsistencies; the politicians approve a general policy but their permanent staff either cannot or will not make sure that it is carried out. In Toronto, the elected councillors approve general policies in the council chamber and then scurry back to their wards to make sure that it is implemented in a way that suits their particular interpretation of what is appropriate for their own ward. This is a feature of policy implementation that is probably unique to municipal government, perhaps unique to large amalgamated municipalities such as Toronto.

Conclusion

In a 2007 book chapter about policy-making in major Canadian cities, Kennedy Stewart and Patrick J. Smith claim that "the capacity of local decision-makers to direct, receive, and act upon sophisticated policy advice is severely hampered by an antiquated approach to local governing."[41] Their entire chapter is based on the premise that the federal and provincial parliamentary systems of government should be the models for municipal policy-making. In particular, municipal political parties are necessary in order for elections to offer clear choices and for councils to make clear decisions. The authors conclude that, of the eight large cities that they study, "only Montreal avoids the pitfalls of non-partisanship, at-large elections, and unlimited election spending and, from an electoral perspective at least, can be considered the study city most likely to play an effective role in the policy analysis process."[42] Each of these "pitfalls" were examined in Chapter 9, so they will not be reviewed here. The problem with Stewart and Smith's analysis is that they do not examine the kinds of issues with which city governments actually have to deal.

The objective of this chapter has been to show that policy-making is different in Canadian municipalities from policy-making at other levels, in large part because the issues are different. Unless we pay attention to the nature of the issues, there is no justification for assuming that one set of political structures is different from another. The unique features of municipal issues for policy-making are that they involve responding to federal and provincial initiatives; engaging in direct competition with other municipalities for jobs and growth; responding to citizen initiatives from both inside and outside the municipality, often without significant resources to implement real change; and having to make decisions about the built environment, especially public infrastructure, that cannot be reversed for many decades.

Stewart and Smith favour large councils elected by wards, with high salaries and appropriate staff for each individual member of council. This is exactly the structural environment that has enabled city councillors in Toronto to become so intimately involved in the implementation of municipal policies within their own wards. In Stewart and Smith's ideal world, Toronto city councillors should be spending their time analyzing and debating the big policy issues that confront the city of Toronto. There are many urban issues (the future of the waterfront; social assistance) that they cannot decide because other levels of government are the main players. Other issues (investment in new regional transit infrastructure) transcend the city's boundaries. Councillors are left with other more local issues (traffic flow, trees, bicycle paths) that are of crucial importance to the residents who elect them. This is why they get so involved in policy implementation. To understand municipal policy-making in Canada, it is not sufficient simply to wish that it was more like other levels of government. The job of the political scientist is to understand, not to wish. Municipal policy-making in Canada is not "immature," as Stewart and Smith claim. It is simply different.

RESOURCES

Go to the website of your local municipality and find the agenda for a recent council meeting. Pick an issue on the agenda that looks interesting to you. How do you think this item made it to the council's agenda? Find out all you can about this issue by looking at the documentation that is linked to the agenda and/or by searching local media and blogs. Then check the council minutes for the same meeting and see what the council decided about this agenda item. In larger municipalities you might be able to watch a video of the meeting.

STUDY QUESTIONS

1. What do we mean when we say that municipalities are both *policy-takers* and *policy-makers*?
2. Do you think municipalities should have more legal authority to make deals with potential investors to attract new businesses to their communities? Why or why not?
3. What is *policy diffusion*? Why is it especially important in municipal policy-making?
4. What makes the municipal policy-making process different from the same process at the federal and provincial levels in Canada?

CHAPTER 13

Senior Management and Labour Unions

Without employees to advise them or to implement their decisions, mayors and municipal councils are powerless, regardless of how much support they have in their respective communities. Municipal employees implement council decisions. As we shall see, some people have argued that much municipal work should be contracted out to the private sector. But even if a Canadian municipal council accepted such advice and decided to contract out almost everything, it would still need at least some management employees to advise it about the contracts, to manage the competition for awarding them, and to monitor them once they were agreed.

In this chapter we first look at what is distinctive about the work of senior municipal managers. We then focus on the position of *city manager* or *chief administrative officer* (CAO), paying special attention to Montreal where the position (known as directeur-général in Quebec) has been under a great deal of stress due to scandals relating to corruption in the construction industry. Towards the end of the chapter, we consider the issues of contracting out and public–private partnerships and how municipal policy on these issues has been affected in Canada by the strength of municipal unions.

Distinctive Features of Municipal Management

As we learned in Chapter 1, municipal employees technically are not civil servants because they are not servants of the Crown. They are, however, clearly part of the public sector. Statistics Canada reports that 3,632,000 Canadians were employed in 2011 in the public sector, which includes schools, colleges, universities, and hospitals. Of this number,

609,000 worked in *local general government* (municipal government and associated special-purpose bodies, but not school boards) and another 68,000 worked in local government business enterprises. More people are employed by local general government than by either the federal government or the provincial governments collectively, but school boards and health and social service institutions each employ more people than general local governments.[1]

More so than at the federal and provincial levels, senior municipal managers tend to be functional specialists. Senior civil servants at the federal and provincial levels have usually been educated as generalists and expect that they will move around from one department to another as part of their career progression. Municipal managers often get their first municipal jobs because they were educated as engineers, land-use planners, lawyers, or accountants and then progress through the management hierarchy in the same functional specialization, although not necessarily in the same municipality. By definition, the highest management position in a municipality has no functional specialization, so people initially recruited to such positions often have only limited preparation. Generalists tend to get hired by the very smallest municipalities, which might have only one or two managers in total, or by the very largest, which can afford to hire policy analysts and research assistants in the offices of the very senior managers.

As we have seen in previous chapters, unlike most federal and provincial civil servants, municipal managers are not responsible to a single political master, a minister of the Crown. In a strong city-manager system, department heads have the luxury of considering themselves to report only to the city manager, but in most municipalities, all department heads also report to the council as a collective entity. Reporting to a group of people rather than a single person makes any manager's job more difficult, especially when various members of the governing body often differ publicly from each other in their basic objectives and priorities. In any event, even in a strong city-manager system, the city manager reports to the council as a whole, which makes the job more politically complex than that of most deputy ministers at other levels.

Finally, as we have seen in Chapter 9, municipal councils carry out most of their business in public. Much of this business involves receiving written and oral reports from senior managers. As a result, unlike that of their federal and provincial counterparts, the work of senior municipal managers is very much a matter of public record, not just in writing but also at locally televised council meetings where they are called on to answer questions from councillors who might not have properly read or understood their agenda material or who wish to use the manager in scoring a political point against an opponent.

The Role of City Managers and CAOs[2]

To understand the positions of city manager and CAO, we must go back to the Progressive reformers at the end of the nineteenth century (see Chapter 9). These are the same people who argued for small municipal councils and non-partisan at-large elections. They wanted as much as possible to remove politics from municipal government. In many ways, their most important municipal innovation was the *council–manager plan*, a system of municipal government in which the mayor's position became largely ceremonial, the council's jobs were to set broad policy and appoint a city manager, and the city manager's job was to do everything else. The establishment of such a position was seen as crucial for removing undue political influence from city administration, breaking the power of the urban political machines, and bringing professional management to urban government.

The first municipal general manager in the United States was appointed for Staunton, Virginia, in 1908. This was "the first municipal post with the title of manager, whereby a single, appointed official would have responsibility for the day-to-day management of the civic adminis-tration."[3] Staunton became the ideal model for the reformers who advo-cated for the council–manager plan throughout the United States and Canada. Sumpter, South Carolina, appointed a city manager in 1912 and Westmount, Quebec, appointed one in 1913, becoming the third council–manager municipality in North America.[4] In a pure council–manager system, the manager appoints all the department heads and is directly and solely responsible for all the management documents that flow to council, including the proposed annual municipal budget.

In 1914 the International City Managers' Association (ICMA) was formed to promote the council–manager plan. Except in the very largest of American cities, where strong mayor systems still predominate, ICMA has been remarkably successful and has extended its efforts throughout the Western world. On its website, the ICMA describes its recent history in these words:

> During the 1960s, the profile of local government began to show sig-nificant changes. Not only were there complex new problems created, but variations in organizations and structure became evident. Some cities, towns, and counties began providing for an appointed official

responsible for overall administrative affairs without adopting the council–manager plan as it was originally conceived. Likewise, the development of councils of governments and regional councils brought new and innovative structures to local government. It became obvious to ICMA that, in many cases, the positions being developed did not significantly vary from the role of the traditional professional positions provided for in the council–manager form of government.

In July 1969, the International City Managers' Association changed its name to the International City Management Association and began the process of recognizing local governments that provide for positions of professional management while retaining a form of government other than the council–manager plan. To distinguish them from those recognized as council–manager communities, these newly recognized places were designated "general management" communities. Criteria were established for recognition and the individuals in these local government management positions were made eligible for corporate membership in ICMA. More recently, in 1986, ICMA completed the same process for recognizing state/provincial associations of local governments.

In May 1991, members voted to change ICMA's constitutional name to the International City/County Management Association, reflecting the membership of the Association and recognizing the evolution in county government professionalism.[5]

Many Canadian city managers and CAOs have been active in ICMA. In 2013–14, Simon Farbrother, the city manager of Edmonton, served as president of the ICMA. All major Canadian municipalities now have either a city manager or a CAO, or a *directeur-général*, as the position is known in Quebec. Regardless of the title used, the actual authority granted to the holder of the position varies significantly. Municipal acts in the various provinces and the relevant bylaw in each municipality can provide an outline of the legal situation, but even when all this research is done, much depends on the culture of the municipal organization and the management style of the particular individual. In any event, there are no major Canadian municipalities in which the city manager or CAO has as much authority as envisioned by the original designers of the council–manager plan.

When Things Go Wrong

Most of the time things go right in municipal administration: council receives good advice from municipal managers and makes a decision; managers then implement the decision relatively efficiently. Municipalities are human institutions, however, and things occasionally go wrong. When they do, we usually learn more about what happened than we do when things went right. Much can be learned from two judicial inquiries into municipal mismanagement in Ontario in the 2000s.[6] However, in recent years, the major Canadian municipality with the most managerial turmoil has been Montreal. Between 2006 and 2013, Montreal lived with four different mayors and five directors-general (not counting interim directors-general). Most of the changes related in one way or another to allegations of corruption or other forms of wrongdoing. In this portion of the book we are concerned with directors-general, not mayors. The reasons for the departures of some of them present us with important examples of what can go wrong. Each of the five directors-general are discussed briefly below:[7]

1. Robert Abdallah (2003–6). Abdallah left his position with two years remaining on his contract, without stating any reasons. In 2013, during testimony to the Charbonneau Commission of Inquiry on the Awarding and Management of Public Contracts in the Construction Industry in Quebec, Mayor Gérald Tremblay testified that he fired Abdallah because he had received information about Abdallah's involvement in corrupt practices.[8] In 2012, testimony at the Charbonneau inquiry stated that Abdallah participated in schemes to defraud the city of millions of dollars. Abdallah has denied the accusations.[9]

2. Claude Léger (2006–9). Legér resigned after the city's auditor-general released a report stating that a contract to install water meters in Montreal had been grossly mismanaged, so much so that the Quebec Provincial Police launched a corruption investigation.[10] Léger testified at the Charbonneau inquiry that he had been suspicious about improper practices among politicians and subordinates concerning various contracts, including the one for water meters and that he regretted not properly informing Mayor Tremblay about his suspicions. He claimed that he was reluctant to do anything because he was worried about losing his job.[11]

3. Louis Roquet (2010–11). The auditor-general accused Roquet of intercepting his emails and of improperly divulging one of his confidential reports to Telus, a company involved in upgrading the city's phone system. There were also reports that his relations with members of the executive committee were poor. He resigned for "personal reasons" after having been in the job for less than two years.[12]

4. Guy Hébert (2012–13). Hébert was director-general for only 15

months. Mayor Michael Applebaum (who himself resigned shortly thereafter when charged with various offences relating to corruption) demanded Hébert's resignation after it was revealed that
Hébert had asked the Quebec government to fire the Montreal police chief.[13] Reasons for Hébert's actions were not entirely clear but
they appeared to relate mostly to labour relations between the city
and the police union. The union was glad to see Hébert go.

5.   Alain Marcoux (2013–) When Denis Coderre was elected mayor
     in November 2013, he arranged for the appointment of 68-year-old
     Alain Marcoux as director-general. Marcoux had been minister
     of municipal affairs in the government of René Lévesque. More
     recently he had been director-general of Quebec City since 2006.[14]
     Will the combination of Coderre and Marcoux bring probity and
     stability? That is the big question.

A great deal has been going wrong in the last few years in the municipal government of Montreal. Much of it is now being investigated by the
Charbonneau inquiry into the construction industry in Quebec. When
the final report of the inquiry is released, we shall likely have a much
clearer idea of the nature and extent of the city of Montreal's political
and managerial problems.

Contracting Out

Many of the examples of bad municipal management in Ontario and
Quebec referred to in the previous section resulted from one form or
another of contracting out. Municipalities contracted for services, but
the contracts were not awarded strictly according to the rules. In the
final analysis, municipal taxpayers were cheated. But not all companies that provide services to municipalities break the rules. Some provide
excellent value for money. One of the main challenges in municipal management is to discover the circumstances under which contracting out is
appropriate and when it is not.

The first point to make is that contracting out is nothing new.
Every time a municipality consults an outside lawyer or expert, it is
contracting out, because it is purchasing a service that could in theory
be provided by its own employees, current or potential. Often there
are extremely good reasons why special expertise is obtained in this
way; it would simply be far too expensive to employ highly trained specialists in a particular issue whose special skills might be needed only
once every few years. Similarly, if a municipality needs to clean the
windows on a high-rise city hall, no one is likely to complain if it hires

a specialized company to do the job. No one expects banks to employ window cleaners as permanent employees. Why should anyone expect municipalities to do so?

But what about the idea that municipalities should contract out almost everything they do? This idea has been seriously advanced from time to time, especially in the 1990s when confidence in the ability of governments to do almost anything was at a very low ebb. The issue is politically charged because contracting out is often seen—quite rightly in many cases—as an attack on unionized labour. If municipal workers have high wages because they are unionized, and if a private company can perform the same work at a cheaper price because its workers are not unionized, it is not surprising that unions would fight contracting out. The role of unions on this issue is something we shall return to in the next section of this chapter. In the meantime, there are other important issues to be examined in relation to contracting out.

Garbage collection is a municipal function that causes many battles about contracting out. In 2001, James C. McDavid at the University of Victoria reported on results of a cross-Canada survey about the contracting out of garbage collection. Except in Quebec, he found that contracting out was usually less expensive, especially in smaller municipalities. Lowest costs seemed to be found in municipalities that combined public provision and contracting out, suggesting that direct competition between public and private providers placed downward pressure on costs.[15] But such findings do little to resolve the debate because McDavid did not collect data on wage levels or ages of workers. Some citizens do not want garbage collectors to be non-unionized young workers who will be let go when they age and become less physically productive. Where municipal workers are doing the job, this is precisely why municipal unions are so resistant to contracting out. In a similar study of residential recycling collection services reported in 2008, McDavid and Mueller found little difference in cost between public and private providers. Notably, private provision predominated: 77 per cent of the providers were private companies.[16] As this is a relatively recent municipal service, private providers were often contracted at the beginning, before unions were able to negotiate their own role.

Because of all the negative attention Toronto mayor Rob Ford attracted to himself in 2013, it is easy to forget that he actually was successful in partially implementing one of his campaign promises from 2010. He had pledged to contract out garbage collection in Toronto beyond the area (the pre-amalgamation city of Etobicoke) for which there was already contracting out. In 2011, Toronto city council voted to contract out its garbage collection between Etobicoke and Yonge Street. The city's unionized employees previously doing this work were re-assigned. After a shaky start, the company that won the seven-year contract (Green for Life Environmental East) is now receiving fewer complaints per capita than the city is for the area east of Yonge Street in which it still collects. The city is expected to save $11 million a year as a result of the contract for the area west of Yonge Street. All of this information comes from the *Toronto Star*,[17] a newspaper that has been otherwise relentlessly critical of Mayor Ford.

The city of Winnipeg has also recently contracted out its garbage collection to a company (Emterra Environmental) that collects recycling materials in the same trucks. In 2013 the company's workers successfully organized to join the same union, the Canadian Union of Public Employees (CUPE), which represents Winnipeg's city workers. It is still not known whether Emterra workers will eventually obtain the same pay and working conditions as city workers.[18]

Water services (supply of drinking water and sewage) are considerably more controversial.[19] In Toronto, for example, any hint of moving towards opening the door to private companies has met with immediate resistance from labour unions, environmentalists, and Canadian nationalists concerned with maintaining public control over freshwater resources. But elsewhere there has been considerable movement. Perhaps the best-known case is Hamilton, Ontario, where in 1995 the regional government contracted out the operation of all its water services to a subsidiary of Philip Environmental, a locally based company. The decision was based as much on a strategy for local economic development as it was on saving money. The idea was that the contract with Hamilton would help Philip develop a national and international presence in what looked like a fast-developing marketplace. The contract guaranteed cost savings to the city, new investment, and the continuation of the unionized jobs in the facilities. But all did not go smoothly. The city underestimated the costs of monitoring the contract. Sewage spills caused lawsuits and embarrassment all around. By the late 1990s, Philip was laying off workers, and those who were left were complaining of deteriorating equipment. Most significant of all, Philip Environmental, a company with many other investments, ran into financial difficulty and was acquired cheaply by a subsidiary of Enron Corporation, a company that would soon go bankrupt in circumstances that showed its whole operation to be built on financial fraud. American Water Services Canada, a company ultimately owned by a German utility, took over from the Enron subsidiary and tried to keep the contract. In anticipation of its expiry, Hamilton city council (which had replaced the regional government as a result of amalgamation) voted narrowly to put the contract out for tender, but no company came up with a proposal that was satisfactory to the city. In September 2004 the city council voted to take direct control of the operation of the water services.[20] In retrospect Hamilton's experience with contracting out can only be assessed as disastrous.

But this type of experience has not been universal. A great many Canadian municipalities successfully contract out the management of various parts of their water services. Since 2006, Veolia Water Canada (a French company once known as Vivendi) has managed water services for the municipality of Brockton, Ontario. The initial five-year contract was renewed for another five years in 2011.[21] Brockton is notable because it is an amalgamated municipality that includes Walkerton, the town where, in 2000, contaminated water supplied by a public body run by incompetents killed at least seven people and caused severe illness in hundreds more.[22]

Public–Private Partnerships

Veolia Water Canada has a different kind of arrangement with Moncton, New Brunswick. In the 1990s it designed, built, and paid for a new water treatment facility for Moncton. In return, Veolia obtained the exclusive right to sell water to the city for 20 years.[23] This arrangement is just one of many different ways in which partnerships can be worked out. Details will vary with each project, depending in large measure on what municipalities are looking for. In the case of the Moncton project, the city was looking both for specialized expertise in the design and construction of the plant and for a financing mechanism that enabled the city to avoid having to borrow large sums. Although generally recognized as a success, the Moncton–Veolia partnership has been criticized by John Loxley for being more costly to the city than is commonly believed. He claims that the whole project was made financially viable only because Veolia received special treatment from the Canada Revenue Agency on sales tax and depreciation rules. He ultimately argues that Moncton actually would have been better off borrowing the necessary funds and building the plant itself. For accounting purposes, no borrowing occurred, but the practical impact on Moncton's financial obligations were the same.[24]

In Regina in 2013, municipal voters had an opportunity to decide on whether their municipality would pursue a public–private partnership to build a new sewage treatment plant. After receiving a report[25] from consultants in January 2013, the Regina city council voted to begin the process of acquiring a partner for the $224 million facility. Probably the most important reason for making this decision was that a 25-per cent federal subsidy, which was announced in June, required significant private involvement. CUPE countered with its own study[26] which argued that, even after the contribution from the federal government, the partnership option was more expensive. According to CUPE, all of the financial benefits claimed in the city's consultants' report resulted from an overestimation of the cost of the risk to be taken by the private partners. Opponents of the council decision launched a petition calling for a referendum on the subject. City council decided to hold one on 25 September 2013.[27] With a 31 per cent turnout, 57 per cent of the voters approved the project.[28] Voters in Regina probably now know more about public–private partnerships than residents of any other city in Canada.

How to quantify risk is a major issue in the assessment of any public–private partnership, including the ones just discussed in Moncton and Regina. A partnership formed in the early 2000s that was mostly about minimizing municipal risk involved the John Labatt Centre (now Budweiser Gardens) in downtown London, Ontario. The arena was a crucial part of the city's plan for downtown revitalization, and the land on which it was built was owned by the municipality. No private company would take on a project like this in downtown London without public backing. The city would not take on the project because it did not want to get into the highly specialized and financially risky business of building and operating an arena. In his study of London's downtown revitalization efforts, Timothy Cobban reports that:

> City council agreed in May 2000 to build the arena with a consortium whose principal partners included Ellis-Don Construction Ltd., a large construction firm with origins in London. The city's responsibilities under the agreement included providing the land for the arena and $31.72 million of the project's total capital costs. The private sector partners were required to provide $10 million and pay the city $45.5 million over fifty years, with full ownership of the arena transferring to the city at the end of the fifty-year agreement.[29]

The arena is operated by Philadelphia-based Global Spectrum Management (whose parent company also owns the Philadelphia Flyers hockey team and 76ers basketball team), which was also part of the original public–private partnership. Financially, the arena has been a huge success. The city has been criticized for structuring the partnership in such a way that the municipality does not gain directly from this success. But the whole point of the agreement was to protect the city from undue risk if it was not successful. In this sense the partnership met the city's objectives, not to mention the fact that the arena clearly has helped meet the city's revitalization objectives.

A more significant project involving both a $480 million new arena and downtown revitalization was negotiated in 2013 in Edmonton. The partnership is between the city and Daryl Katz, the owner of the Edmonton Oilers hockey team.[30] Building of the new arena did not start until early 2014, so it is too early to make any assessment. The general plan is that the city will own the facility, but that it will mainly be paid for by rent from the Oilers, by a special tax (community revitalization levy) that will be paid by neighbouring property owners, and by a surcharge on tickets.

The main lesson to be learned from this discussion of contracting out and public–private partnerships is that today's city managers require a wide variety of skills in order to navigate through all the various tools at their disposal to meet city objectives. They need to understand all the complexities of the kinds of financial arrangements that have just been discussed. They can, of course, receive specialized advice from outside lawyers and accountants, and wise ones will undoubtedly do so for big projects. Ironically, seeking such outside guidance is yet another form of contracting out.

Municipal Unions

Managers also have to deal with unions. Although unions have no particular interest in the contracting out of specialized professional work, they are highly sensitive to proposals to contract out the work that is normally done by their members. Municipal unions are important for a wide range of reasons, not the least of which is that many citizens think most about municipal services when unions threaten to strike or actually do withdraw the services of their members.

Collective Bargaining

Municipal unions have received very little attention from Canadian political scientists.[31] In 1978, T.J. Plunkett and G.M. Betts wrote a text on Canadian municipal management that briefly considered "Employer–Employee Relations and Collective Bargaining." Their opening paragraph is almost as relevant today as it was then:

> There was a time when local governments as employers established jobs and positions, assigned tasks, set wages, determined hours of work and other working conditions, and promoted, disciplined, and discharged

staff at will without reference to their employees. But those days have long since passed in most urban communities. Yet, despite the fact that some groups of public service employees have been organized as trade union locals for more than three decades, elected and appointed officials have been slow to recognize the overall impact that unionization has had, and will continue to have, upon local government administration and practice. As a result, many municipalities still appear to tolerate employee unions as aberrations from the norm and tend to deal with them on an ad hoc basis during contract negotiations rather than develop a cohesive on-going strategy to promote effective and harmonious labour/management relations.[32]

Katherine Graham wrote a book chapter entitled "Collective Bargaining in the Municipal Sector" in 1995. She claims that "municipalities' generally narrow approach to the human resource management function was likely a contributing factor to the significant spread of unionization in the municipal public service by the 1960s, with the Canadian Union of Public Employees (CUPE) emerging as by far the most dominant municipal union."[33] In 2013, CUPE was the largest union in Canada[34] and municipal workers, as well as workers in health and educational institutions, remain its primary base of membership. Graham raises two issues that appear to place municipalities at a disadvantage when bargaining with unions. Both relate to employer disunity. The first variant of the problem is that there are many municipalities and often just one strong union— CUPE. The union provides its local negotiators with considerable data about settlements in other municipalities, and each local attempts to "whipsaw" better settlements than those obtained elsewhere. Naturally, the municipalities respond by sharing information through municipal associations, but they generally do not seem as effective or united as CUPE. In many ways, the most innovative management response to this problem has been in the Vancouver area where Metro Vancouver actually handles labour relations not only for its own employees but also for 15 of the 22 constituent municipalities. In 2013 it was managing over 60 collective agreements.[35]

Another source of management disunity derives from what is sometimes called *multilateral bargaining*.[36] In this situation, participants in the bargaining process know that it is ultimately impossible for management to remain united. Unity, or solidarity, is always a potential problem for unions as well, but except in the most unusual of circumstances, local union negotiators are in complete control of the process. Negotiators for municipal management, on the other hand, know that strong elements on the local council, often including the mayor, are not always completely removed from the negotiating process, regardless of what they might say in public. Indeed, some municipal politicians are closely allied to labour interests and are particularly vulnerable to union efforts to crack open an apparently united management position. In contrast, it is rare for a union in the private sector to expect to have allies on a private company's board of directors.

A third problem for municipal management is that some contract settlements are determined by arbitration. Graham does not discuss this scenario directly because she was writing about non-uniformed municipal workers—that is, workers who are not members of police or fire services. Regardless of the existence or strength of police boards as special-purpose bodies (see Chapter 4), municipal police officers are paid by municipalities mostly from revenues that the municipalities must raise themselves. The same observation applies to fire personnel, for whom there generally are no special-purpose bodies. Police and fire personnel have no legal right to go on strike, but they do have very strong local unions, albeit ones that are usually more limited by provincial legislation in their ability to affiliate with larger organizations like CUPE. In the event that management and union negotiators are unable to reach agreement for police and fire labour contracts, the outstanding issues are usually sent to arbitration. Concerning wage levels, arbitrators frequently award higher settlements than what other unions obtain in the absence of compulsory arbitration.[37] One generous arbitration for one service leads to pressure for others to "catch up"—which in turn creates higher goals for other unions to strive for. Municipal politicians complain frequently about arbitrated settlements for police and fire, but there appears to be little they can do short of launching a full-scale attack on police officers and firefighters, which is not an attractive option for anyone seeking re-election.

Labour Support for Municipal Candidates

In chapters 9 and 10 we examined some of the incentives for and evidence of close connections between the land development industry and municipal councillors. Incentives for municipal unions to take an active role in municipal politics are equally strong, not just because of concerns about wage levels and working conditions but also about matters of wider public interest such as contracting out and public–private partnerships. Canada has a long history of labour involvement in municipal elections, especially during the first half of the twentieth century (see discussion in Chapter 9 about the role of the CCF in Vancouver), but the most significant recent involvement of labour in municipal politics has been seen in British Columbia and Ontario in the early 2000s.[38] In the 2006 Ontario municipal elections, local labour councils affiliated with the Canadian Labour Congress:

> held a series of strategy sessions, campaign manager and candidate schools, public speaking and media courses, and political organizer training sessions in 21 cities across the province. . . . This unprecedented political mobilization at the local level produced a slate of 438 endorsed candidates in 60 different municipalities. On election day, 217 labour-endorsed candidates were either elected or acclaimed to local councils or school boards in Ontario.[39]

In Guelph, labour-endorsed candidates won the mayoralty and a majority on city council. Prominent labour-endorsed mayors who were elected in 2006 were David Miller in Toronto and John Rodriguez (a former federal NDP MP) in Greater Sudbury. However, Miller did not run in 2010 and Rodriguez was defeated.

To understand the unions' political objectives, it is especially important to understand what they were concerned about when they were interviewing candidates who were seeking endorsement:

> A typical interview would involve quizzing candidates about their positions on a number of contentious issues, including municipal procurement, privatization, contracting out, and commitment to public transit. Most candidates were also asked if they had ever, or would ever, cross a picket line. Labour councils were not simply looking to endorse candidates who answered all the questions correctly. Rather, in addition to being satisfied that a candidate was committed to a labour-friendly platform, labour councils were interested in a candidate's overall credibility. After all, if a candidate had no hope of winning, an endorsement from a labour council might have had an adverse effect on the credibility of the CLC's municipal campaign overall. After labour councils interviewed prospective candidates and handed out endorsements accordingly, the CLC dispatched trained union members to carry labour's message to CLC-affiliated locals in various targeted communities.[40]

The Canadian Labour Congress continues to remind the members of its affiliated unions that "Municipalities Matter" and that members "should volunteer for candidates who support you."[41] In any future calculations about labour involvement in municipal elections it is likely that the Toronto municipal strike in the summer of 2009 will be considered of crucial importance. It was not a happy experience for anybody. David Miller's decision not to seek re-election in 2010 seemed to result from being perceived by many Toronto voters as being too favourable to the union and by union leaders as not favourable enough. Whatever his accomplishments as mayor, many residents will only remember the inconveniences brought about by the strike and by his apparent weakness in dealing with union demands. In any event, as we saw in Chapter 9, the campaign financing rules in Toronto for the 2010 election were different from 2006: neither corporations nor unions were allowed to contribute. However, such a rule has no effect on unions' rights to endorse candidates or to encourage members to support them.

Is Municipal Work a "Safe Harbour"?

Fifty years ago, unions were successfully enabling organized private-sector workers in North America to become middle-class consumers. Public-sector unions barely existed, and working for a municipal government, especially in "outside" jobs (garbage collection, street cleaning, park maintenance, and the like), meant being close to the bottom of the labour hierarchy. Now, all of that has changed. Victories won by unions in the private sector have been dramatically eroded. Globalization has caused thousands of manufacturing jobs in North America simply to move elsewhere. Union leaders have faced the grim choice of watching the jobs leave or making concession after concession to try to preserve them. In the public sector, changes have repositioned unions differently: they have gone from victory to victory such that public-sector employment now offers considerable advantages in terms of wage levels, benefits, and security. As noted earlier, of the three levels of government in Canada, the local level employs the most workers, and dramatically so if we include the education and health sectors.

This means that the debate about public-sector employment really is about *local* public-sector employment. The debate is about the extent to which we should tolerate growing disparities between the public and private sectors. People with different political views and values will no doubt differ about whether the current public or private model is the one to follow. What must concern the student of the local public sector are the implications of the disparities if they persist and grow.

An American scholar, John D. Donahue, addresses this issue in his provocative book, *The Warping of Government Work*.[42] Donahue presents a great deal of evidence from the United States to demonstrate that public-sector jobs requiring relatively low-level skills (e.g., office clerks, janitors) pay significantly more than equivalent private-sector jobs, while jobs requiring high-level skills (lawyers, high-level managers) pay significantly less. As a result, employment offered by the public sector is extremely attractive for the less-skilled while it becomes increasingly unattractive to highly skilled employees. The difficulty of recruiting and retaining highly skilled people, according to Donahue, explains the increasing tendency for public organizations to contract out much of their high-end work to consultants. The same organizations also try to contract out work performed by the less-skilled, but they meet huge resistance from powerful public-sector unions. The stakes are exceptionally high for the unions because in many ways these unionized public-sector jobs represent most of the few remaining examples of the great union victories of the second half of the twentieth century.

Donahue refers to government jobs as *safe harbours* for workers in the storm of globalization. He notes that the role of public-sector unions in American politics has become increasingly controversial:

> Anyone looking to wax indignant about aspects of American politics could work through a long list of more deserving candidates before directing their outrage towards workers banding together to defend their middle-class jobs. The main reason for discussing public-sector unions' rapid shift from the sidelines to the front lines of politics is that it so vividly illustrates how a government job has become something millions of Americans will fight to defend. This development is both a sorry commentary on the status of the middle class within the private sector, and a chronic impediment to delivering on the public sector's imperatives of efficiency, flexibility, and performance.[43]

Performance standards are crucial to understanding why municipal unions are so important in the context of the work that senior management in local government is supposed to do. In the private sector, managers can enhance efficiency by outsourcing jobs, say, to China. They are rewarded well for their work; while jobs are lost at home, prices are reduced in the big-box stores, and the capitalist system appears to be working. But the public-sector manager can do no such thing. Proposals to contract out even minimal amounts of work are resisted at every turn—understandably so, as Donahue reminds us. The public sector appears increasingly inefficient, which in turn provokes more anger both from lower-income citizens not engaged in public-sector employment and from private-sector, high-income earners who bemoan the inability of the public sector to be as ruthlessly competitive as they are.

What has all this got to do with Canada? In a careful analysis of data on union membership in both the United States and Canada, Leo Troy concludes that, although much is different about labour law and labour statistics between the United States and Canada, trends in the two countries are converging: private-sector unions are declining while public-sector unions are at least holding their own.[44] Although the issues raised by Donahue might be more acute in the United States, they are of great importance in Canada—and likely to become more so in the future.

What this means is that some of the most profound issues facing Canadian society are being fought out in municipalities. We are used to hearing about the importance of municipal policies for the environment or for economic competitiveness. But if municipal government is one of the few remaining places where less-skilled workers can obtain jobs that are relatively well paid, with decent benefits and security, what do we expect our municipalities to do in collective bargaining? To some extent at least, their role is to try to obtain concessions from the unions in order to save money for taxpayers. So far, however, they have not been very successful because CUPE and other unions have remained strong. Eventually, public resentment about the special advantages of public-sector employment might become too great for politicians to ignore. The election of Rob Ford in Toronto in 2010 on a promise of eliminating "the gravy train" was in many ways a scarcely veiled attack on municipal unions. Was his election a harbinger of things to come or will working- and middle-class Canadians themselves begin to seek ways to ensure that they too have access to the wages and benefits that the municipal unions have tried so hard to protect? Answering this question will be key not just to the future of local government and politics but to Canadian politics in general.

Conclusion

Municipal managers face many remarkably challenging and complex issues. Unlike federal and provincial civil servants, they do their job largely in public and for multiple political masters. They face a constant barrage of criticism for not spending taxpayers' money more efficiently, but they face overwhelming constraints when they try to take steps to do so. Over the last two or three decades, they have been pressured to be innovative and entrepreneurial while at the same time they were not supposed to upset vested interests, especially unions. The contracting out of municipal work to private companies has been prescribed by many as a way to bring the discipline of the private sector to public services. But as we have seen in this chapter, Canadian experiences with contracting out have not always been positive, and they have caused considerable controversy. Although contracting out clearly leads to a reduction in the total number of municipal employees, it does not eliminate the need for competent municipal managers. In fact, it likely *increases* the need because, in order to ensure that it reaps any efficiencies, the municipal government needs to know as much about what is going on with the contract as the contracting company does. One of the many criticisms of the Regina public–private partnership was that the city's assumptions apparently leave it "without a dime budgeted for its costs in administering the operations contract and enforcing compliance."[45]

Collective agreements are among the most important constraints on municipal managers. Too often these agreements have been seen simply as the public-sector equivalent of private-sector collective agreements. But the political dynamics of labour relations are much different in municipalities, and the stakes have become much higher. There has been almost no academic research on collective bargaining in Canadian municipal government. We have emphasized how so much municipal business is carried out in public, but collective bargaining is done behind closed doors, as are councils' deliberations about their bargaining strategies. How are final decisions made about negotiating positions that might provoke a strike or about concessions that might end one? What is the politicians' role, especially the role of those who are known to have the political support of the unions with whom the municipality is negotiating? For citizens who want to know how their municipal governments work and what their significance is to the functioning of our wider society, these are the kinds of questions to which we should have some answers. Unfortunately, we do not.

In the final analysis, decisions about the remuneration and treatment of municipal workers depend on societal values expressed by municipal councillors who are elected by voters. But these values are affected by scarce resources. We cannot give everyone what he or she wants.

RESOURCES

For contrasting views about the merits of privatization and contracting out, see the websites of the Canadian Council for Public–Private Partnerships at www.pppcouncil.ca, and the "privatization watch" conducted by the Canadian Union of Public Employees at http://cupe.ca/privatizationwatch?list=articles&date=2010

STUDY QUESTIONS

1. What makes the job of city manager or CAO of a major Canadian municipality different from that of a senior civil servant in the federal or provincial governments?
2. Would you favour the contracting out of the management and operation of the water supply system in your municipality? Why or why not?
3. Should municipal workers doing similar jobs as those available in the private sector be paid more? Explain your reasoning.

PART IV
FINANCIAL ISSUES

CHAPTER 14

Budgets, Grants, and User Fees

"Follow the money" is advice commonly given to any investigative reporter trying to find out what is going on in complex organizations. Often such advice is directed at tracking down various forms of corruption or conflicts of interest. But it applies just as well to understanding government at any level. The serious student needs to understand how public funds are used and where they come from. The aim of this chapter is to enable such understanding with respect to Canadian local government. We look first at the various sources of information about Canadian local government finance and how we can best make use of them. Next we will use some of these sources to analyze what Canadian local governments spend their money on and why. Then we will review the sources of local government revenues, emphasizing grants from other levels of government and user fees, and reserving a full discussion of the municipal property tax until the next chapter. Finally, we will discuss the financing of water supply systems as a case in point about the politics of user fees and government grants.

This part of the book is not meant for financial managers; it should be readily understandable to people without technical knowledge of accounting and bookkeeping. One hopes that municipal councillors and senior managers are familiar with the material, although many such people are more likely to know about the financial intricacies of their own municipalities rather than some of the broader issues and perspectives presented here. Even financial professionals often do not look at the wider political perspective in which their work takes place. Because this book is grounded in political science rather than in accounting or financial management, its approach to the subject should be accessible to all.[1]

Local Government Finances

All three levels of government in Canada collect data about local government finances. If one's interest is in a particular municipality, the best source is the website of that municipality because it will have the most detailed information. However, not all municipalities structure and present their financial information in the same way. The best way to compare financial information from municipalities in the same province is to use data collected from the relevant provincial ministry concerned with municipal affairs. Statistics Canada collects local government financial data for the entire country. These data are comparable but are lacking in detail. For example, the data from Statistics Canada can be compared by province but not across individual municipalities. Because this book addresses Canadian local government in general and aims at making interprovincial comparisons, the financial data from Statistics Canada will be most useful.

The two main kinds of financial information, each of which is available from all three levels of government, are:

1. Statements of assets and liabilities, or balance sheets. Such information is meant to convey measures of wealth or indebtedness at one particular point in time.
2. Statements of revenues and expenditures. These show the amount of money received or spent for particular purposes over a particular period of time, most often one year.

Assets and Liabilities

Statements of assets and liabilities are crucially important for businesses because they are an important way of stating how much a business is worth. They list the value of everything that the company owns and then list all the companies' debts or financial obligations. (Assets minus liabilities equal net worth; if liabilities exceed assets, the result is net indebtedness.) These statements are less important for municipalities, primarily because municipalities are not bought and sold. However, for financial professionals interested in providing funds to finance municipal debt, statements of assets and liabilities provide important information about the potential capacity of a municipality to repay its debt. Provincial legislation for municipalities in Canada requires them to comply with generally accepted accounting principles for local governments as determined by the Public Sector Accounting Board (PSAB), which is affiliated with the Canadian Institute of Chartered Accountants. Starting with 2009, municipalities were required to include in their statements of assets and liabilities the depreciated value of their physical assets, such as roads, sewers, buildings, and the like. Prior to 2009, and unlike business corporations' statements, the value of such physical assets was not included. Superficially, the new system makes municipalities look wealthier than they were prior to the change in accounting procedures. However, in the real world, nothing has changed, especially because most municipal physical assets cannot realistically be bought and sold. What likely is most significant about the change is that if municipalities do nothing between the issuance of two statements (usually a period of one year) to renew or refurbish their physical assets, they will rightly be seen as suffering a reduction in the net value of their assets because the value of what they have will have depreciated (in the same way that a car depreciates in value each year that it is used). The expectation is that including depreciation into statements of assets and liabilities will force municipal politicians and senior managers to pay more attention to ensuring that their physical assets are renewed at least at the same rate as those assets depreciate. In any event, Figure 14.1, which tracks the value of non-financial assets owned by each of the three levels of governments, shows that the value of such assets owned by local governments (including school boards) is higher than those owned by provincial governments, and much higher than those owned by the federal level. What this figure is really showing is the importance of local governments for the ownership of Canada's built infrastructure.

It is still too early to tell what effect, if any, the accounting changes will have on municipal financial decision-making. Canadian municipal statements of assets and liabilities for periods prior to 2009 did not include physical (or tangible) assets. Among other things, this means that their liabilities invariably were greater than their assets. Using data from Statistics Canada that includes school boards,[2] Figure 14.2 shows that, as far as *net financial worth* is concerned, Canadian local governments have become somewhat more indebted since 1991. However, their *net worth* has increased dramatically during the period 1991–2013. Net worth includes all the non-financial assets that they own (as shown in Figure 14.1), minus their financial debt (i.e., the extent to which their net financial worth is negative).

Statements of Revenues and Expenditures

As noted previously, these statements report on the sources of revenue and the purposes of expenditures for a given period of time, usually a year. Annual municipal budgets are very similar to these statements except that the statements look to the past and budgets look to the future.

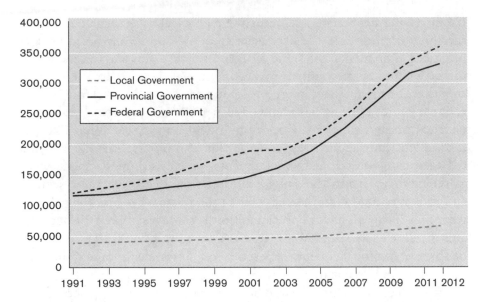

Figure 14.1   Non-financial Assets of Three Levels of Canadian
Government, 1991–2012 ($ X 1,000,000)

Source: Statistics Canada, CANSIM Table 385-0032 Government finance statistics, statement of government
operations and balance sheet, 2014. Reproduced on an "as is" basis with the permission of Statistics Canada.

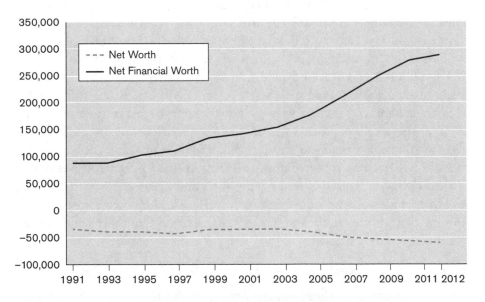

Figure 14.2   Net Worth and Financial Worth of Canadian Local
Governments, 1991–2012 ($ X 1,000,000)

Source: Statistics Canada, CANSIM Table 385-0032 Government finance statistics, statement of government
operations and balance sheet, 2014. Reproduced on an "as is" basis with the permission of Statistics Canada.

Using data from Statistics Canada, we shall be focusing on municipal revenues and expenditures. The data we use in the sections that follow are for what Statistics Canada calls *local general government*, which includes municipal governments and their associated boards and commissions, but not school boards. The data include both operating and capital revenues and expenditures, which is not the usual municipal way of presenting financial data. Later in this chapter we make the necessary distinctions between financial transactions for operating purposes and those for capital. For now we need only note that, although legislation in all the provinces prevents municipalities from running operating deficits, it is possible for them to spend more than they take in for any given year, if capital expenditures are included.

Municipal Expenditures

Since 2008, Statistics Canada no longer collects data relating to government expenditures by function. Table 14.1 shows expenditure data for selected provinces. For each province, these data derive from the respective provincial government and are not strictly comparable. It is clear from the numbers in this table's figures that municipal expenditures are dominated by roads and public transit, water supply and sewage, and public protection (police and fire services). Only in Ontario are there significant expenditures for "health, social services, and housing."

Municipal Revenues

Statistics Canada still collects data on local-government sources of revenue,[3] but because such data includes revenues for school boards (which is high and almost all of which is from provincial transfers), it is not of much value in understanding municipal revenues. Once again, for this purpose, we must rely on data from provincial governments (Table 14.2), which are not strictly comparable.[4]

The two main kinds of own-source revenues are *property taxes* and *user fees*. All of the next chapter will be devoted to issues relating to the property tax, because it is of crucial importance to understanding municipal government and politics in Canada. A discussion of the politics behind the pricing and selling of municipal water ends this chapter. Water is the most important commodity for which Canadian municipalities charge user fees. For our purposes now, all we need to know is that property taxes are the most important source of municipal revenue and that user fees are next in importance. Together these own-source revenues comprise well over half of municipal revenue. Provincial transfers are also significant, but their importance in Ontario derives

Table 14.1 Municipal Spending by Function, Selected Provinces[a]

Spending by Function[b]	British Columbia		Ontario		Alberta		Quebec		Nova Scotia		Manitoba	
	Per Capita	% of Total	Per Capita	% of Total	Per Capita	% of Total	Per Capita	% of Total	Per Capita	% of Total	Per Capita	% of Total
	$	%	$	%	$	%	$	%	$	%	$	%
General government	196	12.3	133	4.6	336	12.9	226	11.6	230	16.8	189	12.0
Protection, (fire and police, etc.)	386	24.3	477	16.7	454	17.4	345	17.8	354	25.8	353	22.4
Health, social services, and housing	13	0.8	864	30.3	121	4.6	24	1.2	34	2.5	6	0.4
Planning and development	48	3.0	61	2.1	113	4.3	102	5.3	—	—	52	3.3
Roads, streets, parking, and public transit	159	10.0	652	22.8	729	27.9	503	26.0	322	23.5	548	34.7
Parks, recreation, and culture	253	15.9	268	9.4	342	13.1	253	13.1	141	10.3	140	8.9
Water and sewer	198	12.4	283	9.9	263	10.1	200	10.3	—	—	208	13.2
Solid waste management and recycling	61	3.9	96	3.3	114	4.4	104	5.4	—	—	—	—
Other services	43	2.7	22	0.8	136	5.2	30	1.6	227	16.5	38	2.4
Environmental health	—	—	—	—	—	—	10	0.5	69	5.1	44	2.8
Environmental development	—	—	—	—	—	—	—	—	—	—	—	—
Amortization[c]	235	14.8	0	0.0	0	0.0	139	7.2	—	—	—	—
TOTAL	1,591	100.0	2,854	100.0	2,610	100.0	1,937	100.0	1,371	100.0	1,578	100.0

a Data for British Columbia, Ontario, and Alberta municipalities are for 2010. Data for Nova Scotia, Manitoba, and Quebec municipalities are for 2009.

b The provincial data are not always organized according to these functions, so the authors of this report reorganized the provincial data into these functions.

c Amortization expenditures were reported as a separate category of expenditures in two provinces, but are included in the functional spending categories in the other provinces.

— Data were not listed for these expenditure categories.

Source: Harry Kitchen and Enid Slack, "Property Taxes and Competitiveness in British Columbia," a report prepared for the BC Expert Panel on Business Tax Competitiveness, 11 May 2012, p.5, available at www.fin.gov.bc.ca/docs/expert_panel_submissions/Business%20Property%20Tax%20Competitiveness%20Report.pdf almost exclusively from the fact that Ontario municipalities receive large provincial transfers to help cover municipal responsibilities for social services and public health, responsibilities that are largely provincial in other provinces. Federal transfers are relatively insignificant in all provinces, notwithstanding the federal government's sharing of gas-tax revenues (see Chapter 3). The fact that Table 14.2 shows some provinces as receiving no federal transfers simply reflects different accounting practices in the different provinces.

PILs are *payments-in-lieu* of taxes paid to municipal governments by the federal and provincial governments to compensate for property taxes, which they are not legally obligated to pay. These are discussed further in the next chapter.

Municipal Budgets

Adopting the annual municipal budget is often the most important function performed by a municipal council in any given year. The budget is a complex document, even in relatively small municipalities. In larger ones it can be hundreds of pages long and almost impossible for the outsider to comprehend.[5] Figure 14.3 is a helpful introduction.

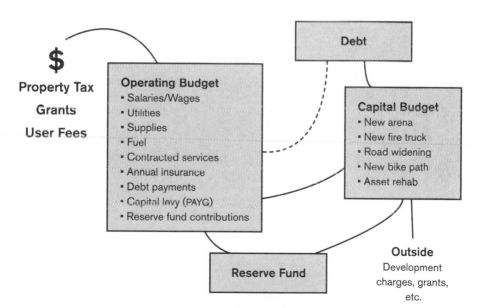

Figure 14.3 How the Municipal Budget Works

Source: City of London, Ontario

Table 14.2 Municipal Revenue by Source, Selected Provinces[a]

Revenue Source	British Columbia		Ontario		Alberta		Quebec[b]		Nova Scotia		Manitoba	
	Per Capita	% of Total	Per Capita	% of Total	Per Capita	% of Total	Per Capita	% of Total	Per Capita	% of Total	Per Capita	% of Total
	$	%	$	%	$	%	$	%	$	%	$	%
Property taxation and PILs	803	46.0	1,271	38.2	1,325	39.4	1,565	64.12	919	65.8	853	40.2
User fees	605	31.1	605	18.2	709	21.1	323	12.2	186	13.3	572	27.0
Federal transfers	45	2.3	169	5.1	78	2.3	—	—	—	—	109	5.2
Provincial transfers	123	6.3	693	20.8	613	18.2	382	15.7	166	12.0	296	14.0
Transfers from other local governments	26	1.3	59	1.8	17	0.5	—	—	—	—	—	—
Developer contributions	180	9.3	—	—	37	1.1	34	1.4	—	—	—	—
Investment income	48	2.5	—	—	101	3.0	2	0.1	—	—	62	2.9
Other	23	1.2	531	15.9	585	17.4	134	5.5	114	8.1	228	10.8
TOTAL	1,942	100.0	3,328	100.0	3,364	100.0	2,440	100.0	1,396	100.0	2,121	100.0

a Data for British Columbia, Ontario, and Alberta municipalities are for 2010. Data for Nova Scotia, Manitoba, and Quebec municipalities are for 2009.

b All federal transfers must pass through the provincial government.

— data were not listed in these categories.

Source: Harry Kitchen and Enid Slack, "Property Taxes and Competitiveness in British Columbia," a report prepared for the BC Expert Panel on Business Tax Competitiveness, 11 May 2012, p. 7, available at: www.fin.gov.bc.ca/docs/expert_panel_submissions/Business%20Property%20Tax%20Competitiveness%20Report.pdf

The first point to note is that there are really two budgets—one for operating expenses and one for capital. The budgets are linked by debt payments and reserve funds. One of Canada's foremost experts on municipal finance, Harry Kitchen, acknowledges that "[t]he use for municipal purposes of the term 'capital' varies somewhat from municipality to municipality" and that "[s]ome types of expenditure defy ready classification."[6] New construction clearly is a capital expenditure and so is a major rehabilitation of, say, a municipal arena or city hall; routine maintenance is not. Buying land and purchasing new vehicles are capital expenditures; the purchase of routine office supplies is not. As noted previously, provincial legislation prevents municipalities from budgeting for operating deficits. Municipalities are allowed to borrow to finance capital costs, but such borrowing is generally regulated by the relevant provincial government. It is important to realize that although federal and provincial governments in Canada make budgetary distinctions between capital and operating costs, they are rolled together when budgetary deficits or surpluses are reported. Only at the municipal level are such clear distinctions made between budgets for operating and capital expenses.

A great deal of academic literature relates to both how public-sector budgeting works and how it should work. Regardless of innumerable plans to make budgeting decisions more rational and comprehensive, the process remains fundamentally political, in that elected officials make decisions about controversial items based on their own political instincts and calculations rather than on the basis of elaborate assessments performed by their staff. However, most of what is contained in most governmental budgets is not controversial at all—it simply reflects the continuation of ongoing programs that no one much wants to change, or even can change. This status quo certainly is true of municipal budgets.

Attempting to find the beginning of the annual budgetary process is like attempting to determine whether the chicken comes before the egg. Everyone involved in the process knows that the political acceptability of the budget will be determined ultimately by the extent to which it results in changes to property tax levels that are acceptable to the voters who elect the councillors. If it looks like increased tax revenues will be available in the following year, the heads of various municipal departments will discover new projects and programs that they cannot live without. If funds look scarce and they wish to protect their own positions, they will not be foolish enough to launch crusades for new expenditures. Despite the fact that staff budget proposals are invariably adjusted to suit political reality, the formal part of the process begins with such requests. The requests are collected by senior municipal financial officials and reviewed by the city manager or CAO. The degree of involvement by councillors or council committees at this stage varies from place to place. In municipalities with strong city managers, it will be kept to a minimum. In any event, the proposed operating and capital budgets are formally released either by the municipal administration or by a council committee. They are then discussed and debated by council committees and/or the full council, and are approved, usually with relatively minor changes. In most years in most places there is public controversy about a few particular aspects of the budgets; rarely does that process provoke significant discussion about major policy choices.

As suggested in Figure 14.3 on page 295, many aspects of the operating budget are determined by prior commitments. In particular, a municipality must meet its scheduled payments on accumulated debt. Although payment for the original project that caused the debt counts as a capital expense, the actual debt repayments are in the operating budget because they are recurring financial obligations. Similarly, ongoing municipal commitments for salaries of councillors and many staff members, as well as ongoing maintenance and other expenses, cannot possibly be avoided. In times past (and still today in very small municipalities) each municipal department would have an operating budget comprising the kinds of items shown in Figure 14.3: salaries, supplies, utilities, fuel, and so on. Most proposals over the years to make budgeting more meaningful and effective have involved replacing such *line items* with budgets relating to particular objectives. Thus, a municipal recreation department would budget instead for declared objectives such as providing a certain number of supervised swimming pool hours, a certain number of places available in sports programs, and specified programs in disadvantaged neighbourhoods. The theory here is that, if politicians want to cut or expand the department's budget, they do so by adjusting the levels of service as proposed in the budget. In reality, however, not all departmental costs can be allocated to particular programs. In any event, most policy-makers really do want to know how much money particular units are spending on such line items as salaries, supplies, and travel. Most budgets now include information about both program costs and line items, which contributes to the budget's size and complexity.

In addition to providing for debt repayment and for ongoing expenses, operating budgets often make direct contributions to the capital budget for particular projects (*pay-as-you-go*—just like using extra available cash to pay for a new car rather than borrowing money to pay for it) or to reserve funds (which, as the name implies, are like special savings accounts individuals might establish to enable a special purchase at some time in the future). Sometimes provincial legislation or regulations require that municipalities establish particular reserve funds for particular purposes and specify a formula for determining the payments into the fund and the circumstances under which the funds can be withdrawn. Other reserve funds are completely voluntary, and some are designed to cover unusual and unforeseen operating costs, such as a winter requiring unusually high costs for snow removal. If a reserve fund is voluntary, then nothing stops a municipal council from "raiding the reserves" to finance normal operating costs when times are tough—a well-known technique for avoiding sudden and dramatic tax increases in a particular year (though if practised regularly, this completely negates the purpose of having reserve funds in the first place).

Most municipalities are financially cautious. They establish reserve funds for some purposes, the proceeds of which they may invest in short-term securities so as to generate additional income for the fund. Simultaneously, they borrow money for other projects at a fixed rate for a term that roughly matches the expected life of the project. This leads to the common municipal practice of borrowing money for some purposes and investing it for others, not unlike a couple who choose to borrow money for a home (mortgage) and at the same time put aside savings by investing in bonds for their retirement. Although Figure 14.2 on page 292 indicates that the net financial worth of Canadian local governments is negative, compared to their federal and provincial counterparts, Canadian local governments are in excellent financial shape. Complaints from citizens about local indebtedness are often misplaced. Such complaints usually do not take account of the value of reserve funds. More importantly, no serious financial analyst suggests that borrowing to acquire capital goods is a bad idea; quite the contrary. If we only construct a new facility with money we have already saved, current taxpayers are effectively subsidizing future users of the facility.[7] This situation is quite different from one in which the federal government runs a deficit to pay for current operating costs, in which case future taxpayers are subsidizing current ones.

During the Great Depression of the 1930s, many Canadian municipalities effectively went bankrupt because they could not repay loans that had been taken out to construct new infrastructure that ultimately was not needed.[8] Because municipal bankruptcies negatively affected the creditworthiness of the provinces in which they were located, all provinces eventually took action to prevent reckless municipal borrowing. Furthermore, as we saw in Chapter 10, municipalities in most provinces (but not so much in Quebec) eventually required developers to construct and pay for municipal infrastructure within new subdivisions, thereby passing the cost and risk from themselves to developers and eventually on to homeowners. Like all governments and corporations, the credit-worthiness of municipalities is evaluated by credit-rating agencies, the same agencies that failed in their task in 2008 with respect to many large American financial institutions. Municipalities with high credit ratings can borrow money at lower rates than municipalities with low credit rat-ings, but high credit ratings most often are achieved by not having to borrow money; consequently, the benefits are often overstated, especially by financially conservative municipal politicians. High municipal credit ratings also are achieved by having diverse and stable local economies. Money loaned to a municipality with such an economy is almost cer-tain to be paid back, which is not necessarily likely for an isolated one-industry town where the one industry is in danger of shutting down. The potential financial risk in such situations explains why, in some new one-industry towns, the main industry has no choice but to build much municipal infrastructure itself.

Figure 14.3 shows that capital budgets also receive funds from development charges. The evolution of these charges was described in Chapter 10. They involve property owners (usually developers) being required to pay a municipal charge for each lot on which new buildings are constructed. The idea is that the revenue from these charges will be used to finance the additional municipal capital costs associated with the new buildings. That is why the revenue from these charges is shown in Figure 14.3 as being connected with the capital budget rather than the operating budget. In reality, most revenue from development charges goes into reserve funds before being spent directly on municipal capital acquisitions.

Multi-year planning for budgeting is always desirable, especially in relation to capital spending. In any well-run municipality, capital budgets carefully outline the sequencing of new capital projects, for both financial and engineering reasons. For example, if a road needs to be widened or reconstructed, it makes sense to renew underground piping at the same time, thereby saving both money and disruption. Of course, the need for some capital projects cannot always be determined in advance (rebuild-ing destruction caused by a natural disaster, for example) and everyone has to acknowledge the right of municipal councillors to depart from a pre-established capital plan if political priorities change (for example, councillors' pledge to building a new performing arts centre that had been rejected by a previous council). Multi-year planning is always sub-ject to change.

Ordinary citizens generally care little about the intricacies of capital and operating budgets, reserve funds, and credit ratings. What they generally want are the highest possible level of services and facilities in their municipality with the lowest possible level of property taxes and user charges. As we saw in Chapter 2, balancing these conflicting demands is one of the main reasons we have elected local governments in the first place. During the budgetary process, council members are placed under the most pressure regarding these issues. Often they are criticized for attempting to cut too deeply, such that services considered important by many people are felt to be under threat. More often they are criticized for allowing levels of user fees and property taxes to become too high.

User Fees

Even if it were desirable, it is not possible to finance all government services by user fees. Services that cannot possibly be financed by user fees are what economists call *public goods*. When a public good is provided, it is available to everybody whether some people want it or not: the good cannot be divided and it cannot be consumed. Classic examples of public goods are street lighting and defence against external threats. The only way to finance these services is through compulsory taxation. If we tried to charge citizens for these services, some would rationally conclude that they need not pay because, once provided, the benefits of the service cannot be denied to anybody. The end result likely would be that everyone would end up with a lower level of street lighting or of defence than they really wanted.

At the core of any economic analysis of government is the provision of public goods, because private markets simply cannot provide them at the optimal level or develop a mechanism whereby those goods will be financed. Debates about exact definitions of public goods can become quite silly (Can we dispense with public police forces by expecting people to provide their own bodyguards?), and we need not explore all the intricacies. There can be little doubt that local governments provide real public goods that could not possibly be financed by user fees. Clearest examples are goods like snow removal, safe and comfortable public spaces, and measures to prevent the spread of disease by infected rodents. An almost universal temptation is to add to this list by including such expensive items as education and health care. It is completely possible to charge fees for these services and even to have them provided by private entrepreneurs, so these goods are not public goods, although powerful grounds exist for having governments provide them or at least contribute to the costs of their provision. These grounds relate to the *positive externalities* that accrue to us all from an educated population and to a sense of fundamental fairness and equity (prevalent in most societies) that people should not die or suffer as a result of being unable to afford medical care. Services like health and education are called *merit goods*; they are not public goods in the sense described above, but they are so important to the well-being of our societies that governments take action to make sure that the appropriate people receive the required level of services. Precisely because these services are not public goods, it is usually relatively easy for citizens to purchase additional (or different) levels of the service if they so desire. As we have seen in Chapter 4, local governments in Canada are heavily involved in the provision of basic levels of public education through school boards.

As we also saw in Chapter 4, some goods cannot be provided efficiently by competing private suppliers. Distribution systems for water, sewage, natural gas, and electricity are prime examples. In an unregulated environment, one supplier soon would become dominant in a given territory because it is simply too expensive (and disruptive) for competitors to build competing systems. In the absence of regulation, the dominant supplier could make huge profits by taking advantage of the *natural monopoly* that would inevitably result. Governments either take over these services themselves or tightly regulate the private monopoly suppliers. In particular, they regulate the *tolls* that these suppliers levy. The goods in question frequently are referred to as *toll goods*. Canadian local governments are heavily involved in some toll goods, especially water supply and sewage. The ways in which Canadian municipalities levy charges for these particular goods will be explored more fully in the next section of this chapter.

Roads and public transit are toll goods as well. It is practically impossible to have competing private road systems within the same territory. Competing private bus and taxi companies are more feasible, but competing private fixed-rail systems within a single city are just as improbable as competing road systems. The big issue at the local level for roads and public transit is the level of the toll. Historically, toll roads in Canada were quite common, but almost all road tolls were abolished over time, in part because the collection of the tolls added to traffic delays. As we all know, changes in technology now make it possible for road tolls to be charged without causing traffic to stop. A *congestion charge* is now levied on all private motor vehicles entering central London in England, and there is much talk about the desirability of such a charge in Canada's largest cities.[9] It is bound to be a major issue in urban politics in the years ahead. The mirror image of this debate is taking place with respect to public transit. Public transit systems were initially self-financing, with most operated by private companies. Now, they are municipally operated in Canada (except TransLink in Vancouver). Yet no one argues for higher tolls (or fares) so that these systems can become totally self-financing. For environmental reasons, and to ease roadway congestion, the much more common argument is that government subsidies for public transit should be increased.

In certain circumstances municipalities also provide private goods, ones that are also commonly provided in the private marketplace. For example, they might operate golf courses, which will be at least partially in competition with private ones. Municipalities owning convention centres or community halls likely will be in competition with local hotels. Usually, the municipal facility has the greatest capacity and is designed to attract large meetings whose delegates will stay overnight in local hotels. However, in order to maximize business, municipal facilities are sometimes tempted to go after smaller events as well, which puts them in direct competition with meeting facilities in hotels. Invariably, municipal competition in an otherwise private marketplace becomes a local political issue. A common solution is for the municipality to adopt a business strategy for these facilities aimed at avoiding direct competition with local business rather than maximizing municipal revenue. Other local taxpayers will then claim that municipalities cannot operate businesses very well!

Only a tiny portion of municipal revenue from the sale of goods and services derives from goods and services that are also provided privately. Most such municipal revenue comes from goods and services for which municipalities are the only or the dominant supplier. The initial decision that a municipality must make about financing a particular service is whether to charge user fees at all. For many services, as we have seen, such fees are not technically possible. For others, such as roads, fees might now be technically possible, but are, for the moment at least, not politically possible. And for others, such as garbage collection, debate in many communities still rages on.

Advocates of user fees for garbage collection make the plausible argument that they will cause residents to be more careful about the amounts of garbage they leave at the curb. This reasoning loses some of its force if the amount of garbage each household throws out is not carefully measured. Weighing garbage and recording where it comes from will likely add to the cost of collection. Selling tags for bags solves this problem, but encourages people to stuff each bag as full as it can get. If tags are priced to cover the complete cost of collection and disposal, including all costs associated with the life cycle of a landfill site, they could become high enough to cause some people to try to dispose of their garbage illegally, thereby causing more costs and undermining the original purpose of adopting the user fees in the first place. To make the issue even more complicated, in most municipalities, owners of commercial and high-rise residential buildings must arrange and pay for their own garbage collection, often from private companies, and they receive no relief from property tax for themselves paying for a service that single-family homes usually receive as part of their overall package of tax-supported municipal services.

Once a municipality has decided to charge user fees for a service, it faces difficult issues about how to set the price. In private businesses, the obvious strategy is to set a price for a service that will, over a given period of time, maximize the financial position of the business. Municipalities do not have such a luxury. The political constraints on maximizing profits from such private services as municipal golf courses and reception rooms are fairly obvious. But there are constraints on the pricing of toll goods as well. For example, if municipalities decided to maximize their revenues by charging as much as they could get away with for the supply of piped water, they could make a great deal of money. In fact, no municipal council would agree to such a strategy, because it would lead to howls of outrage both from businesses that use large amounts of water and from poverty activists who would rightly claim that no one should be denied drinking water in a country such as Canada because they are unable to pay for it. Even if municipalities decide to charge only for the *real cost* of a service, they still face difficult issues.

The first issue pertains to knowing the real cost of all aspects of providing a service, which is basically an accounting problem that is not insurmountable. The more difficult issue relates to the difference between *average-cost pricing* and *marginal-cost pricing*. Average-cost pricing is easy to understand. The municipality simply takes the total cost of providing the service, divides it by the number of anticipated number of users, and the quotient is the price. In the real world, this is often what is done in an attempt to set a price based on full-cost recovery, and there is nothing wrong with such an approach. Potential problems arise if the service involved requires major capital investments, such as sewage treatment plants. If a large plant with surplus capacity has already been built, then the *marginal* cost of treating additional sewage will be less than the average cost. The municipality and the consumer both will be better off if the pricing is based on the marginal cost.

If, however, taking in additional sewage will require the building of a new treatment plant, average-cost pricing will be too low because it will not generate enough revenue to cover the cost of a new plant. In this case, the municipality can only cover its costs if it adopts marginal-cost pricing. Harry Kitchen points out that calculating the marginal cost of providing service for each single additional user is impossible. Instead, public officials can approximate marginal-cost pricing by dividing "all of the additional costs associated with providing an increased level of service by the number of additional users. Each user is charged the average of the incremental total costs."[10]

A variant of this approach is *peak-period pricing*. Public transit systems are stretched to the limit during rush hours and have surplus capacity at other times of the day. Higher charges during rush hours discourage people from travelling at that time if they have a choice, thereby reducing the need for extra capacity. To the extent that people still use the system at rush hour, extra funds are generated that add to the system's capacity. All these considerations could go by the wayside, however, if the overall public policy objective is to get commuters out of their cars during rush hours. If this is the paramount objective, it might not be such a good idea to raise public transit fares for precisely these journeys. The optimal pricing of local public services is far from being a strictly technical or mathematical issue.

Harry Kitchen joins most other economists in being a great advocate of user fees, where they are technically feasible, on the grounds that such fees lead to the most efficient use of society's resources. In the Canadian context, Kitchen argues that their use in local government should be extended not only to the services already discussed but also within certain aspects of municipal recreation programs, public libraries, and police and fire services.[11] A common objection to extending user fees within such services as recreation programs is that the cost will fall disproportionately on the poor, who would likely have to pay a higher share of their total income for municipal recreation than rich people would. In the language of economics, such charges would be *regressive*. Kitchen responds to such a concern by stating that "This claim . . . is about as relevant as the claim that the prices of milk and movie tickets are regressive."[12] He and other economists suggest that if society is concerned that poor people need more money, it is more efficient to have central governments increase personal transfer payments to them and let them decide to how to spend it rather than to provide subsidized local services to everybody, whether they really want them or not. The problem, of course, is that central governments generally do not provide sufficient payments to poor people such that those individuals do not have to worry about the cost of municipal user fees. Consequently there will always be demands that at least some municipal user fees be adjusted so that they are not so onerous for the poor.

Financing Water[13]

Providing safe and clean piped drinking water and removing dirty water and sewage are arguably the most important functions carried out by urban municipalities. Important as these functions are, they do not meet the technical definition of a *public good* because it is easy to exclude people who do not pay. In fact, water and sewage are examples of toll goods because there can be only a single network of pipes for each function in a given territory. Toll goods can be provided by private companies. As we saw in Chapter 4, Canada's first urban water supply systems were owned and operated by companies holding franchises issued by municipal councils. In the early days of communal water supply, the provision of a constant water pressure to city-owned fire hydrants was at least as important as piping water to private purchasers. The level of domestic water rates was closely linked to the terms of the deal concerning the fire hydrants as worked out between the city and the company.

After decades of local wrangling and after approval by ratepayers and the Ontario legislature, the Toronto city council finally purchased that city's private water supply system in 1872.[14] In other cities, private ownership was not an inevitable first step. The Hamilton city council built its own system in the 1850s after it became evident that private entrepreneurs were not interested.[15] In London, Ontario, a private water company was formed in 1854, but it went out of business the following year after its one source of water had completely dried up; the pond on which it relied was fed only by surface drainage.[16] London's first functioning system was built by the municipality and began operations in 1879.[17] Similar stories can be told for virtually every city and town in the country: private water companies may have started water supply systems, but those supply systems eventually became municipal. Sewage systems have always been municipally owned and operated.

Municipalities—and other levels of government—face many decisions about how to finance these systems. The decisions comprise three main issues:

1. financing by general tax revenues or by usage;
2. if financing by usage, what kind of rate structure to adopt;
3. the role of subsidies for capital investments.

Financing by General Tax Revenues or by Usage

The almost universal consensus among economists and environmentalists is that water consumption should be paid for by user fees. Their position is that if households and businesses pay for the water they consume, they will pay more attention to conservation, and municipalities will receive more accurate signals about how much water is really needed. This is important not just for water policy, but for energy policy as well: considerable amounts of electricity are needed to purify water and to move it around at desirable pressures. Without water meters, however, conservation programs become much more difficult because there is no financial incentive for individual consumers to conserve. In many communities in Canada water meters have never been installed, or they have not been installed for individual units in multi-family buildings. The issue is whether continued investment in meters is necessary.

The main objection to charging people for the use of water is that it is not a commodity that people normally can choose to do without; because it is required for sustenance and sanitation, everyone should be entitled to whatever is required for these purposes. However, no one who adopts such a position argues that people have a right to unlimited amounts of water for unessential purposes, such as watering lawns or washing cars, or that businesses that use water for industrial processes should not pay for what they use. Among the Canadian provinces, water metering seems least popular in Quebec, where in 2006 only 16.5 per cent of residences had water meters while the percentage for Canada as a whole was 63.1.[18] In Sherbrooke, Quebec, water meters were actually removed following municipal amalgamation in 2002, in part because some of the outlying amalgamated municipalities did not have meters.[19] A Quebec government commission charged with investigating a wide range of issues relating to water claimed that, unless costs for water were much higher than they are in Quebec, there is little evidence that user charges reduce consumption.[20] The commission concluded that:

> Although trends in opinion largely favour user charges, the Commission does not think it would be wise to insist cities put in place such a measure. The costs of investment and planning as well as the social costs of such a measure (fees beyond the capacity of some to pay; the difficulty of allocating costs to tenants in multi-family dwellings; the risks to hygiene) cast doubt on its universal effectiveness. From the standpoint of the argument of equitability (each paying for his own consumption) the Commission discerns confusion between the terms "equitable" and "equal."

"Equitability" should be thought of in the sense of solidarity. In some places, where municipal policy already provides for user fees, it is no longer appropriate to intervene because a form of consensus, both of understanding and acceptance, has already been achieved locally. But in these cases we should prohibit municipalities from disconnecting residents from the water supply because of failure to pay their bills and provide other means (emergency funds, or other strategies) of resolving difficulties.[21]

A much more common view was expressed in 2005 by an Ontario "expert panel" on *water strategy*:

The benefits of conservation programs and price signals are largely lost unless customers are metered. But metering does not benefit just water services. Customers benefit too, through the assurance that they are paying only for the amount of water that they use. Metering also reminds them of the cost of waste.

When meters are installed, consumption drops: Environment Canada's Municipal Water Use and Pricing survey shows, for example, that residential per capita water use is consistently lower for metered municipalities across all size ranges.[22]

There is no metering for sewage. However, many municipalities establish a sewage charge on the basis of metered water consumption,[23] thereby creating a further incentive not to use water because the price increases dramatically. In the case of water that is not returned via the sewage system (lawn and garden watering, car washing), the user pays for sewage treatment anyway.

Different Kinds of Rate Structures

Most municipalities that charge for water on the basis of usage employ a *constant unit rate*; the amount charged per unit is the same no matter how much is used. But there are good arguments for varying the rate depending on usage. Municipalities that use a *declining block rate* charge less per unit as volume used increases. The obvious argument against this approach is that it appears to encourage consumption but, as Kitchen points out, "a declining block rate system may be appropriate if it is small customers who are responsible for the inefficient water use in a system, since by charging a higher price to the small customer than the large one it gives the small customer a greater incentive to conserve water."[24]

Increasing block rates work in the opposite way. Costs per unit increase as consumption increases:

> This pricing tool may be appropriate for residential customers who as a customer class are the main cause of peak demand [summer lawn watering], and for industrial users if limitations on the availability of water justify shifting the cost burden to largest users. It should be possible to set the price differences from block to block in a way that would give the customer a clear and strong economic incentive to conserve water.[25]

A *humpback block rate* charges relatively low-volume users higher unit rates for increased use, so as to discourage consumption by residential users; and it charges lower unit rates to high-volume industrial users to whom providing water is relatively cheap on a unit basis because of the very high volumes. Other rate variations involve changing the rates according to the time of year, or *excess-use* rates that apply to everyone when volumes consumed exceed a prescribed threshold.[26] All of these rate structures, except the *constant unit rate*, have the potential to reflect a form of marginal pricing, although decision-makers might not necessarily explicitly justify their decisions using this vocabulary. In other words, a municipality with excess capacity for supplying water will likely want to use a declining block rate, while one that has limited current capacity is more likely to adopt a rate structure that acts more strongly to reduce consumption in peak periods. Deciding on rate structures for water consumption is one of the more important financial actions that municipal councils take.

Subsidies for Capital Investments

Economists who urge that water use be metered and paid for as a commodity invariably believe that the price should reflect the full cost of providing the water (and the sewage treatment if such costs are meant to be included in the water charge). Full-cost pricing means that the price must cover capital investments. It is obvious, however, that consumers should not pay for the cost of a new treatment plant in their water rates during the year that the plant is constructed. One of the important functions that accountants and other financial experts perform is figuring out how to spread out these costs fairly over the life of the investment. The task can be difficult, but the challenges are far from insurmountable.

Water purification and sewage treatment plants, together with their associated pipeline networks, are key features of any country's physical infrastructure. In the last few decades in Canada there has been a great deal of attention paid to claims that such infrastructure is deteriorating faster than municipalities can reinvest in it, and that federal and provincial governments should provide increased grants to municipalities for infrastructure renewal.[27] Since the financial crisis of 2008, national governments in many advanced industrial democracies (including Canada) have allocated large sums of money for *shovel-ready* infrastructure projects to provide jobs and ameliorate the effects of the recession. It appears that many people support such programs while simultaneously believing that consumers should pay the full cost of water and/or sewer systems through user charges. But holding both these beliefs at the same time is not consistent. Subsidizing the costs of water infrastructure through grants means that metered consumers are not paying the full costs of water.[28]

On its Infrastructure Canada website, the federal government states that its investments in water infrastructure are designed to:

- Improve the safety, management, reliability and efficiency of Canada's drinking water treatment and distribution systems;
- Increase the number of households with access to safe drinking water that meets or exceeds the *Guidelines for Canadian Drinking Water Quality*;
- Improve protection and management of drinking water sources;
- Improve conservation of water.[29]

The same website lists hundreds of capital grants throughout the country for various water-related infrastructure projects. Each dollar spent on such projects reduces the likelihood that Canadians will pay the full cost of the water they are using.

An important Ontario expert panel written in 2005, before the latest round of grants, described the problems with capital subsidies:

> The sad reality . . . is that over-generous grants actually caused many of the problems in Ontario's water sector today. These are still with us in the form of plants that were built or enlarged unnecessarily and municipalities struggling to operate plants that are too big for their customer base. The impact on attitudes has been equally damaging; numerous municipalities appear to be delaying important work that needs to be done to move to full-cost recovery because of an expectation that senior government grants will solve their problems.[30]

In many cases, this is exactly what happened in the years that followed.

With respect to how the pricing of water should be affected by capital grants, the same report stated that "When looking at replacing large assets, even if an existing system was largely paid for with senior government grants, the only prudent assumption in setting prices is that the municipality will one day have to pay for replacements through its own revenues."[31] However, a municipality that priced water high so as to build up its reserves to replace an existing plant would weaken its own potential case later on that it needed new rounds of grants to replace the subsidized infrastructure that had run its course. As noted in the Ontario report, "Municipalities such as Perth and [Greater] Sudbury that have, admirably, acted without benefits of grants to maintain their systems properly are understandably concerned that others who were less forward-thinking will be rewarded with catch-up money."[32]

Despite the recommendations of economists and rational policymakers, it is difficult to see how this problem can be avoided. Federal and provincial governments could proclaim that there will be no new capital grants for water infrastructure, but it is unlikely they would be believed. Meanwhile, some municipalities, especially in Quebec, will continue on without water meters and will not even pretend to charge residents and businesses on the basis of their actual use of water. Others will claim to do so, but will remain on the lookout for capital grants so that they do not really have to. Others will charge the full price for water and add on surcharges for the cost of sewage. Most will stumble along with some combination of all these different approaches, with municipal councillors only addressing the issues in a serious way when something appears to be going wrong.

There is a reason, however, by which such a hybrid approach can be justified, even for those who generally advocate full-cost pricing. Water supply systems, as we have seen earlier, are not in place solely to provide water for residential and business consumers. They are also necessary for fighting fires. Even if humans did not need water for drinking and sanitation, municipal fire departments would require readily available supplies of water. For such purposes, municipalities are an important consumer of the same commodity that they produce. Having water available for fighting fires is close to being a public good, for which user fees are not possible. In these circumstances, it is easier to appreciate the strength of arguments made in Quebec that, because we need water pipes in the ground to fight fires anyway, it makes no sense to have consumers pay the full cost of the system based on the amount of water they consume.[33] Such a view, surprisingly, is echoed by the Ontario expert panel, which is otherwise highly favourable to full user-pay systems. The panel states that it:

does not assume that the indirect costs to the water system that make it suitable for firefighting—oversizing mains, building storage capacity, adding hydrants and keeping pressure at a high enough level—should automatically be included in water rates. There is a good argument that firefighting is a service to property, not a water or a wastewater service, and therefore the general tax base should pay the excess costs of water systems that result from firefighting needs.[34]

Taking all these factors into account, it is hardly surprising that the pricing of water is a highly complex matter.

Conclusion

Most of the material presented in this chapter, especially perhaps in Figure 14.2, should lead readers to believe that Canadian municipalities are quite well off. Indeed, much evidence supports such a position. Municipal balance sheets appear to be strong, and some municipal infrastructure—even if it needs more maintenance than it has often received—has surplus capacity. Some of the important services municipalities provide can be financed by user charges, and almost everyone seems to agree that such financing, which by definition is not a form of taxation, is economically efficient. Furthermore, the potential exists for increased reliance on user charges, especially with respect to road pricing in our big cities.

But an uncomfortable truth remains. The taxes Canadians pay on property are among the highest in the world, thereby adding significantly to the cost of housing and to the cost of doing business. Students of Canadian local government need to know as much as possible about property taxes, the subject of the next chapter.

RESOURCES

On the website of the municipality in which you live or in which you have a particular interest, seek out information concerning the most recent municipal budget. Having read this far in this book, you probably already know more about Canadian municipal government than most newly elected councillors. Imagine yourself in this position, and try to determine the extent to which you think you could make intelligent decisions about the budget on behalf of the people who elected you. Think about what additional information you might like to have and how it could be provided.

STUDY QUESTIONS

1. What does the *net financial worth* of a municipality mean? Why do you think the net financial worth of Canadian local government went down between 1991 and 2013?

2. What is the difference between a municipality's operating budget and its capital budget? How are the two connected?

3. Should major municipal arterial roads be paid for by tolls? Explain your reasoning.

4. Do you favour full-cost pricing for water? Explain your reasoning. Why do you think that federal and provincial governments continue to provide subsidies for capital costs related to municipal water supply and sewage systems?

CHAPTER 15

The Property Tax

The property tax is of great importance for Canadian local governments because it is the main source of their revenue. It is also of obvious importance to anyone who owns property, because paying the tax is a significant cost, sometimes so significant that it causes people to sell a property that they would otherwise like to keep. But the property tax is important for renters as well, both for people who rent their residential accommodation and for people who operate businesses in rental property. Tracing the impact (or *incidence*) of the property tax is a major concern of urban economists that has practical implications for public policy. All we need realize at this point is that the property tax is not merely a technical or financial issue that concerns municipal administrators and large property owners. It is important to everyone. We all notice those few extra cents in sales tax that are added to our every purchase. But some aspects of how property taxes work likely have far more direct impact on how we actually live our lives.

In this chapter we first explore how municipalities in a given year determine how much property tax revenue they need. We then look at how this overall amount gets translated into a charge on individual property owners. Although relatively simple in principle, this process becomes much more complex as it is implemented in the real world, and the resulting complexities are the subject of the third section of this chapter. Finally, we compare the advantages and disadvantages of the property tax with other proposed municipal taxes.

How Much Property Tax?

We saw in the previous chapter that much of the annual municipal budgetary process is ultimately determined by the expected impact of proposed expenditures on future property tax levels. But let us briefly forget this real-world intrusion and assume unrealistically that municipal budgets are set solely on the basis of what municipal councillors want to spend. If this were the case, the process would comprise three distinct phases:

1. A set of calculations about all desired operating expenditures, including payments for debt charges and reserve funds. In many municipalities some of these expenditures will be requisitions from special-purpose bodies (or upper-tier municipalities) that municipalities are required to pay.
2. A set of calculations concerning all of the incoming revenue from all non-property-tax funds. In the last chapter we saw that the most important of these are user fees and transfers from other governments.
3. The amount by which the result of the first set of calculations exceeds the result of the second is the amount of funds that the municipality has to raise from its own taxes, which in Canada are almost exclusively property taxes.

Compared to the budgetary processes of other levels of government, this process, although it requires many calculations and assumptions, is relatively simple. There can be no decision about whether the budget will project an operating deficit (or surplus) because municipalities are required to adopt balanced operating budgets (always including expenses for debt charges and contributions to reserve funds). Usually, decisions about the mix of various kinds of tax increases are irrelevant because the property tax is the only one available. As we saw in the previous chapter, municipalities have to decide from time to time about whether particular services (garbage collection or roads, for example) should be paid for by user charges or property tax revenues, and they have to make difficult decisions about levels of user fees. But once such decisions are made, the property tax generally will be the mechanism whereby shortfalls will be covered.

As previously indicated, decisions about how much property tax revenue is needed in a given year are never as clear as the three-stage process described above would suggest. Municipal councillors know that if they approve a new subsidized recreation program, property tax will be increased. They know that sometimes if they assume new recreation programs will be fully paid for by user charges, then there might be insufficient demand for the program. A decision about the program's fate, not surprisingly, is never made solely on the basis of the program's inherent virtues. Often decision-makers have to consider all three stages of the process at once. Another factor that councillors have to consider is whether or not the municipality is growing. If there is much new growth and therefore many new buildings to be taxed, then perhaps increases in the total amount of property tax revenues needed to balance the budget are not a major problem, unless the growth itself generates new municipal operating expenditures, which it usually does. But if the municipality is not growing, increased demands for property tax revenue will be difficult to meet.

As we move ahead, let us assume that the municipal budgetary process is at a point where all three stages described above have been completed. How are these decisions translated into tax bills for individual property owners?

Determining Tax Payable for Individual Property Owners

The amount of tax payable for each individual property owner is determined by the assessed value of the property and by the property tax rate set by the council. Each of these factors is discussed in this section.

Unlike income taxes or sales taxes, property taxes are not levied as the direct result of any transaction. They are levied annually on the property owner even if the owner does absolutely nothing other than continue to own the property. Until about 50 years ago, property taxes in many provinces were levied on *all* personal property, including cars, artwork, jewellery, furniture, and the like. But taxes on the value of all property were exceptionally difficult to collect because it was impossible for any government accurately to determine who owned what and how much it was all worth. It is much easier to tax *real* property—buildings and land. As discussed in Chapter 10, municipal governments know who owns each parcel of real property because the land registry is public and available to all. If ownership is not recorded at the registry, the owner has no proof that he or she owns the land—so there is no way that an owner can escape the tax on real property, other than simply not to pay it. If payment is not made over a specified period of time, the municipality can confiscate the property for non-payment of taxes. Unlike sales taxes and income taxes, it is virtually impossible to escape paying property taxes—which makes it a very attractive tax from the viewpoint of any government.

The only circumstance in which property owners might rationally walk away from their properties by not paying their taxes is if the value to them of the property is less than the total amount of taxes owing.

This can happen if the difference between the taxes payable and the outstanding mortgage is greater than the value of the property. Such a circumstance can occur when lenders make unwise loans at a time when property values are declining (which is exactly what happened in the US prior to the 2008 financial crash). It can also happen when industrial property is found to contain toxic pollutants from previous industrial activities. Sometimes the costs of the required treatment of such *brownfield* sites are greater than the projected value of the property after the cleanup. In these circumstances, municipalities can be stuck with a property that has a negative value. Provincial laws, however, have made it much more difficult for industrial polluters to avoid liability in this way.

Assessment

The biggest problem with the property tax is determining, for tax purposes, how much a property is worth. Taxes on sales or incomes are easier because there is much less room for dispute about how much was paid for a particular item at a store or how much income a person received from his or her employer. If a particular property has been sold recently, the amount paid is usually recorded in the land registry and is a matter of public record. But as we all know, many properties are held by the same owner for decades, so direct information about their current market value is simply not available.

One way to solve this problem is to base the assessed value for tax purposes on some factor other than its current value. Many such factors have been used in the past, and most have been deficient in one way or another. We shall return to some of these factors when we look later at possible ways of reforming property assessment. Let us assume for now that the assessment of property is to be done on the basis of its market value, which is generally the case in all Canadian municipalities. Market value is easy to calculate if a property has been recently sold or if similar properties in nearby locations have been recently sold. But many properties do not fall into these categories, an extreme example being Toronto's CN Tower. It is very difficult to determine its market value in any given year unless it was bought and sold. Similar problems arise for thousands of industrial and commercial properties, not to mention unusual residential properties. In the case of some industrial properties, it is not even clear where the building ends and large-scale equipment begins, especially if the building is built around the equipment. (Disputes about such matters are highly technical and help line the pockets of lawyers and consultants, but those disputes need not concern us here.) For residential properties, in-ground swimming pools are generally considered real property, while above-ground ones are not.

It is obviously difficult for any government to assess the approximate market value of each property within its jurisdiction. There is lots of room for conflict and disagreement between property owners and the assessors, but such disputes place property owners in a conflicted situation: normally—and especially when they want to sell—they want everybody to consider their properties to be highly valuable and worth more than they paid for them; but, when it comes to property assessment for tax purposes, they want the government to consider the value of their properties to be as low as possible. Assessors keep extensive data relating to sales of different kinds of properties in different locations. They also keep track of applications from property owners for building permits. If owners add space to their house or extensively renovate, they are likely to see the assessed value of their property increase. This leads to a significant criticism of one of the impacts of the property tax: it discourages owners from upgrading buildings or, at a minimum, it discourages them from applying for the required permits, which are designed to force all builders to meet the appropriate zoning and building code requirements.

The assessment of property for tax purposes is carried out directly by the provincial government in some provinces, by arm's-length provincial agencies in others, or by municipalities themselves under close provincial supervision.[1] All provinces have in place mechanisms to allow property owners to appeal the assessed value of their properties. For owners of multiple properties, or of especially valuable ones, the outcomes of such appeals can be very important. For individual homeowners, such appeals can be frustrating and expensive, but sometimes victory can seem to make it worthwhile.

Rates

When the assessment process is complete within a municipality for any given year, the municipal council can then set its tax rate. In its simplest terms, the rate is the total amount of money a municipality needs to raise from the property tax divided by the total assessed value of all the properties within its boundaries. For any individual property-owner, the amount of tax payable in a given year is the product of the rate and the assessed value of his or her property. A typical example in Canada would be a home assessed at a value of $300,000 having to pay tax at a rate of .015 (1.5 per cent), leading to an annual tax bill of $4,500. Such a calculation should illuminate two simple truths:

1. If everybody's property value doubles, and if the assessment process captures the increase for everybody, then the municipality can cut its rate in half and still raise the same amount of money. Despite a common view that that this is unlikely to happen, in fact, it generally does. Municipalities cannot leave the rate the same while property values generally increase because for everybody who does not sell property in that year the increase in property values is simply a gain on paper. Unless property owners remortgage their houses at the higher value, they do not magically have new resources with which to pay property tax increases. This is different from income taxes where the more one makes, the more one can pay, because the income earner actually has more financial resources as his or her income increases. It is true, of course, that some people make a great deal of profit when they sell a property, but if or how to tax that profit has nothing to do with the property tax. (This is an income tax matter. Gains on the sale of a property used as a main residence are not subject to income tax in Canada; gains on the sale of all other properties are.)

2. If assessments change at the same rate for everybody in a given year, such changes are unlikely to have any appreciable impact on the amount of property taxes people pay because rates likely will change inversely to changes in property values. Therefore, people should not be concerned if the assessed value of their property goes up by 10 per cent while everybody else's is going up by the same rate. They do have cause for concern, however, if the assessed value of everyone else's property goes down by 10 per cent and theirs stays the same. In such circumstances, the municipal council will have to raise the rate by 10 per cent simply to maintain the same revenues, and the person whose property maintained its value would be facing a 10 per cent tax increase. Such an example reinforces the idea that the interaction between rates and assessed values means that property owners need to pay attention not simply to the increase or decrease in the assessed value of their property but how it is changing *in relation to the assessed value of other properties.*

To consider another important matter in analyzing property taxes, let us assume that a house worth $300,000 in one municipality is worth $600,000 in an analogous location in another municipality. Such an assumption is totally realistic, because we all know that house prices vary dramatically from city to city—between Winnipeg and Vancouver, for example. If house prices are generally twice as high in Vancouver as in Winnipeg, it certainly does not follow that the costs of providing municipal services will be twice as high in Vancouver. In fact, there is no reason to expect such costs to be much different (except perhaps for snow removal). Assuming market-value assessment in both cities, we should therefore expect property tax *rates* to be lower in Vancouver, perhaps by half, because the rates apply to a much larger average assessment. But this is of little practical consequence because the total taxes paid by owners of similar houses would be roughly similar in each city. If we were to measure the property tax burden in terms of the ratio of tax paid to value of houses, it would seem as though Vancouver homeowners were subject to a relatively low tax burden, but such an outcome results solely from the fact that housing prices are higher in Vancouver. If we want to measure relative property tax burdens among different cities, we should not do so by looking at houses of similar value. We should compare houses of similar size, quality, and relative location.

So far we have assumed that municipalities charge a single tax rate on all properties. In fact, this is not generally the case. Many provinces allow municipalities to vary the rate among different *classes* of property.[2] Examples of classes of property are single-family residential, multi-family residential, commercial, and industrial. In general in Canada, owners of single-family residences have received the best deal from municipalities, presumably because they comprise the most voters in any municipal election and councillors have the greatest immediate incentive to please them. However, these same councillors are usually under pressure to attract investment and jobs, so one would think that they would want to lower rates on industrial properties.[3] Recently, provincial governments seem to have become more sensitive about industrial property tax rates and, in some cases, have required municipalities to narrow the gap between industrial and residential rates.

Despite the fact that the property tax is, in many ways, an ideal mechanism for financing many municipal services, some significant problems and issues must be understood by anybody who wants to understand the main financial issues facing Canadian municipalities. The most important of these issues are addressed in the sections that follow.

Alternative Assessment Systems

Despite the use of different names, all provinces base their assessment system on the perceived market value of properties at the time of assessment.[4] But such systems are always controversial, in part because property owners object to having their assessment go up if they make improvements to their house. If they bought expensive artwork instead, they would not have to pay an annual tax based on the value of the art. The way around this problem is to base the assessment on the perceived value of the land, rather than on both the land and the building(s). Such a system is called *site-value assessment*. It has been used in the past in parts of Ontario and western Canada and is still in use in some countries of the British Commonwealth.[5] Such a system has many virtues, especially for those who want dense urban development to combat urban sprawl. No one would use developable land as a parking lot in a downtown core for very long if they were paying the same property taxes as the owner of a high-rise building next door. The idea that taxing land—and land alone—is the most suitable form of taxation is associated with Henry George, a nineteenth-century American political economist whose views are still supported today by a disparate band of environmentalists, libertarians, and egalitarians.[6] The most obvious problem with this scheme is assessing the value of land without the buildings that are on it. Assessment problems are even greater than with market-value assessment.

A quite different kind of assessment system is known as *unit-value assessment*. In this system, there are no subjective judgments by assessors. Assessment is based solely on the amount of land owned and the size of the buildings that are on it. The two factors can be combined using whatever arithmetical formula might be desired by the taxing authority. By encouraging small living units on small lots, this system is attractive for environmental reasons. However, if implemented, it would likely have some strange distributional effects. Compared with market-value assessment, relatively small homes on small lots in highly desirable areas of cities would likely see significant tax decreases, while larger homes on larger lots lived in by larger families in peripheral suburban areas would see tax increases. Making such a change would not be appealing to any provincial or municipal politician.

It is possible, of course, to combine aspects of these different systems by using complex formulas. But the more complex the formula, the less likely it will be understood. The great virtue of market-value assessment is that it is readily understood. From the point of view of the government, another advantage is that dissatisfied property owners must argue that their property is worth less than the assessor says it is—not an attractive proposition for those who treasure their real estate. We are not likely to see departures from market-value assessment in Canada anytime soon.

Exempt Property and Payments-in-Lieu of Taxes

The federal and provincial governments cannot tax each other.[7] Because municipalities derive their authority from provincial legislatures, it follows that municipalities cannot tax federal property. It also follows that municipalities cannot tax provincial property unless the provincial legislature specifically allows such taxation. Provincial legislation also prevents municipalities from taxing provincially funded institutions such as hospitals (except in New Brunswick) and colleges and universities.[8] But federal and provincial buildings and institutions consume municipal services. For some services, they pay user charges like anybody else. But they also rely on municipal roads and police and fire services, for which there generally are no user charges. In order to compensate municipalities for the provision of these services, the federal and provincial governments pay what are called *payments-in-lieu of taxes*, an attempt to cover municipal costs resulting from the operation of these services. It is important to note that, ultimately, the federal and provincial governments decide how much they will pay—not the municipalities.

Provincial legislation generally excludes places of worship and charitable institutions from having to pay municipal property taxes. In these cases, municipalities are effectively providing services free and are, therefore, offering a form of subsidy. Decisions about which properties qualify for the exemption generally are made provincially. But municipalities can decide to make grants to local organizations that are deemed to be serving some kind of public purpose; they could make grants to cover property taxes. The problem for the organizations, however, is that such grants need to be approved annually, while a property tax exemption is much more permanent. Compared to other forms of property, farmland is subject to less property tax in all provinces except Newfoundland and Labrador, and Prince Edward Island.[9]

Over the course of Canadian municipal history the most controversial property tax exemptions have related to railroads and to manufacturing. In the mid- and late nineteenth century, municipalities competed desperately with each other to attract railroads. One way they did this was to offer incentives, both outright financial grants and exemptions from paying property tax. Such policies soon extended to investors in manufacturing plants whose factory outputs often were needed to make the railroads profitable. If only a very few municipalities granted tax exemptions, little harm was done. In fact, to the extent that the exemptions caused new jobs to be created in a particular place—stimulating other kinds of property investment, including residences and retail outlets—they might well have led to an increase in local property tax revenue. However, problems resulted when most, or all, municipalities started doing the same thing. No municipality was better able to compete for investment in these circumstances, and all have lost property tax revenue from businesses.

Precisely because of this "race-to-the-bottom" dynamic, provinces eventually eliminated the ability of municipalities to offer such exemptions.[10] If any tax exemptions were to be offered, provinces tended to want to make the offers themselves. However, with the rise of globalization in the late twentieth century, many municipalities found it difficult to compete with other jurisdictions around the world, especially in the United States, which still had considerable freedom to attract footloose capital investment by offering a variety of tax holidays.[11] Various kinds of special economic zones have been established within cities around the world to attract businesses by making tax concessions. Although there have been occasional demands that Canadian provinces should move in the same direction, little has come of them. Canadian municipalities can do very little, if anything, to exempt businesses from paying property taxes.

In Canada the more common complaint is that home-owning voters have offloaded an unfair property tax burden onto local businesses, particularly since businesses generally cannot make use of many municipal services, notably garbage collection. Provincial policy within Ontario and in the city of Vancouver has been explicitly aimed at phasing in more equal treatment of businesses.[12] This has painful consequences for municipal councillors because it means that, in any given year until the phase-in is complete, residential tax-rate increases are higher than the average increase that the municipality requires to balance its budget.

Who Pays?

In legal terms, we know who pays the property tax: the registered owner of each property. But to determine the real impact of the property tax, it is important to have some idea about who really pays in practice. For example, our views of the property tax are likely to be quite different depending on whether we think the owner of a low-rent apartment building pays from his/her own funds or whether we think the owner simply passes on the cost of the tax to the tenants through rents. What really happens depends on a great many factors: the state of the rental market; the potential mobility of renters; or whether we are looking at the short or long term.[13]

If few housing alternatives are available and if renters with short-term leases are not in a position to move, then it is likely that the property owner could easily pass on any tax increases to the tenants. But let us imagine an alternative situation, with a number of similar apartment units in different buildings on both sides of a municipal border and frequent movement by tenants out of the buildings. Due to factors other than the level of municipal services provided, the annual property tax rate (as a percentage of the market value of the building) increases in the first municipality at a rate faster than the second. What happens here? Clearly the landlord in the first municipality cannot charge significantly higher rents because he or she will end up with few or no tenants. Because rents must remain roughly equal in both municipalities, the landlord pays. This will have the effect of driving down the value of the buildings in the first municipality. As a result, someone buying these buildings at their reduced prices will actually make the same amount of profit (other things being equal) as the landlord in the second municipality. In these circumstances we say that the differences in the property tax levels are *capitalized*, because the differences in levels affect the value of the different properties in the marketplace. When property tax differentials are capitalized, they are not being passed on to tenants; instead, they are absorbed by property owners. Even assuming high vacancy rates and mobile tenants, however, we must be careful in drawing conclusions. If property taxes were increased to provide accessible recreational facilities to a nearby apartment building, tenants would be willing to pay more in rent and the tax increases could be passed on. In this case, the value of the property would not go down as a result of higher taxes because the higher taxes would be producing a direct benefit to the property in question, and ultimately to the renters.

The issue of who really pays property taxes is important for provincial public policy in Canada because almost all provinces have some kind of scheme to provide property tax relief to low-income homeowners. In Ontario and Quebec, renters are eligible as well.[14] Data from the 1990s show that, for homeowners, the lower the gross family income, the higher the percentage of such income that is absorbed by the property tax. In British Columbia in 1992, the poorest (bottom decile) home-owning families spent 12.55 per cent of their income on property taxes. In Newfoundland and Labrador, the richest (top decile) spent only 0.79 per cent on property taxes.[15] Economists refer to a tax as *regressive* when it absorbs a higher proportion of poor people's income than that of rich people. The relief schemes for property tax in various provinces are designed to soften the regressive nature of the property tax. Especially targeted are home-owning senior citizens. After paying off their mortgages and reaching retirement, some are forced to consider selling their family home because of high property taxes. Various schemes are now in place to reduce the likelihood of such forced sales, because no politician wants to be held responsible for senior citizens having to leave their homes because of the burden of high property taxes.

If property taxes on rental units really are passed on to renters, then schemes for property tax relief are manifestly unfair if they apply only to low-income homeowners. This is precisely why determining the incidence of the property tax is such an important practical policy issue. In Ontario, the provincial government assumes that 25 per cent of residential rents are spent on property taxes, and renters are treated as though they were homeowners for property tax relief purposes.

Other Demands on the Property Tax

In Chapter 4 we noted that some special-purpose bodies are able to make a direct charge on the municipal treasury. Whatever they decide they need in a given year, municipalities are required to pay, subject only to some form of provincial appeal mechanism. In these cases, such costs are integrated directly into the municipal budget and there is no reason for those who pay property taxes to know about them unless the municipality decides to launch some kind of publicity campaign about costs that it cannot control. But there is another mechanism whereby a special-purpose body can raise local funds: it can itself set a tax rate on the value of assessed property and charge the tax directly, even if the municipality might still collect the tax on its behalf. This is the way elected school boards in Canada traditionally have raised local funds to finance local schools.

As we saw in Chapter 4, only in Quebec do school boards have the authority to levy their own property taxes. However, there are provincially mandated property taxes (mostly for educational purposes) in all provinces except Quebec. In the last few decades, provincial governments have acted to restrict or eliminate the taxing authority of school boards because of concerns about intra-provincial equity and because there was evidence that school boards—responding to constant pressure for increased expenditures on education—were *crowding out* municipalities from the property tax base.[16] Provinces that levy taxes on property for educational purposes are generally committed to decreasing the level of such taxes over time so that much of the pressure on municipalities caused by crowding out is easing. Nevertheless, as many municipal politicians search for tax sources that add to the property tax, it is surprising that they do not also stress that, in all provinces except Nova Scotia, they do not even have exclusive access to the tax most often considered their own—the property tax.

Alternatives to the Property Tax

As we noted in Chapter 3, Canadian municipalities in the past in some provinces have had access both to the sales tax and to income taxes. But the last vestiges of such access were abolished in Quebec in 1964. More recently, especially in the early 2000s, Canadian municipal leaders made a valiant effort to widen their taxation opportunities. Again, as we saw in Chapter 3, in 2007 Toronto was successful in obtaining the authority to tax personal vehicle registrations, land transfers, public entertainment, tobacco products, and alcohol served in bars and restaurants, but it has so far taxed only vehicles and land transfers. At the urging of Mayor Ford, the Toronto city council has since abolished the city tax on vehicle registrations. In this section we examine the case for municipal alternatives to the property tax. In order to do so, we must first understand municipal complaints about excessive reliance on the property tax.

Nobody in municipal government wants to get rid of the property tax. After all, it generates impressive revenues, is virtually impossible to avoid, and is quite closely linked to most of the main municipal functions, which usually involve property in one way or another. But the main complaint is that it is not sufficiently *elastic*, which means that it is not sufficiently responsive to changes in the overall economy. This is perceived as a problem by municipal officials when the economy is growing, as it was in the early 2000s. It would appear to be much less of a problem after the economic slowdown caused by the financial crisis in 2008.

When the economy is growing, revenue from sales taxes and income taxes increases automatically. Politicians need do nothing but watch the extra funds flow in as incomes increase and people buy more goods. Although the people paying the higher taxes might complain, they do so from a position of increasing wealth, so the political impact of the higher taxation is minimal. But people and businesses have to pay property tax even if they are not enjoying increases in income and not purchasing anything. If the value of their properties is increasing faster than the average in their municipality, then their property tax burden actually increases even though they have no additional funds. In such circumstances, if a municipal council wants to increase the property tax rate, it will face howls of opposition, not necessarily from everybody, but certainly from those whose incomes are not increasing (seniors, for example). It is in this sense that property tax revenues are *inelastic*.

A related problem pointed to by critics of the property tax is that non-residents of a city who use its resources—commuters or tourists—pay nothing, at least not directly. Commuters pay income tax on the money that they earn in the city, but it all goes to the federal and provincial governments. These same commuters, as well as tourists, make purchases in the city, but again all the goods and services tax (GST) and sales tax revenue goes to the federal and provincial governments. Why should a municipality spend money to encourage job creation and promote tourism when other levels of government reap the financial rewards? Part of the answer, of course, is that municipalities do benefit indirectly. Owners of office buildings, hotels, and major stores that serve commuters and tourists pay property tax like anyone else—and they likely would not have invested in such property were they not confident that that their buildings would be profitable. But once the buildings are built, very little of the funds generated by their occupants actually finds its way into municipal coffers.

Advocates of municipal sales or income taxes aim to fix this problem. They assume, first of all, that such taxes would be collected using the same bureaucratic apparatus that has already been established by the federal and provincial governments. The idea is that municipalities would be allowed to set their own rate that would be added to the existing rates and that funds collected from the municipal rate would automatically be turned over to the relevant municipality, just as the federal government collects provincial income taxes (outside Quebec) and turns the funds over to the relevant province. The cost of collection would be negligible, except that chain stores, which do not now have to worry about the municipality in which sales took place, would then have to contend with much more detailed reporting requirements. Municipal boundaries would become much more important than they already are, because there would often be different levels of sales and income taxes on each side, which would affect shopping and retail development decisions.

If municipal income taxes were levied by the municipality in which the worker resided, then the problem of taxing commuters would not be addressed. But if employees were taxed by the municipality in which they worked, then collection would be complicated by the need to distribute the revenue to a municipality different from the one in which he or she lived. These problems are by no means insurmountable, but they do indicate that municipal income taxes could not be implemented easily in the Canadian context, even if they do exist in many other countries.[17]

Another solution would be simply to allocate shares of federal and provincial income and sales taxes to municipalities, in much the same way that the federal gas tax is currently shared (see Chapter 3). The difficulty here is that this is not really a new municipal tax at all; it is really just a disguised form of transfer payment. Such a new transfer program might well be desirable, but it would do nothing to solve the original perceived problem: that municipalities get little in return for any investment they make to bring in outsiders. If taxes were shared on the basis of where they were collected, however, administrative problems of the kind referred to in the previous paragraph would emerge—and municipalities would have no freedom themselves to try to influence tax-payers' behaviour or to increase their own revenues through the adjustment of their own rates.

Another possibility is a municipal tax on the occupancy of hotel rooms. Such taxes already exist in Vancouver and Montreal.[18] Although not a huge generator of revenue, hotel occupancy taxes at least directly compensate the municipality for some of the costs associated with hosting visitors. The problem, of course, is that many local businesses want municipalities to do all they can to attract visitors, and levying a tax especially directed at them does not look like a desirable policy. It is surely no accident that the tax exists in precisely the two large Canadian cities that are most attractive to visitors anyway. It is hard to disagree with Harry Kitchen, who writes: "municipalities should be given the opportunity to implement this type of tax. Presumably, if they get it wrong and drive tourists or conventions away, they will soon correct for this error in judgment."[19]

Conclusion

This discussion of alternatives to the property tax raises larger questions about the future role of Canadian municipalities. If they are ever to levy such alternative taxes, then mayors, councillors, and senior municipal staff will have to make some very complex policy judgments about how to maximize revenue while mixing the taxes in such a way as to optimally advance the municipality's other policy interests, such as economic development and local environmental protection. We shall address this issue of municipal policy capacity in the final chapter.

The important lessons from this chapter are paradoxical. On the one hand, everyone acknowledges that the property tax has many virtues as the main source of municipal revenue and that, whatever reforms might come in the future, it will remain as the financial bedrock of Canadian municipalities, especially now that school boards are no longer significant players in the same arena. On the other hand, there are constant complaints about the property tax: it is inelastic; it is unfair to low-income earners; and its burdens on individual property-owners can increase, even in years where their incomes decrease. Furthermore, the assessment system inevitably produces some results that are arbitrary, if not perverse, causing aggrieved property owners to have to launch frustrating and worrisome appeals. Correcting a problem for one property can well produce new inequities for neighbours. With all these problems, it might seem surprising that the system survives. But it does—because most of the alternatives are considerably worse.

RESOURCES

Perhaps the most comprehensive website relating to property tax in Canada is operated by Ontario's Municipal Property Assessment Corporation. Although its emphasis is obviously on assessment in Ontario, it contains a wealth of information on many issues that are also important in other provinces. See www.mpac.on.ca

STUDY QUESTIONS

1. What do members of a municipal council need to know before they decide how much property tax they need to collect in a particular year?
2. Is it possible for the assessed value of a property to go up in a given year but for the total taxes payable to go down? Explain your reasoning.
3. What are the advantages and disadvantages of charging property tax only on the value of land and not on the combined value of land and buildings?
4. What additional taxation authority do you believe Canadian municipalities should have? Explain your reasoning.
5. Pick a property with which you are familiar to find out how property tax works in particular cases. Assessments of properties for tax purposes are in the public domain, so you can find out how to access them from the Web or from the relevant municipality. Does the assessment seem fair to you? What is the tax rate on the property? How much, if any, is charged explicitly for public education, either by the province or by a school board?

CHAPTER 16

Conclusion: Canadian Local Government in Comparative Perspective

Studying local government inevitably involves comparisons. This is particularly so in Canada because each province and territory has its own local-government system. Throughout this book we have seen that the various provincial systems are alike in some respects and different in others. For example, British Columbia is probably the province in which municipalities are the least regulated and controlled while Ontario is clearly at the opposite end of this spectrum. Making such distinctions—and explaining them—is the essence of the comparative method. One possible explanation for the difference between British Columbia and Ontario is that Ontario municipalities carry out more governmental functions than those in British Columbia. Why? Perhaps because Ontario is much more populous. Or perhaps Ontario municipalities have less autonomy because Ontario's historical origins date back to the period immediately after the American Revolution, and its first settlers were highly suspicious of the kind of local autonomy the American revolutionaries believed in. Perhaps local autonomy in British Columbia is more respected because this province, because of its distance from central Canada, was always more closely linked to the US. In comparative political analysis, possible explanations for one phenomenon invariably lead to new questions about others.

This book has been resolutely focused on Canada. Such an approach makes perfect sense if its sole purpose is to enable Canadians to better understand their own systems of local government. But the book has another purpose as well: to introduce students to the role of local government within democratic societies generally. The implicit assumption is that students need to understand one system (or set of similar systems in the same country) before they can start making meaningful comparisons.

In this final chapter we have the luxury of beginning to place Canadian local government in a wider comparative perspective.

We shall do this by examining four different variables, each of which has been thoroughly explored in the Canadian context in different places within this book. The four variables—which, as we shall see, are all interconnected—are: governmental functions; autonomy; multiple-purpose versus single-purpose authorities; and size. Discussions of each of these variables follow, and each discussion leads to other variables and questions which are crucial for the study of comparative local government.

Governmental Functions

What is it that local governments in different countries actually do? This is an important question. To answer it, however, we must begin by examining two other questions, the first of which has dominated much political analysis in the entire world over at least the last four decades: How can we explain that governments in general are seen as being less capable of improving the quality of life in our societies than they used to be? Answers to this question involve the terms *neo-liberalism* and *globalization*. Neo-liberalism has been described as a "cousin" of globalization.[1] It is "a theory and practice of running the economy in a way that frees markets from state and bureaucratic control."[2] Globalization is connected to neo-liberalism in that, starting in the 1980s, the common prescription from international organizations and consultants for most national problems relating to governance was to advocate a reduction in regulation and taxes to stimulate the wealth-generating capacity of the marketplace. As a result of the impact of neo-liberalism and globalization, citizens' faith in the capacities of governments to solve problems has been dramatically reduced. For many neo-liberals, however, different actions by many local governments are preferable to one big action by a central government. This is why in some countries it seems that, while the functions of government in general seem to have been reduced, the functions of local governments seem to have increased. This process is part of what is often referred to as *rescaling*, which is what happens when globalization and the liberalization of markets cause authority and policy to be redefined in different ways for different territories.[3] Rescaling takes place when different levels of government, governments with different boundaries, or different special-purpose bodies take on new functions. It is highly relevant to each of the four variables to be discussed in this chapter.

Even when governments retain responsibility for carrying out a wide range of functions, neo-liberals believe that, where possible, governments should contract out the actual delivery of these functions to the private sector. In Chapter 13 we examined some of the ways in which debates about this issue have played out in Canada. Any attempt to compare local governments across countries must examine the extent to which local governments in different countries contract out the functions that have been assigned to them. Explaining such differences is not easy, and often causes the analyst to address much broader national issues such as the political power of left-of-centre political parties and trade unions.

Comparing local-government functions in different countries requires that we have a common definition of local government that holds up across different countries. For Canada, this issue was addressed in Chapter 1, where we made it clear that Canadian provinces were *not* local governments. The justification for this is that Canada (like the United States, Germany, Spain, and Switzerland) is a federation in which the constituent units of the federation (provinces) have an equal constitutional status to that of the government of the country as a whole. Governments of large regions within some countries (Italy, France) do not have such constitutional status and are therefore local by just about any definition. Some comparative analysts are interested in the relative strength of *sub-national* governments within countries; they are not especially interested in the niceties of federal constitutions. By this definition Canadian sub-national governments (provinces and local governments) are very strong indeed, because collectively they provide the vast majority of Canadian government functions. However, using the definition of *local* employed in this book for Canada, our local governments are relatively weak in functional terms. Even in Ontario, the province where local governments have the most functions of any in Canada, local-government involvement in child-protection services and in specialized services for physically and mentally disabled children and adults is very limited. Instead the provincial government generally contracts directly with various local non-governmental agencies and organizations to provide the services. In most European countries, such services would be seen as being at the core of the social-service mission of local government. In the Canadian context we must remember that, outside Ontario, local governments have even less involvement in other social services: limited or no responsibility for welfare payments, employment services, social housing, child daycare, and services for senior citizens.

This relatively limited functional responsibility of Canadian local government helps explain why political parties are not as involved in local government as they are in other countries and perhaps why some citizens seem uninterested. The functional responsibility of Canadian *municipal* government—as we shall see again in the next section of this chapter—is even more limited, because, unlike municipalities in Europe, Canadian cities and towns have no responsibility for public education. As we have seen throughout this book, however, Canadian local governments, especially municipalities, have considerable functional responsibility for the built environment, a matter of constantly increasing importance as more and more Canadians find themselves living in cities. Developers, as shown in Chapter 10, have a huge interest in how the built environment is regulated and controlled, which, especially in the absence of political parties, goes a very long way to explain their importance within the municipal political process. The functions that local governments are expected to carry out go a long way to explain their politics. We see this even more dramatically when we examine the next variable.

Multi-Purpose versus Single-Purpose Authorities

As we have seen in Chapter 4, local-government functions can be carried out either by multi-purpose authorities we generally call municipalities or by single- (special-) purpose authorities such as school boards, police services boards, or regional health authorities. When we compare local-government systems across countries we generally want to determine the relative importance of these two different types of local governments. We also want to keep in mind that in some countries and some Canadian provinces (British Columbia, Ontario, Quebec, and New Brunswick) some municipal structures are divided into two (or more) tiers or levels. If special-purpose bodies exist within the same territories as two-tier municipal structures, as they do in many parts of Canada, the whole system can be exceptionally complex and difficult to understand. Why was such a system ever constructed?

Major cities do not have simple arrangements for municipal government. The underlying reason for this is that different functions of urban government require different boundaries. Institutions for the planning of outward regional development in big cities require different boundaries from institutions that are established to run a system of inner-city neighbourhood parks. Sometimes all of these different functions are forced to coexist within the same municipal boundaries or within the somewhat less rigid arrangements allowed by two-tier systems. But ultimate flexibility is provided by having different boundaries for different special-purpose bodies responsible for different governmental functions. The fact that both Metrolinx for Toronto and Hamilton and TransLink for the Vancouver area have their own unique boundaries for regional transit purposes is a perfect illustration of this point. That they exist, and that they are responsible for such an important function of government, indicates why the institutional arrangements for urban government are often as complex as they are.

As we saw in Chapter 4, there are other reasons for having single-purpose authorities: some are essentially operating businesses and they are separated from the municipality in the hope that those businesses can be run more efficiently as distinct entities; others (like port and airport authorities) exist because they are essentially intergovernmental in nature. Still others exist because the people most concerned with a particular function (policing, for example) are more distrustful of elected municipal politicians than they are of supervising provincial ministries for their function. In other words, for such people, functional autonomy is more important than local autonomy. This brings us to our next variable.

Autonomy

In legal terms, the ultimate form of political autonomy is sovereignty. By definition, no local government is sovereign. But if a city government performs a great many government functions without much central control, has access to sufficient financial resources to pay for them, and has some form of constitutional protection, then it would likely have much more real (as opposed to legal) governmental power than many of the world's sovereign states. As we have seen, especially in Chapter 3, no Canadian municipality comes close to being autonomous in the sense of having a large degree of independent governmental power. Their functions are generally limited, as is their access to resources. They are generally subject to considerable provincial control. Furthermore, they have no constitutional guarantees of autonomy.

In Chapter 3 we noted that the legal authority and independence of many American municipal corporations are recognized in the constitutions of their respective states. Such an arrangement is known as *home rule*. Because Canadian provinces do not have written constitutions, there can be no home rule in this sense in Canada. The so-called charters for some big Canadian cities are nothing more than ordinary provincial statutes aimed especially at those large cities. Despite having less *legal* autonomy than American cities, there is an important sense in which Canadian city governments are free of the *economic* control exerted by big business over their American counterparts. For example, because Canadian provinces prevent city governments from making tax concessions to existing and potential businesses, they cannot yield to business demands for such concessions.

In democratic political systems outside North America, municipal governments *are* specifically recognized in the national constitution and are guaranteed a minimum degree of autonomy within the overall state structure into which they are unquestionably fully integrated. They are usually directly involved in more government functions than are North American municipalities. When citizens are looking for just about any government service, they turn instinctively to their municipality and they are usually looking in the right place. The only way such a system can work is if some of the services are tightly controlled and subsidized by the central government. Ironically, the more functions a municipality administers, the less autonomous in most of its day-to-day operations it is likely to be. But such a lack of autonomy is not inconsistent with a form of constitutional protection.

Outside North America, where most countries have relatively disciplined and ideologically based political parties operating at all levels, including the local, the existence of such parties generally limits the capacity of particular municipalities for independent action. For example, if the French socialist party controls a large number of major French municipalities, these municipalities are unlikely to attempt any major initiatives that are outside the general political program of the socialist party. Socialist party members who are elected to office will be expected to work toward common purposes regardless of the level of government to which they are elected.[4]

Compared to other countries, Canada's municipalities might seem to lack autonomy because they have relatively few functions and resources and no constitutional recognition. But because of the official absence of provincial political parties at the local level, they have considerable political autonomy. Except in Ontario, where the Ontario Municipal Board is very powerful, municipalities have broad autonomy with respect to how they control the built environment. Paradoxically however, issues relating to size, the last of our variables, have in recent decades been the biggest threat to Canadian municipal autonomy.

Size

As we saw in chapters 6 and 8, many Canadian provincial and big-city governments have been greatly concerned about the size of Canadian municipalities. The main argument has been that municipalities need to be bigger in order to carry out their assigned functions more effectively and efficiently. Provincial governments in Manitoba, Nova Scotia, Ontario, and Quebec have been so obsessed with this issue that they took huge political risks to create larger urban municipalities through legislated amalgamations. In some countries, such forced amalgamations would have violated the national constitution. In the United States, they would have violated many state constitutions, and they certainly would have violated long-standing American political practices and conventions that place great store in local autonomy. Many European countries, most recently Denmark, have experienced similar rounds of forced amalgamations. In these countries, however, a major concern has been *functional capacity*. How can municipalities be expected to provide many of the specialized social services of a welfare state if they are too small to be able to hire the necessary specialized workers? Such concerns were obviously less relevant in Canada where these services are generally not municipal responsibilities. Even in Ontario, municipal amalgamations were not necessary for social-service and major infrastructure purposes because such services were usually already being provided by upper-tier regional authorities (see Chapter 7). France, with its more than 33,000 communes (lowest-tier municipalities), is an example of a country that has resisted the desire to increase the size of the basic units of municipal government. Instead, the national government simply adds more tiers and more special-purpose authorities.

The claim has often been made that neo-liberalism was responsible for the wave of municipal amalgamations (described in Chapter 8) that swept over eastern Canada in the 1990s.[5] The amalgamations themselves are clearly a form of *rescaling*, because the whole purpose of an amalgamation is to create a municipal government with a dramatically larger territory or scale. The problem with attributing the amalgamations of the 1990s to neo-liberalism, however, is that, as we saw in Chapter 8, provincially legislated amalgamations go back to the 1930s in Canada, long before the term *neo-liberalism* had been coined. More importantly, the amalgamations in Windsor and Winnipeg were unequivocally meant to benefit residents of poorer municipalities rather than to strengthen the operation of the private market. The same is true of the Quebec amalgamations of the early 2000s. Anyone familiar with the *public-choice* approach to local government described in Chapter 7 will recognize that this approach, rather than the consolidationist one, best fits with neo-liberalism. Even though Mike Harris's government in Ontario clearly espoused a neo-liberal ideology, its efforts to create larger municipal governments were the opposite of neo-liberal. Is it possible that Harris and his government simply did not know what they were doing?[6]

Students of comparative local government will always be fascinated by the question of size. Few scholars today take the time to consider the ideal size of a country because we recognize that the sizes of the world's countries have been settled not by rational calculation but by wars, colonial explorers, and diplomatic bargaining. Municipal boundaries, on the other hand, are often more pliable; they certainly have been in Canada. This provides opportunities to meaningfully speculate, as Aristotle did, on the ideal size of a political community. Nevertheless, in most countries, including Canada, it is now hard to find much that is rational in our current municipal boundaries. As we have seen, even in Calgary and Winnipeg—where, among our major cities, the closest correlation exists between a continuous built-up urban area and a single municipality—there is now so much urban development taking place outside the central-city boundaries that policy-makers are having to explore other possibilities for the governance of the city-region. Small size does not in itself mean that a municipal government is incapable of providing responsive and responsible control of the built environment. Nor does large size not guarantee such government. Despite the desirability of cross-national comparisons on this and many other related issues, Canada itself provides such diversity in the size of its urban and rural municipalities that, even by restricting ourselves to Canadian experiences, we should be able to discover a great deal more about the impact of size on local government than we already have.

Why Canadian Local Government Is Important

If we looked at the broad range of functions of Canadian local governments a hundred years ago compared to today, we would be forced to conclude that local government has become less important over the last century, especially relative to provincial governments. A hundred years ago municipalities were universally regarded as the last resort for public social assistance, but now they are not. School boards once had enormous autonomy to shape the nature of public schooling in their communities, but now most decisions about funding and curriculum are made in provincial capitals. Although these basic facts must never be forgotten as we assess the current role of local government, we need not focus exclusively on such examples of reductions of local autonomy, especially because, in terms of social equity at least, they are perfectly justified.

As has been emphasized repeatedly, local governments have considerable control over our built environment. A hundred years ago, when a much higher proportion of Canadians lived in rural areas and small towns, controlling the built environment was not nearly as important as managing the settlement of new agricultural land, especially in the West. But the urban nature of current Canadian life means that the quality of the built environment is crucial to all of us, particularly to citizens with special concerns about the environment and the quality of urban design. Subject to broad provincial control, our municipalities determine where new suburban development will take place. Subject to much less provincial control, they determine design standards for this development and the mechanisms for financing the required infrastructure. They determine the level of public protection for old buildings and the kind of development that is allowed or not allowed in our downtowns. (Many of these matters were explored in Chapter 10.) Municipalities also determine where roads and streets are built, how wide they will be, how well they will be maintained, and how they will accommodate pedestrians and cyclists. Subject to federal and provincial environmental standards, they determine how our water will be supplied, how our sewage will be treated, the conditions under which solid waste will be collected, and how it will disposed of.

Municipal governments, as discussed in Chapter 4, have varying levels of direct control over local police services. But even where direct municipal control is minimal (as in Ontario), local special-purpose bodies fill the gap. In every city in the country there are hugely sensitive issues about how the police relate to local residents, and much more opportunity exists than is usually acknowledged for local citizens, through the appropriate channels, to have a greater role in determining what the police do and how they do it. Unlike police services, fire services are invariably under direct municipal control, but for them, too, important local decisions must be made about how their personnel are to be deployed, especially as first responders in medical emergencies.

Other local special-purpose bodies, many with few direct connections to municipalities, have significant control over ports and airports, and still others are crucial for the planning and provision of regional public transit. Even health services are being decentralized and made more subject to forms of local control, although progress here is not nearly as fast as many experts had hoped or predicted.

With all these crucial attributes of urban life so vitally dependent on decisions of local governments of one form or another, why would anyone possibly suggest that either the services themselves or the local governments are somehow not important? Susan Phillips has claimed that municipalities are being transformed from providers of "hard" services (e.g., of roads and sewers rather than of social services) to democratic governments.[7] But the hard services she refers to are crucially important for urban life and they are provided democratically. As was noted in Chapter 2, all of these hard services, in theory, could be provided directly by provincial governments without having local governments at all. Local governments ensure that decisions about these key services are made by local people who are accountable in some way to local citizens.

Anyone who thinks that making local democratic decisions about hard services is easy or routine has not watched the agonies that local councils often go through in making such decisions. How much do we subsidize public transit systems to provide weekend service to people who have no other way of getting around a medium-sized city where most people have cars? Do we build a larger sewage treatment plant than we need now in the expectation that our community will grow? Do we widen an arterial road to ease traffic flow even if it means decreased property values and quality of life for residents in nearby houses? Do we maintain a policy of low industrial water rates just because a major consumer and employer threatens to leave if the rates are raised? Do we close a local school where enrolment is declining so as to redirect badly needed resources elsewhere, even if it means that a community or neighbourhood might wither and die? These are not hypothetical issues. They are faced regularly and repeatedly by municipal councillors and school board members whose levels of education and technical background are no greater than that of most readers of this book. And (except in some cities in British Columbia and Quebec) they have no party caucus or leader telling them what to do. Arguably, as we saw in Chapter 10, some of them are told what to do by developers and other groups associated with the property industry. But all of these factors are powerful reasons for political scientists, the media, and informed citizens to pay attention to the day-to-day business of local government rather than to write it off as boring and irrelevant.

Assessing Canadian Local Government

As we saw in Chapter 5, there is considerable evidence in Canada, especially for Toronto, that provincial governments are increasingly making the key strategic decisions about the long-term futures of Canadian city-regions. This is not bad news for local government; it is good news. It means that municipalities need not constantly be enlarged or reorganized in the vain hope that one day their boundaries will perfectly match the apparent functional requirements of our growing urban areas. It means, instead, that they can get on with the business of providing all the various services and regulations expected of them. Sometimes they will do this in co-operation with their municipal neighbours, either through various kinds of relatively informal agreements or by establishing new inter-municipal special-purpose bodies for the joint provision of particular services. Sometimes the provincial—and even the federal—government will be closely involved, requiring that municipal officials be highly skilled and knowledgeable with respect to intergovernmental negotiating. But negotiating on behalf of municipalities in the intergovernmental arena does not inevitably mean pleading for financial assistance or new taxation authority. As indicated in chapters 14 and 15, municipalities have considerable resources to finance their own activities both by charging appropriate user fees and by levying property taxes.

How can ordinary citizens relate to local governments, especially amid the complexity that characterizes Canadian local government? One approach is for local officials to continue to try to design new ways to engage local citizens in civic participation. As suggested in Chapter 10, provoking such participation when homeowners feel threatened by a particular municipal undertaking has never been a problem. But convincing these same people to attend public meetings to discuss matters of broad local interest has always been a different matter. Perhaps the Internet, social networking programs, or other devices that have not yet been invented will one day make possible a level of local engagement that theorists of local participatory engagement have so far only dreamed about.

In the meantime, we must never forget the municipal councillors and mayors whom we generally elect every four years (see chapters 9 and 11). These mayors and councillors are at the very core of our system of local government. Most elected municipal officials are ordinary people, sometimes frustratingly so from the standpoint of their lack of expertise. They become involved in municipal politics because they know many people (sometimes through political parties), because they have become neighbourhood leaders around a particular issue, because they have sought out a particularly visible form of community service, or because they see it as a way of making a (usually modest) income before moving on to something bigger and better and more lucrative. Whatever their motives, they are charged with balancing the professional concerns of municipal staff with the usually parochial concerns of local residents, the concerns of local employers with those of environmentalists, the concerns of those who want or need high levels of expensive municipal services with those who want low taxes and user charges. If local citizens know and understand what their mayors and councillors are doing, both within their own municipalities and within the various local special-purpose bodies and other governmental agencies with which they are connected, and if citizens vote in accordance with their evaluations of the officials' performance, then our system of local government is performing as it should in accordance with the reasons for having systems of local government.

Needless to say, the system is riddled with flaws. Voter turnout is abysmally low, and many of those individuals who do vote appear to have very little understanding of the key issues and how the candidates relate to them. A few (but by no means the majority) of the people elected to municipal office seem somehow less than ordinary and quite incapable of grappling seriously with many of the difficult issues facing municipal councils. More so than at other levels of government, there will always be proposals to fix problems of apparently unsatisfactory municipal decision-making by changing the internal structures and/or the external boundaries of the relevant municipality. Much of this book has been devoted in one way or another to describing, assessing, and analyzing the relative merits of such proposals. Ultimately, however, municipal governments must be judged by the extent to which they do what the majority of their residents want done. By this simple measure, Canadian local government probably succeeds.

RESOURCES

This book did not outline various theoretical approaches to urban politics at the beginning because there is no such approach, or combination of approaches, that is especially helpful in understanding all of Canadian local government as it has been discussed here. Some theoretical approaches, such as *public choice* and *regime theory*, were introduced when and where they were relevant. For many theorists of urban politics broadly defined, some of the institutional issues discussed here would be considered quite unimportant, and some important theoretical issues (such as rescaling) have scarcely been touched. For alternative approaches to those used in this book, see the writings by Boudreau, Keil, Bradford, and Phillips listed in the Bibliography, as well as the writings that these authors cite.

STUDY QUESTIONS

1. What are the connections among globalization, neo-liberalism, and rescaling? How do these concepts help you understand what has happened in Canadian cities and local governments over the last 30 years?
2. What factors must we consider when trying to compare the relative autonomy of municipalities in different countries?
3. Would you ever stand as a candidate for election to a municipal council? Why or why not?

NOTES

Introduction

1. For an excellent survey of the work of Canadian political scientists on Canadian cities, see Zack Taylor and Gabriel Eidelman, "Canadian Political Science and the City: A Limited Engagement," *Canadian Journal of Political Science* 43, 4 (December 2010): 961–81.
2. For Canadian urban geography, see Trudi Bunting, Pierre Filion, and Ryan Walker, eds., *Canadian Cities in Transition: New Directions in the Twenty-First Century*, 4th ed. (Toronto: Oxford University Press, 2010); for urban sociology, see Louis Guay and Pierre Hamel, *Urban Sociology* (Toronto: Oxford University Press, 2014).

Chapter 1

1. For a brief account of the historical evolution of the Corporation of the City of London, see the following entry on its website: www.cityoflondon.gov.uk/about-the-city/history-and-heritage/mansion-house/Pages/History-of-the-Government-of-the-City-of-London.aspx .
2. For a review of the historical origins of municipal government in Canada, see Kenneth Grant Crawford, *Canadian Municipal Government* (Toronto: University of Toronto Press, 1954), ch. 2.
3. Hendrik Hartog, *Public Property and Private Power: The Corporation of the City of New York in American Law, 1730–1870* (Chapel Hill: University of North Carolina Press, 1983). For a more general discussion of "a political theory of the corporation," see David Ciepley, "Beyond Public and Private: Toward a Political Theory of the Corporation," *American Political Science Review* 107, 1(2013): 139–58.
4. Section 15(b) of the Ontario Freedom of Information and Protection of Privacy Act, as quoted in Ontario, Ministry of the Attorney General, Information and Privacy Commissioner, *Final Order PO-1915-F*, 22 June 2001.
5. Ibid.
6. *Godbout v. Longueuil (City)*, [1997] 3 S.C.R. 844.
7. But the four Ontario counties of Brant, Haldimand, Norfolk, and Prince Edward are all single-tier.
8. Statistics Canada, *Financial Information System (FMS) 2004*, Catalogue no. 68F0023XIB, p. 131.
9. Warren Magnusson, "The Local State in Canada: Theoretical Perspectives," *Canadian Public Administration* 28, 4 (1985): 575–99.
10. Crawford, *Canadian Municipal Government*, 59.

Chapter 2

1. David Bulger and James Sentance, "Prince Edward Island," in Andrew Sancton and Robert Young, eds., *Foundations of Governance: Municipal Government in Canada's Provinces* (Toronto: University of Toronto Press, 2009), 314–44.
2. For a full discussion criticizing assumptions about the inherent virtues of political decentralization, see Daniel Treisman, *The Architecture of Government: Rethinking Political Decentralization* (Cambridge: Cambridge University Press, 2007). See also Gerry Stoker, "Introduction: Normative Theories of Local Government and Democracy," in Desmond King and Gerry Stoker, eds., *Rethinking Local Democracy* (Houndsmills, Basingstoke, Hampshire: Macmillan, 1996), 1–25.
3. For a discussion of this and related issues, see Ronald J. Oakerson, *Governing Local Public Economies: Creating the Civic Metropolis* (Oakland, CA.: ICS Press, 1999), esp. 16.

4. For a discussion of allocative efficiency in the Canadian context, see Harry Kitchen, *Municipal Revenue and Expenditure Issues in Canada*, Canadian Tax Paper 107 (Toronto: Canadian Tax Foundation, 2002), ch. 3.

5. Charles Tiebout, "A Pure Theory of Local Expenditure," *Journal of Political Economy* 64 (1956): 416–24. For background on how Tiebout developed his approach, see William A. Fischel, *The Homevoter Hypothesis: How Home Values Influence Local Government Taxation, School Finance, and Land-use Policies* (Cambridge, MA.: Harvard University Press, 2001), 76–80. For a relatively recent survey of the public choice approach to American local government, see Oakerson, *Governing Local Public Economies*. Those at the lower end of the socio-economic scale—poor people—often are not in position to "vote with their feet," and since they usually are not property owners in any case, their concerns and needs can get pushed aside in the public choice model. For a broad discussion of the importance of "exit" options for democratic theory, see Mark E. Warren, "Voting with Your Feet: Exit-based Empowerment in Democratic Theory," *American Political Science Review* 105, 4 (2011): 683–701.

6. John Stuart Mill, *Considerations on Representative Government* (London, UK: Parker, Son, and Bourn, 1861), 275.

7. Paul E. Peterson, *City Limits* (Chicago: University of Chicago Press, 1981), ch. 6.

8. Alan Norton, *International Handbook of Local and Regional Government* (Brookfield, VT: Edward Elgar, 1994). For more recent information, see the website of United Cities and Local Governments (UCLG), The Global Network of Cities, Local and Regional Governments, at www.uclg.org/en.

9. David Siegel, "Ontario," in Andrew Sancton and Robert Young, eds., *Foundations of Governance*, 20–69.

10. André Côté and Howard Tam, *Affordable Housing: Mobilizing Private Capital in an Era of Public Constraint*, IMFG Perspectives, No. 3, Munk School of Global Affairs at the University of Toronto, 2013, p. 3. See also Jason Hackworth and Abigail Moriah, "Neoliberalism, Contingency and Urban Policy: The Case of Social Housing in Ontario," *International Journal of Urban and Regional Research* 30, 3 (1996): 510–27.

11. The following discussion of municipal functions in Canada is an updated version of the account found in Andrew Sancton, "Introduction," in Sancton and Young, eds., *Foundations of Governance*, 6–8. Research on this subject was part of the project on Public Policy in Municipalities, based at the University of Western Ontario, funded by the Social Sciences and Humanities Research Council of Canada (SSHRC), and headed by Robert Young.

12. Calgary Homeless Foundation, http://calgaryhomeless.com/10-year-plan/.

Chapter 3

1. These documents can be found at http://laws.justice.gc.ca/en/const/index.html .

2. Government of Canada, National Capital Commission, *The Capital of Canada: How Should It Be Governed* (Ottawa, 1974), I, 14. For a recent discussion of issues facing the National Capital Commission and the cities of Ottawa and Gatineau, see Rupak Chattopadhyay and Gilles Paquet, eds., *The Unimagined Federal Capital: Challenges for the Federal Capital Region* (Ottawa: Invenire Books, 2011).

3. School boards will be explored more fully in Chapter 4.

4. David M. Cameron, "Provincial Responsibilities for Municipal Government," *Canadian Public Administration* 23, 2 (1980): 222–35. and Zack Taylor, "If Different, then Why? Explaining the Divergent Development of Canadian and American Local Governance," *International Journal of Canadian Studies* 49 (2014): 53-79. See also the articles by Warren Magnusson cited in the Resources section of this chapter. For a recent discussion of home rule in the US, see Jesse J. Richardson, Jr., "Dillon's Rule is from Mars, Home Rule is from Venus: Local Government Autonomy and the Rules of Statutory Construction," *Publius: The Journal of Federalism* 41, 4 (2011): 662–85.

5. C. Richard Tindal, S. Nobes Tindal, Kennedy Stewart, and Patrick J. Smith, *Local Government in Canada*, 8th ed. (Toronto: Nelson, 2013), 203.

6. Ibid., 206. See also, Joseph Garcea, "The Empowerment of Canadian Cities: Classic Canadian Compromise," *International Journal of Canadian Studies* 49 (2014): 81-104.

7. For details, see www.scics.gc.ca/english/view.asp?x=1 .

8. For BC's Agricultural Land Commission, see www.alc.gov.bc.ca/ .

9. John G. Chipman, *A Law Unto Itself: How the Ontario Municipal Board Has Developed and Applied Land-Use Planning Policy* (Toronto: University of Toronto Press, 2002), 10–11.

10. Ibid., 12.

11. For a detailed analysis of the effect of the OMB on municipal decision-making in the city of Toronto, see Aaron A. Moore, *Planning Politics in Toronto: The Ontario Municipal Board and Urban Development* (Toronto: University of Toronto Press, 2013).

12. Serge Belley et al., "Quebec," in Andrew Sancton and Robert Young, eds., *Foundations of Governance: Municipal Government in Canada's Provinces* (Toronto: University of Toronto Press, 2009), 122.

13. Carey Doberstein, "Institutional Creation and Death: Urban Development Agreements in Canada," *Journal of Urban Affairs* 33, 5 (2011): 529–47.

14. *Canada (Attorney General) v. PHS Community Services Society*, 2011 SCC 44, [2011] 3 S.C.R. 134. For background, see Eugene J. McCann, "Expertise, Truth, and Urban Policy Mobilities: Global Circuits of Knowledge in the Development of Vancouver, Canada's 'Four Pillar' Drug Strategy" in *Environment and Planning* A 40 (2008): 885–904.

15. Harry Kitchen, *Municipal Revenue and Expenditure Issues in Canada*, Canadian Tax Paper No. 107 (Toronto: Canadian Tax Foundation, 2002), 226.

16. For links to each of the agreements, see http://www.infrastructure.gc.ca/prog/agreements-ententes/index-eng.html#gtf-fte. For more information on how municipalities originally obtained their share of this tax, see Erika Adams and Allan M. Maslove, "The Federal Gas Tax Cession: From Advocacy Efforts to 13 Signed Agreements" in Katherine Graham and Caroline Andrew, eds., *Canada in Cities: The Politics and Policy of Federal-Local Governance* (Montreal and Kingston: McGill-Queen's University Press, 2014).

17. Vincent Ostrom, Robert Bish, and Elinor Ostrom, *Local Government in the United States* (San Francisco: ICS Press, 1988), 88–9.

18. David Reevely, "City Asks Province for Power to Levy Tolls on Highway 174," *Ottawa Citizen*, 12 June 2013.

19. Eric Champagne, "Tracking the Growth of the Federal–Municipal Infrastructure Program under Different Political Regimes" in Caroline Andrew and Katherine Graham, eds., *Canada in Cities: The Politics and Policy of Federal–Local Governance* (Montreal and Kingston: McGill-Queen's University Press, 2014).

20. For details, see Government of Canada, Budget 2013, at www.budget.gc.ca/2013/doc/themes/infrastructure-eng.html .

21. Barbara Wake Carroll, "Housing Policy in the New Millennium: The Uncompassionate Landscape," in Edmund P. Fowler and David Siegel, eds., *Urban Policy Issues: Canadian Perspectives*, 2nd ed. (Toronto: Oxford University Press, 2002), 69–89.

22. Government of Canada, Employment and Social Development, Canada, "Terms and Conditions of the Homelessness Partnering Strategy," www.hrsdc.gc.ca/eng/communities/homelessness/funding/terms.shtml. See also Fran Klodawsky and Lenore Evans, "Homelessness on the Federal Agenda: Progressive Architecture but No Solution in Sight" in Caroline Andrew and Katherine Graham, eds., *Canada in Cities: The Politics and Policy of Federal–Local Governance* (Montreal and Kingston: McGill-Queen's University Press, 2014).

23. John A. Chenier, "The Evolving Role of the Federation of Canadian Municipalities," *Canadian Public Administration* 52, 3 (2009): 395–416.

24. For sustainability initiatives by the FCM, see www.fcm.ca/home/programs/green-municipal-fund.htm .

25. Zachary Spicer, "Institutional Policy Learning and Formal Federal–Urban Engagement in Canada," *Commonwealth Journal of Local Governance*, 7 (2010): 99–119.

26. Andrew Sancton, "The Urban Agenda," in Herman Bakvis and Grace Skogstad, eds., *Canadian Federalism: Performance, Effectiveness, and Legitimacy*, 3rd ed. (Toronto: Oxford University Press, 2012), 302–19. See also Robert Young and Kelly McCarthy, "Why Do Municipal Issues Rise on the Federal Policy Agenda in Canada?", *Canadian Public Administration* 52, 3 (2009): 347–70; Christopher Stoney and Katherine A.H. Graham,

"Federal–Municipal Relations in Canada: The Changing Organizational Landscape," *Canadian Public Administration* 52, 3 (2009): 371–94. For a valuable collection of essays on federal involvement with municipalities, see Katherine Graham and Caroline Andrew, eds., *Canada in Cities: The Politics and Policy of Federal–Local Governance* (Montreal and Kingston: McGill-Queen's University Press, 2014).

27.   For composition of the board of directors of the Association of Municipalities of Ontario, see www.amo.on.ca/About/Board-of-Directors.aspx. For a recent analysis of provincial-local relations in Ontario, see André Côté and Michael Fenn, "Provincial-Municipal relations in Ontario: Approaching the Inflection Point" IMFG Papers on Municipal Finance and Governance, No.17, Munk School of Global Affairs at the University of Toronto, 2014.

Chapter 4

1.   Ronald A. Manzer, *Public Schools and Political Ideas: Educational Policy in Historical Perspective* (Toronto: University of Toronto Press, 1994), 52; David M. Cameron, *Schools for Ontario: Policy-making, Administration, and Finance in the 1960s* (Toronto: University of Toronto Press, 1972), 34–5.

2.   Cameron, *Schools for Ontario*, 36.

3.   Joseph P. Viteritti, ed., *When Mayors Take Charge: School Governance in the City* (Washington: Brookings Institution Press, 2009).

4.   H.C. Barnard, *A History of English Education from 1760*, 2nd ed. (London: University of London Press, 1964), 210.

5.   Manzer, *Public Schools*, 60.

6.   Ibid., 54.

7.   Quebec, Forum sur la démocratie et la gouvernance des commissions scolaires (February 2008), p.9, see www.mels.gouv.qc.ca/fileadmin/site_web/documents/PSG/politiques_orientations/RapportForumTMI.pdf . There were no general elections for school boards in Quebec between 2007 and November 2014. See Québec, Assemblée nationale, *Débats*, 24 April 2013.

8.   P.C. Stenning, "The Role of Police Boards and Commissions as Institutions of Municipal Police Governance," in C.D. Shearing, ed., *Organizational Police Deviance* (Toronto: Butterworths, 1981), 165.

9.   Ibid., 168; N. Rogers, "Serving Toronto the Good: The Development of the City Police Force, 1834–84," in Victor L. Russell, ed., *Forging a Consensus: Historical Essays on Toronto* (Toronto: University of Toronto Press, 1984), 122–3; John C. Weaver, *Crimes, Constables, and Courts: Order and Transgression in a Canadian City, 1816–1970* (Montreal and Kingston: McGill-Queen's University Press, 1995), 87.

10.   Robert L. Bish and Eric G. Clemens, *Local Government in British Columbia*, 4th ed. (Vancouver: Union of British Columbia Municipalities, 2008), 99–102 Available at www.ubcm.ca/assets/library/Publications/Local~Government~in~British~Columbia/LGBC-All.pdf .

11.   Québec, Statutes, Charter of the Ville de Montréal, Chapter C-11.4, s.72-4 and 106-17. It is actually Montreal's "agglomeration" council that appoints the municipal representatives on the public safety committee. For details, see Chapter 8.

12.   Ontario, Ministry of the Attorney General, The Ipperwash Inquiry, Vol. 2, *Policy Analysis* (2007), ch. 12, at www.attorneygeneral.jus.gov.on.ca/inquiries/ipperwash/report/vol_2/index.html .

13.   M.E. Beare and T. Murray, eds. *Police and Government Relations: Who's Calling the Shots?* (Toronto: University of Toronto Press, 2007).

14.   Quoted in Ontario, *Policy Analysis*, 311.

15.   Quoted ibid., 312.

16.   Ibid., 313.

17.   Ontario, Report of the Royal Commission on Metropolitan Toronto, Vol. 2: *Detailed Findings and Recommendations* (1977), 279.

18.   Susan Eng, "Commentary," in Beare and Murray, eds., *Police and Government Relations*, 290–4. For more on this point, see John Sewell, *Police in Canada: The Real Story* (Toronto: James Lorimer, 2010), especially ch. 8.

19. Ontario, *Policy Analysis*, 328. For further discussion, see Andrew Sancton, "Democratic Policing": Lessons from Ipperwash and Caledonia, *Canadian Public Administration* 55, 3 (2012): 365–83.

20. John W. Morden, *Independent Civilian Review into Matters, Relating to the G20 Summit: Report* (Toronto: Toronto Police Services Board, 2012), ch.1. www.tpsb.ca/g20/ICRG20 Mordenreport.pdf. Reprinted with permission.

21. Ibid., 208.

22. Ibid., 234.

23. Ibid., 234 and 236.

24. Ibid., 238. Reprinted with permission.

25. See Section 485 of the Vancouver Charter, which can be found at www.bclaws.ca/ EPLibraries/bclaws_new/document/LOC/freeside/--%20V%20--/Vancouver%20 Charter%20SBC%i201953%20c.%2055/00_Act/vanch_24.xml#section485 .

26. Vancouver Board of Parks and Recreation, *Annual Report* 2011, http://former.vancouver .ca/parks/info/publications/VPBAnnualReport2011.pdf .

27. Sections 492 and 493 of the Vancouver Charter.

28. Christopher Armstrong and H.V. Nelles, *Monopoly's Moment: The Organization and Regulation of Canadian Utilities, 1830–1930* (Philadelphia: Temple University Press, 1986), 12. For more on the history of Montreal's water supply, see Michèle Dagenais, "At the Source of a New Urbanity: Water Networks and Power Relations in the Second Half of the Nineteenth Century" in Stéphane Castonguay and Michèle Dagenais, *Metropolitan Natures: Environmental Histories of Montreal* (Pittsburgh: University of Pittsburgh Press, 2011) 101–14.

29. Armstrong and Nelles, *Monopoly's Moment*, 37.

30. Ibid., 75–6.

31. See Ontario, Ontario Distribution Sector Review Panel, *Renewing Ontario's Electricity Distribution Sector: Putting the Consumer First* (December 2012), and Stephen Fyfe, Mark Garner, and George Vegh, *Mergers by Choice, Not Edict: Reforming Ontario's Electricity Distribution Policy*, C.D. Howe Institute Commentary No. 376 (March 2013).

32. Toronto Transit Commission, *Annual Report 2011*, www.ttc.ca/PDF/About_the_TTC/ TTC_Annual Report_ap.pdf .

33. Toronto Administrative Structure, www.toronto.ca/divisions/pdf/org_chart.pdf , 16 September 2013.

34. In 2013, six were elected officials within the Montreal city council. The seventh was the mayor of the suburban municipality of Dollard-des-Ormeaux. For more details about municipal organization in the Montreal area, see Chapter 8.

35. Frances Frisken, "A Triumph for Public Ownership; The Toronto Transportation Commission, 1921 53," in Russell, ed , *Forging a Consensus*, 249. For a history of rapid-transit proposals in Toronto, see Ed Levy, *Rapid Transit in Toronto: A Century of Plans, Progress, Politics & Paralysis*, a webbook published by the Neptis Foundation, available at: http://levyrapidtransit.ca.

36. Frisken, "A Triumph," 262–4.

37. Frances Frisken, *The Public Metropolis: The Political Dynamics of Urban Expansion in the Toronto Region, 1994–2003* (Toronto: Canadian Scholars' Press, 2007), 84.

38. For details, see Conservation Ontario at www.conservation-ontario.on.ca/ .

39. Bish and Clemens, *Local Government in British Columbia*, 127–34. For a more recent and critical commentary, see a consultant's study for TransLink's Mayors' Council: Acuere Consulting et al, *Translink Governance Review* (March 2013) available at www.scribd .com/doc/131890569/TransLink-Governance-Review. For the most recent legislative amendments in 2014, see Bills 22 and 23 available at: www.leg.bc.ca/40th2nd/3rd_read/ gov23-3.htm.

40. The information on this special-purpose body is updated from Andrew Sancton, Rebecca James, and Rick Ramsay, *Amalgamation vs. Inter-municipal Cooperation: Financing Local and Infrastructure Services* (Toronto: ICURR Press, 2000).

41. See Martin Horak, "Success and Failure in Multilevel Governance in Toronto," in Martin Horak and Robert Young, eds., *Sites of Governance: Multilevel Governance and Policy Making in Canada's Big Cities* (Montreal and Kingston: McGill-Queen's University Press, 2012), 248–52; and Gabriel Eidelman, *Three's Company: A Review of Waterfront Toronto's Tri-Government Approach to Revitalization* (Toronto: The Mowat Centre, 2013).

42. See also Gordon Hamilton, "Port Metro Vancouver approves first of two controversial coal export projects," *Vancouver Sun*, 25 January 2013. For more on the multilevel governance of Vancouver's port and associated infrastructure, see Thomas A. Hutton, "'Multilevel Governance and Urban Development in Vancouver," in Horak and Young, eds., *Sites of Governance*, 271–4.

43. Tom Urbaniak, *Her Worship: Hazel McCallion and the Development of Mississauga* (Toronto: University of Toronto Press, 2009), 186–9.

44. Ibid., 186.

45. The municipal appointments are formally made by the Communauté métropolitaine de Montréal, an upper-tier level of metropolitan government (discussed in Chapter 7), which also assigns municipal costs of the commuter rail system to its member municipalities on the basis of each municipality's share of total assessed property.

46. The three authorities joined forces in December 2012 to make a common presentation to the federal government about the need for renewed infrastructure funds. See www.bigmove.ca/wp-content/uploads/2013/05/Canadas-RTA-Delivering-Real-Results-for -Canadians1.pdf.

47. www.bigmove.ca.

48. For a discussion of Nova Scotia that contains helpful general analysis and references, see Martha Black and Katherine Fierlbeck, "Whatever Happened to Regionalization: The Curious Case of Nova Scotia," *Canadian Public Administration* 49, 4 (2006): 506–27. For Ontario, see Ontario, Ombudsman, *The LHIN Spin: Investigation into the Hamilton Niagara Haldimand Brant Local Health Integration Network's Use of Community Engagement in its Decision-making Process*, August 2010. For the abolition of regional health authorities in Alberta in 2008, see Susan Ruttan, "Supersized: Forged in Secrecy, Alberta's New Health Superboard Continues the Dismantling of Public Healthcare," *Alberta Views* (Nov. 2009), 32–7. Nova Scotia is consolidating its nine regional health authorities into one effective 1 April 2015. See: novascotia.ca/news/ release/?id=20140724002.

49. Québec, Pacte 2000, *Rapport de la Commission nationale sur les finances et la fiscalité locales* (1999), 290–2. For subsequent developments in the regionalization of health care in Quebec, see Elisabeth Martin, Marie-Pascale Pomey, and Pierre-Gerlier Forest, "One Step Forward, One Step Back: Quebec's 2003–04 Health and Social Services Regionalization Policy, *Canadian Public Administration* 53.4 (December 2010), 467–88.

50. Dale Richmond and David Siegel, eds, *Agencies, Boards, and Commissions in Canadian Local Government* (Toronto: Institute of Public Administration of Canada, 1994).

Chapter 5

1. Louis Wirth, "Urbanism as a Way of Life," *American Journal of Sociology* 44 (1938): 3–24.

2. Harry H. Hiller, "Introduction: Urbanization and the City," in Harry H. Hiller, ed., *Urban Canada*, 2nd ed. (Toronto: Oxford University Press, 2010), xii.

3. See Statistics Canada, www12.statcan.gc.ca/census-recensement/2011/ref/dict/geo049a-eng.cfm. *See also*, Henry A. Puderer, *Urban Perspectives and Measurement*, Statistics Canada Geography Working Paper Series (2009), Catalogue no. 92F0138M—No. 2009001, available at www.statcan.gc.ca/pub/92f0138m/92f0138m2009001-eng.pdf.

4. Statistics Canada, www12.statcan.gc.ca/census-recensement/2011/ref/dict/table-tableau/ table-tableau-1-eng.cfm.

5. Statistics Canada, www12.statcan.gc.ca/census-recensement/2011/ref/dict/geo049a-eng .cfm .

6. Statistics Canada, *Canada's Rural Population Since 1851: Population and Dwelling Counts, 2011 Census*, Catalogue no. 98-310-X2011003, available at www12.statcan.gc.ca/census-recensement/2011/as-sa/98-310-x/98-310-x2011003_2-eng.pdf .

7. Calculated from data found at Statistics Canada, www12.statcan.gc.ca/census-recensement/2011/dp-pd/hlt-fst/pd-pl/Table-Tableau.cfm?LANG=Eng&T=801&S=51&O=A .

8. For details, see Statistics Canada, www12.statcan.gc.ca/census-recensement/2011/ref/ dict/geo009-eng.cfm . Cores with populations of more than 50,000 but that do not generate a population of more than 100,000 remain as CAs.

9. Ray D. Bollman and Heather A. Clemenson, "Structure and Change in Canada's Rural

Demography: An Update to 2006 with Provincial Detail," *Rural and Small Town Analysis Bulletin*, Statistics Canada, Nov. 2008, Catalogue no. 21-006-X; available at Statistics Canada, www.statcan.gc.ca/pub/21-006-x/21-006-x2007007-eng.pdf.

10. Statistics Canada, www12.statcan.gc.ca/census-recensement/2011/ref/dict/geo009-eng.cfm .

11. Larry S. Bourne, John N.H. Britton, and Deborah Leslie, "The Greater Toronto Region: The Challenges of Economic Restructuring, Social Diversity, and Globalization," in Larry S. Bourne et al., eds., *Canadian Urban Regions: Trajectories of Growth and Change* (Toronto: Oxford University Press, 2011), 239.

12. Calculated from data at Statistics Canada, www12.statcan.gc.ca/census-recensement/2011/dp-pd/prof/index.cfm?Lang=E.

13. Ontario, Ministry of Municipal Affairs and Housing, www.mah.gov.on.ca/Page187.aspx. For a substantial part of the political background to the adoption of the Greenbelt legislation, see L. Anders Sandberg, Gerda R. Wekerle, and Liette Gilbert, *The Oak Ridges Moraine Battles: Development, Sprawl, and Nature Conservation in the Toronto Region* (Toronto: University of Toronto Press, 2013).

14. Ontario, Ministry of Infrastructure, "Growth Plan for the Greater Golden Horseshoe, 2006," www.placestogrow.ca/index.php?option=com_content&task=view&id=9&Itemid=14 . For a discussion of the political background to the policy, see Gabriel Eidelman, "Managing Urban Sprawl in Ontario: Good Policy or Good Politics," *Politics and Policy* 38, 6 (2010): 1211–36. For a recent assessment, see Rian Allen and Philippa Campsie, *Implementing the Growth Plan for the Greater Golden Horseshoe: Has the Strategic Regional Vision Been Compromised?* (Toronto: Neptis Foundation, 2013), available at: www.neptis.org/publications/implementing-growth-plan-greater-golden-horseshoe. See also, Edward Relph, *Toronto: Transformations in a City and its Region* (Philadelphia: University of Pennsylvania Press, 2014), ch.9.

15. Robert Lewis, *Manufacturing Montreal: The Making of an Industrial Landscape, 1850 to 1930* (Baltimore: Johns Hopkins University Press, 2000).

16. For a discussion of the "global cities" literature from a Canadian perspective, see Peter V. Hall, "The Global Imperative," in Trudi Bunting, Pierre Filion, and Ryan Walker, eds., *Canadian Cities in Transition: New Directions in the Twenty-first Century*, 4th ed. (Toronto: Oxford University Press, 2010), 56–69. For a thoughtful and dissenting perspective on competitiveness, see Neil Brenner and David Wachsmuth, "Territorial Competitiveness: Lineages, Practices, Ideologies" in Bishwapriya Sanyal et al eds., *Planning Ideas that Matter: Livability, Territoriality, Governance, and Reflective Practice* (Cambridge MA: MIT Press, 2012): 179 204.

17. For more discussion of this subject, see Chapter 12.

18. Erin Tolley and Robert Young, eds. *Immigration Settlement Policy in Canadian Municipalities* (Montreal and Kingston: McGill-Queen's University Press, 2011) and Caroline Andrew et al, eds. *Immigration, Integration, and Inclusion in Ontario Cities* (Montreal and Kingston: McGill-Queen's University Press, 2012).

19. Eric Fong, "Immigration and Race in the City," in Harry Hiller, ed., *Urban Canada*, 2nd ed. (Toronto: Oxford University Press, 2010), 132 54.

20. Evelyn Peters, ed., *Urban Aboriginal Policy Making in Canadian Municipalities* (Montreal and Kingston: McGill-Queen's University Press, 2011).

21. Alison Bain, "Re-Imaging, Re-Elevating, and Re-Placing the Urban: The Cultural Transformation of the Inner City in the Twenty-First Century," in Trudi Bunting, Pierre Filion, and Ryan Walker, eds., *Canadian Cities in Transition: New Directions in the 21st Century*, 4th ed., (Toronto: Oxford University Press, 2010), 262–75.

Chapter 6

1. For a more detailed discussion of this hypothetical example, see Andrew Sancton, *The Limits of Boundaries: Why City-Regions Cannot Be Self-governing* (Montreal and Kingston: McGill-Queen's University Press, 2008), 59–64.

2. For information on the property tax, see Chapter 15.

3. Andrew Sancton, *Governing the Island of Montreal: Language Differences and Metropolitan Politics* (Berkeley: University of California Press, 1985), 23.

4. Paul-André Linteau, *Histoire de Montréal depuis la Confédération* (Montreal: Boréal, 1992), 75.

5. Sancton, *Governing the Island of Montreal*, 26–7.

6. Paul-André Linteau, *The Promoters' City: Building the Industrial Town of Maisonneuve, 1883–1918* (Toronto: James Lorimer, 1985).

7. E.W. Villeneuve, quoted in Andrew Sancton, "Montreal," in Warren Magnusson and Andrew Sancton, eds., *City Politics in Canada* (Toronto: University of Toronto Press, 1983), 64.

8. Ibid.

9. Calculated from data in Table 1 of the Appendix in Magnusson and Sancton, eds., *City Politics in Canada*, 321.

10. This account is based on Sancton, *Governing the Island of Montreal*, 93–101.

11. James Lightbody, "Edmonton," in Magnusson and Sancton, eds., *City Politics in Canada*, 283.

12. Ibid., 259.

13. Ibid., 276.

14. T.J. Plunkett and James Lightbody, "Tribunals, Politics, and the Public Interest: The Edmonton Annexation Case," *Canadian Public Policy* 8, 2 (1982): 207. Reprinted with permission.

15. Lionel D. Feldman, "Editor's Note," in Lionel D. Feldman, ed., *Politics and Government of Urban Canada*, 4th ed. (Toronto: Methuen, 1981), 431.

16. Calculated from data in Table 1 of the Appendix in Magnusson and Sancton, eds., *City Politics in Canada*, 321.

17. Plunkett and Lightbody, "Tribunals, Politics, and the Public Interest," 216. Reprinted with permission.

18. City of Edmonton, "Submission to the Local Authorities Board of Alberta: Written Argument," September 1980. For details of the area in question, see P.J. Smith and H.L. Diemer, "Equity and the Annexation Process," in P.J. Smith, ed., *Edmonton: The Emerging Metropolitan Pattern* (Victoria, BC: University of Victoria Department of Geography, 1978), 263–89.

19. Alberta lab as quoted in Plunkett and Lightbody, "Tribunals, Politics, and the Public Interest," 217. Reprinted with permission.

20. Ibid., 218.

21. Ibid.

22. Lightbody, "Edmonton," 278.

23. Statistics Canada, *2011 Census of Canada*.

24. The City of Edmonton, "Annexation Proposal," www.edmonton.ca/city_government/urban_planning_and_design/proposed-annexation-lands-south-edmonton.aspx .

25. Timothy W. Cobban, *Cities of Oil: Municipalities and Petroleum Manufacturing in Southern Ontario, 1860–1960*, © University of Toronto Press, 2013, p. 15.

26. Ibid., 230. Reprinted with permission of the publisher.

27. Ibid., 24.

28. Ibid., 42. Reprinted with permission of the publisher.

29. Ibid., 71–2.

30. For more details, see John F. Meligrana, "The Politics of Municipal Annexation: The Case of London's Territorial Ambitions during the 1950s and 1960s," *Urban History Review* 29, 1 (2000): 91–103.

31. Ontario Municipal Board, ffm 7054, 9 May 1960, 37.

32. Ibid., 11.

33. Ibid., 25–6.

34. Ibid., 31–2.

35. Ibid., 32.

36. Ibid., 35–6.

37. Ibid., 7.

38. City of London, "Proposal for Boundary Adjustments," 18 November 1988, transmittal letter. For more details of this case, see Andrew Sancton, "Negotiating, Arbitrating, Legislating: Where Was the Public in London's Boundary Adjustment?" in Katherine A. Graham and Susan D. Phillips, eds., *Citizen Engagement: Lessons in Participation from Local Government* (Toronto: Institute of Public Administration of Canada, 1998), 163–87.

39. Letter from John Sweeney, Ontario Minister of Municipal Affairs, to M.C. Engels, London city administrator, 25 April 1990.
40. Ontario, Ministry of Municipal Affairs, Office of the Greater London Area Arbitrator, "Co-opportunity: Success through Co-operative Independence," April 1992, Appendix 1.
41. Ibid., 1.
42. As quoted in the *London Free Press*, 27 April 1992.
43. Ibid.
44. Geoff Ghitter and Alan Smart, "Mad Cows, Regional Governance, and Urban Sprawl: Path Dependence and Unintended Consequences in the Calgary Region," *Urban Affairs Review* 44, 5 (2009): 628.
45. Richard Parker, "Calgary: A Uni-City at 50 Years," *Plan Canada* 45, 3 (2005): 29–31.
46. Max Foran, *Expansive Discourses: Urban Sprawl in Calgary, 1945–1978* (Edmonton: University of Alberta Press, 2009), ch. 5.
47. Ibid., 44.
48. Ibid., 52.
49. Ibid., 53.
50. Sancton, *The Limits of Boundaries*, 76.
51. Kerry Benjoe, "RMs to discuss concerns," *The Leader-Post* (Regina), 9 January 2014.
52. In the United States, state governments have not intervened, making the annexation option much more relevant. For a passionately argued case in favour of annexation in American cities, see David Rusk, *Cities without Suburbs, A Census 2010 Perspective*, 4th ed. (Washington DC: Woodrow Wilson Centre Press, 2013).
53. For details, see Zachary Spicer, "Regional organization and the dynamics of inter-municipal cooperation. policy coordination between Ontario's separated cities and counties," Ph.D. thesis, University of Western Ontario, 2013.

Chapter 7

1. A huge academic literature exists on the government of the London metropolitan area. See, for example, Ben Pimlott and Nirmala Rao, *Governing London* (Oxford: Oxford University Press, 2002).
2. David C. Hammack, *Power and Society: Greater New York at the Turn of the Century* (New York: Russell Sage Foundation, 1982).
3. For elaboration, see G. Ross Stephens and Nelson Wikstrom, *Metropolitan Government and Governance: Theoretical Perspectives, Empirical Analysis, and the Future* (New York: Oxford University Press, 2000), ch. 2.
4. The urban application of the public-choice approach is especially associated with the work of Vincent Ostrom and Elinor Ostrom and their students at the Workshop in Political Theory and Policy Analysis at Indiana University. A much broader public-choice perspective is concerned with applying market principles to all forms of political analysis. In this perspective, the work of such authors as James Buchanan, Gordon Tullock, Mancur Olson, Kenneth Arrow, and William Niskanen is especially important.
5. For a summary, see Stephens and Wikstrom, *Metropolitan Government and Governance*, ch. 6.
6. For a Canadian example of this kind of analysis, complete with references to all the relevant American academic literature, see Robert L. Bish, *Organization and Opportunities: Local Government Services Production in Greater Saint John*, The AIMS Urban Futures Series, Paper #4 (Halifax: Atlantic Institute for Market Studies, 2004), available at www.aims.ca/site/media/aims/bish.pdf_. For a general discussion in an international context, see Santiago Lago-Peñas and Jorge Martinez-Vazquez, eds., *The Challenge of Local Government Size: Theoretical Perspectives, International Experience and Policy Reform* (Cheltenham UK: Edward Elgar, 2013).
7. For elaboration on these points, see Ronald J. Oakerson, *Governing Local Public Economies: The Civic Metropolis* (Oakland, CA: ICS Press, 1999).
8. Frances Frisken, *The Public Metropolis: The Political Dynamics of Urban Expansion in the Toronto Region, 1924–2003* (Toronto: Canadian Scholars' Press, 2007), 55.
9. Ibid.

10. Andrew Sancton, *Governing the Island of Montreal: Language Differences and Metropolitan Politics* (Berkeley: University of California Press, 1985), 28.

11. Frisken, *The Public Metropolis*, 68.

12. Unless otherwise noted, this discussion of Metro Toronto is based on material in Andrew Sancton, *Governing Canada's City-Regions* (Montreal: Institute for Research on Public Policy, 1994), 77–8.

13. Frisken, *The Public Metropolis*, 81.

14. As quoted ibid., 124. See also Ian Milligan, "'This Board Has a Duty to Intervene': Challenging the Spadina Expressway through the Ontario Municipal Board, 1963–1971," *Urban History Review* 39.2 (Spring 2011), 25–39, available at www.erudit.org/revue/uhr/2011/v39/n2/1003460ar.pdf.

15. Meyer Brownstone and T.J. Plunkett, *Metropolitan Winnipeg: Politics and Reform of Local Government* (Berkeley: University of California Press, 1983), 18–32.

16. S. George Rich, "Winnipeg: Innovations in Governing a Metropolis," in R. Charles Bryfogle and Ralph R. Krueger, eds., *Urban Problems*, revised ed. (Toronto: Holt, Rinehart, and Winston, 1975), 344.

17. Ibid., 344–6.

18. Stewart Fyfe, "Local Government Reform in Toronto: 1853–1973," in Bryfogle and Krueger, eds., *Urban Problems*, revised ed., 362. Holt, Rinehart and Winston, 1971.

19. Tom Urbaniak, *Her Worship: Hazel McCallion and the Development of Mississauga* (Toronto: University of Toronto Press, 2009), 36.

20. For a discussion of Mayor McCallion's role as mayor, see Chapter 11. The discussion both here and in Chapter 11 relies heavily on Tom Urbaniak's superb biography, *Her Worship*, which is must reading for any student of Canadian urban politics.

21. Ibid., 208.

22. Ibid., 210–11.

23. Ibid., 214.

24. Ibid., 216.

25. Three "restructured counties" subsequently were created in Oxford, Lambton, and Grey. The main feature of the restructuring was that the cities of Woodstock, Sarnia, and Owen Sound were no longer "separated" and became part of their respective county systems.

26. Sancton, *Governing the Island of Montreal*, 28–30, 38–9.

27. Ibid., 108–9.

28. Quoted ibid., 110.

29. Ibid., 132–5.

30. Ibid., 132–43.

31. Ibid., 147.

32. For information about the three different categories of MRCS after 2002, see Serge Belley et al., "Quebec," in Andrew Sancton and Robert Young, eds., *Foundations of Governance: Municipal Government in Canada's Provinces* (Toronto: University of Toronto Press, 2009), 76–7.

33. Ibid., 78. See also Marie-Ève Lafortune and Jean-Pierre Collin, "Building Metropolitan Governance: The Case of the Communauté métropolitaine de Montréal," *Canadian Public Administration* 54.3 (September 2011), 399–420; and Mariona Tomas, *Penser métropolitain: La bataille politique du Grand Montréal* (Québec: Les presses de l'Université du Québec, 2012).

34. For a recent assessment, see Brian Walliser, Gary Paget, and Michelle Dann, "New Pathways to Effective Regional Governance: Canadian Reflections," in Graham Sansom and Peter McKinlay, eds., *New Century Local Government: Commonwealth Perspectives* (London: Commonwealth Secretariat, 2013), 145–68.

35. Patrick J. Smith and Kennedy Stewart, "British Columbia," in Sancton and Young, eds., *Foundations of Governance*, 282–313. See especially the references in footnotes 4–7 on pp. 306–7.

36. Patrick J. Smith, "Even Greater Vancouver: Metropolitan Morphing in Canada's Third-Largest City Region," in Don Phares, ed., *Governing Metropolitan Regions in the 21st Century* (Armonk, NY: M.E. Sharpe, 2009), 142.

37. Mike Harcourt and Ken Cameron, with Sean Rossiter, *City Making in Paradise: Nine Decisions that Saved Vancouver* (Vancouver: Douglas & McIntyre, 2007), ch. 4.

38. Metro Vancouver, Regional Growth Strategy, www.metrovancouver.org/planning/development/strategy/Pages/default.aspx.
39. For a recent expression of this view, see Hoi Kong, "Toward a Federal Legal Theory of the City," *McGill Law Journal* 56.3 (2012), 474–517.
40. British Columbia, *Forsaken: Report of the Missing Women Commission of Inquiry*, Wally T. Oppal, Commissioner (2012), IV, 151–3.
41. For a list, see New Brunswick, Commissioner on the Future of Local Governance (Jean-Guy Finn), *Building Stronger Local Governments and Regions: An Action Plan for the Future of Local Governance in New Brunswick* (2008), 6.
42. New Brunswick, "Governance of the New Regional Service Commissions," *Environment and Local Government*, www2.gnb.ca/content/gnb/en/departments/elg/local_government/content/promos/action_plan_local_governance/governance.html.
43. Edward C. LeSage Jr, "Municipal Reform in Alberta: Breaking Ground at the New Millennium," in Joseph Garcea and Edward C. LeSage Jr, eds., *Municipal Reform in Canada: Reconfiguration, Re-empowerment, and Rebalancing* (Toronto: Oxford University Press, 2005), 69–70.
44. *Alberta Capital Region Governance Review, Final Report: An Agenda for Action, 2000.* Government of Alberta. Reprint with permission.
45. Ibid., 19.
46. LeSage, "Municipal Reform in Alberta," 74.
47. Capital Region Board, www.capitalregionboard.ab.ca.
48. Calgary Regional Partnership, *Calgary Metropolitan Plan* (2009), 17.
49. Error! Hyperlink reference not valid.Mario Vigliotti, "High River Leaves Calgary Partnership," *High River Times*, 15 April 2013.
50. Information derived from the *2011 Census of Canada* and from the websites of the city of Airdrie and town of Cochrane.
51. For a summary of the different political factors and arguments relating to Bill 28, read the debates in the Alberta legislature at www.assembly.ab.ca/documents/isysmenu.html.

Chapter 8

1. For brief descriptions of events in Britain, Australia, and New Zealand, see Andrew Sancton, *Merger Mania: The Assault on Local Government* (Montreal and Kingston: McGill-Queen's University Press, 2000), 84–8. For Denmark, see Jens Blom-Hansen, "Local Government in Denmark and the 2007 Municipal Reform," in Antti Moisio, ed., *Rethinking Local Government: Essays on Municipal Reform* (Helsinki: VATT Publications, 2012), ch.3, available online at www.vatt.fi/file/vatt_publication_pdf/j61.pdf.
2. Andrew Sancton, Rebecca James, and Rick Ramsay, *Amalgamation vs. Inter-municipal Cooperation: Financing Local Infrastructure Services* (Toronto: ICURR Press, 2000), ch. 6.
3. Larry Kusilek and Trevor Price, "Ontario Municipal Policy Affecting Local Autonomy: A Case Study Involving Windsor and Toronto," *Urban History Review* 16, 3 (1988): 257.
4. Ibid., 257–8.
5. Ibid., 259.
6. Ibid., 260.
7. Ibid., 261, 268–9.
8. Ibid., 261.
9. As quoted ibid., 262.
10. Ibid.
11. Kenneth Grant Crawford, *Canadian Municipal Government* (Toronto: University of Toronto Press, 1954), 70.
12. Sancton, *Merger Mania*, 51–7.
13. Meyer Brownstone and T.J. Plunkett, *Metropolitan Winnipeg: Politics and Reform of Local Government* (Berkeley: University of California Press, 1983).
14. Ibid., 41.
15. Quoted ibid., 42.
16. Quoted ibid.
17. Tom Carter, "Manitoba," in Andrew Sancton and Robert Young, eds., *Foundations of Governance: Municipal Government in Canada's Provinces* (Toronto: University of Toronto

Press, 2009), 250–2. For further analysis of the federal presence in Winnipeg, see Christopher Leo et al., "Multilevel Governance without Municipal Government," in Martin Horak and Robert Young, eds., *Sites of Governance: Multilevel Governance and Policy Making in Canada's Big Cities* (Montreal and Kingston: McGill-Queen's University Press, 2012), ch.11.

18. For details, see Andrew Sancton, *Governing Canada's City-Regions* (Montreal: Institute for Research on Public Policy, 1994), 26.

19. Calculated from Statistics Canada, *2011 Census of Canada*.

20. For the law establishing the partnership, see www.canlii.org/en/mb/laws/stat/ccsm-c-c23/latest/ccsm-c-c23.html.

21. Allan O'Brien, *Municipal Consolidation in Canada and Its Alternatives* (Toronto: ICURR Press, 1993), 24.

22. Quoted in Sancton et al., *Amalgamation vs. Inter-municipal Cooperation*.

23. For an evaluation and further discussion, see ibid., ch. 5. In 2008, the provincial government established regional waste management boards. The one serving the St. John's area is Eastern Regional Service Board. For details see Eastern Waste Management, www.easternwaste.ca/about-us.

24. John Crossley, "Municipal Reform in Prince Edward Island: Uneven Capacity and Reforms," in Joseph Garcea and Edward C. LeSage Jr, eds., *Municipal Reform in Canada: Reconfiguration, Re-empowerment, and Rebalancing* (Toronto: Oxford University Press, 2005), 228.

25. John C. Robison, "Public Participation in Restructuring Local Government to Create the City of Miramichi," in Katherine A. Graham and Susan D. Phillips, eds., *Citizen Engagement: Lessons in Participation from Local Government* (Toronto: Institute of Public Administration of Canada, 1998), ch. 9; and Igor Vojnovic, "Municipal Consolidation, Regional Planning, and Fiscal Accountability," *Canadian Journal of Regional Science* 23, 1 (2000): 49–72.

26. Daniel Bourgeois, "Municipal Reform in New Brunswick: To Decentralize or Not To Decentralize," in Garcea and LeSage, eds., *Municipal Reform*, 247.

27. Ibid.

28. George Betts, "Municipal Restructuring, New Brunswick Style: The Saint John Experience," *Municipal World* 51, 9 (1997): 3–8.

29. *The Globe and Mail*, 28 October 1994.

30. Sancton et al., *Amalgamation vs. Inter-municipal Cooperation*, ch. 5.

31. This account of the Halifax amalgamation follows Andrew Sancton, "Reducing Costs by Consolidating Municipalities: New Brunswick, Nova Scotia, Ontario," *Canadian Public Administration* 39, 3 (1996): 275–8. Full references for this material can be found there. See also Vojnovic, "Municipal Consolidation."

32. Halifax Regional Municipality, www.halifax.ca/BoundaryReview/archive.html.

33. Igor Vojnovic, "The Fiscal Distribution of the Provincial–Municipal Service Exchange in Nova Scotia," *Canadian Public Administration* 42, 2 (1999): 512–41.

34. Robert G. Finbow, "Submerging the Urban: Halifax in a Multilevel Governance System," in Horak and Young, *Sites of Governance*, ch.4.

35. For details, see Sancton, *Merger Mania*, 93–101. See also Ian Stewart, "The Dangers of Municipal Reform in Nova Scotia," in Peter Clancy et al., *The Savage Years: The Perils of Reinventing Government in Nova Scotia* (Halifax: Formac, 2000), 199–227.

36. James C. McDavid, "The Impacts of Amalgamation on Police Services in the Halifax Regional Municipality," *Canadian Public Administration* 45, 4 (2002): 538–65.

37. John Ibbitson, *Promised Land: Inside the Mike Harris Revolution* (Toronto: Prentice-Hall, 1997).

38. The material that follows, until the discussion of Kawartha Lakes, is based on Andrew Sancton, "Amalgamations, Service Realignment, and Property Taxes: Did the Harris Government Have a Plan for Ontario's Municipalities?" *Canadian Journal of Regional Science* 33, 1 (2000): 137–42.

39. Material on Kawartha Lakes was originally published in French. See Andrew Sancton, "Fusions et défusions municipales au Québec et en Ontario," in François Pétry, Éric Bélanger, and Louis M. Imbeau, eds., *Le parti Libéral: Enquête sur les réalisations du gouvernement Charest* (Québec: Les Presses de l'Université Laval, 2006), 321–38.

40. The former chief of staff to the Minister of Municipal Affairs at the time has dismissed

this possible reason for the amalgamation as "nonsense." Frances Frisken, *The Public Metropolis: The Political Dynamics of Urban Expansion in Toronto, 1924–2003* (Toronto: Canadian Scholars' Press, 2007), 241.

41. For more details, see Sancton, *Merger Mania*, 125–7. Full references can be found there.

42. Although there might not have been chaos in the delivery of services, there was much confusion (and worse) behind the scenes. For details, see Toronto Computer Leasing Inquiry/Toronto External Contracts Inquiry (the Bellamy Inquiry) *Report* (2005).

43. Toronto City Summit Alliance, *Enough Talk: An Action Plan for the Toronto Region*, April 2003: 4, available at www.civicaction.ca/sites/default/files/TCSA_report.pdf .

44. Enid Slack and Richard M. Bird, "Merging Municipalities: Is Bigger Better?" in Moisio, ed., *Rethinking Local Government*, 114.

45. Ibbitson, *Promised Land*, 248, 250.

46. Martin Horak, "The Power of Local Identity: C4LD and the Anti-amalgamation Mobilization in Toronto," Research Paper 195, Centre for Urban and Community Studies at the University of Toronto, 1998; and Julie-Anne Boudreau, *The Megacity Saga* (Montreal: Black Rose, 2000). For Horak's broader assessment of overall "rescaling" in Toronto, see his "State Rescaling in Practice: Urban Governance Reform in Toronto," *Urban Research & Practice* 6, 3 (2013): 311–28.

47. *East York (Borough) v. Ontario* (1997), [1998] 36 O.R. (3d) 733 [1998]. For more details, see Beth Moore Milroy, "Toronto's Legal Challenge to Amalgamation," in Caroline Andrew, Katherine A. Graham, and Susan Phillips, eds., *Urban Affairs: Back on the Policy Agenda* (Montreal and Kingston: McGill-Queen's University Press, 2002), 157–78.

48. For more details on all these changes, see Sancton, *Merger Mania*, ch. 6.

49. Zachary Spicer, "Post-amalgamation Politics: How Does Consolidation Impact Community Decision-making?" *Canadian Journal of Urban Research* 21.2 (2012), 90–111.

50. David Siegel, "Ontario," in Sancton and Young, eds., *Foundations of Governance*, 28.

51. Ibid., 30.

52. Serge Belley et al., "Quebec," in Sancton and Young, eds., *Foundations of Governance*, 72, 75.

53. Material in this subsection is an English-language version of part of Sancton, "Fusions et défusions." For more references, see the French-language publication. See also Mariona Tomàs, *Penser métropolitain: La bataille politique du Grand Montréal* (Montreal: Presses de l'Université du Québec, 2012), especially ch. 4.

54. Quebec, *Pacte 2000: Rapport de la Commission nationale sur les finances et la fiscalité locales* (Québec: Gouvernement du Québec, 1999).

55. As quoted in Kathleen Lévesque, "25 élus dirigeront la suprarégion de Montréal," *Le Devoir*, 15 June 1999, A1. Author's translation.

56. Québec, Municipal Affairs and Greater Montreal, *Municipal Reorganisation: Changing the Ways to Better Serve the Public* (Québec: Gouvernement du Québec, 2000).

57. Québec, Ministère des Affaires municipales, *Regroupements municipaux dans la région métropolitaine de Montréal: Recommandations du mandataire* (2000), at www.mamrot .gouv.qc.ca/pub/organisation_municipale/historique/reorganisation_loi170/rap_mand_ ber.pdf, 6–7. Author's translation.

58. I was a consultant for the city of Westmount in 1999–2000. My work for Westmount resulted in the publication of *Merger Mania: The Assault on Local Government* (Montreal and Kingston: McGill-Queen's University Press, 2000). At the time that Mayor Trent responded to the Bernard report, I had no contractual relationship with Westmount. For Peter Trent's fascinating personal account of this entire process, see his *The Merger Delusion: How Swallowing Its Suburbs Made an Even Bigger Mess of Montreal* (Montreal and Kingston: McGill-Queen's University Press, 2012).

59. Henry Milner and Pierre Joncas, "Montreal: Getting through the Megamerger," *Inroads* 11 (2002): 49–63.

60. For an extended analysis along these lines, see Andrew Sancton, "Why Municipal Amalgamations? Halifax, Toronto, Montreal," in Robert Young and Christian Leuprecht, eds., *Municipal–Federal–Provincial Relations in Canada* (Montreal and Kingston: McGill-Queen's University Press, 2004), 119–38.

61. Material in this subsection is an English-language version of part of Sancton, "Fusions et défusions." For detailed references, see the French-language publication. See also Tomàs, *Penser métropolitain*, ch.5.

62. "Editorial: Demergers Still an Issue," *The Gazette* (Montreal), 18 March 2003.

63. Jean-Pierre Collin and Mélanie Robertson, "The Borough System of Consolidated Montréal: Revisiting Urban Governance in a Composite Metropolis," *Journal of Urban Affairs* 27, 3 (2005): 307–30.

64. Henry Aubin, "Those Pesky Mergers," *The Gazette* (Montreal), 15 March 2003.

65. Lawrence Poitras, "La défusion municipale au Québec," Report from the Montreal law office of Borden Ladner Gervais, 17 March 2003, 35.

66. Ibid., 72.

67. Le Directeur Générale Des Élections du Québec, www.electionsquebec.qc.ca/english/municipal/election-results/2004-referendums.php.

68. Ville de Montréal, *Rapport officiel du recensement des votes*, election-montreal.qc.ca/user-files/file/fr/Actualites-documentation/20091103-Resultats-Sommaires.pdf, 1 November 2009.

69. Jean-Philippe Meloche and François Vaillancourt, *Public Finance in Montreal: In Search of Equity and Efficiency*, Institute on Municipal Finance & Governance (IMFG), IMFG Papers on Municipal Finance and Governance, No.15 (Toronto: University of Toronto, Munk Centre of Global Affairs, 2013), available online at http://munkschool.utoronto.ca/imfg/uploads/259/1483_imfg_no_15_online_final_(2).pdf.

70. Ibid, 11.

71. Trent, *The Merger Delusion*, 537.

72. Belley et al., "Quebec," in Sancton and Young, *Foundations of Governance*, 76.

73. Joseph Garcea, "Saskatchewan's Municipal Reform Agenda: Plethora of Processes and Proposals but Paucity of Products," in Garcea and LeSage, eds., *Municipal Reform in Canada*, 83–105. In September 2013, the Manitoba legislature enacted a law that would require all 92 municipalities with fewer than 1000 residents to amalgamate so that the population of the amalgamated municipality would exceed 1000. See http://web2.gov.mb.ca/laws/statutes/2013/pdf/c01013.pdf.

Chapter 9

1. Floyd Hunter, *Community Power Structure* (Chapel Hill: University of North Carolina Press, 1953).

2. Nelson W. Polsby, *Community Power and Political Theory*, 2nd ed. (New Haven: Yale University Press, 1980); Alan Harding, "The History of Community Power," in Jonathan S. Davies and David L. Imbroscio, eds., *Theories of Urban Politics*, 2nd ed. (Los Angeles: Sage, 2009), 27–39.

3. David M. Rayside, *A Small Town in Modern Times: Alexandria, Ontario* (Montreal and Kingston: McGill-Queen's University Press, 1991).

4. Ira Katznelson, *City Trenches: Urban Politics and the Patterning of Class in the United States* (New York: Pantheon, 1981).

5. For a fuller discussion, with extensive references, see Warren Magnusson, "Introduction," in Warren Magnusson and Andrew Sancton, eds., *City Politics in Canada* (Toronto: University of Toronto Press, 1983): 13–20.

6. Paul E. Peterson, *City Limits* (Chicago: University of Chicago Press, 1981), ch. 6. This argument has more recently been advanced by J. Eric Oliver et al., *Local Elections and the Politics of Small-Scale Democracy* (Princeton, NJ: Princeton University Press, 2012).

7. Donald Gutstein, "Vancouver," in Magnusson and Sancton, eds., *City Politics in Canada*, 196.

8. For a discussion of the election that brought Larry Campbell to power, see Fred Cutler and J. Scott Matthews, "The Challenge of Municipal Voting: Vancouver 2002," *Canadian Journal of Political Science* 38, 2 (June 2005): 359–82.

9. Timothy Lloyd Thomas, *A City with a Difference: The Rise and Fall of the Montreal Citizens' Movement* (Montreal: Véhicule Press, 1997).

10. Henry Milner, "Gérald Tremblay and the Tragedy of Public Life in Montreal," *Inroads*, 33 (Summer/Fall 2013): 101–7.

11. Élection Montréal, *Je vote pour ma ville, Montréal*, www.resultats-election-montreal.ca.

12. For a pre-2013 account of the role of municipal political parties in Quebec, see Anne Mévellec and Manon Tremblay, "Les partis politiques municipaux: la

"westminsterisation" des villes du Québec?" *Recherches sociographiques* 54, 2 (2013): 325–47.

13 James Lightbody, "Finding the Trolls under Your Bridge: The New Case for Party Politics in Canadian Cities," *Journal of Canadian Studies* 34, 1 (1999): 172–83.

14. Jean-Philippe Meloche and Patrick Kilfoil, *La taille du conseil municipal et le coût de représentation démocratiques dans les principales villes du Québec et du Canada* (Montreal: CIRANO, 2013) available at www.cirano.qc.ca/pdf/publication/2013s-38.pdf.

15. Quoted in Nova Scotia Utility and Review Board, Decision 2011-NSUARB-119 (July 2011), 13, available at www.canlii.org/en/ns/nsuarb/doc/2011/2011nsuarb119/2011nsuarb119.html?searchUrlHash=AAAAAQAPTINVQVJCLU1CLTEwLTA2AAAAAAE. In the same year, the NSUARB reduced the size of the Cape Breton regional council from 16 to 12.

16. Ibid.

17. Quoted in ibid., 24.

18. For the argument that immigrants who are non-citizens should have the right to vote in municipal elections, see Graeme Cook and Patti Tamara Lenard, "Making Politics more Welcoming," *Literary Review of Canada*, June 2013: 25–6.

19. Ontario Municipal Board, Decision No. 0605, 8 March 2003.

20. Calculated from information posted at the time on the city of Ottawa website.

21. Le Directeur Général des Élections du Québec, "Criteria related to the delimitation of municipal electoral districts," www.electionsquebec.qc.ca/english/municipal/electoral-map/criteria-for-delimitation.php .

22. NSUARB, Decision 2011 NSUARB 196, (20 December 2011): 47, available at www.canlii.org/en/ns/nsuarb/doc/2011/2011nsuarb196/2011nsuarb196.html?searchUrlHash=AAAAAQAPTINVQVJCLU1CLTEwLTA2AAAAAAE.

23. Ontario Municipal Board, Decision #3072, 22 November 2005.

24. For a recent discussion, see Robert Williams, ". . . we think it is the last time," *Municipal World* 122, (11 November 2012): 39–42.

25. Paul J. Bedford, "Reconsidering the Ward System of Governance," *Ontario Planning Journal* 20, 6 (2005): 25–7.

26. Patrick J. Smith and Kennedy Stewart, "British Columbia," in Andrew Sancton and Robert Young, eds., *Foundations of Governance: Municipal Government in Canada's Provinces* (Toronto: University of Toronto Press, 2009), 299.

27. Vancouver, "A City of Neighbourhoods: Report of the 2004 Electoral Reform Commission."

28. Ibid., 16–17.

29. Irene Bloemraad, "Diversity and Elected Officials in the City of Vancouver," in Caroline Andrew et al., eds., *Electing a Diverse Canada: The Representation of Immigrants, Minorities, and Women* (Vancouver: University of British Columbia Press, 2008), 61.

30. M. Rick O'Connor, *Open Local Government: How Crucial Legislative Changes Impact the Way Municipalities Do Business in Canada*, 2nd ed. (St. Thomas, ON: Municipal World, 2004), 23–5.

31. Ibid., 28–9.

32. The ombudsman has used this definition in a number of his reports. For a list of all of them, see www.ombudsman.on.ca/Investigations/Municipal-Meetings/Cases.aspx . For a legal argument criticizing the ombudsman's position, see the Appendix to Ontario Ombudsman, "Investigation into whether members of Council for the City of London held an improper closed meeting on February 23, 2013," available at www.ombudsman.on.ca/Files/sitemedia/Images/Reports/London_BT_Final-EN_1.pdf.

33. British Columbia Ombudsperson, *Open Meetings: Best Practices Guide for Local Governments* (September 2012), available at www.integritybc.ca/wp-content/uploads/2013/07/Open_Meetings_Best_Practices_Guide_for_Local_Governments-Ombudsperson-2013.pdf.

34. Stanley M. Makuch and John Jackson, "Freedom of Information in Local Government in Ontario," *Research Publication 7 for the Commission on Freedom of Information and Individual Privacy* (May 1979), 111.

35. For a more detailed discussion of some of the issues involved, see Andrew Sancton and Paul Woolner, "Full-time Municipal Councillors: A Strategic Challenge for Canadian Urban Government," *Canadian Public Administration* 33, 4 (1990): 482–505. For a discussion of councillor remuneration in Canada, see Kurt Schobel, "How Much is Enough? A Study of Municipal Councillor Remuneration," *Canadian Public Administration* 57, 1 (2014): 138-53.

36. Mariana Valverde, *Everyday Life on the Street: City Governance in an Age of Diversity* (Chicago: University of Chicago Press, 2012).

37. Mississauga Judicial Inquiry, *Updating the Ethical Infrastructure* (2011), p.171, available at www.mississaugainquiry.ca/report/index_pdf.html.

38. Ontario Superior Court of Justice, *Doug Craig v. Her Majesty the Queen in Right of Ontario*, 2013 ONSC 5349, 14.

39. Union of BC Municipalities (UBCM) and Local Government Management Association (LGMA) of BC. "BCCA Decision on Conflict of Interest – Some Questions to Consider," www.ubcm.ca/assets/Resolutions~and~Policy/Policy/Governance/03-Conflict%20 of%20Interest%20Schlenker%20Decision%20Info%20Bulletin.pdf.

40. Joseph Kushner, David Siegel, and Hannah Stanwick, "Ontario Municipal Elections: Voting Trends and Determinants of Electoral Success in a Canadian Province," *Canadian Journal of Political Science* 30, 3 (1997): 539–53.

40. Joseph Kushner and David Siegel, "Why Do Municipal Electors Not Vote?" *Canadian Journal of Urban Research* 15, 2 (2006): 264–77.

41. Kushner et al., "Ontario Municipal Elections."

42. For a recent discussion of this in the American context, see J. Eric Oliver et al., *Local Elections and the Politics of Small-Scale Democracy* (Princeton: Princeton University Press, 2012).

43. Andrew et al., eds., *Electing a Diverse Canada*.

44. Erin Tolley, "Do Women 'Do Better' in Municipal Politics? Electoral Representation across Three Levels of Government," *Canadian Journal of Political Science* 44, 3 (September 2011): 573–94.

45. Myer Siemiatycki, *The Diversity Gap: The Electoral Under-Representation of Visible Minorities* (Toronto: Ryerson Centre for Immigration and Settlement, 2011), available at http://diversecitytoronto.ca/wp-content/uploads/Final-Report.pdf.

46. For a description of the state of affairs in 2010, see British Columbia, Union of British Columbia Municipalities, "Local Government Elections Task Force, Campaign Financing in B.C. Local Elections," available at www.localelectionstaskforce.gov.bc.ca/ library/Campaign_Finance_Overview.pdf.

47. City of Toronto, "Contribution Rules and Fund-Raising," www1.toronto.ca/wps/portal/ contentonly?vgnextoid=eeed92a2b594c310VgnVCM10000068d60f89RCRD&vgnextch annel=72c5715242ccd310VgnVCM1000006cd60f89RCRD#acceptable.

48. Union of British Columbia Municipalities, www.localelectionstaskforce.gov.bc.ca/li-brary/Campaign_Finance_Overview.pdf, p. 14.

49. Robert MacDermid, "Funding City Politics: Municipal Campaign Funding and Property Development in the Greater Toronto Area," CSJ Foundation for Research and Education and Vote Toronto, January 2009, 39, available at www.socialjustice.org/ uploads/pubs/FundingCityPolitics.pdf.

Chapter 10

1. Material on London was originally collected as part of a research project from 1990 to 1995, called "Does Local Government Matter? Community Policy-Making in London, Ontario," funded by the Social Sciences and Humanities Research Council of Canada. Most of the findings remain unpublished, except for Andrew Sancton and Byron Montgomery, "Municipal Government and Residential Land Development: A Comparative Study of London, Ontario in the 1920s and 1980s," in Frances Frisken, ed., *The Changing Canadian Metropolis* (Berkeley: Institute of Governmental Studies, University of California, 1994), vol. 2, 777–98. Some of the material in the early sections of this chapter derives from this publication.

2. Ian M. Rogers, *Canadian Law of Planning and Zoning* (Toronto: Carswell, 1973), 75.

3. Ibid., 76.

4. Ontario, Committee on Taxation, *Report* (Toronto: Queen's Printer, 1967), vol. 2, 310.

5. For the most thorough exposition of this view in the Canadian context, see Pamela Blais, *Perverse Cities: Hidden Subsidies, Wonky Policy, and Urban Sprawl* (Vancouver: UBC Press, 2010).

6. For a full list of all the relevant land-use planning terminology in the various provinces, see Gerald Hodge and David L.A. Gordon, *Planning Canadian Communities: An Introduction to the Principles, Practice, and Participants*, 5th ed. (Toronto: Nelson, 2008), 218–19.

7. Aaron A. Moore addresses this issue in the Toronto context in *Planning Politics in Toronto: The Ontario Municipal Board and Urban Development* (Toronto: University of Toronto Press, 2013), especially ch. 7.

8. Michael R. Pearce, Carman Cullen, Donna Green, and Chow-Hou Wee, *The London Retailing Study* (London, ON: City of London, 1984), 332–3.

9. Ibid., 335.

10. For a case study in the east end of Toronto (Scarborough) that is an exception, see Vanessa Parlette and Deborah Cowen, "Dead Malls: Suburban Activism, Local Spaces, Global Logistics," *International Journal of Urban and Regional Research* 35, 4 (July 2011): 794–811.

11. Jane Jacobs, *The Death and Life of Great American Cities* (New York: Random House, 1961).

12. Edward Glaeser, *Triumph of the City: How Our Greatest Invention Makes Us Richer, Smarter, Greener, Healthier, and Happier* (New York: Penguin, 2011), 147.

13. Christopher Klemek, *The Transatlantic Collapse of Urban Renewal: Postwar Urbanism from New York to Berlin* (Chicago: University of Chicago Press, 2011).

14. Danielle Robinson, "'The Streets Belong to the People': Expressway Disputes in Canada, c. 1960–75'" (Ph.D. thesis, McMaster University, 2012).

15. Pierre Gauthier, Jochen Jaeger, and Jason Prince, eds., *Montréal at the Crossroads: Superhighways, the Turcot and the Environment* (Montreal: Black Rose, 2009).

16. For a powerful analysis, using Toronto as an example, see Margaret Kohn, "What is Wrong with Gentrification?" *Urban Research and Practice* 6, 3 (November 2013): 297–310.

17. Warren Magnusson, "Toronto," in Andrew Sancton and Warren Magnusson, eds., *City Politics in Canada* (Toronto: University of Toronto Press, 1983), 118–26.

18. The rest of this section closely follows Moore's account, especially pp. 104–19.

19. Ibid., p.166.

20. Hodge and Gordon, *Planning Canadian Communities*, 5th ed., ch. 12.

21. William A. Fischel, *The Homevoter Hypothesis: How Home Values Influence Local Government Taxation, School Finance, and Land-Use Policies* (Cambridge, MA: Harvard University Press, 2001).

22. John R. Logan and Harvey L. Molotch, *Urban Fortunes: The Political Economy of Place* (Berkeley: University of California Press, 1987).

23. Paul Peterson, *City Limits* (Chicago: University of Chicago Press, 1981).

Chapter 11

1. James P. Feehan et al., "Newfoundland and Labrador," in Andrew Sancton and Robert Young, eds., *Foundations of Governance: Municipal Government in Canada's Provinces* (Toronto: University of Toronto Press, 2009), 478.

2. Jeromy Anton Farkas, "Growing the Democratic Toolbox: City Council Vote Tracking," *Calgary: The Manning Foundation for Democratic Education*, 20 September 2013, pp. 5, 10, available at www.counciltracker.ca/sourcefiles/MFDEDemocraticToolboxReport. pdf.

3. Allan Levine, "Stephen Juba: The Great City Salesman," in Allan Levine, ed., *Your Worship: The Lives of Eight of Canada's Most Unforgettable Mayors*, © 1989 James Lorimer and Company Limited. Reprinted with permission.

4. Ibid.

5. Ibid., 76.

6. Ibid., 78.

7. Ibid., 95.

8. Statistics Canada, *2011 Census of Canada*.

9. Tom Urbaniak, *Her Worship: Hazel McCallion and the Development of Mississauga*, © University of Toronto Press, 2009.

10. Ibid., 9.

11. Ibid., 235.

12. Ibid., 9.

13. Ibid., 107. Reprinted with permission of the publisher.

14. Ibid., 226.

15. Ibid., 237. Reprinted with permission of the publisher.

16. Ibid., 238. See also, Tom Urbaniak, "Studying Mayoral leadership in Canada and the United States," *International Journal of Canadian Studies* 49 (2014): 205-27.

17. Robert E. Lang and Jennifer B. LeFurgy, *Boomburbs: The Rise of America's Accidental Cities* (Washington: Brookings Institution Press, 2006).

18. Urbaniak, *Her Worship*, 238.

19. Ibid., 237-8.

20. Robert A. Dahl, *Who Governs? Democracy and Power in an American City* (New Haven: Yale University Press, 1961).

21. Clarence Stone, *Regime Politics: Governing Atlanta, 1946–1988* (Lawrence, KS: University Press of Kansas, 1989), 3.

22. Ibid., 4.

23. Karen Mossberger, "Urban Regime Analysis," in Jonathan S. Davies and David L. Imbroscio, eds., *Theories of Urban Politics*, 2nd ed. (Los Angeles: Sage, 2009), 40–54.

24. Douglas W. Rae, "Two Cheers for Very Unequal Incomes: Toward Social Justice in Central Cities," in Clarissa Rile Hayward and Todd Swanstrom, eds., *Justice and the American Metropolis* (Minneapolis, MN: University of Minnesota Press, 2011), 119.

25. Christopher Leo, "Global Change and Local Politics: Economic Decline and the Local Regime in Edmonton," *Journal of Urban Affairs* 17, 3 (1995): 277–99; Timothy Cobban, "The Political Economy of Urban Development: Downtown Revitalization in London, Ontario, 1993–2002," *Canadian Journal of Urban Research* 12, 2 (2003): 231–48; Christopher Leo, "Are There Urban Regimes in Canada? Comment on: Timothy Cobban's 'The Political Economy of Urban Development: Downtown Revitalization in London, Ontario, 1993–2002,'" *Canadian Journal of Urban Research* 12, 2 (2003): 344–8; Timothy Cobban, "Timothy Cobban's Reply to Christopher Leo's Comment 'Are There Urban Regimes in Canada?'" *Canadian Journal of Urban Research* 12, 2 (2003): 349–52; Kristin R. Good, *Municipalities and Multiculturalism: The Politics of Immigration in Toronto and Vancouver* (Toronto: University of Toronto Press, 2009); and Ahmed Allahwala, Julie-Anne Boudreau, and Roger Keil, "Neo-Liberal Governance: Entrepreneurial Municipal Regimes in Canada," in Trudi Bunting, Pierre Filion, and Ryan Walker, eds., *Canadian Cities in Transition: New Directions in the Twenty-First Century* (Toronto: Oxford University Press, 2010), 210–24.

26. Douglas Yates, *The Ungovernable City: The Politics of Urban Problems and Policy Making* (Cambridge, MA: MIT Press, 1977), 165.

27. Darren MacDonald, "A recipe for dysfunctional local government," *Sudbury Northern Life*, 16 September 2013.

28. Marianne Matichek, quoted ibid.

29. Martin Horak, "Governance Reform from Below: Multilevel Politics and the 'New Deal' in Toronto, Canada," *Human Settlements and Dialogue* Series 4 (Nairobi: UN-HABITAT, 2008).

30. Nick Ternette, "Glen Murray's Failed New Deal," *Canadian Dimension* 38, 5 (September–October 2004), available at http://canadiandimension.com/articles/1961.

31. Emmanuel Brunet-Jailly, "Vancouver: The Sustainable City," *Journal of Urban Affairs* 30, 4 (2008): 375–88.

32. Robert Young, "Multilevel Governance: Benefits, Costs, Possibilities," presentation to the *Workshop on Cities and Multilevel Governance—American and Canadian Perspectives*, annual meeting of the Canadian Political Science Association, Ottawa, 27 May 2009.

33. Roger Tassé, "Review of Toronto Port Authority Report," October 2006, at www.tc.gc.ca/media/documents/policy/tpa.pdf.

34. Calculated from data at Toronto, www1.toronto.ca/wps/portal/contentonly?vgnextoid=4113c36902f5d310VgnVCM1000006cd60f89RCRD.

35. This was the subject of the Mississauga Judicial Inquiry into Mayor McCallion's alleged conflicts of interest. See Chapter 9 for details.

36. This analysis was inspired by Marcus Gee, "When it comes to Ford, we are a city of enablers," *The Globe and Mail*, 9 November 2013. Gee wrote: "The Fords like to say that the

elite class in this town is too powerful. In fact, it is too weak. What passes for a Toronto elite didn't dare challenge Mr. Ford for fear of being called, well, elitists."

37. "Hashtag Mayor," *The Walrus* (November 2013), available at http://thewalrus.ca/hashtag-mayor.

Chapter 12

1. For examples, see Edmund P. Fowler and David Siegel, eds., *Urban Policy Issues: Canadian Perspectives*, 2nd ed. (Toronto: Oxford University Press, 2002).

2. In the Canadian context, see Michael Howlett, M. Ramesh, and Anthony Perl, *Studying Public Policy: Policy Cycles and Policy Subsystems*, 3rd ed. (Toronto: Oxford University Press, 2009), and Leslie A. Pal, *Beyond Policy Analysis: Public Issue Management in Turbulent Times*, 5th ed. (Toronto: Nelson, 2014).

3. For an especially helpful discussion of this topic in an American context, see James H. Svara, "The Shifting Boundary between Elected Officials and City Managers in Large Council-Manager Cities," *Public Administration Review* 59, 1 (February 1999): 44–53.

4. Eric A. Nordlinger, *On the Autonomy of the Democratic State* (Cambridge, MA: Harvard University Press, 1981).

5. Pal, *Beyond Policy Analysis*, 5th ed., 2.

6. Daniel Henstra, ed., *Multilevel Governance and Emergency Management in Canadian Municipalities* (Montreal and Kingston: McGill-Queen's University Press, 2013).

7. Kurt Peacock and Robert MacKinnon, "Federal Land Transfers in New Brunswick," in Michael C. Ircha and Robert Young, eds., *Federal Property Policy in Canadian Municipalities* (Montreal and Kingston: McGill-Queen's University Press, 2013), ch. 3.

8. For details about Metrolinx and TransLink, see Chapter 4 of this book. For more on the multilevel politics of transit in Vancouver and Toronto, see Thomas A. Hutton, "Multilevel Governance and Urban Development: A Vancouver Case Study," and Martin Horak, "Multilevel Governance in Toronto: Success and Failure in Canada's Largest City," in Martin Horak and Robert Young, eds., *Sites of Governance: Multilevel Governance and Policy Making in Canada's Big Cities* (Montreal and Kingston: McGill-Queen's University Press, 2012), 263–98 and 228–62.

9. Christopher Leo and Kathryn Anderson, "Being Realistic about Urban Growth," *Journal of Urban Affairs* 28, 2 (2006): 169–89. See also Neil Bradford and Allison Bramwell, eds., *Governing Urban Economies: Innovation and Inclusion in Canadian City Regions* (Toronto: University of Toronto Press, 2014).

10. The best known version of this argument is contained in John R. Logan and Harvey L. Molotch, *Urban Fortunes: The Political Economy of Place* (Berkeley, CA: University of California Press, 1987).

11. Paul E. Peterson, *City Limits* (Chicago: University of Chicago Press, 1981), ch. 7.

12. Paul G. Lewis and Max Neiman, *Custodians of Place: Governing the Growth and Development of Cities* (Washington, DC: Georgetown University Press, 2009).

13. See www.hampstead.qc.ca/uploads/files/docs/plan_zonage_0.pdf.

14. (Toronto: University of Toronto Press, 2013), 72–92.

15. Mario Polèse, "Urban-Development Legends," *City Journal* 21, 4 (2011), available at www.city-journal.org/2011/21_4_urban-development.html.

16. William M. Rohe, *The Research Triangle: From Tobacco Road to Global Prominence* (Philadelphia, PA: University of Pennsylvania Press, 2011).

17. Jen Nelles, *Comparative Metropolitan Policy: Governing beyond Local Boundaries in the Imagined Metropolis* (New York: Routledge, 2012), ch. 7.

18. Jean Harvey and Robert Young, eds., *Image-building in Canadian Municipalities* (Montreal and Kingston: McGill-Queen's University Press, 2012).

19. Horak, "Multilevel Governance in Toronto," pp.242–3.

20. Richard Florida, *Who's Your City? How the Creative Economy is Making Where to Live the Most Important Decision of Your Life* (Toronto: Random House Canada, 2008).

21. For the argument that Florida is mistaken in the direction of causality, see Enrico Moretti, *The New Geography of Jobs* (Boston and New York: Houghton Mifflin Harcourt, 2012), 188–93. For Florida's reply to Moretti and others, see "What Critics Got Wrong about Creative Cities," at www.theatlanticcities.com/jobs-and-economy/2012/05/what

-critics-get-wrong-about-creative-cities/2119. For a discussion in the context of Toronto's Distillery District, see Vanessa Mathews, "Incoherence and Tension in Culture-led Redevelopment," *International Journal of Urban and Regional Research* 38, 3 (May 2014):1019–1036.

22. Harry M. Kitchen, *The Role for Local Governments in Economic Development* (Toronto: Ontario Economic Council, 1985).

23. Harold Wolman, "Local Economic Development Policy: What Explains the Divergence between Political Analysis and Political Behaviour?" *Journal of Urban Affairs*, 10, 1 (1988): 19–28.

24. Polèse, "Urban Development Legends." For an argument that the most important function of municipalities in promoting economic growth is to provide high quality urban infrastructure, see Christopher Kennedy, *The Evolution of Great World Cities: Urban Wealth and Economic Growth* (Toronto: University of Toronto Press, 2011).

25. But see Katherine A. Graham and Susan D. Phillips, eds., *Citizen Engagement: Lessons in Participation from Local Government* (Toronto: Institute of Public Administration of Canada, 1998) and Katherine A.H. Graham, "The Paradox of Participation: An Overview of Public Participation and Local Government in Canada" in Andrew Sancton and Chen Zhenming, eds., *Citizen Participation at the Local Level in Canada and China* (Boca Raton FL: CRC Press, 2014), ch.2.

26. Donley T. Studlar, *Tobacco Control: Comparative Politics in the United States and Canada* (Peterborough, ON: Broadview Press, 2002), 150.

27. Region of Waterloo, "Blue Box & Blue and Grey Cart Recycling Programs," available at www.regionofwaterloo.ca/en/aboutTheEnvironment/Blue_Box_Recycling.asp. For waste diversion generally, see Jeffrey Garkowski and Charles Hostovsky, "Policy versus Practice in Municipal Solid Waste Diversion: The Role of the Waste Crisis in Ontario Waste Planning," *Canadian Journal of Urban Research*, 20, 1 (2011): 81–102.

28. Sarah Pralle, "The Mouse that Roared: Agenda Setting in Canadian Pesticide Politics," *Policy Studies* Journal, 34, 2 (2006): 179.

29. Charles R. Shipan and Craig Volden, "Policy Diffusion: Seven Lessons for Scholars and Practitioners," *Public Administration Review*, 72, 6 (2012): 788–96.

30. Ontario, "The law," *Pesticide Licences and Permits*, available at www.ene.gov.on.ca/environment/en/category/pesticides/index.htm.

31. Prashan Ranasinghe and Mariana Valverde, "Governing Homelessness through Land-Use: A Sociolegal Study of the Toronto Shelter Zoning By-Law," *Canadian Journal of Sociology*, 31, 3 (2006): 325–49.

32. Peterson, *City Limits*, 180. For a more recent discussion that uses a broader definition of *redistribution*, see Clayton P. Gillette, *Local Redistribution and Local Democracy* (New Haven, CT: Yale University Press, 2011).

33. For a discussion of the hiring of outside consultants to assist with planning policy, see Bessma Momani and Luna Khirfan, "Explaining the Use of Planning Consultants in Ontario Cities," *Canadian Public Administration* 56, 3 (September 2013): 391–413.

34. In 2013, the Calgary city council unanimously endorsed the city's "poverty reduction strategic plan." See www.enoughforall.ca. A critical analysis is contained in Angela MacLeod Irons, *Noble Frustration: The Many Practical Problems with Municipal Poverty Initiatives* (Calgary: The Manning Foundation, 2013), available at www.manningfoundation.org/Docs/Noble-Frustrations.pdf. See also Martin Horak and Marilyn Dantico, "The Limits of Local Redistribution: Neighbourhood Regeneration Initiatives in Toronto and Phoenix," and Martin Horak and Aaron A. Moore, "Policy Shift without Institutional Change: The Precarious Place of Neighbourhood Revitalization in Toronto." For a recent Canadian discussion of symbolic politics, see Michael J. Prince, "Self-regulation, Exhortation, and Symbolic Politics," in Glen Toner, Leslie A. Pal, and Michael J. Prince, eds., *Policy: From Ideas to Implementation* (Montreal and Kingston: McGill-Queen's University Press, 2010), 77–108.

35. I am indebted to my colleague, Richard Vernon, for drawing my attention to this concept. See Stephen Holmes, *Passions and Constraint* (Chicago: University of Chicago Press, 1995), ch. 5.

36. Aaron A. Moore, *Planning Politics in Toronto: The Ontario Municipal Board and Urban Development* (Toronto: University of Toronto Press, 2013), 49. For a further discussion, see Aaron A. Moore, "Comparing the Politics of Urban Development in American

and Canadian Cities: The Myth of the North-South Divide," *International Journal of Canadian Studies* 49 (2014): 229-49.

37. Calculated from Statistics Canada, Table 385-0032, "Government finance statistics, statement of government operations and balance sheet," quarterly.

38. Jeffrey L. Pressman and Aaron Wildavsky, *Implementation: How Great Expectations in Washington are Dashed in Oakland: Or, Why it's Amazing that Federal Programs Work at All, This Being a Saga of the Economic Development Administration as Told by Two Sympathetic Observers who Seek to Build Morals on a Foundation of Ruined Hopes.* (Berkeley, CA: University of California Press, 1973). For a recent Canadian example, see Mario Levesque, "Build it . . . *if you can!*": Discretion, Building Inspectors and Part 8 of Ontario's 2006 Building Code," *Canadian Journal of Urban Research* 20, 1 (2011):103–30.

39. Levesque ("Build it") discusses the implementation locally in Ontario of changes in the National Building Code. Ironically, although the changes were meant to increase local flexibility, Levesque shows that concerns about municipal liability among municipal employees caused them to be very reluctant to approve the kinds of new installations that the changes at the national level contemplated.

40. Mariana Valverde, *Everyday Life on the Street: City Governance in an Age of Diversity* (Chicago: University of Chicago Press, 2012).

41. "Immature Policy Analysis: Building Capacity in Eight Major Canadian Cities," in Laurent Dobuzinskis, Michael Howlett, and David Laycock, eds., *Policy Analysis in Canada: The State of the Art* (Toronto: University of Toronto Press, 2007), 265.

42. Ibid., 278.

Chapter 13

1. Statistics Canada, "Public sector employment, wages and salaries (employees)," available at www.statcan.gc.ca/tables-tableaux/sum-som/l01/cst01/govt54a-eng.htm.

2. For a valuable commentary on this subject, see David Siegel, "The Leadership Role of the Municipal Chief Administrative Officer," *Canadian Public Administration* 50, 2 (2010): 139–61. See also Patrick Eamonn O'Flynn and Tim A. Mau, "A Demographic and Career Profile of Municipal CAOs in Canada: Implications for Local Governance," *Canadian Public Administration* 57, 1 (2014): 154-70 and David Siegel, *Leaders in the Shadows: The Leadership Qualities of Municipal Chief Administrative Officers* (Toronto: University of Toronto Press, forthcoming in 2015).

3. Thomas J. Plunkett, *City Management in Canada: The Role of the Chief Administrative Officer* (Toronto: Institute of Public Administration of Canada, 1992), 13.

4. Ibid., 16.

5. Excerpted from "History of the ICMA and the Local Government Management Profession" at icma.org. Accessed November 28, 2013 and used by permission, copyright ICMA 2014.

6. City of Waterloo Judicial Inquiry, *Final Report of the Commissioner* (2003); and Toronto Computer Leasing Inquiry/Toronto External Contracts Inquiry, *Report* (2005).

7. This listing is based on Monique Beaudin, "City Manager has history of controversy," *The Gazette* (Montreal), 19 March 2013.

8. Henry Milner, "Gérald Tremblay and the Tragedy of Public Life in Montreal," *Inroads*, 33 (Summer/Fall 2013): 106.

9. Beaudin, *The Gazette*, 19 March 2013.

10. Montreal, "Report of the General Auditor to city council and the agglomeration council concerning the audit of the entire process involving the acquisition and installation of water meters in IBIs, as well as the optimization of the entire Montréal agglomeration water network," (September 2009), available at http://ville.montreal.qc.ca/pls/portal/docs/PAGE/VERIFICATEUR_EN/MEDIA/DOCUMENTS/RCE_ANGLAIS_INTERNET.PDF.

11. Québec, La commission d'enquête sur l'octroi et la gestion des contrats publics dans l'industrie de la construction [Charbonneau Inquiry], Transcripts, 11 March 2013, p.161, available at www.ceic.gouv.qc.ca/fileadmin/Fichiers_client/fichiers/Transcriptions/2013 -03/Transcription_audience_CEIC_2013-03-11.pdf.

12. Jeanne Corriveau, "Louis Roquet démissionne," *Le Devoir* (Montreal), 20 December 2011.

13. Beaudin, *The Gazette*, 19 March 2013.

14. Tommy Chouinard, "Montréal: Alain Marcoux déviant directeur-général," *La Presse* (Montreal), 26 November 2013.

15. James C. McDavid, "Solid Waste Contracting-out, Bidding Practices, and Competition, among Canadian Local Governments," *Canadian Public Administration* 44, 1 (2001): 1–25. See also Benjamin Dachis, *Picking Up Savings: The Benefits of Competition in Municipal Waste Services*, C.D. Howe Institute Commentary No. 308, September 2010.

16. James C. McDavid and Annette E. Mueller, "A Cross-Canada Analysis of the Efficiency of Residential Recycling Services," *Canadian Public Administration* 51, 4 (2008): 569–88.

17. Daniel Dale, "Garbage outsourcing generates fewer complaints than municipal collectors," *Toronto Star*, 13 May 2013.

18. Aldo Santin, "Outside workers at Emterra agree to join CUPE Local 500," *Winnipeg Free Press*, 21 August 2013.

19. Kathryn Furlong and Karen Bakker, "The Contradictions in 'Alternative' Service Delivery: Governance, Business Models, and Sustainability in Municipal Water Supply," *Environment and Planning C: Government and Policy* 28, 2 (2010): 349–68.

20. Frank K. Ohemeng and John K. Grant, "When Markets Fail to Deliver: An Examination of the Privatization and Deprivatization of Water and Wastewater Services Delivery in Hamilton, Canada," *Canadian Public Administration* 51, 3 (2008): 475–99. See also John Loxley with Salim Loxley, *Public Service Private Profits: The Political Economy of Public-Private Partnerships in Canada* (Halifax and Winnipeg: Fernwood, 2010), pp.161–70.

21. Municipality of Brockton, "Water and Sewer," www.brockton.ca/en/our-services/water-and-sewer.asp.

22. Ontario, *Report of the Walkerton Inquiry* (Toronto: Queen's Printer for Ontario, 2002).

23. David Cameron, "The Relationship between Different Ownership and Management Regimes and Drinking Water Safety," Discussion Paper for the Walkerton Inquiry, June 2001, 127–8.

24. Loxley, *Public Service Private Profits*, 151–9.

25. Deloitte, *City of Regina Wastewater Treatment & Plant Expansion Upgrade Project: Delivery Model Assessment*, 22 January 2013, available at www.regina.ca/opencms/export/sites/regina.ca/residents/open-government/.media/pdf/waste-water-treatment-plant---deloitte-report.pdf.

26. Hugh Mackenzie, *Flushing Money Away: Why the Privatization of the Wastewater Treatment Plant is A Bad Idea*, 6 May 2013, available at: http://cupe.ca/updir/Regina_Waste_Water_Treatment_Plant_Report.pdf.

27. For the city's website presenting its side of the case, see City of Regina, www.regina.ca/residents/sewage-treatment-plant/facts-and-background.html.

28. "Wastewater Treatment Plant Referendum, Official Summary of Results, 25 September 2013," available at www.reginareferendum.ca/opencms/export/sites/regina.ca/residents/open-government/.media/pdf/official-summary-of-referendum-results.pdf.

29. Timothy Cobban, "The Political Economy of Urban Redevelopment: Downtown Revitalization in London, Ontario, 1993–2002," *Canadian Journal of Urban Research* 12, 1 (2003): 240.

30. For financial details, see The City of Edmonton, www.edmonton.ca/city_government/projects_redevelopment/the-agreement.aspx.

31. An exception is James R. McVittie, "Local Government Unionism in Ontario 1935–1963: Study of the Determinants of Union Growth," Ph.D. thesis, University of Western Ontario, 1991.

32. T.J. Plunkett and G.M. Betts, *The Management of Canadian Urban Government: A Basic Text for a Course in Urban Management* (Kingston, ON: Institute of Local Government, Queen's University, 1978), 283–4.

33. Katherine Graham, "Collective Bargaining in the Municipal Sector," in Gene Swimmer and Mark Thompson, eds., *Public Sector Collective Bargaining in Canada: Beginning of the End or End of the Beginning?* (Kingston, ON: Industrial Relations Centre, Queen's University, 1995), 182–3.

34. CUPE, http://cupe.ca/about.

35. Metro Vancouver, "Labour Relations and Collective Agreements," www.metrovancouver.org/services/labour/Pages/default.aspx.

36. Graham, "Collective Bargaining in the Municipal Sector," 191.

37. Richard L. Jackson, "Police and Firefighter Labour Relations," in Swimmer and Thompson, eds., *Public Sector Collective Bargaining*.
38. Larry Savage, "Organized Labour and Local Politics: Ontario's 2006 Municipal Elections," *Labour/Le Travail* 62 (Fall 2008), 174.
39. Ibid.
40. Ibid., 175.
41. Canadian Labour Congress, www.canadianlabour.ca/action-center/municipality-matters .
42. John D. Donahue, *The Warping of Government Work* (Cambridge, MA: Harvard University Press, 2008).
43. Ibid., 79.
44. Leo Troy, *The Twilight of the Old Unionism* (Armonk, NY: M.E. Sharpe, 2004), 111–38.
45. Greg Fingas, "Troubling questions about the city's P3 plan," *Regina Leader-Post*, 8 August 2013.

Chapter 14

1. An excellent example of such writing relating to the federal government is David A. Good, *The Politics of Public Money: Spenders, Guardians, Priority Setters, and Financial Watchdogs inside the Canadian Government* (Toronto: University of Toronto Press, 2008).
2. International Monetary Fund, *Government Finance Statistics Manual 2001*, p.14, available at www23.statcan.gc.ca/imdb-bmdi/document/5174_D4_T9_V1-eng.pdf.
3. CANSIM Table 3850032.
4. For example, Table 14.2 shows no "developer contributions" for Ontario. But developers in Ontario do make significant "contributions" in the form of development charges, though these go directly into capital expenditures (as we shall see in the next section of this chapter). Such contributions are obviously accounted for differently in other provinces.
5. For an assessment of the comprehensibility of budgets in various major municipalities, see Benjamin Dachis and William B.P. Robson, *Holding Canada's Cities to Account: An Assessment of Municipal Fiscal Management*, C.D. Howe Institute Backgrounder No.145 (November 2011), available at www.cdhowe.org/pdf/Backgrounder_145.pdf ; and (by the same authors), *Baffling Budgets: Canada's Cities Need Better Financial Reporting*, C.D. Howe Institute Commentary No. 397 (January 2014), available at www.cdhowe.org/pdf/Commentary_397.pdf.
6. Harry M. Kitchen, *Municipal Revenue and Expenditure Issues in Canada*, Canadian Tax Paper No.107 (Toronto: Canadian Tax Foundation, 2002), 187.
7. Kyle Hanniman, *Borrowing Today for the City of Tomorrow? Municipal Debt and Alternative Financing*, Institute on Municipal Finance and Governance, University of Toronto (2013), available at http://munkschool.utoronto.ca/imfg/uploads/254/imfg_1453borrowingtoday_final_web_sept_12.pdf.
8. For details, see Richard M. Bird and Almos Tassonyi, "Constraining Subnational Fiscal Behavior in Canada: Different Approaches, Similar Results?" in Jonathan Rodden et al., eds., *Fiscal Decentralization and the Challenge of Hard Budget Constraints* (Cambridge MA: MIT Press, 2003), pp. 85–132.
9. Catherine Althaus, Lindsay M. Tedds, and Allen McAvoy, "The Feasibility of Implementing a Congestion Charge on the Halifax Peninsula: Filling the 'Missing Link' of Implementation," *Canadian Public Policy* 37-4 (2011): 541 61; and Harry Kitchen, *Financing Roads and Public Transit in the Greater Toronto and Hamilton Area*, An Independent Study Commissioned by the Residential and Civil Construction Alliance of Ontario (January 2013), available at www.rccao.com/news/files/RCCAO_JAN2013_REPORT_LOWRES.pdf.
10. Kitchen, *Municipal Revenue and Expenditure Issues*, 127.
11. Ibid., 147–52.
12. Ibid., 152.
13. For a broad survey of pricing and related issues, together with a comprehensive bibliography, see Kathryn Furlong and Karen Bakker, "Governance and Sustainability at a

Municipal Scale: The Challenge of Water Conservation," *Canadian Public Policy* 37-2 (2011): 220–37.

14. Christopher Armstrong and H.V. Nelles, *Monopoly's Moment: The Organization and Regulation of Canadian Utilities, 1830–1930* (Philadelphia: Temple University Press, 1986), 18.

15. Ibid., 32.

16. E.V. Buchanan, *London's Water Supply: A History* (London, ON: London Public Utilities Commission, 1968), 9.

17. Ibid, 86.

18. Environment Canada, *2010 Municipal Water Use Report*, http://publications.gc.ca/collections/collection_2010/ec/En11-2-2006-eng.pdf.

19. Furlong and Bakker, "Governance and Sustainability," 223.

20. Quebec, Bureau d'audiences publiques sur l'environnement, Rapport de la Commission sur la gestion de l'eau au Québec, Tome 2, *L'eau, ressource à protéger, à partager et à mettre en valeur* (Québec, 2000), 105.

21. Ibid., 105–6. Author's translation. The quotation begins (in English) "Although trends in opinion ... of resolving difficulties."

22. Ontario, Ministry of Public Infrastructure Renewal, Water Strategy Expert Panel, *Watertight: The Case for Change in Ontario's Water and Wastewater System* (Toronto: Queen's Printer for Ontario, 2005), 55. © Queen's Printer for Ontario, 2005. Reproduced with permission.

23. For details, see Kitchen, *Municipal Revenue and Expenditure Issues*, 141.

24. Ibid., 132.

25. Ibid., 133.

26. Ibid., 134–5.

27. Federation of Canadian Municipalities, *Canadian Infrastructure Report Card*, Volume 1: 2012, Municipal Roads and Water Systems, available at www.fcm.ca/Documents/reports/Canadian_Infrastructure_Report_Card_EN.pdf. For a dissenting view, see Philip Bazel and Jack Mintz, "The Free Ride is Over: Why Cities, and Citizens, Must Start Paying for Much-needed Infrastructure," *University of Calgary School of Public Policy Research Papers* 7–14 (May 2014)

28. Steven Renzetti and Colin Busby, "Water Pricing: Infrastructure Grants Hinder Necessary Reform," *Policy Options* (July–August 2009): 32–5.

29. Infrastructure Canada, "Building Canada Fund – Funding Categories in Detail," www.infrastructure.gc.ca/prog/bcf-fcc-categ-details-eng.html#envir.

30. Ontario, *Watertight*, 50.

31. Ibid., 58.

32. Ibid., 50. © Queen's Printer for Ontario, 2005. Reproduced with permission.

33. Pierre J. Hamel, "Les compteurs d'eau résidentiels: une mauvaise idée," *Bulletin de la ligue des droits et libertés* (Spring 2006): 22–3.

34. Ontario, *Watertight*, 59. © Queen's Printer for Ontario, 2005. Reproduced with permission.

Chapter 15

1. Harry Kitchen, "Municipal Taxes and User Fees," in Heather Kerr, Ken McKenzie, and Jack Mintz, eds., *Tax Policy in Canada* (Toronto: Canadian Tax Foundation, 2012), p. 9:7.

2. Harry Kitchen, *Municipal Revenue and Expenditure Issues in Canada*, Canadian Tax Paper 107 (Toronto: Canadian Tax Foundation, 2002), 67–72.

3. For a discussion of these conflicting pressures in the Ontario context, see Richard M. Bird, Enid Slack, and Almos Tassonyi, *A Tale of Two Taxes: Property Tax Reform in Ontario* (Cambridge MA: Lincoln Institute of Land Policy, 2012), especially ch. 9.

4. Kitchen, *Municipal Revenue and Expenditure Issues*, 64.

5. Ibid., 79.

6. Center for the Study of Economics, www.ourcommonwealth.org. See also Francis K. Peddle, *Cities and Greed: Taxes, Inflation and Land Speculation* (Ottawa: Canadian Research Committee on Taxation, 1994).

7. Constitution Act, 1867, s. 125.
8. Kitchen, *Municipal Revenue and Expenditure Issues*, 64.
9. Ibid., 64.
10. For Ontario, see Elizabeth Bloomfield, "Municipal Bonusing of Industry to 1930," *Urban History Review* 9, 3 (1981): 59–76; Timothy W. Cobban, *Cities of Oil: Municipalities and Petroleum Manufacturing in Southern Ontario, 1860-1960* (Toronto: University of Toronto Press, 2013).
11. John D. Donahue, *Disunited States* (New York: Basic Books, 1997).
12. Kitchen, *Municipal Revenue and Expenditure Issues*, 109–12. See also Bird et al., *A Tale of Two Taxes.*
13. Ibid., 85–90.
14. Ibid., 76–7.
15. Ibid., 94.
16. Wade Locke and Almos Tassonyi, "Shared Tax Bases and Local Public Expenditure Decisions," *Canadian Tax Journal* 41, 5 (1993): 941–57. For a discussion of the impact of the provincial property tax for education on businesses in Ontario, British Columbia, and Alberta, see Adam Found and Peter Tomlinson, *Hiding in Plain Sight: The Harmful Impact of Provincial Business Property Taxes*, Commentary No.368, C.D. Howe Institute (December 2012), available at www.cdhowe.org/hiding-in-plain-sight-the-harmful-impact-of-provincial-business-property-taxes/19828.
17. Enid Slack, "Revenue Sharing Options for Canada's Hub Cities," a report prepared for the Meeting of Canada's Hub City Mayors, 17–18 September 2004, available at http://munkschool.utoronto.ca/imfg/uploads/137/revenuesharingoptions.pdf.
18. Kitchen, *Municipal Revenue and Expenditure Issues*, 229.
19. Ibid.

Chapter 16

1. Julie-Anne Boudreau, Roger Keil, and Douglas Young, *Changing Toronto: Governing Urban Neoliberalism* (Toronto: University of Toronto Press, 2009), 27. See also, Valentina Capurri, "'Residents' or 'Taxpayers'? Rob Ford's Mayoral Campaign and the Meaning of Urban Citizenship," *Canadian Journal of Urban Research* 22, 2 (Winter 2013):1–17.
2. Boudreau, Keil, and Young, *Changing Toronto.*, 25.
3. Julie-Anne Boudreau, "Intergovernmental Relations and Polyscalar Social Mobilization," in Robert Young and Christian Leuprecht, eds., *Municipal–Federal–Provincial Relations in Canada* (Montreal and Kingston: McGill-Queen's University Press, 2006), 162.
4. For a valuable book that places Canadian urban politics in a comparative perspective with France and other major countries, see Michael Keating, *Comparative Urban Politics: Power and the City in the United States, Canada, Britain and France* (Brookfield, VT: Edward Elgar, 1991).
5. Boudreau et al., *Changing Toronto*, ch. 4. Although the book as a whole is about "governing urban neoliberalism," and Chapter 4 is about the amalgamation, the word *neoliberalism* is not used in the chapter, except in the very last sentence where it is not applied to the amalgamation.
6. Andrew Sancton, "Why Municipal Amalgamations? Halifax, Toronto, Montreal," in Young and Leuprecht, eds., *Municipal–Federal–Provincial Relations*, 119–37.
7. Susan D. Phillips, "'You Say You Want an Evolution?' From Citizen to Community Engagement in Canadian Cities," in Emmanuel Brunet-Juilly and John F. Martin, eds., *Local Government in a Global World: Australia and Canada in Comparative Perspective* (Toronto: University of Toronto Press, 2010), 71.

BIBLIOGRAPHY

Acuere Consulting et al. *Translink Governance Review* (March 2013), available at www.scribd.com/doc/131890569/TransLink-Governance-Review.

Adams, Erika and Allan M. Maslove. "The Federal Gas Tax Cession: From Advocacy Efforts to 13 Signed Agreements" in Katherine Graham and Caroline Andrew, eds., *Canada in Cities: The Politics and Policy of Federal-Local Governnance.* Montreal and Kingston: McGill-Queen's University Press, 2014.

Alberta, Municipal Affairs, Alberta Capital Region Governance Review. *Final Report: An Agenda for Action.* Edmonton, 2000.

Allahwala, Ahmed, Julie-Anne Boudreau, and Roger Keil. "Neo-Liberal Governance: Entrepreneurial Municipal Regimes in Canada," in Trudi Bunting, Pierre Filion, and Ryan Walker, eds., *Canadian Cities in Transition: New Directions in the Twenty-First Century,* 4th ed. Toronto: Oxford University Press, 2010, pp. 210–24.

Allen, Rian, and Philippa Campsie. *Implementing the Growth Plan for the Greater Golden Horseshoe: Has the Strategic Regional Vision been Compromised?* Toronto: Neptis Foundation, 2013.

Althaus, Catherine, Lindsay M. Tedds, and Allen McAvoy. "The Feasibility of Implementing a Congestion Charge on the Halifax Peninsula: Filling the 'Missing Link' of Implementation," *Canadian Public Policy* 37-4 (2011): 541–61.

Andrew, Caroline, et al., eds., *Electing a Diverse Canada: The Representation of Immigrants, Minorities, and Women.* Vancouver: University of British Columbia Press, 2008.

———. *Immigration, Integration, and Inclusion in Ontario Cities.* Montreal and Kingston: McGill-Queen's University Press, 2012.

Armstrong, Christopher, and H.V. Nelles. *Monopoly's Moment: The Organization and Regulation of Canadian Utilities, 1830–1930.* Philadelphia: Temple University Press, 1986.

Bain, Alison. "Re-Imaging, Re-Elevating, and Re-Placing the Urban: The Cultural Transformation of the Inner City in the Twenty-First Century," in Trudi Bunting, Pierre Filion, and Ryan Walker, eds., *Canadian Cities in Transition.* Toronto: Oxford University Press, 2010, pp. 262–75.

Barnard, H.C. *A History of English Education, from 1760,* 2nd ed. London: University of London Press, 1964.

Bazel, Philip and Jack Mintz. "The Free Ride is Over: Why Cities, and Citizens, Must Start Paying for Much-needed Infrastructure," *University of Calgary School of Public Policy Research Papers* 7–14 (May 2014).

Beare, M.E., and T. Murray, eds. *Police and Government Relations: Who's Calling the Shots?* Toronto: University of Toronto Press, 2007.

Bedford, Paul J. "Reconsidering the Ward System of Governance," *Ontario Planning Journal* 20, 6 (2005): 25–7.

Belley, Serge et al. "Quebec," in Andrew Sancton and Robert Young, eds., *Foundations of Governance: Municipal Government in Canada's Provinces.* Toronto: University of Toronto Press, 2009, pp. 70–137.

Betts, George. "Municipal Restructuring, New Brunswick Style: The Saint John Experience," *Municipal World* 51, 9 (1997): 3–8.

Bird, Richard M., and Almos Tassonyi. "Constraining Subnational Fiscal Behavior in Canada: Different Approaches, Similar Results?" in Jonathan Rodden et al., eds., *Fiscal Decentralization and the Challenge of Hard Budget Constraints.* Cambridge, MA: MIT Press 2003, pp. 85–132.

Bird, Richard M., Enid Slack, and Almos Tassonyi. *A Tale of Two Taxes: Property Tax Reform in Ontario.* Cambridge, MA: Lincoln Institute of Land Policy, 2012.

Bish, Robert L. *Organization and Opportunities: Local Government Services Production in Greater Saint John.* The AIMS Urban Futures Series, Paper #4. Halifax: Atlantic Institute for Market Studies, 2004.

Bish, Robert L., and Eric G. Clemens. *Local Government in British Columbia,* 4th ed. Vancouver: Union of British Columbia Municipalities, 2008.

Black, Martha, and Katherine Fierlbeck. "Whatever Happened to Regionalization? The Curious Case of Nova Scotia,"

Canadian Public Administration 49, 4 (2006): 506–27.

Blais, Pamela. *Perverse Cities: Hidden Subsidies, Wonky Policy, and Urban Sprawl.* Vancouver: UBC Press, 2010.

Bloemraad, Irene. "Diversity and Elected Officials in the City of Vancouver," in Andrew et al., eds., *Electing a Diverse Canada: The Representation of Immigrants, Minorities, and Women.* Vancouver: University of British Columbia Press, 2008, pp. 46–69.

Blom-Hansen, Jens. "Local Government in Denmark and the 2007 Municipal Reform," in Antti Moisio, ed., *Rethinking Local Government: Essays on Municipal Reform.* Helsinki: VATT Publications, 2012, ch.3.

Bloomfield, Elizabeth. "Municipal Bonusing of Industry to 1930," *Urban History Review* 9, 3 (1981): 59–76.

Bollman, Ray D., and Heather A. Clemenson. "Structure and Change in Canada's Rural Demography: An Update to 2006 with Provincial Detail." Statistics Canada Research Paper, Agriculture and Working Paper Series, December 2008, Catalogue no. 21–601–M, No. 90.

Boudreau, Julie-Anne. *The Megacity Saga.* Montreal: Black Rose, 2000.

———. "Intergovernmental Relations and Polyscalar Social Mobilization," in Robert Young and Christian Leuprecht, eds., *Municipal–Federal–Provincial Relations in Canada.* Montreal and Kingston: McGill-Queen's University Press, 2006, pp. 161–80.

Boudreau, Julie-Anne, Roger Keil, and Douglas Young. *Changing Toronto: Governing Urban Neoliberalism.* Toronto: University of Toronto Press, 2009.

Bourgeois, Daniel. "Municipal Reform in New Brunswick: To Decentralize or Not To Decentralize," in Joseph Garcea and Edward C. LeSage Jr, eds., *Municipal Reform in Canada: Reconfiguration, Re-empowerment, and Rebalancing.* Toronto: Oxford University Press, 2005, pp. 242–68.

Bourne, Larry S., John N.H. Britton, and Deborah Leslie, "The Greater Toronto Region: The Challenges of Economic Restructuring, Social Diversity, and Globalization," in Larry S. Bourne et al., eds., *Canadian Urban Regions: Trajectories of Growth and Change.* Toronto: Oxford University Press, 2011.

Bradford, Neil, and Allison Bramwell, eds. *Governing Urban Economies: Innovation and Inclusion in Canadian City Regions.* Toronto: University of Toronto Press, 2014.

Brenner, Neil and David Wachsmuth. "Territorial Competiveness: Lineages, Practices, Ideologies" in Bishwapriya Sanyal et al., eds., *Planning Ideas that Matter: Livability, Territoriality, Governance, and Reflective Practice.* Cambridge MA: MIT Press, 2012, pp. 179–204.

British Columbia. *Forsaken: Report of the Missing Women Commission of Inquiry.* Wally T. Oppal, Commissioner (2012).

British Columbia Ombudsperson. *Open Meetings: Best Practices Guide for Local Governments* (September 2012).

Brownstone, Meyer, and T.J. Plunkett. *Metropolitan Winnipeg: Politics and Reform of Local Government.* Berkeley: University of California Press, 1983.

Brunet-Jailly, Emmanuel. "Vancouver: The Sustainable City," *Journal of Urban Affairs* 30, 4 (2008): 375–88.

Buchanan, E.V. *London's Water Supply: A History.* London, ON: London Public Utilities Commission, 1968.

Bulger, David, and James Sentance. "Prince Edward Island," in Andrew Sancton and Robert Young, eds., *Foundations of Governance.* 2009, pp. 314–44.

Bunting, Trudi, Pierre Filion, and Ryan Walker, eds. *Canadian Cities in Transition: New Directions in the Twenty-First Century.* Toronto: Oxford University Press, 2010.

Bunting, Trudi, and Tod Rutherford. "Transitions in an Era of Globalization and World City Growth," in Trudi Bunting and Pierre Filion, eds., 2006, pp. 65–85.

Calgary Regional Partnership. *Calgary Metropolitan Plan.* 2009.

Cameron, David. "The Relationship between Different Ownership and Management Regimes and Drinking Water Safety." Discussion Paper for the Walkerton Inquiry, June 2001.

Cameron, David M. *Schools for Ontario: Policy-making, Administration, and Finance in the 1960s.* Toronto: University of Toronto Press, 1972.

———. "Provincial Responsibilities for Municipal Government," *Canadian Public Administration* 23, 2 (1980): 222–35.

Canada, National Capital Commission. *The Capital of Canada: How Should It Be Governed?* Ottawa, 1974.

Capurri, Valentina. "'Residents' or 'Taxpayers'? Rob Ford's Mayoral Campaign and the Meaning of Urban Citizenship," *Canadian Journal of Urban Research* 22, 2 (Winter 2013): 1–17.

Carroll, Barbara Wake. "Housing Policy in the New Millennium: The Uncompassionate Landscape," in Edmund P. Fowler and David Siegel, eds., *Urban Policy Issues: Canadian Perspectives*, 2nd ed. Toronto: Oxford University Press, 2002: 69–89.

Carter, Tom. "Manitoba," in Sancton and Young, 2009, pp. 223–81.

Champagne, Eric. "Tracking the Growth of the Federal-Municipal Infrastructure Program under Different Political Regimes," in Caroline Andrew and Katherine Graham, eds., *Canada in Cities: The Politics and Policy of Federal-Local Governance*. Montreal and Kingston: McGill-Queen's University Press, 2014.

Chattopadhyay, Rupak and Gilles Paquet, eds. *The Unimagined Canadian Capital: Challenges for the Federal Capital Region* (Ottawa: Invenire Books, 2011).

Chenier, John A. "The Evolving Role of the Federation of Canadian Municipalities," *Canadian Public Administration* 52, 3 (2009): 395–416.

Chipman John G. *A Law unto Itself: How the Ontario Municipal Board Has Developed and Applied Land-Use Planning Policy*. Toronto: University of Toronto Press, 2002.

Ciepley, David. "Beyond Public and Private: Toward a Political Theory of the Corporation," *American Political Science Review* 107, 1 (2013): 139–58.

Cobban, Timothy. "The Political Economy of Urban Development: Downtown Revitalization in London, Ontario, 1993–2002," *Canadian Journal of Urban Research* 12, 2 (2003): 231–48.

———. "Timothy Cobban's Reply to Christopher Leo's Comment 'Are There Urban Regimes in Canada?'" *Canadian Journal of Urban Research* 12, 2 (2003): 349–52.

———. *Cities of Oil: Municipalities and Petroleum Manufacturing in Southern Ontario, 1860–1960*. Toronto: University of Toronto Press, 2013.

Collin, Jean-Pierre, and Mélanie Robertson. "The Borough System of Consolidated Montréal: Revisiting Urban Governance in a Composite Metropolis," *Journal of Urban Affairs* 27, 3 (2005): 307–30.

Cook, Graeme, and Patti Tamara Lenard, "Making Politics More Welcoming," *Literary Review of Canada*, (June 2013): 25–6.

Côté, André, and Howard Tam. *Affordable Housing: Mobilizing Private Capital in an Era of Public Constraint*. IMFG Perspectives,

No. 3, Munk School of Global Affairs at the University of Toronto, 2013.

Côté, André and Michael Fenn. "Provincial-Municipal relations in Ontario: Approaching the Inflection Point" *IMFG Papers on Municipal Finance and Governance*, No. 17, Munk School of Global affairs at the University of Toronto, 2014.

Crawford, Kenneth Grant. *Canadian Municipal Government*. Toronto: University of Toronto Press, 1954.

Crossley, John. "Municipal Reform in Prince Edward Island: Uneven Capacity and Reforms," in Joseph Garcea and Edward C. LeSage, eds., *Municipal Reform in Canada*. Toronto: Oxford University Press, 2005, pp. 218–41.

Cutler, Fred, and J. Scott Matthews, "The Challenge of Municipal Voting: Vancouver 2002," *Canadian Journal of Political Science* 38, 2 (June 2005): 359–82.

Dachis, Benjamin. *Picking Up Savings: The Benefits of Competition in Municipal Waste Services*. Toronto: C.D. Howe Institute Commentary No. 308, September 2010.

Dachis, Benjamin, and William B.P. Robson. *Holding Canada's Cities to Account: An Assessment of Municipal Fiscal Management*. C.D. Howe Institute Backgrounder No.145, November 2011.

———. *Baffling Budgets: Canada's Cities Need Better Financial Reporting*. C.D. Howe Institute Commentary No. 397, January 2014.

Dagenais, Michèle. "At the Source of a New Urbanity: Water Networks and Power Relations in the Second Half of the Nineteenth Century," in Stéphane Castonguay and Michèle Dagenais, eds., *Metropolitan Natures: Environmental Histories of Montreal*. Pittsburgh: University of Pittsburgh Press, 2011, pp. 101–14.

Dahl, Robert A. *Who Governs? Democracy and Power in an American City*. New Haven: Yale University Press, 1961.

Deloitte. *City of Regina Wastewater Treatment & Plant Expansion Upgrade Project: Summary of Delivery Model Assessment*, 22 January 2013.

Doberstein, Carey. "Institutional Creation and Death: Urban Development Agreements in Canada," *Journal of Urban Affairs* 33, 5 (2011): 529–47.

Donahue, John D. *Disunited States*. New York: Basic Books, 1997.

———. *The Warping of Government Work*.

Cambridge, MA: Harvard University Press, 2008.

Eidelman, Gabriel. "Managing Urban Sprawl in Ontario: Good Policy or Good Politics," *Politics and Policy* 38, 6 (2010): 1211–36.

———. *Three's Company: A Review of Waterfront Toronto's Tri-Government Approach to Revitalization.* Toronto: The Mowat Centre, 2013.

Eng, Susan. "Commentary," in Beare and Murray, eds., *Police and Government Relations*, 2007, pp. 290–4.

Farkas, Jeromy Anton. "Growing the Democratic Toolbox: City Council Vote Tracking," Calgary: The Manning Foundation for Democratic Education, 20 September 2013.

Federation of Canadian Municipalities. *Canadian Infrastructure Report Card Volume 1: 2012, Municipal Roads and Water Systems.*

Feenan, James P. et al. "Newfoundland and Labrador," in Sancton and Young, eds., *Foundations of Governance: Municipal Governance in Canada's Provinces.* 2009, pp. 453–86.

Feldman, Lionel, ed. *Politics and Government of Urban Canada: Selected Readings,* 4th ed. Toronto: Methuen, 1981.

Finbow, Robert G. "Submerging the Urban: Halifax in a Multilevel Governance System," in Horak and Young, eds., *Sites of Governance,* 2012, ch.4.

Fischel, William A. *The Homevoter Hypothesis: How Home Values Influence Local Government Taxation, School Finance, and Land-use Policies.* Cambridge, MA: Harvard University Press, 2001.

Florida, Richard. *Who's Your City? How the Creative Economy is Making Where to Live the Most Important Decision of Your Life.* Toronto: Random House Canada, 2008.

———. "What Critics Get Wrong about Creative Cities" at www.theatlanticcities. com/jobs-and-economy/2012/05/what -critics-get-wrong-about-creative-cities/ 2119.

Fong, Eric. "Immigration and Race in the City," in Harry Hiller, ed., *Urban Canada,* 2nd ed. Toronto: Oxford University Press, 2010, pp. 131–54.

Foran, Max. *Expansive Discourses: Urban Sprawl in Calgary, 1945–1978.* Edmonton: University of Alberta Press, 2009.

Found, Adam, and Peter Tomlinson. *Hiding in Plain Sight: The Harmful Impact of Provincial Business Property Taxes.*

Commentary No. 368, C.D. Howe Institute, December 2012.

Fowler, Edmund P., and David Siegel, eds. *Urban Policy Issues: Canadian Perspectives,* 2nd ed., Toronto: Oxford University Press, 2002.

Frisken, Frances. "A Triumph for Public Ownership: The Toronto Transportation Commission," in Victor L. Russell, ed., *Forging a Consensus: Historical Essays on Toronto.* Toronto: University of Toronto Press, 1984.

———. *The Public Metropolis: The Political Dynamics of Urban Expansion in the Toronto Region, 1924–2003.* Toronto: Canadian Scholars' Press, 2007.

Furlong, Kathryn, and Karen Bakker. "The Contradictions in 'Alternative' Service Delivery: Governance, Business Models, and Sustainability in Municipal Water Supply," *Environment and Planning C: Government and Policy* 28, 2 (2010): 349–68.

———. "Governance and Sustainability at a Municipal Scale: The Challenge of Water Conservation," *Canadian Public Policy* 37-2 (2011): 220–37.

Fyfe, Stephen, Mark Garner, and George Vegh, *Mergers by Choice, Not Edict: Reforming Ontario's Electricity Distribution Policy,* C.D. Howe Institute Commentary No.376, March 2013.

Fyfe, Stewart. "Local Government Reform in Ontario: 1853–1973," in R. Charles Bryfogle and Ralph R Krueger, eds., *Urban Problems,* revised ed. Toronto: Holt, Rinehart, and Winston, 1975, pp. 352–66.

Garcea, Joseph. "The Empowerment of Canadian Cities: Classic Canadian Compromise," *International Journal of Canadian Studies* 49 (2014): 81–104.

Garcea, Joseph, and Edward C. LeSage Jr, eds. *Municipal Reform in Canada: Reconfiguration, Re-empowerment, and Rebalancing.* Toronto: Oxford University Press, 2005.

Garkowski, Jeffrey and Charles Hostovsky, "Policy versus Practice in Municipal Solid Waste Diversion: The Role of the Waste Crisis in Ontario Waste Planning," *Canadian Journal of Urban Research,* 20, 1 (2011): 81–102.

Gauthier, Pierre, Jochen Jaeger, and Jason Prince. *Montréal at the Crossroads: Superhighways, the Turcot and the Environment.* Montreal: Black Rose, 2009.

Ghitter, Geoff, and Alan Smart. "Mad Cows, Regional Governance, and Urban Sprawl: Path Dependence and Unintended

Consequences in the Calgary Region," *Urban Affairs Review* 44, 5 (2009): 617–45.

Gillette, Clayton P. *Local Redistribution and Local Democracy*. New Haven, CT: Yale University Press, 2011.

Glaeser, Edward. *Triumph of the City: How Our Greatest Invention Makes Us Richer, Smarter, Greener, Healthier, and Happier*. New York: Penguin, 2011.

Good, David A. *The Politics of Public Money: Spenders, Guardians, Priority Setters, and Financial Watchdogs inside the Canadian Government*. Toronto: University of Toronto Press, 2008.

Good, Kristin R. *Municipalities and Multiculturalism: The Politics of Immigration in Toronto and Vancouver*. Toronto: University of Toronto Press, 2009.

Graham, Katherine A. "Collective Bargaining in the Municipal Sector," in Gene Swimmer and Mark Thompson, eds., *Public Sector Collective Bargaining in Canada: Beginning of the End or End of the Beginning?* Kingston, ON: Industrial Relations Centre, Queen's University, 1995.

———. "The Paradox of Participation: An Overview of Public Participation and Local Government in Canada" in Andrew Sancton and Chen Zhenming, eds., *Citizen Participation at the Local Level in Canada and China* (Boca Raton FL: CRC Press, 2014), ch.2.

Graham, Katherine and Caroline Andrew, eds. *Canada in Cities: The Poltics and Policy of Federal-Local Governance*. Montreal and Kingston: McGill-Queen's University Press, 2014.

Graham, Katherine A., and Susan D. Phillips, eds. *Citizen Engagement: Lessons in Participation from Local Government*. Toronto: Institute of Public Administration of Canada, 1998.

Guay, Louis and Pierre Hamel. *Urban Sociology*. Toronto: Oxford University Press, 2014.

Gutstein, Donald. "Vancouver," in Warren Magnusson and Andrew Sancton, eds., *City Politics in Canada*. Toronto: University of Toronto Press, 1983, pp. 189–221.

Hackworth, Jason and Abigail Moriah, "Neoliberalism, Contingency and Urban Policy: The Case of Social Housing in Ontario," *International Journal of Urban and Regional Research* 30,3 (1996): 510–27.

Hall, Peter V. "The Global Imperative," in Bunting, Filion, and Walker, eds., *Canadian Cities in Transition*, 2010, pp. 56–69.

Hamel, Pierre J. "Les compteurs d'eau résidentiels: une mauvaise idée," *Bulletin de la ligue des droits et libertés* (Spring 2006): 22–3.

Hammack, David C. *Power and Society: Greater New York at the Turn of the Century*. New York: Russell Sage Foundation, 1982.

Hanniman, Kyle. *Borrowing Today for the City of Tomorrow: Municipal Debt and Alternative Financing*. Institute on Municipal Finance and Governance at the University of Toronto (2013).

Harcourt, Mike, and Ken Cameron, with Sean Rossiter. *City Making in Paradise: Nine Decisions That Saved Vancouver*. Vancouver: Douglas & McIntyre, 2007.

Harding, Alan. "The History of Community Power," in Jonathan S. Davies and David L. Imbroscio, eds., *Theories of Urban Politics*, 2nd ed. Los Angeles: Sage, 2009, pp. 27–39.

Hartog, Hendrik. *Public Property and Private Power: The Corporation of the City of New York in American Law, 1730–1870*. Chapel Hill: University of North Carolina Press, 1983.

Harvey, Jean, and Robert Young, eds. *Image-building in Canadian Municipalities*. Montreal and Kingston: McGill-Queen's University Press, 2012.

Henstra, Daniel, ed., *Multilevel Governance and Emergency Management in Canadian Municipalities*. Montreal and Kingston: McGill-Queen's University Press, 2013.

Hiller, Harry H. "Introduction," in Harry H. Hiller (2010: xii–xxi) ed. *Urban Canada*, 2nd ed. Toronto: Oxford University Press, 2010.

Hodge, Gerald, and David L.A. Gordon. *Planning Canadian Communities: An Introduction to the Principles, Practice, and Participants*, 5th ed. Toronto: Nelson, 2008.

Holmes, Stephen. *Passions and Constraint*. Chicago: University of Chicago Press, 1995.

Horak, Martin. "The Power of Local Identity: C4LD and the Anti-amalgamation Mobilization in Toronto." Research Paper 195, Centre for Urban and Community Studies, University of Toronto, 1998.

———. *Governance Reform from Below: Multilevel Politics and the 'New Deal' in Toronto, Canada*. Human Settlements and Dialogue Series 4. Nairobi: UN-HABITAT, 2008.

———. "Success and Failure in Multilevel Governance in Toronto," in Horak and Young, eds., *Sites of Governance*, 228–62.

——. "State Rescaling in Practice: Urban Governance Reform in Toronto," *Urban Research & Practice* 6,3 (2013): 311–28.

Horak, Martin, and Marilyn Dantico. "The Limits of Local Redistribution: Neighbourhood Regeneration Initiatives in Toronto and Phoenix," *International Journal of Canadian Studies* 49 (2014), pp. 135–58.

Horak, Martin, and Aaron A. Moore. "Policy Shift without Institutional Change: The Precarious Place of Neighborhood Revitalization in Toronto," in Clarence Stone et al., *In a New Era: The Politics of Neighborhood Revitalization in the Post-industrial City.* Chicago: University of Chicago Press, forthcoming.

Horak, Martin and Robert Young, eds., *Sites of Governance: Multilevel Governance and Policy Making in Canada's Big Cities.* Montreal and Kingston: McGill-Queen's University Press, 2012.

Howlett, Michael, M. Ramesh, and Anthony Perl. *Studying Public Policy: Policy Cycles and Policy Subsystems,* 3rd ed. Toronto: Oxford University Press, 2009.

Hunter, Floyd. *Community Power Structure.* Chapel Hill: University of North Carolina Press, 1953.

Hutton, Thomas A. "Multilevel Governance and Urban Development in Vancouver," in Horak and Young, eds., *Sites of Governance,* 263–98.

Ibbitson, John. *Promised Land: Inside the Mike Harris Revolution.* Toronto: Prentice-Hall, 1997.

International Monetary Fund, *Government Finance Statistics Manual 2001.*

Irons, Angela Macleod. *Noble Frustrations: The Many Practical Problems with Municipal Poverty Initiatives.* Calgary: The Manning Foundation, 2013.

Jackson, Richard L. "Police and Firefighter Labour Relations," in Gene Swimmer and Mark Thompson, eds., *Public Sector Collective Bargaining in Canada: Beginning of the End or End of the Beginning?* Kingston, ON: Industrial Relations Centre, Queen's University, 1995.

Jacobs, Jane. *The Death and Life of Great American Cities.* New York: Random House, 1961.

Katznelson, Ira. *City Trenches: Urban Politics and the Patterning of Class in the United States.* New York: Pantheon, 1981.

Keating, Michael. *Comparative Urban Politics: Power and the City in the United States, Canada, Britain and France.* Brookfield, VT: Edward Elgar, 1991.

Kennedy, Christopher. *The Evolution of World Cities: Urban Wealth and Economic Growth.* Toronto: University of Toronto Press, 2011.

Kitchen, Harry M. *The Role for Local Governments in Economic Development.* Toronto: Ontario Economic Council, 1985.

——. *Municipal Revenue and Expenditure Issues in Canada.* Canadian Tax Paper 107, Toronto: Canadian Tax Foundation, 2002.

——. "Municipal Taxes and User Fees," in Heather Kerr, Ken McKenzie, and Jack Mintz, eds., *Tax Policy in Canada.* Toronto: Canadian Tax Foundation, 2012, ch.9.

——. *Financing Roads and Public Transit in the Greater Toronto and Hamilton Area.* An Independent Study Commissioned by the Residential and Civil Construction Alliance of Ontario (January 2013).

Klemek, Christopher. *The Transatlantic Collapse of Urban Renewal: Postwar Urbanism from New York to Berlin.* Chicago: University of Chicago Press, 2011.

Klodawsky, Fran and Lenore Evans. "Homelessness on the Federal Agenda: Progressive Architecture but No Solution in Sight" in Caroline Andrew and Katherine Graham, eds., *Canada in Cities: The Politics and Policy of Federal–Local Governance.* Montreal and Kingston: McGill-Queen's University Press, 2014.

Kohn, Margaret. "What is Wrong with Gentrification?" *Urban Research & Practice* 6, 3 (November 2013): 297–310.

Kong, Hoi. "Toward a Federal Legal Theory of the City," *McGill Law Journal* 56,3 (2012): 474–517.

Kushner, Joseph, and David Siegel. "Why Do Municipal Electors Not Vote?" *Canadian Journal of Urban Research* 15, 2 (2006): 264–77.

Kushner, Joseph, David Siegel, and Hannah Stanwick. "Ontario Municipal Elections: Voting Trends and Determinants of Electoral Success in a Canadian Province," *Canadian Journal of Political Science* 30, 3 (1997): 539–53.

Kusilek, Larry, and Trevor Price. "Ontario Municipal Policy Affecting Local Autonomy: A Case Study Involving Windsor and Toronto," *Urban History Review* 16, 3 (1988): 255–70.

Lafortune, Marie-Ève, and Jean-Pierre Collin. "Building Metropolitan Governance: The Case of the Communauté métropolitaine de Montréal," *Canadian Public Administration* 54, 3 (September 2011): 399–420.

Lago-Peñas, Santiago and Jorge Martinez-Vazquez, eds. *The Challenge of Local Government Size: Theoretical Perspectives, International Experience and Policy Reform.* Cheltenham UK: Edward Elgar, 2013.

Lang, Robert E., and Jennifer B. LeFurgy. *Boomburbs: The Rise of America's Accidental Cities.* Washington: Brookings Institution Press, 2006.

Leo, Christopher. "Global Change and Local Politics: Economic Decline and the Local Regime in Edmonton," *Journal of Urban Affairs* 17, 3 (1995): 277–99.

———. "Are There Urban Regimes in Canada? Comment on Timothy Cobban's 'The Political Economy of Urban Development: Downtown Revitalization in London, Ontario, 1993–2002,'" *Canadian Journal of Urban Research* 12, 2 (2003): 344–8.

Leo, Christopher, and Kathryn Anderson. "Being Realistic about Urban Growth," *Journal of Urban Affairs* 28, 2 (2006):169–89.

Leo, Christopher et al. "Multilevel Governance without Municipal Government," in Horak and Young, eds., *Sites of Governance*, Montreal and Kingston: Queen's University Press, 2012, ch.11.

LeSage, Edward C., Jr. "Municipal Reform in Alberta: Breaking Ground at the New Millennium," in Joseph Garcea and Edward C. LeSage Jr, eds., *Municipal Reform in Canada*, 2005, pp. 57–82.

Levesque, Mario. "'Build it . . . if you can!': Discretion, Building Inspectors and Part 8 of Ontario's 2006 Building Code," *Canadian Journal of Urban Research*, 20, 1 (2011): 103–30.

Levine, Allan. "Stephen Juba, the Great City Salesman," in Allan Levine, ed., *Your Worship: The Lives of Eight of Canada's Most Unforgettable Mayors.* Toronto: James Lorimer, 1989, 67–96.

Levy, Ed. *Rapid Transit in Toronto: A Century of Plans, Progress, Politics & Paralysis*, a web-book published by the Neptis Foundation, available at: http://levyrapidtransit.ca.

Lewis, Paul G. and Max Neiman, *Custodians of Place: Governing the Growth and Development of Cities.* Washington, DC: Georgetown University Press, 2009.

Lewis, Robert. *Manufacturing Montreal: The Making of an Industrial Landscape, 1850 to 1930.* Baltimore, MD: Johns Hopkins University Press, 2000.

Ley, David, and Heather Frost. "The Inner City," in Bunting and Filion, eds. *Canadian Cities in Transition*, 3rd ed. (2006: 192–210).

Lightbody, James. "Edmonton," in Magnusson and Sancton, eds., *City Politics in Canada.* 1983, pp. 255–90.

———. "Finding the Trolls under Your Bridge: The New Case for Party Politics in Canadian Cities," *Journal of Canadian Studies* 34, 1 (1999): 172–83.

Linteau, Paul-André. *The Promoters' City: Building the Industrial Town of Maisonneuve, 1883–1918.* Toronto: James Lorimer, 1985.

———. *Histoire de Montréal depuis la Confédération.* Montreal: Boréal, 1992.

Locke, Wade, and Almos Tassonyi. "Shared Tax Bases and Local Public Expenditure Decisions," *Canadian Tax Journal* 41, 5 (1993): 941–57.

Logan, John R., and Harvey L. Molotch. *Urban Fortunes: The Political Economy of Place.* Berkeley: University of California Press, 1987.

Loxley, John, with Salim Loxley. *Public Service, Private Profits: The Political Economy of Public-Private Partnerships in Canada.* Halifax and Winnipeg: Fernwood, 2010.

MacDermid, Robert. "Funding City Politics: Municipal Campaign Funding and Property Development in the Greater Toronto Area." The CSJ Foundation for Research and Education and Vote Toronto, January 2009.

Mackenzie, Hugh. *Flushing Money Away: Why the Privatization of the Wastewater Treatment Plant Is a Bad Idea.* 6 May 2013.

Makuch, Stanley M., and John Jackson. "Freedom of Information in Local Government in Ontario," Research Publication 7 for the Commission on Freedom of Information and Individual Privacy (May 1979).

Martin, Elisabeth, Marie-Pascale Pomey, and Pierre Gerlier Forest. "One Step Forward, One Step Back: Quebec's 2003–04 Health and Social Services Regionalization Policy," *Canadian Public Administration* 53, 4 (December 2010), 467–88.

Mathews, Vanessa. "Incoherence and Tension in Culture-led Redevelopment," *International Journal of Urban and Regional Research* 38, 3 (May 2014), 1019-1036.

McCann, Eugene, J. "Expertise, Truth, and Urban Policy Mobilities: Global Circuits of Knowledge in the Development of Vancouver, Canada's 'Four Pillar' Drug Strategy," in *Environment and Planning A* 40 (2008): 885–904.

McDavid, James C. "Solid-waste Contracting-out, Bidding Practices, and Competition among Canadian

Local Governments," *Canadian Public Administration* 44, 1 (2001): 1–25.

———. "The Impacts of Amalgamation on Police Services in the Halifax Regional Municipality," *Canadian Public Administration* 45, 4 (2002): 538–65.

McDavid, James C., and Annette E. Mueller. "A Cross-Canada Analysis of the Efficiency of Residential Recycling Services," *Canadian Public Administration* 51, 4 (2008): 569–88.

McVittie, James R. "Local Government Unionism in Ontario 1935–1963: Study of the Determinants of Union Growth," Ph.D. thesis, University of Western Ontario, 1991.

Magnusson, Warren. "Introduction," in Magnusson and Sancton, eds., *City Politics in Canada*. 1983, pp. 3–57.

———. "Toronto," in Magnusson and Sancton, eds., *City Politics in Canada*, 1983, pp. 94–139.

———. "The Local State in Canada: Theoretical Perspectives," *Canadian Public Administration* 28, 4 (1985): 575–99.

———. "Protecting the Right of Local Self-Government," *Canadian Journal of Political Science* 38, 4 (2005): 897–922.

———. "Urbanism, Cities, and Local Self-Government," *Canadian Public Administration* 48, 1 (2005): 96–123.

Magnusson, Warren, and Andrew Sancton, eds. *City Politics in Canada*. Toronto: University of Toronto Press, 1983.

Manzer, Ronald A. *Public Schools and Political Ideas: Educational Policy in Historical Perspective*. Toronto: University of Toronto Press, 1994.

Meligrana, John F. "The Politics of Municipal Annexation: The Case of London's Territorial Ambitions during the 1950s and 1960s," *Urban History Review* 29, 1 (2000): 91–103.

Meloche, Jean-Philippe, and Patrick Kilfoil. *La taille du conseil municipal et le coût de représentation démocratiques dans les principales villes du Québec et du Canada*. Montreal: CIRANO, 2013.

Meloche, Jean-Philippe, and François Vaillancourt. *Public Finance in Montreal: In Search of Equity and Efficiency*, IMFG Papers on Municipal Finance and Governance, No.15, University of Toronto Munk Centre of Global Affairs, 2013.

Mévellec, Anne, and Manon Tremblay. "Les partis politiques municipaux: la 'westminsterisation' des villes du Québec?" *Recherches sociographiques* 54, 2 (2013): 325–47.

Mill, John Stuart. *Considerations on Representative Government*. London: Parker, Son, and Bourn, 1861.

Milligan, Ian. "'This Board has a Duty to Intervene': Challenging the Spadina Expressway through the Ontario Municipal Board, 1963–1971," *Urban History Review* 39, 2 (Spring 2011): 25–39.

Milner, Henry. "Gérald Tremblay and the Tragedy of Public Life in Montreal," *Inroads*, 33 (Summer/Fall 2013): 101–7.

Milner, Henry, and Pierre Joncas. "Montreal: Getting through the Megamerger," *Inroads* 11 (2002): 49–63.

Milroy, Beth Moore. "Toronto's Legal Challenge to Amalgamation," in Caroline Andrew, Katherine A. Graham, and Susan Phillips, eds., *Urban Affairs: Back on the Policy Agenda*. Montreal and Kingston: McGill-Queen's University Press, 2002, 157–78.

Mississauga Judicial Inquiry. *Updating the Ethical Infrastructure* (2011).

Momani, Bessma, and Luna Khirfan. "Explaining the Use of Planning Consultants in Ontario Cities," *Canadian Public Administration* 56, 3 (September 2013): 391–413.

Montreal, City of, "Report of the General Auditor to city council and the agglomeration council concerning the audit of the entire process involving the acquisition and installation of water meters in IBIs, as well as the optimization of the entire Montréal agglomeration water network" (September 2009), available at http://ville.montreal.qc.ca/pls/portal/docs/PAGE/VERIFICATEUR_EN/MEDIA/DOCUMENTS/RCE_ANGLAIS_INTERNET.PDF.

Moore, Aaron A. *Planning Politics in Toronto: The Ontario Municipal Board and Urban Development*. Toronto: University of Toronto Press, 2013.

———. "Comparing the Politics of Urban Development in American and Canadian Cities: The Myth of the North-South divide," *International Journal of Canadian Studies* 49 (2014): 229–49.

Morden, John W. *Independent Civilian Review into Matters Relating to the G20 Summit: Report*. Toronto: Toronto Police Services Board, 2012, ch.1. www.tpsb.ca/g20/ICRG20Mordenreport.pdf.

Moretti, Enrico. *The New Geography of Jobs*. Boston and New York: Houghton Mifflin Harcourt, 2012.

Mossberger, Karen. "Urban Regime Analysis," in Jonathan S. Davies and David L. Imbroscio, eds., *Theories of*

Urban Politics, 2nd ed. Los Angeles: Sage, 2009, 40–54.

Moisio, Antti, ed. *Rethinking Local Government: Essays on Municipal Reform.* Helsinki: VATT Publications, 2012.

Nelles, Jen. *Comparative Metropolitan Policy: Governing beyond Local Boundaries in the Imagined Metropolis.* New York, Routledge, 2012.

New Brunswick, Commissioner on the Future of Local Governance (Jean-Guy Finn). *Building Stronger Local Governments and Regions: An Action Plan for the Future of Local Governance in New Brunswick* (2008).

Nordlinger, Eric A. *On the Autonomy of the Democratic State.* Cambridge, MA: Harvard University Press, 1981.

Norton, Alan. *International Handbook of Local and Regional Government.* Brookfield, VT: Edward Elgar, 1994.

Oakerson, Ronald J. *Governing Local Public Economies: Creating the Civic Metropolis.* Oakland, CA: ICS Press, 1999.

O'Brien, Allan. *Municipal Consolidation in Canada and Its Alternatives.* Toronto: ICURR Press, 1993.

O'Connor, M. Rick. *Open Local Government: How Crucial Legislative Changes Impact the Way Municipalities Do Business in Canada,* 2nd ed. St. Thomas, ON: Municipal World, 2004.

O'Flynn, Patrick Eamonn and Tim A. Mau, "A Demographic and Career Profile of Municipal CAOs in Canada: Implications for Local Governance," *Canadian Public Administration* 57, 1 (2014): 154–70

Ohemeng, Frank J., and John K. Grant, "When Markets Fail to Deliver: An Examination of the Privatization and Deprivatization of Water and Wastewater Services Delivery in Hamilton, Canada," *Canadian Public Administration* 51, 3 (2008): 475–99.

Oliver, J. Eric, et al. *Local Elections and the Politics of Small-Scale Democracy.* Princeton, NJ: Princeton University Press, 2012.

Ontario. *Report of the Royal Commission on Metropolitan Toronto, Vol. 2: Detailed Findings and Recommendations.* Toronto, 1977.

———. *Report of the Walkerton Inquiry.* Toronto: Queen's Printer for Ontario, 2002.

Ontario, Committee on Taxation. *Report.* Toronto: Queen's Printer, 1967.

Ontario, Ministry of the Attorney General. The Ipperwash Inquiry, Vol. 2: *Policy Analysis.* Toronto, 2007.

Ontario, Ministry of Public Infrastructure

Renewal, Water Strategy Expert Panel. *Watertight: The Case for Change in Ontario's Water and Wastewater System.* Toronto: Queen's Printer for Ontario, 2005.

Ontario, Ombudsman. *The LHIN Spin: Investigation into the Hamilton Niagara Haldimand Brant Local Health Integration Network's Use of Community Engagement in Its Decision-making Process.* Toronto, August 2010.

Ontario, Ontario Distribution Sector Review Panel. *Renewing Ontario's Electricity Distribution Sector: Putting the Consumer First,* December 2012.

Ostrom, Vincent, Robert Bish, and Elinor Ostrom. *Local Government in the United States.* San Francisco: ICS Press, 1988.

Pal, Leslie A. *Beyond Policy Analysis: Public Issue Management in Turbulent Times,* 5th ed. Toronto: Nelson, 2014.

Parker, Richard. "Calgary: A Uni-City at 50 Years," *Plan Canada* 45, 3 (2005): 29–31.

Parlette, Vanessa and Deborah Cowen. "Dead Malls: Suburban Activism, Local Spaces, Global Logistics," *International Journal of Urban and Regional Research* 35, 4 (July 2011): 794–811.

Peacock, Kurt and Robert MacKinnon, "Federal Land Transfers in New Brunswick," in Michael C. Ircha and Robert Young, eds. *Federal Property Policy in Canadian Municipalities.* Montreal and Kingston: McGill-Queen's University Press, 2013, ch. 3.

Peddle, Francis K. *Cities and Greed: Taxes, Inflation and Land Speculation.* Ottawa: Canadian Research Committee on Taxation, 1994.

Peters, Evelyn J., ed. *Urban Aboriginal Policy Making in Canadian Municipalities.* Montreal and Kingston: McGill-Queen's University Press, 2011.

Peterson, Paul E. *City Limits.* Chicago: University of Chicago Press, 1981.

Phillips, Susan D. "'You Say You Want an Evolution?' From Citizen to Community Engagement in Canadian Cities," in Emmanuel Brunet-Jailly and John F. Martin, eds., *Local Government in a Global World: Australia and Canada in Comparative Perspective.* Toronto: University of Toronto Press, 2010, 55–80.

Pimlott, Ben, and Nirmala Rao. *Governing London.* Oxford: Oxford University Press, 2002.

Plunkett, Thomas J. *City Management in Canada: The Role of the Chief Administrative Officer.* Toronto: Institute of Public Administration of Canada, 1992.

Plunkett, Thomas J., and G.M. Betts. *The Management of Canadian Urban Government: A Basic Text for a Course in Urban Management.* Kingston, ON: Institute of Local Government, Queen's University, 1978.

Plunkett, Thomas J., and James Lightbody. "Tribunals, Politics, and the Public Interest: The Edmonton Annexation Case," *Canadian Public Policy* 8, 2 (1982): 207–21.

Poitras, Lawrence. "La défusion municipale au Québec," Report from the Montreal law office of Borden, Ladner, Gervais, 17 March 2003.

Polèse, Mario. *The Wealth and Poverty of Regions: Why Cities Matter.* Chicago: University of Chicago Press, 2009.

———. "Urban Development Legends," *City Journal* 21, 4 (2011).

Polsby, Nelson W. *Community Power and Political Theory,* 2nd ed. New Haven, CT: Yale University Press, 1980.

Pralle, Sara. "The Mouse that Roared: Agenda Setting in Canadian Pesticide Politics," *Policy Studies* Journal, 34, 2 (2006).

Pressman, Jeffrey L. and Aaron Wildavsky. *Implementation: How Great Expectations in Washington are Dashed in Oakland; or, Why it's Amazing that Federal Programs Work at All, This Being a Saga of the Economic Development Administration as Told by Two Sympathetic Observers Who Seek to Build Morals on a Foundation of Ruined Hopes.* Berkeley: University of California Press, 1973.

Prince, Michael J. "Self-regulation, Exhortation, and Symbolic Politics," in Glen Toner, Leslie A. Pal, and Michael J. Prince, eds. *Policy: From Ideas to Implementation.* Montreal and Kingston: McGill-Queen's University Press, 2010, pp. 77–108.

Pudcrei, Henry A. *Urban Perspectives and Measurement,* Statistics Canada Geography Working Paper Series (2009), Catalogue no. 92F0138M — No. 2009001, available at www.statcan.gc.ca/pub/92f0138m/92f0138m2009001 eng.pdf.

Québec. *Pacte 2000: Rapport de la Commission nationale sur les finances et la fiscalité locales.* Quebec, 1999.

Quebec, Bureau d'audiences publiques sur l'environnement, Rapport de la Commission sur la gestion de l'eau au Québec, Tome 2. *L'eau, ressource à protéger, à partager et à mettre en valeur.* Quebec, 2000.

Quebec, Municipal Affairs and Greater Montreal. *Municipal Reorganisation: Changing the Ways to Better Serve the Public.* Quebec: Gouvernement du Québec, 2000.

Quebec, Ministère des Affaires Municipales. *Regroupements municipaux dans la région métropolitaine de Montréal: Recommandations du mandataire.* Quebec, 2000.

Rae, Douglas W. "Two Cheers for Very Unequal Incomes: Toward Social Justice in Central Cities," in Clarissa Rile Hayward and Todd Swanstrom, eds., *Justice and the American Metropolis.* Minneapolis: University of Minnesota Press, 2011.

Ranasinghe, Prashan, and Mariana Valverde. "Governing Homelessness Through Land-use: A Sociological Study of the Toronto Shelter Housing By-law," *Canadian Journal of Sociology* 31, 3 (2006): 325–49.

Rayside, David M. *A Small Town in Modern Times: Alexandria, Ontario.* Montreal and Kingston: McGill-Queen's University Press, 1991.

Relph, Edward. *Toronto: Transformations in a City and its Region.* Philadelphia: University of Pennsylvania Press, 2014.

Renzetti, Steven, and Colin Busby. "Water Pricing: Infrastructure Grants Hinder Necessary Reform," *Policy Options* (July–August, 2009): 32–5.

Rich, S. George. "Winnipeg: Innovations in Governing a Metropolis," in R. Charles Bryfogle and Ralph R. Krueger, eds., *Urban Problems,* revised ed. Toronto: Holt, Rinehart, and Winston, 1975, 341–51.

Richardson, Jesse J. Jr. "Dillon's Rule is from Mars, Home Rule is from Venus: Local Government Autonomy and the Rules of Statutory Construction," *Publius: The Journal of Federalism* 41, 4 (2011): 662–85.

Richmond, Dale, and David Siegel, eds. *Agencies, Boards, and Commissions in Canadian Local Government.* Toronto: Institute of Public Administration of Canada, 1994.

Robinson, Danielle. "'The Streets Belong to the People': Expressway Disputes in Canada, c. 1960–75," Ph.D. thesis, McMaster University, 2012.

Robison, John C. "Public Participation in Restructuring Local Governments to Create the City of Miramichi," in Graham and Phillips, eds., *Citizen Engagement,* pp. 188–99.

Rogers, Ian M. *Canadian Law of Planning and Zoning.* Toronto: Carswell, 1973.

Rogers, N. "Serving Toronto the Good: The Development of the City Police Force,

1834–84," in Victor L. Russell, ed., *Forging a Consensus: Historical Essays on Toronto*. Toronto: University of Toronto Press, 1984.

Rohe, William H. *The Research Triangle: From Tobacco Road to Global Prominence*. Philadelphia: University of Pennsylvania Press, 2011.

Rusk, David. *Cities without Suburbs, A Census 2010 Perspective*, 4th ed. Washington DC: Woodrow Wilson Centre Press, 2013.

Ruttan, Susan. "Supersized: Forged in Secrecy, Alberta's New Health Superboard Continues the Dismantling of Public Healthcare," *Alberta Views* (November 2009): 32–7.

Sancton, Andrew. "Montreal," in Magnusson and Sancton, eds., *City Politics*, pp. 58–93.

———. *Governing the Island of Montreal: Language Differences and Metropolitan Politics*. Berkeley: University of California Press, 1985.

———. *Governing Canada's City Regions*. Montreal: Institute for Research on Public Policy, 1994.

———. "Reducing Costs by Consolidating Municipalities: New Brunswick, Nova Scotia, Ontario," *Canadian Public Administration* 39, 3 (1996): 267–89.

———. "Negotiating, Arbitrating, Legislating: Where Was the Public in London's Boundary Adjustment?" in Graham and Phillips, eds., *Citizen Engagement*, pp. 163–87.

———. "Amalgamations, Service Realignment, and Property Taxes: Did the Harris Government Have a Plan for Ontario's Municipalities?" *Canadian Journal of Regional Science* 33, 1 (2000): 135–56.

———. *Merger Mania: The Assault on Local Government*. Montreal and Kingston: McGill-Queen's University Press, 2000.

———. "Why Municipal Amalgamations? Halifax, Toronto, Montreal," in Young and Leuprecht, eds., *Municipal–Federal–Provincial Relations in Canada*, pp. 119–37.

———. "Fusions et défusions municipales au Québec et en Ontario', in François Pétry, Éric Bélanger, and Louis M. Imbeau, eds., *Le Parti Libéral: Enquête sur les Réalisations du Gouvernement Charest*. Québec: Les Presses de l'Université Laval, 2006, 321–38.

———. *The Limits of Boundaries: Why City-Regions Cannot Be Self-governing*. Montreal and Kingston: McGill-Queen's University Press, 2008.

———. "The Urban Agenda," in Herman Bakvis and Grace Skogstad, eds., *Canadian Federalism: Performance, Effectiveness, and Legitimacy*, 3rd ed. Toronto: Oxford University Press, 2008, 302–19.

———. "Introduction," in Andrew Sancton and Robert Young, eds., *Foundations of Governance: Municipal Governance in Canada's Provinces*. Toronto: University of Toronto Press, 2009, pp. 3–19.

———. "Democratic Policing: Lessons from Ipperwash and Caledonia," *Canadian Public Administration* 55, 3 (2012): 365–83.

Sancton, Andrew, Rebecca James, and Rick Ramsay. *Amalgamation vs. Inter-municipal Cooperation: Financing Local and Infrastructure Services*. Toronto: ICURR Press, 2000.

Sancton, Andrew, and Byron Montgomery. "Municipal Government and Residential Land Development: A Comparative Study of London, Ontario in the 1920s and 1980s," in Frances Frisken, ed., *The Changing Canadian Metropolis*, Vol. 2. Berkeley, CA: Institute of Governmental Studies, University of California, 1994, 777–98.

Sancton, Andrew, and Paul Woolner. "Full-time Municipal Councillors: A Strategic Challenge for Canadian Urban Government," *Canadian Public Administration* 33, 4 (1990): 482–505.

Sancton, Andrew, and Robert Young, eds. *Foundations of Governance: Municipal Governance in Canada's Provinces*. Toronto: University of Toronto Press, 2009.

Savage, Larry. "Organized Labour and Local Politics: Ontario's 2006 Municipal Elections," *Labour/Le Travail* 62 (Fall 2008): 171–85.

Schobel, Kurt. "How Much is Enough? A Study of Municipal Councillor Remuneration," *Canadian Public Administration* 57, 1 (2014): 138–53.

Sewell, John. *Police in Canada: The Real Story*. Toronto: Lorimer, 2010.

Shipan, Charles R., and Craig Volden. "Policy Diffusion: Seven Lessons for Scholars and Practitioners," *Public Administration Review* 72, 6 (2012): 788–96.

Siegel, David. "Ontario," in Sancton and Young, eds., *Foundations of Governance*, pp. 20–69.

———. "The Leadership Role of the Municipal Chief Administrative Officer," *Canadian Public Administration* 50, 2 (2010): 139–61.

———. *Leaders in the Shadows: The Leadership Qualities of Municipal Chief Administrative Officers*. Toronto: University of Toronto Press, forthcoming in 2015.

Siemiatycki, Myer. *The Diversity Gap: The Electoral Under-Representation of Visible Minorities.* Toronto: Ryerson Centre for Immigration and Settlement, 2011.

Slack, Enid. "Revenue Sharing Options for Canada's Hub Cities," a report prepared for the Meeting of Canada's Hub City Mayors. 17–18 September 2004.

Slack, Enid, and Richard M. Bird, "Merging Municipalities: Is Bigger Better?" in Antti Moisio, ed., *Rethinking Local Government* (2012).

Smith, P.J., and H.L. Diemer. "Equity and the Annexation Process," in P.J. Smith, ed., *Edmonton: The Emerging Metropolitan Pattern.* Victoria, BC: University of Victoria Department of Geography, 1978, 263–89.

Smith, Patrick J. "Even Greater Vancouver: Metropolitan Morphing in Canada's Third-Largest City Region," in Don Phares, ed., *Governing Metropolitan Regions in the 21st Century.* Armonk, NY: M.E. Sharpe, 2009, 237–63.

Smith, Patrick, and Kennedy Stewart. "British Columbia," in Sancton and Young, eds., *Foundations of Governance,* pp. 282–313.

Spicer, Zachary. "Institutional Policy Learning and Formal Federal-Urban Engagement in Canada," *Commonwealth Journal of Local Governance* 7 (2010): 99–119.

———. "Post-amalgamation Politics: How Does Consolidation Impact Community Decision-making?" *Canadian Journal of Urban Research* 21.2 (2012): 90–111.

———. "Regional Organization and the Dynamics of Inter-municipal Cooperation: Policy Coordination between Ontario's Separated Cities and Counties," Ph.D. thesis, University of Western Ontario, 2013.

Statistics Canada. Rural and Small Town Analysis Bulletin, Nov. 2008, Catalogue no. 21–006X01–M.

———. *2011 Census of Canada.*

———. *Canada's Rural Population Since 1851: Population and Dwelling Counts, 2011 Census,* Catalogue no. 98-310-X2011003.

Stenning, P.C. "The Role of Police Boards and Commissions as Institutions of Municipal Police Governance," in C.D. Shearing, ed., *Organizational Police Deviance.* Toronto: Butterworths, 1981.

Stephens, G. Ross, and Nelson Wikstrom. *Metropolitan Government and Governance: Theoretical Perspectives, Empirical Analysis, and the Future.* New York: Oxford University Press, 2000.

Stewart, Ian. "The Dangers of Municipal Reform in Nova Scotia," in Peter Clancy et al., *The Savage Years: The Perils of Reinventing Government in Nova Scotia.* Halifax: Formac, 2000, pp. 199–227.

Stewart, Kennedy and Patrick J. Smith. "Immature Policy Analysis: Building Capacity in Eight Major Canadian Cities," in Laurent Dobuzinskis, Michael Howlett, and David Laycock, eds., *Policy Analysis in Canada: The State of the Art.* Toronto: University of Toronto Press, 2007.

Stoker, Gerry. "Introduction: Normative Theories of Local Government and Democracy," in Desmond King and Gerry Stoker, eds., *Rethinking Local Democracy.* Houndsmills, Basingstoke, Hampshire: Macmillan, 1996, pp. 1–25.

Stone, Clarence. *Regime Politics: Governing Atlanta, 1946–1988.* Lawrence: University Press of Kansas, 1989.

———. "Rethinking the Policy-Politics Connection," *Policy Studies* 26, 3 and 4 (2005): 241–60.

Stoney, Christopher, and Katherine A.H. Graham. "Federal–Municipal Relations in Canada: The Changing Organizational Landscape," *Canadian Public Administration* 52, 3 (2009): 371–94.

Studlar, Donley T. *Tobacco Control: Comparative Politics in the United States and Canada.* Peterborough, ON: Broadview Press, 2002.

Svara, James H. "The Shifting Boundary between Elected Officials and City Managers in Large Council-Manager Cities," *Public Administration Review* 59, 1 (February 1999): 44–53.

Tassé, Roger. *Review of the Toronto Port Authority Report.* October 2006.

Taylor, Zack. "If Different, then Why? Explaining the Divergent Development of Canadian and American Local Governance," *International Journal of Canadian Studies* 49 (2014): 53–79.

Taylor, Zack and Gabriel Eidelman, "Canadian Political Science and the City: A Limited Engagement," *Canadian Journal of Political Science* 43, 4 (December 2010): 961–81.

Ternette, Nick. "Glen Murray's Failed New Deal," *Canadian Dimension* 38, 5 (September–October 2004). At canadiandimension.com/articles/1961.

Thomas, Timothy Lloyd. *A City with a Difference: The Rise and Fall of the Montreal Citizens' Movement.* Montreal: Véhicule Press, 1997.

Tiebout, Charles. "A Pure Theory of Local

Expenditure," *Journal of Political Economy* 64 (1956): 416–24.

Tindal, C. Richard et al. *Local Government in Canada*, 8th ed. Toronto: Nelson, 2013.

Tolley, Erin. "Do Women 'Do Better' in Municipal Politics? Electoral Representation across Three Levels of Government." *Canadian Journal of Political Science* 44, 3 (September 2011): 573–94.

Tolley, Erin, and Robert Young, eds., *Immigration Settlement Policy in Canadian Municipalities*. Montreal and Kingston: McGill-Queen's University Press, 2011.

Tomas, Mariona. *Penser métropolitain: La bataille politique du Grand Montréal* (Québec: Les presses de l'Université du Québec, 2012.

Toronto Computer Leasing Inquiry/Toronto External Contracts Inquiry. *Report*. 2005.

Trent, Peter. *The Merger Delusion: How Swallowing its Suburbs Made an even Bigger Mess of Montreal*. Montreal and Kingston: McGill-Queen's University Press, 2012.

Treisman, Daniel. *The Architecture of Government: Rethinking Political Decentralization*. Cambridge: Cambridge University Press, 2007.

Troy, Leo. *The Twilight of the Old Unionism*. Armonk, NY: M.E. Sharpe, 2004.

Urbaniak, Tom. *Her Worship: Hazel McCallion and the Development of Mississauga*. Toronto: University of Toronto Press, 2009.

———. "Studying Mayoral Leadership in Canada and the United States," *International Journal of Canadian Studies* 49 (2014): 205–27.

Valverde, Mariana. *Everyday Life on the Street: City Governance in an Age of Diversity*. Chicago: University of Chicago Press, 2012.

Vancouver. "A City of Neighbourhoods: Report of the 2004 Electoral Reform Commission," 2004.

Viteritti, Joseph P., ed. *When Mayors Take Charge: School Governance in the City*. Washington: Brookings Institution Press, 2009.

Vojnovic, Igor. "The Fiscal Distribution of the Provincial-Municipal Service Exchange in Nova Scotia," *Canadian Public Administration* 42 (1999): 512–41.

———. "Municipal Consolidation, Regional Planning, and Fiscal Accountability," *Canadian Journal of Regional Science* 23, 1 (2000): 49–72.

Walisser, Brian, Gary Paget, and Michelle Dann, "New Pathways to Effective Regional Governance: Canadian Reflections," in Graham Sansom and Peter McKinlay, eds., *New Century Local Government: Commonwealth Perspectives*. London: Commonwealth Secretariat, 2013, 145–68.

Warren, Mark E. "Voting with Your Feet: Exit-based Empowerment in Democratic Theory," *American Political Science Review* 105, 4 (2011): 683–701.

Waterloo, City of, Judicial Inquiry. *Final Report of the Commissioner*. 2003.

Weaver, John C. *Crimes, Constables, and Courts: Order and Transgression in a Canadian City, 1816–1970*. Montreal and Kingston: McGill-Queen's University Press, 1995.

Williams, Robert. " . . . we think it is the last time," *Municipal World* 122, 11 (November 2012): 39–42.

Wirth, Louis. "Urbanism as a Way of Life," *American Journal of Sociology* 44 (1938): 3–24.

Wolman, Harold. "Local Economic Development Policy: What Explains the Divergence between Political Analysis and Political Behaviour?" *Journal of Urban Affairs* 10, 1 (1988): 19–28.

Yates, Douglas. *The Ungovernable City: The Politics of Urban Problems and Policy Making*. Cambridge, MA: MIT Press, 1978.

Young Robert, and Christian Leuprecht, eds. *Municipal–Federal–Provincial Relations in Canada*. Montreal and Kingston: McGill-Queen's University Press, 2006.

Young, Robert, and Kelly McCarthy. "Why Do Municipal Issues Rise and Fall on the Federal Policy Agenda in Canada?" *Canadian Public Administration* 52, 3 (2009): 347–70.

INDEX

Abdallah, Robert, 272
Aboriginal governance, xv
Aboriginal people, in cities and CMAs, 88
administration. *see* management and
  managers
administrative tribunals, 33–5
Agence métropolitaine de transport (AMT),
  68
agricultural land, in annexations, 93, 103–4
airport authorities, 66–8
Alberta: CMAs, 85–6; Edmonton and
  annexations, 99; expenditures and
  revenues, 294, 296; Local Authorities
  Board (LAB), 97–9; mayors, 228; number
  of municipalities, 9; regional partnerships,
  134–6; social services provision, 23
Alberta Capital Regional Alliance (ACRA),
  135
Alexandria, ON, 174–5
Allen Road, Toronto, 119
allocative efficiency, 16–17
amalgamations: British Columbia, 138, 170;
  Cape Breton and Halifax, NS, 146–9;
  commissioners in, 151–2; creation, 336; de-
  amalgamations, 153–4, 165–9; definition,
  91–2; financial aspects, 147, 149, 155–6;
  linguistic aspects, 162, 163, 164; Montreal,
  QC, 162–5, 168–9; New Brunswick,
  146; Ontario, 149–61, 336; opposition
  to, 153–4, 156–8; PEI, 145–6; provincial
  governments, generally, 138, 169, 336;
  Quebec government, 141, 161–3, 168–9,
  336; St. John's, NL, 144–5; Toronto,
  ON, 154–9; "voluntary", 152–3; wards
  population, 186–7; Windsor, ON, 139–41,
  336; Winnipeg's Unicity, 142–4, 336
ambulance services, 24
annexations: arbitration, 105–6; and
  boundaries, 91, 92–3; Calgary, AB, 107–9;
  definition, 91–2; Edmonton, AB, 96–100,
  109; financial issues, 95, 96; limits and
  alternatives to, 112–13; London, ON,
  100–6; Montreal, QC, 94–6; Ontario
  government in, 104–6, 109–10; process
  and mechanisms, 92–4, 109–10; and public
  policy, 102–3; Regina, SK, 109; Toronto,
  ON, 117
arbitration, 105–6, 280
arenas, 277–8
assets and liabilities, 290–1, 292
Atlanta, GA, 174, 237–8, 239
at-large elections, 188–90

autonomy, 250–1, 330, 334–5
average-cost pricing, 304–5

Baldwin Act (Canada, 1849), 5
bankruptcies, 95, 140
Barrie, ON, 109–10
Barrie–Innisfil Boundary Adjustment Act
  (Ontario, 2009), 109–10
Beaumont, AB, 100
Bédard Report (QC), 162
Berger, Thomas R., 189–90
Bernard, Louis, and report, 163–4
Betts, G.M., 278–9
big-box stores, 212
Bill 24 (Quebec, 2000), 161
Bill 26 (Ontario, 1996), 150–1, 152
Bill 28 (Alberta, 2013), 136
Bill 170 (Quebec, 2000), 161, 164
Billy Bishop Toronto City Airport, 66, 67, 243
Bird, Richard M., 156
blockbusting by developers, 216
Board of Public Utilities (Alberta), 108.
  see also Local Authorities Board (LAB)
  (Alberta)
boards of commissioners, 230–1
Borins, Justice Stephen, 157–8
Bouchard, Lucien, and government, 162–3,
  164
boundaries, 91, 92–3, 188, 333–4
Bourque, Pierre, 161–2, 165, 166, 180
branding, 257
Brant, John, 105–6
Britain, 3–7, 48, 53
British Columbia: amalgamations, 138, 170;
  central funding of local government, 36;
  conflict of interests, 197; council meetings,
  193–4; expenditures and revenues, 294,
  296; land-use regulation, 33–4; municipal
  parties, 180–1; number of municipalities,
  9; police boards, 51–2; regional districts, 8,
  129–33, 137; regulation of municipalities,
  330; social services provision, 23–4;
  TransLink, 62–3
British North America Act, 27, 49
Brockton, ON, 276
brokers, mayors as, 239–40
budgets: capital and operating budgets,
  295–301; description, 295–301;
  precommitment, 263–4, 298; and property
  tax, 315–16; reserve funds, 298–9. see also
  finances and financing
Budweiser Gardens, 277–8

Buffalo Pound Water Administration Board, 63–4
built environment, control by municipality, 25, 263, 337–8
businesses, property tax, 322–3

C4LD (Citizens for Local Democracy), 157
Cadillac-Fairview company, 211
Calgary, AB, 24, 107–9, 135–6, 183, 245–7
Calgary Regional Partnership (CRP), 135–6
Cambridge, ON, 196–7
Cameron, Donald, 146–7
Campbell, Gordon, 179
Campbell, Larry, 179, 241–2
Campeau Corporation, 212
Canada Marine Act (1998), 65
Canadian Charter of Rights and Freedoms, 6–7, 49, 157–8
Canadian Intergovernmental Conference Secretariat, 32
Canadian Labour Congress, 281
Canadian Union of Public Employees (CUPE), 277, 279
Cape Breton, NS, 146–7
Cape Breton Regional Municipality, 147
capital budgets, 295–301
capital investments subsidies, 309–12
Capital Region Board (CRB) (Alberta), 135
Capital Region Growth Plan: Growing Forward (CRB), 135
census, as resource, 89
census agglomerations (CA), 79–80
census metropolitan areas (CMAs):
    consolidationist vs. public-choice approaches, 113–17; description, 79–81; population, 80–1, 84, 86–8; and provinces, 84, 85–6. see also specific CMAs
central governments. see federal government; provinces and provincial governments
Charbonneau Commission of Inquiry, 272–3
Charest, Jean, and government, 165, 166, 168–9
Charlottetown, PEI, 145–6
Charter of the French Language (QC), 162, 164
charters, for cities, 4, 30, 94, 334
Chatham–Kent, ON, 151–2
chief administrative officers (CAO), 270–3
cities: branding, 257; charters, 4, 30, 94, 334; definition in Canada, 87; development vs. preservation, 214–16; dowtown shopping areas, 211–13; financial role, 24; and globalization, 86–8; immigration and ethnic makeup, 87–8; inner-city neighbourhoods, 216–17; new reform movement, 217–20; old buildings, 213–15
citizens: in local decision-making, 19–21; meetings and consultations, 222–3; and neighbourhood changes, 223–4; new

reform movement, 218, 220; participation, 19–21, 142–3, 218, 222–4, 340; policy-making in municipalities, 258–62; resistance to development, 215; and subdivisions, 209
Citizens for Local Democracy (C4LD), 157
city managers, role, 270–1
City of Toronto Act (1997), 150, 252
Civic Action League, 179
Civic Party, 179–80, 181
CMAs. see census metropolitan areas (CMAs)
Cobban, Timothy, 100–1, 256, 277
Coderre, Denis, 180, 273
collective and multilateral bargaining, 278–80, 285
commercial property, 210–13
Committee of Progressive Electors (COPE), 179, 218–19
committees of the whole, 190–1
committee systems in municipalities, 190–1
Common Sense Revolution (CSR) in Ontario, 150
communities of interest, in wards, 187–8
community economic development, 257
community power, in councils, 174–5
commuters, 79–80, 327
conditional grants, 253
conditional transfers, 35–7
condominiums, 220–2
conflict of interests, 196–7
conservation authorities, in Ontario, 61–2
consolidation, Metro Toronto, 118
consolidationist position, 112–15, 116–17
Constitution, and role of governments, 27–9
Constitution Act, 1867 and 1982, 27, 29, 49
contracting out, 273–6, 284–5
Co-operative Commonwealth Federation (CCF), 178–9
core, 79
corruption, 272
councillors: on committees, 191; conflict of interests, 196–7; contributions from developers, 219–20; as employees, 194–6; meetings, 192–4, 223, 240; minority representation, 198–9; numbers of, 182–4, 185; role, 340–1
council–manager plan, 270
councils: committee systems, 190–1; costs, 183; decision making, 174–6, 182, 188–91, 237; and development, 201, 217–18, 219–20, 224, 255; executive committees, 230–2; openness of meetings and votes, 192–4; policy-making, 250–1; population and councillors, 182–3, 185; size, 182–5; structure and composition, 182, 198–9; terms of office, 197. see also councillors; elections (municipal); mayors
counties, 7–8
Craig, Mayor, 196–7

Crawford, K. Grant, 141
creative class, 257
Croll, David, 140
Crombie, David, 218
Cuff, George B., 230–1
Cumming, Lorne, 117

Dahl, Robert, 237
Davis, Bill, 119
de-amalgamations, 153–4, 165–9
Death and Life of Great American Cities, The (Jacobs), 215
decision making: and citizens, 19–21; councils, 174–6, 182, 188–91, 237; and power, 174–5; urban pluralism and regimes, 237–9
Denmark, 336
denominational rights, 29, 48–9
dense development, 209
Developers, The (Lorimer), 220
developers and development industry: campaign funding, 200; and citizens, 215, 223; commercial property, 210–13; condominiums, 220–2; contributions, 219–20; and councils, 201, 217–18, 219–20, 224, 255; development charges, 206–7, 300; financing of infrastructure, 208–9; infrastructure development, 205–7; inner-city neighbourhoods, 216–17; old buildings into new ones, 213–15; and politics, 178, 201; Stoneybrook subdivision, 207–10; studies of, 220; subdivision agreements, 205–7; in Toronto, ON, 220–2; urban reform movement, 217–20
Dillon's rule, 30
directeur-général, 271–3
Donahue, John D., 282–3
Doré, Jean, 180
downtown shopping areas, 211–13
Drapeau, Jean, 96, 179–80, 181, 241
drinking water. see water supply and services

economies of scale, 15–16
economies of scope, 18
economy: efficiency of local government, 15–18; globalization and competitiveness, 86–8; growth policies, 254–5; influence on councils, 175–6; old buildings vs. new in cities, 213–14; policy-making in municipalities, 254–8; precommitment, 263–4; urban-development legends, 256–7
Edmonton, AB, 96–100, 109, 134–5, 278
education: constitutional aspects, 29, 49; denominational rights, 48–9; linguistic rights, 49–50; as merit goods, 301–2; property tax, 325; responsibility for, 24, 48; school boards, 48–50; for urban and rural areas, 78
efficiency of local government, 15–18, 20

elections (municipal): at-large, 188–90; campaign financing, 199–200; elites in, 175; mayors, 228; minority representation, 198–9; non-partisan approach, 178; terms of office, 197–9; Toronto, ON, 158–9; turnout, 198; and unions, 280–2; Vancouver, BC, 188–90; voters mobilization, 176; in wards, 185–90
election system in Canada, 185–6
electricity provision, 59–60
Emergency Management Act (Ontario, 2002), 252–3
employees, 250–1, 252, 268–70, 327
Enabling Regional Growth Boards Act (Bill 28) (Alberta, 2013), 136
England, 3–7, 48, 53
environmentalism, 219
Essex Border Utilities Commission (EBUC), 139
Europe, 332–3, 336
Eves, Ernie, 153
executive committees, 230–2
expenditures, 10–11, 290, 291–5
expressways, 119, 215–16
externalities, 38–40

Farbrother, Simon, 271
fares. see user fees and user-fee services
farmland, in annexations, 93, 103–4
federal government: constitutional role, 27–9; funding of local government, 36; infrastructure programs, 253–4; intergovernmental special-purpose bodies, 65–8; involvement in local issues, 38–41; and mayors, 242–3; municipal regulations, 28; national parties in local politics, 176–7; non-financial assets, 291–2; policy-making in municipalities, 253–4; presence in municipalities, 42–3; subsidies, 40–1; taxation, 322, 327–8; transfers, 293–5, 296
Federation of Canadian Municipalities (FCM), 41–3, 44
Fewer Municipal Politicians Act (Ontario, 1999), 159–60
finances and financing: assets and liabilities, 290–1, 292; capital investments subsidies, 309–12; data presentation, 290; debt in municipalities, 208–9; expenditures and revenues, 10–11, 290, 291–5, 296; infrastructure of subdivisions, 208–9; by local improvement taxes, 204–5; net worth and net financial worth, 291–2; payments-in-lieu (PILs), 295, 296, 322–3; provinces' role, 35–7; rates structures, 308–9; subdivision agreements, 205–7; by tax revenues and usage, 307–8; transfers, provincial and federal, 35–7, 293–5, 296; user fees, 301–6; water supply services, 306–12. see also budgets; property tax

fire services and firefighters, 280, 311, 338
Fischel, William, 223
Florida, Richard, 257
Foran, Max, 108
Ford, Rob: garbage collection, 274–5; public transit, 69; style and policies, 243–5, 246–7; taxation for funding, 37, 326; votes for, 159
Forest Lawn, AB, 107–8
Fort McMurray, AB, 76
fragmentation, 94
France, 335, 336
franchises, 58
fringe development, 93
Frisken, Frances, 117, 119
Frost, Leslie, 117
Fundy Regional Services Commission, 146
Fyfe, Stewart, 121–2

G20 summit (2010), 55–6
garbage collection, 274–5, 303–4
Gardiner Expressway, Toronto, 216
gas tax, 37
gentrification, 217
geographical townships, 7–8
George, Henry, 321
Georgia, US, land use plans, 262
Glaeser, Edward, 213
globalization, 86–8, 331–2
Goldenberg, H. Carl, 118
Goldenberg commission, 118
GO Transit, 69
government: rescaling, 331–2, 336; role in Constitution, 27–9; tri-level relations, 242–3. see also federal government; local government; provinces and provincial governments
governmental entities, 5–8, 9–10
governmental functions, international comparisons, 331–3
Graham, Katherine, 279
Greater Golden Horseshoe: definition and boundaries, 81–2; land use and planning, 82–3; population, 80, 82, 84; provincial policy, 82–5; regional municipalities in, 122
Greater Sudbury, ON, 160
Greater Toronto Airports Authority (GTAA), 67–8
Greater Toronto Area (GTA), 82
Greater Toronto Civic Action Alliance, 156
Greater Vancouver Regional District (GVRD), 130–3
Green, Sidney, 142–3
Greenbelt Act (Ontario, 2005), 82
Greenbelt area, 82–3
Green Municipal Fund, 42
Growth Plan for the Greater Golden Horseshoe, 82–3
Guelph, ON, 281

Halifax, NS, 146–9, 183–4, 187
Halifax Regional Municipality (HRM), 148–9, 183–4
Halton, ON, 124
Hamilton, ON, 69, 160, 275–6, 306
Harcourt, Mike, 179
hard services, 338–9
Harel, Louise, 162, 180
Harper, Stephen, 36, 242–3
Harris, Mike, and government, 150, 152, 155, 156–7, 336
Hayward, C. William, 147–8
heads of council, 228–9. see also mayors
healthcare, 24, 69–70, 301–2
Hébert, Guy, 272–3
heritage property, 214–15
high-rise buildings, 215–17
Hodgson, Chris, 153
homelessness, subsidies, 40–1
Homelessness Partnering Strategy (HPS), 41
home rule, 30, 141, 335–6
Hudson, QC, 259–60
Hyndman, Lou, 134–5

Île-Jésus, QC, 141
immigration, impact on cities, 87–8
Imperial Oil Company, 100–1
implementation, of policy decisions, 264–5
in camera meetings, 192
income taxes, 326–8
incorporated and unincorporated areas, 7–8
independence, 250–1, 330, 334–5
Independent Citizens' Election Committee, 233–4
industrial parks and clusters, 256–7
industry in municipalities, 256–7, 320
infrastructure: development and planning, 205–8; federal and provincial programs, 253–4; financing, 208–9; precommitment, 263–4; subsidies, 40; water supply, 309–10
inner-city neighbourhoods, 216–17
Insite, 36
intergovernmental special-purpose bodies, 64–8
inter-municipal issues and special-purpose bodies, 43–4, 61–4
International City Managers' Association (ICMA), 270–1
Ipperwash occupation, 52–3, 54

Jacobs, Jane, 213, 215–16
John Labatt Centre, 277–8
Juba, Stephen, 232–4, 241
Judicial Committee of the Privy Council, 140–1

Kawartha Lakes, ON, 153–4
Kent County, ON, 151–2

Kitchen, Harry, 153, 297, 305, 308, 328
Kulisek, Larry, 139

land development, policy by municipalities, 202
landownership, registration system, 203
Landry, Bernard, 166
land subdivision. *see* subdivision of land
land use and land-use planning: administrative tribunals, 33–4; citizens participation, 223; Greater Golden Horseshoe, 82–3; infrastructure development, 208; plans by municipality, 262; precommitment, 262–3; shopping malls, 210
Lastman, Mel, 158–9
Laval, QC, 141
Leach, Al, 151, 155
Leduc County, AB, 100
legal authority, municipality and local government, 22–5
Léger, Claude, 272
Levine, Allan, 232, 233
library boards, as special-purpose bodies, 8–9, 57
Linden, Justice Sidney, 52–3, 54–5
Lindsay, ON, 153, 154
linguistic aspects, in amalgamation, 162, 163, 164
linguistic rights, 29, 49–50
Livable Region Plan (LRP) (GVRD), 130
Local Authorities Board (LAB) (Alberta), 97–9, 107–8
local government: administrative tribunals, 33–5; assessment of, 339–41; autonomy, 334–5; and central governments priorities, 39–41; citizens participation, 19–21, 340; competition between, 17–18; complexity of system, 333–4; components, 10; conditional grants, 253; constitutional recognition, 3; definition, 3, 10, 332; differentiation of services, 17; efficiency, 15–18, 20; employment in, 268–9; expenditures and revenues, 10–11; externalities and central governments, 38–40; federal funding, 36; functions, 22–5, 332–3; globalization and neo-liberalism, 87–8, 331–2; hard services, 339; historical origins, 3–7; importance, 337–9; international comparisons, 331–7; legal authority, 23; money and provincial governments, 35–7; municipalities in, 3; own-source revenues, 11; pluralism in, 21–2; policy-making, 252–3; and provinces, 13–22, 35–7; provincial ministries and ministers, 32–3; provincial statutes, 29–32; and trade, 87–8. *see also* municipalities; special-purpose bodies
local improvement taxes, 204–5
London, ON: annexations, 100–6;

communities of interest in wards, 187–8; public–private partnership for arena, 277–8; shopping malls, 210–13; Stoneybrook subdivision, 207–10; water authority and supply, 63, 306
London, UK, 4, 113, 119
London East, ON, 101–2
London Township, ON, 100–1, 102, 104
Longueuil, QC, 6–7
Lorimer, James, 142–3, 220
lower-income residents and homeowners, 209, 217, 324–5
lower-tier municipalities, 8

McCallion, Hazel, 67–8, 124–5, 196, 234–6, 241, 245
McDavid, James C., 149, 274
MacDermid, Robert, 200
McGuinty, Dalton, and government, 153–4, 242–3
McNally, Frederick, 107
McNally Commission and report, 107, 113
Maisonneuve, QC, 95
Makuch, Stanley M., 194
management and managers: city managers and CAO, 270–1; contracting out, 273–6, 284–5; disunity, 279–80; features, 268–70; mismanagement, 271–3; public–private partnerships, 276–8; unions, 278–84
Manitoba: amalgamations, 142–3; campaign financing, 200; central government funding, 36; expenditures and revenues, 294, 296; number of municipalities, 9
Marcoux, Alain, 273
marginal-cost pricing, 304–5
market value of property, 223–4, 317–18, 319–20, 321, 326
Martin, Paul, 241–3
Masonville, ON, 211–12
Matthews Group, 207–8
mayors: as brokers, 239–40; and central governments, 228–9, 242–3; as innovators, 240, 241–2; leadership styles, 239–47; legal status and role, 228–30, 340–1; power of, 229, 231, 232–6, 241, 246–7; system in US, 229
meetings of councils, 192–4, 223, 240
merit goods, 302
Metrolinx, 69
Metropolitan Corporation of Greater Winnipeg, 120–1
"metropolitan problem", 112
Metro Toronto, 117–20, 121, 122–4, 154–5
Metro Vancouver, 130–3
Metro Vancouver 2040 (GVRD), 130
Meyboom, Peter, 151
Miller, David, 66, 158–9, 241–3, 281–2
Mimico, ON, 117
Ministry of Municipal Affairs (ON), 104–5

minorities, in councils, 198–9
Minto Midtown company, 221–2
mismanagement, 271–3
Mississauga, ON, 67–8, 124–5, 196, 234–6
Moncton, NB, 146, 253, 276
Montgomery, AB, 108
Montreal, QC: amalgamations, 162–5, 168–9;
   annexations, 94–6; charter and boundaries,
   94; de-amalgamation, 165–9; executive
   committees, 231–2; managerial turmoil,
   272–3; metropolitan communities, 128–9;
   municipal organization, 167–8; new reform
   movement, 218–19; police, 52, 126–7;
   political parties, 179–80; public transit,
   60–1, 68; as supra-regional government, 8,
   128–9
Montreal Citizens' Movement (MCM), 180,
   218–19
Montreal Island Citizens' Union, 180
Montreal Metropolitan Community (MMC),
   168
Montreal Urban Community (MUC), 126–8
Moore, Aaron A., 220
Moose Jaw, SK, 63–4
Morden, John W., 55–6
multi-purpose authorities, 333–4
Municipal Act (Ontario, 2006), 252
municipal acts, 30
Municipal Boundary Negotiations Act
   (Ontario, 1981), 104
municipal corporations. see municipalities
Municipal Corporations Act (Canada, 1849),
   5
Municipal Corporations Act (UK, 1835), 4
municipalities: amalgamations (see
   amalgamations); annexations (see
   annexations); arrangements, 333–4;
   associations and organizations, 41–5;
   autonomy, 330, 335; budgets (see budgets);
   built environment, 25, 263, 337–8; as CMAs
   and CAs, 79–80; commercial property, 210;
   competition between, 17–18; components
   in Canada, 10; consolidationist vs.
   public-choice approaches, 112–17;
   constitutional authority, 27–9; councillors
   (see councillors); councils (see councils);
   debt, 208–9; development (see developers
   and development industry); economic
   growth, 254–8; efficiency, 15–18;
   elections (see elections (municipal));
   establishment in Canada, 4–5; executive
   committees, 230–2; federal government
   in, 42–3; financial aspects (see finances
   and financing); functions, 22–5, 332–3,
   338–9; as governmental entities, 5–8;
   historical origins, 3–7; homelessness,
   40–1; infrastructure (see infrastructure);
   inter-municipal agreement and issues,
   43–4, 61–4; international comparisons,

335; international competitiveness, 87–8;
   involvement by provinces, 114–15, 116,
   339–40; land development policy, 202; land
   use (see land use and land-use planning);
   legal context, 3–5; in local government,
   3; management (see management and
   managers); mayors (see mayors); number
   by province, 9; old buildings protection
   and development, 213–15; participatory
   mechanisms, 222–3, 340; police boards
   and services, 50–6, 338; policy-making
   (see policy-making); politics (see politics
   (municipal)); precommitment, 262–4;
   private statutes, 31–2; property tax (see
   property tax); provincial laws and statutes,
   5, 6–7, 29–33, 35–6, 140–1; and provincial
   ministries and ministers, 32–3; reform
   movement, 177–8, 218–20; regulation, 330;
   rural, 7–8; size, 335–7; social problems,
   40–1, 261; special-purpose bodies, 61–4;
   subdivision of land (see subdivision of
   land); taxation (see taxation); tier system,
   7–8, 112–13; types of, 7–8; urban areas
   evolving into, 93–4; user fees (see user fees
   and user-fee services); water supply (see
   water supply and services); zoning changes,
   213. see also local government
Municipality of Metropolitan Toronto, 117–
   20, 121, 122–4, 154–5
municipal organizations, 41–5
municipal regional counties (MRCs), 8
Murray, Glen, 241–2

National Airports System, 66
National Capital Commission (NCC), 29
National Household Survey (NHS), as
   resource, 89
natural gas provision, 58–9
natural monopolies, 58–9
natural person powers, 31
neighbourhood groups. see citizens
Nenshi, Naheed, 229–30, 243, 245–7
neo-liberalism, 331–2, 336
net worth and net financial worth, 291–2
New Brunswick: amalgamations, 146;
   federal policy-making, 253; number of
   municipalities, 9; population and CMAs,
   85; regional commissions, 8, 133–4; school
   boards, 49
New Democratic Party (NDP), in local
   politics, 178–9
Newfoundland and Labrador, 9, 49
New Haven, CT, 237
New York City, NY, 113
NIMBY (Not In My Back Yard) syndrome,
   223–4
non-financial assets, 291–2
Non-Partisan Association (NPA), 179, 181,
   189

Novack, Jack, 183–4
Nova Scotia, 9, 146–9, 294, 296

oil refineries, in annexations, 98, 100–2
old buildings, protection *vs.* development,
    213–15
Ontario: amalgamations, 149–61, 336;
    annexations, 104–6, 109–10; bodies
    without municipal involvement, 69;
    campaign financing, 200; conflict of
    interests, 196–7; conservation authorities,
    61–2; council meetings, 192–4, 240;
    counties and townships, 7–8; de-
    amalgamations, 153–4; election turnout,
    198; electricity, 60; expenditures and
    revenues, 294, 296; financial role of
    cities, 24; functions of local government,
    22–3; Greater Golden Horseshoe,
    82–5; labour and politics, 281; land
    registration and subdivision, 203–4;
    land use, 82; local improvement taxes,
    204–5; mayors, 228–9, 240–1; number
    of municipalities, 9; pesticides policy,
    260; police and police boards, 51, 52–3,
    54–5; policy for municipality and local
    government, 252–3; pre-1930 situation,
    139; provincial transfers, 293–5; provincial
    tribunal, 34; regional municipalities, 8,
    121–6; regulation of municipalities, 330;
    rural representation, 160; single-tier
    governments, 121; social services, 22–4;
    special-purpose bodies, 8–9; subdivision
    agreements, 205–7; two-tier municipalities,
    121–6; wards, 186–7, 188; water supply
    systems, 306, 310–12; zoning changes, 213
Ontario Committee on Taxation, 205
Ontario Local Improvement Act (1914), 204
Ontario Municipal Board (OMB):
    annexations, 102–4, land use, 34–5,
    262; Metro Toronto, 117–18; Toronto
    condominiums, 221–2; wards population,
    187–8; zoning changes, 213
Ontario Planning and Development Act
    (1918), 203
Ontario Police Services Act, 53
Ontario Provincial Police (OPP), 52, 54
Ontario Registry Act (1910), 203
Ontario Works, 22–3
operating budgets, 295–301
Ottawa, ON, 29, 39, 160, 187

participation of citizens, 19–21, 142–3, 218,
    222–4, 340
Partnership of the Manitoba Capital Region,
    144
peak-period pricing, 305
Peel, ON, 124–5
pesticides policy, 259–60
Peterson, Paul E., 19, 178, 261

Philip Environmental, 275
Phillips, Susan, 338–9
Places to Grow Act (Ontario, 2005), 82
Plunkett, Thomas J., 124, 278–9
pluralism, 237–9
Poitras, Lawrence, and report, 165–6
Polèse, Mario, 256–8
police boards, as special-purpose bodies, 50–6
policing and police forces: administrative
    tribunals, 35; control by municipality,
    338; jurisidiction and independence of,
    50–1, 52–5; Montreal, QC, 52, 126–7;
    responsibility, 23; Toronto, ON, 51, 55–6;
    unions, 280
policy-making: and autonomy, 250–1;
    citizens' pressure, 258–62; conditional
    grants, 253; councils and staff, 250–1,
    252; criticism about municipality, 265–6;
    decisions implementation, 264–5; diffusion
    and symbolism, 258–62; economic
    pressures, 254–8; federal and provincial
    governments, 251–4; infrastructure
    programs, 253–4; precommitment, 262–4
political parties: mayors, 229–30; Montreal,
    QC, 179–80; municipally, 173–8, 181;
    provincial support, 180–1; in structure of
    councils, 182; Vancouver, BC, 178–9
politics (municipal): contributions from
    developers, 219–20; council–manager
    plan, 270; and development, 178, 201; and
    economic growth, 254–5; national parties
    in, 176–7; overview and conceptualization,
    173–4; reform movement, 177–8; social
    elites and decision makers, 174–6; unions,
    280–2; urban pluralism and urban regimes,
    237–9. *see also* elections (municipal)
population: census as resource, 89; CMAs,
    80–1, 84, 86–8; by council, 182–3, 185;
    and globalization, 86–7; in wards elections,
    186–7
population centres, 75, 78–9. *see also* urban
    areas
port authorities, 65–6
Porter Airlines, 243
power: centres of, 210, 212; in councils, 174–
    5; of mayors, 229, 231, 232–6, 241, 246–7
precommitment, 262–4, 298
Price, Trevor, 139
pricing, 304–5, 308–12
Prince Edward Island, 9, 13, 145–6
private companies, in public services, 58–60
private goods, 303
private statutes, 31–2
Progressive movement, 177–8, 270
Projet Montréal, 180
property tax: alternative assessment systems,
    320–1; assessment, 317–19, 320–1; for
    businesses, 322–3; capitalization, 324;
    criticisms, 326–7, 328–9; determination,

314–20; exempt property, 322–3; for funding municipalities, 36; importance and impact, 314; individual property owners, 316–20; local improvement taxes, 204–5; and market value, 317–18, 319–20, 321, 326; vs. other taxes, 326–8; PILs, 322; rates, 318–20; as revenue, 293, 314–15; special-purpose bodies, 325; who pays, 322–3
provinces and provincial governments: administrative tribunals, 33–5; amalgamations, 138, 169, 336; associations of municipalities, 43; bodies without municipal involvement, 68–70; and built environment, 338; CMAs, 84, 85–6; constitutional role, 27–9; election financing, 199–200; expenditures and revenues, 10–11, 293–4, 296; functions of government, 332; health authorities, 69–70; infrastructure programs, 253–4; involvement in local issues, 38–41; involvement with municipalities, 114–15, 116, 339–40; landownership registration, 203; land use plans, 262; legislation and municipalities, 5, 6–7, 29–33, 35–6, 140–1; local governments' role, 13–22; and local political parties, 180–1; mayors, 228–9, 242–3; meetings of councils, 192; ministries and ministers, 32–3; money and local government, 35–7; non-financial assets, 291–2; number of municipalities, 9; police boards, 50–6; policy-making in municipalities, 251–4; property tax and schools, 325; rural land subdivision, 209–10; school boards, 48–50; size of municipalities, 335–6; social housing, 40–1; statutes relating to local government, 29–32; taxation, 322–3, 324–5, 327–8; transfers, 293–5, 296; wards boundaries, 188. see also specific provinces
Provincial and Territorial Ministers Responsible for Local Government, 32
public-choice approach, 20, 112–13, 115–16
public education. see education
public goods, 301–2
public health, 24
public participation, 142–3, 218, 222–4, 340
public policy, definition, 251
public–private partnerships, 276–8
public sector employment, 268–9
public services, 58, 77–8
public statutes, 32
public transit: investments and policy-making, 254; as special-purpose bodies, 60–1, 62–3, 68, 69; as toll goods, 302–3
public utilities, 24

Quebec (city), 8, 128–9
Quebec (province): amalgamations, 141, 161–3, 168–9, 336; campaign financing, 200; central funding of local government, 36; de-amalgamations, 165–9; executive committees, 231–2; expenditures and revenues, 294, 296; financial role of cities, 24; legislation for municipalities, 127, 128; linguistic aspects and rights, 49, 162, 163, 164; Montreal and annexations, 96; municipal parties, 180–1; municipal regional counties (MRCs), 128; municipal system, 8; number of municipalities, 9; police boards, 52; property tax and schools, 325; reduction in municipalities, 161, 168; school boards, 49–50; supra-regional authorities, 8, 9, 128–9; two-tier systems in, 126–9; unions, 163–4; urban, regional, and metropolitan communities, 126–9; wards, 187, 188; water usage and meters, 307–8
Quebec Municipal Commission, 96

ratepayers' associations. see citizens
rates, structures, 308–9
Rayside, David M., 174–5, 176
RCMP (Royal Canadian Mounted Police), 23, 55
real property, taxation. see property tax
recycling, 259, 260, 274–5
reform movement, 177–8, 217–20, 270
regimes, 236, 237–9, 245
Regina, SK, 63–4, 109, 276–7
religion, 29, 48–9
rental property, taxation, 323–5
rescaling, 331–2, 336
reserve funds, 298–9
residential subdivisions. see subdivision of land
residents' groups, impact on development, 209
revenue: municipal, 293–5, 296; own-source by levels of government, 11; property tax and user fees, 293, 296, 314–15
rezoning, inner-city neighbourhoods, 216–17
roads, as toll goods, 302–3
Robarts, John, 118
Robertson, Gregor, 179
Rodriguez, John, 281
Roquet, Louis, 272
rural areas: annexations, 92–3; conversion to urban land, 203–10; migration to cities, 86–7; municipalities and districts, 7–8; services, 77–8; vs. urban areas, 75–8; in wards population, 186–7

Saint John, NB, 4, 146
St. John's, NL, amalgamation, 144–5
St. John's Metropolitan Area Board, 144–5
sales tax, for funding municipalities, 36–7, 326–8
Saskatchewan, 9, 36, 85–6
Savage, John, 147, 148

Savings and Restructuring Act (Bill 26), Schedule M (Ontario, 1996), 150–1, 152
school boards, as special-purpose bodies, 48–50
schools. *see* education
seniors, housing, 23–4
sewage. *see* water supply and services
Sewell, John, 218, 240–1
Sherwood, SK, 109
shopping malls, 210–13
Siegel, David, 160–1
single-purpose authorities, 333–4. *see also* special-purpose bodies
single-tier system, 112–13, 121
site-value assessment, 321
size of municipalities, international comparisons, 335–7
Slack, Enid, 156
slates, 180, 193–4
slum clearance, 215
Smith, Patrick J., 265–6
smoking policy, 259, 260
social elites, 174–6, 245
social housing, 24, 40–1
social services, 22–4
Société de transport de Montréal (STM), 60
Spadina Expressway, Toronto, 119, 215–16
special committees, 190
special-purpose bodies: definition and functions, 8–10, 47, 71, 338–9; description, 333–4; intergovernmental, 64–8; inter-municipal, 61–4; library boards, 8–9, 57; police boards, 50–6; property tax, 325; school boards, 48–50; transit systems, 60–1, 62–3, 68, 69; user fees, 57–8; utilities and private companies, 57–60; Vancouver Board of Parks and Recreation, 56–7; Winnipeg, MB, 120; without municipal involvement, 68–70
spending, 10–11, 290, 291–5
staff, 230–1, 252, 268–70, 327
standing committes, 190, 191
Statistics Canada: financial data, 290, 291–3; local government defined, 10; population centres and CMAs, 75, 76, 78, 79
Staunton, VA, 270
Stewart, Kennedy, 265–6
Stone, Clarence, 236, 237–8, 239
Stoneybrook subdivision, 207–10, 211
Strathcona, AB, 96–7
Strathcona County, AB, 97–9
subdivision of land: agreements, 205–7; dense development, 209; infrastructure development, 205–7, 208; local improvement taxes, 204–5; London, ON, 207–10; and neighbouring residents, 209; process, 203; and provinces, 209–10
Sullivan, Sam, 179
Summerside, PEI, 145–6

supra-regional municipalities, 8–9, 129
Supreme Court of Canada, municipalities as government, 6–7

taxation: alternatives to property tax, 326–8; and federal government, 322, 327–8; for funding municipalities, 36–7, 326; hotel occupancy, 328; local improvement taxes, 204–5; lower-income homeowners, 324–5; and ownership, 317; payments-in-lieu (PILs), 295, 296, 322–3; rental property, 323–5; sales tax and income taxes, 36–7, 326–8. *see also* property tax
telecommunications services, provision, 58–9
territories of Canada, associations of municipalities, 43
The Electors Action Movement (TEAM), 179, 218
Thompson, Susan, 230
Tiebout, Charles, 18, 115–16
tier system. see single-tier system; two-tier systems
toll goods, 302, 306
Toronto, ON: airports, 66, 67–8, 243; amalgamation, 154–9; annexations, 117; campaign financing, 200; city as government, 5–6; as CMA, 82–3; committees, 191; community councils, 158; condominiums, 220–2; development industry, 220–2; elections, 158–9; expressways, 119, 215–16; financial aspects, 155–6; garbage collection, 274–5; implementation of policy, 265; mayor, 231, 243–5; Metro Toronto, 117–20, 121, 122–3, 154–5; new reform movement, 218; policing and police forces, 51, 55–6; policy, 252; public transit, 60–1, 69, 254; schools and school boards, 48; social elites, 245; taxation for funding, 37, 326; tri-level government relations, 242–3; two-tier government, 117–20, 121, 122–4; urban regime, 245; visible minorities on council, 199; water services, 275, 306. *see also* Greater Golden Horseshoe
Toronto City Summit Alliance, 156
Toronto Island airport, 66, 67, 243
Toronto Police Services Board (TPSB), 55
Toronto Port Authority (TPA), 66
Toronto Transit Commission (TTC), 60–1
tourism, taxation, 327, 328
townships, 7–8
transfers, 35–7, 293–5, 296
transit. see public transit
TransLink, 62–3
Tremblay, Gérald, 165, 166, 180, 272
Trent, Peter, 163–4, 165, 168
tri-level government relations, 242–3
Troy, Leo, 284

two-tier systems: Alberta regional
partnerships, 134–6; BC regional
districts, 129–33, 137; complexity, 333–4;
consolidation *vs.* public choice, 112–17;
Metropolitan Corporation of Greater
Winnipeg, 120–1; Metro Toronto, 117–20,
121, 122–4; New Brunswick regional
commissions, 133–4; Ontario, 121–6;
overview, 112–13; Quebec province, 126–9;
vs. single tier, 112–13; upper and lower, 8

unconditional transfers, 35–7
Unicity amalgamation, 142–4, 336
unincorporated and incorporated areas, 7–8
Union Montreal, 180
unions: arbitration, 280; collective and
multilateral bargaining, 278–80, 285;
contracting out, 274–5, 278; employer
disunity, 279–80; public- vs. private-sector
work, 282–4; Quebec province, 163–4;
support for candidates, 280–2
United States: amalgamations, 336; at-large
elections, 188; home rule, 30, 141, 335–6;
land use plans, 262; national parties in
local politics, 176; public sector unions,
282–4; schools and school boards, 48;
strong-mayor system, 229; urban pluralism
and regimes, 237–9
unit-value assessment, 321
upper-tier municipalities, 8, 9
urban areas: annexations and amalgamations,
91–2; core, 79; creation from rural land,
203–10; definitions, 75–7, 79; evolution
into municipalities, 93–4; *vs.* rural areas,
75–8; services in, 77. *see also* population
centres
Urbaniak, Tom, 234–6, 237
urban municipalities, legal authority, 23
urban pluralism, 237–9
urban reform movement, 177–8, 217–20, 270
urban regimes, 236, 237–9, 245
user fees and user-fee services: finances
and financing, 301–6; garbage collection,
303–4; price-setting, 304–5; public and
toll goods, 301–3, 306; public transit, 60;
as revenue, 293, 296; for special-purpose
bodies, 57–8; water supply, 307
utilities, and special-purpose bodies, 57–60

value of property, 223–4, 317–18, 319–20,
321, 326
Valverde, Mariana, 265
Vancouver, BC: at-large vs. ward elections,
188–90; central governments funding, 36;
as CMA, 133; GVRD/Metro Vancouver, 130–
3; new reform movement, 218–19; political
parties, 178–9; public transit, 62–3, 254;
social housing, 23–4
Vancouver Board of Parks and Recreation,
56–7
Vancouver Port Authority, 66
Vaughan, Adam, 55–6
Veolia Water Canada, 276
visible minorities, in councils, 198–9
Vision Montreal, 180
Vision Vancouver, 179, 181
Voices of Central Ontario (VOCO), 153
votes and voting, 194, 198. *see also* elections
(municipal)

Walkerville, ON, 140
wards, 186–90
water authorities, 63–4
water supply and services: capital investments
subsidies, 309–12; contracting out and
public–private partnerships, 275–7;
finances and financing, 306–12; metering
and usage, 307–8; pricing of water, 309–12
welfare system, 22–4
Westminster, ON, 102, 104–6
Westmount, QC, 163–4, 165, 270
Williams, Robert, 183–4
Windsor, ON, 139–41, 336
Winnipeg, MB: amalgamations, 142–4, 336;
as CMA, 144; Core Area Initiative, 144;
executive committee and structural reform,
230–1; garbage collection, 275; mayor,
230–1, 232–4; Metropolitan Corporation
of Greater Winnipeg, 120–1; Partnership of
the Manitoba Capital Region, 144; social
services, 24; Unicity, 142–4, 336
women, in councils, 198–9
workplaces, 79–80

Yates, Douglas, 239

zoning bylaws, 213, 216–17